The Essential Federalist
and
Anti-Federalist Papers

D0169552

E

The Essential Federalist
and
Anti-Federalist Papers

Edited, with Introduction, by
David Wootton

Hackett Publishing Company, Inc.
Indianapolis/Cambridge

Copyright © 2003 by Hackett Publishing Company, Inc.

All rights reserved
Printed in the United States of America

08 07 06 05 04 03   1 2 3 4 5 6 7

For further information, please address:

Hackett Publishing Company, Inc.
P.O. Box 44937
Indianapolis, IN   46244-0937

www.hackettpublishing.com

Cover design by Abigail Coyle
Interior design by Meera Dash
Composition by William Hartman
Printed at Malloy, Inc.

Library of Congress Cataloging-in-Publication Data

The essential Federalist and anti-Federalist papers / edited
by David Wootton.
       p. cm.
    Includes bibliographical references and index.
    ISBN 0-87220-656-4 (cloth) — ISBN 0-87220-655-6 (paper)
       1. Constitutional history—United States—Sources.
2. Constitutional law—United States.   3. United States—Politics
and government—1783–1789.   I. Wootton, David, 1952–.

KF4515.E85 2003
342.73'024—dc21

                                            2003051109

Contents

Contents   vii

Introduction

Understanding the Constitution

Two texts, a decade apart. One begins "The style [i.e., name] of this confederacy shall be 'The United States of America.'" The other begins "We the people of the United States, in order to form a more perfect union . . ." Between them, the living out of a revolution. One names a political entity that as yet scarcely exists and is intended to serve only limited purposes. In the other, that entity finds its voice. Its first word is "We," identifying itself not as a state, a confederacy, or even a nation, but as a community. Its first noun is "people," declaring itself to be a community of equals. Its first adjective is "perfect," announcing itself to be a community with boundless aspirations, a community to which all the people may contribute and in whose benefits all the people may share.

Of course its aspirations are no sooner stated than compromised—even betrayed. One only has to read as far as Section 2 of Article I to discover that "We" consists of "free persons," as opposed to "Indians not taxed" (the mere payment of taxes is enough to entitle you to be one of "The People") and "other persons." "Other persons" is a euphemism for slaves, but the very fact that the word "slave" is never used in this text, even when the reality of slavery is acknowledged, is an indirect recognition that slavery is at odds with the very principles of freedom the Constitution enunciates. The Articles of Confederation had no need to mention slavery because they applied to the affairs of the thirteen states, not the lives of individuals. The Constitution could not avoid referring to slavery, but slavery was already a peculiar institution: it was confined to certain states, and its legitimacy was contested, and it could therefore be mentioned only indirectly in references to "other persons" and the "migration and importation" of such persons. This second reference is accompanied by a time limit of twenty-one years, an implicit promise that the existence of slavery will have to be reviewed, an implied suggestion that it is at odds with the principles of liberty.

Women too were excluded from this "we," but that, unlike the exclusion of male slaves, did not strike any of its authors as a fundamental problem; it did not even represent an obstacle to be overcome in drafting an acceptable text. There was no need to refer to the exclusion of women, directly or indirectly, for to the authors of the Constitution that exclusion was simply invisible.

The Constitution of the United States—no other political document
has had a greater influence on the life of a people, and no other political
document has so succinctly summarized a wholly new way of thinking
about politics. To understand the Constitution we need to explore its
intellectual origins, the ideas it sought to embody as practical institutions
as they developed over the previous century and more. We need to
acknowledge the complicated process of negotiation and compromise by
which the text of the Constitution was constructed between May 25,
1787, when the Constitutional Convention opened, and September 17 of
that same year, when it completed its work. And we need to follow the
debate on the merits and demerits of the Constitution that broke out
immediately after its text was made public, a debate that lasted from September 1787 until the summer of 1788.

The classic defense of the Constitution is the *Federalist* (published in
installments from October 27, 1787 to May 28, 1788), and it is by reading
the *Federalist* as a reply to anti-Federalist arguments that one can best
begin the study of the Constitution and the ideas it embodies. However,
one cannot get the measure of that remarkable sustained polemic in
defense of a constitution that was still no more than words on paper
unless one has some sense of how much the ideas it contains are new
made, and how much they are simply made new, remade to fit the needs of
the hour.

The argument of this Introduction is that the *Federalist*, like the Constitution, contained few new ideas; but in both the Constitution and the
Federalist, ideas that contemporaries frequently mistook for old ideas
(although many of them were no older than the Founders) were made
new. In 1787 these ideas expressed themselves through two new voices.
One was the voice not of Hamilton, Madison, and the others who labored
over the text of the Constitution, nor of "the Delegates of the United
States of America in Congress assembled" (the voice of the Articles of
Confederation), but of "We the People. . . ." The other was the voice not
of Hamilton, Madison, and Jay, but of an anonymous spokesperson for
this new constitutional idea, a featureless cipher through whom the Constitution speaks—the voice of "Publius." Our task now is to discover what
these voices have to say.

Revolution

The ratification of the Constitution marked the final phase of a revolutionary crisis that had endured for more than a decade. The Declaration
of Independence had been approved on July 4, 1776, but the new state to
which it gave rise came into existence only with the convening of the first

Congress called under the new Constitution on March 4, 1789. We take revolutions, and the principles to which they lay claim—such as popular sovereignty and the right of a new generation to discard the institutions of an outmoded era—so much for granted that we need to start our discussion by acknowledging just how new and challenging revolutionary principles were in 1776.

For centuries, throughout the Middle Ages and the Renaissance, societies had sought to ground political legitimacy in two overlapping principles—divine authorization and ancient tradition. It is sometimes argued that modern political debate began with the Wars of Religion in late–sixteenth-century France. Both in France and in Holland (which fought a war of independence against Spain from 1568 to 1648) polemicists had no difficulty in formulating arguments against tyranny. However, in both countries it was accepted that there were limits to resistance. It might be appropriate to overthrow an evil ruler (whether heretical or tyrannical), but even in a moment of extreme crisis one could not create new political institutions from scratch. Traditional authority should be maintained if possible—a new ruler should take the place of the old. Or, failing that, authority should be exercised by existing institutions with an established legitimacy—magistrates, estates, city councils. In Calvinist Scotland the same assumptions shaped the arguments of monarchomach (i.e., king-killing) theorists such as George Buchanan. (Buchanan wrote *Of the Powers of the Crown in Scotland* [1579] to legitimize the deposition of Mary Queen of Scots.)

It is only with the outbreak of the English Civil War, in 1642, that we find the first theorists prepared to argue that a political crisis could actually dissolve all existing authorities—that subjects could find themselves back in a "state of nature," with the opportunity to establish a new type of political authority from first principles. This is what we now call the doctrine of "popular sovereignty," and its emergence marks the beginning of the transition, in the new nation-state, from subject to citizen. Previously, only the inhabitants of self-governing cities had claimed to rule themselves.

When the people of a large political community rule themselves, some distinction has to be made between the popular assembly (which cannot be constantly in session) and the institutions that carry out its instructions. This distinction, fundamental to modern government, is also a product of the English Civil War and required a wholly new vocabulary: "legislative authority" is a phrase dating from 1642; "legislative power" from 1651 (in Hobbes' *Leviathan*); "the legislature" dates from 1676; "executive power" is a phrase from 1649, while the term "the executive" is a product of the debate on the American Constitution (Madison was using it in 1785); "judicatory power" dates from 1642,

while the term "the judiciary" seems to have been used first in the Constitutional Convention.[1] Only with this new terminology of legislative,
executive, and judicial powers could one both discuss how people might
rule themselves, and ask how the power of government could be limited
by being separated into distinct, independent powers.

The culture of both the Middle Ages and the Renaissance was profoundly backward looking. Present practices were governed by past
precedents; the best (religion, literature, philosophy, or constitutional
design) lay in the past, not the present or future. Suddenly, in the mid-
seventeenth century, a few radical thinkers claimed the right to establish
a new constitution quite unlike any that had preceded it: they insisted
that old forms could be abandoned, and they discussed new forms in
terms of distinct powers. John Locke formulated a modified version of
these arguments in his *Two Treatises,* written as an attack on King
Charles II, and published in 1689 after the overthrow of Charles' brother
King James II in 1688. For later generations this provided the paradig-
matic definition of popular sovereignty. (Locke's account of the separation of powers, on the other hand, was generally assumed to have been
superseded by Montesquieu's.)

Locke was prepared to accept that the best government would be a
form of limited monarchy (for one needed a strong and unified executive),
but during the English Civil War others insisted that monarchs would
always employ their power to thwart the will of the people, and so maintained that only a republican constitution could be legitimate. The Americans were the heirs of this revolutionary tradition—the tradition of
popular sovereignty, separation of powers, and suspicion of monarchy—
passed down through the eighteenth century by True Whigs (the Whigs
being the first national political party, formed to oppose Charles II and
James II) and by others prepared to oppose the British government.

The British state, meanwhile, had been transformed as a result of the
revolution of 1688. The revolution began the long struggle with France
for global predominance, and led to the development of new mechanisms
for concentrating power in the hands of the executive (particularly the
management of patronage and the distribution of pensions and favors),
ultimately perfected by the first Prime Minister, Robert Walpole, who
completed the transformation of the core of the old Whig party into a
party of big government and high taxation. It was this newly powerful
state that sought to extend taxation to the American colonies.

---

1. An earlier, twofold distinction between legislature and executive goes back
to Marsilius of Padua writing in Latin in the fourteenth century, but Marsilius
did not distinguish between the judicial and the executive functions.

Key elements of the radical republican tradition, reconfigured for opposition against a state that was rapidly becoming the first global superpower, found expression in Thomas Paine's *Common Sense* of January 1776, the book that announced the coming revolution.[2] Originally the word "revolution" had implied simply "recurrence," that is, a return or repetition. By the late seventeenth century its meaning had begun to shift. Even as they lived through the events of 1688, contemporaries called them "a revolution," and the term began to be used to refer to the overthrow of a government and its replacement by one based on entirely different principles. After 1776 the new concept of revolution would be firmly established, and both Federalists and anti-Federalists made use of it. "The American war is over: but this is far from being the case with the American revolution," wrote Benjamin Rush in January 1787, calling for a new constitution. "Here is a revolution," said Patrick Henry, opposing the constitution proposed by the Convention, "as radical as that which separated us from Great Britain." The author of the *Federalist* believed the American colonists had "accomplished a revolution which has no parallel in the annals of human society: They reared the fabrics of governments which have no model on the face of the globe."

This revolutionary tradition did not lie only in the immediate past; Federalist 28 reminded readers that "If the representatives of the people betray their constituents, there is then no recourse left but in the exertion of that original right of self-defense, which is paramount to all positive forms of government." In a large country, where the State governments would be prepared to provide leadership in resisting the usurpations of central authority, the people would have the advantage over their rulers. So too Federalist 60 argues that if the federal government were to try to fix elections, there would inevitably be "a popular revolution." If the constitution the *Federalist* advocated failed, it recognized revolution as an appropriate response.

Constitutions

Political analysis as we now know it begins with the composition of Aristotle's *Politics* in the fifth century B.C.E. Aristotle was well aware that political communities are organized in different ways, and he believed that all political systems could be shown to be types or combinations of monarchy, aristocracy, and democracy. Aristotle was also prepared to produce a detailed analysis of the political institutions of particular

---

2. Paine, however, did not share the concern with limiting and separating powers that formed an important strand within the radical tradition.

communities, such as Athens. For Aristotle, the study of constitutions was comparable to the study of biology—it was primarily descriptive rather than normative. Constitutions existed in the real world before they were described by theoreticians, and even if one could identify tactics and strategies that would encourage stability and produce just government, there was still no reason why an individual should feel obliged to approve or sustain any particular constitutional arrangement.

Two thousand years later we find, at last, the idea of a written constitution. (One might look for precursors of this idea outside politics, in the regulations governing organizations such as the Franciscans and Dominicans, or the statutes of medieval universities.) The earliest proposal for a written constitution (leaving aside such American texts as the "Fundamental Orders of Connecticut," 1639, and the "Massachusetts Body of Liberties," 1641, as not being intended for independent states) comes from the extreme radicals of the Parliamentary army, the Levellers, in 1645. They proposed an "Agreement of the People," a written constitution recognizing certain inalienable rights (such as freedom of religious conscience), and establishing a government controlled by the people. Having put their signature to such an agreement, citizens would be bound to preserve and maintain it. Briefly, England actually was governed under a written constitution, the Instrument of Government (1653–7). This was a modern constitution in that it distinguished between "the supreme legislative authority" and the rest of government, but it lumped together "the exercise of the chief magistracy, and the administration of the government." The idea of an independent judiciary had yet to be clearly formulated. Although real power lay in the hands of the Lord Protector, Oliver Cromwell, the Instrument claimed legitimacy from the assent of Parliament. (Marchamont Nedham first defended the Instrument, and then, in his *The Excellency of a Free State* [1656, reprinted in 1767], which was known to John Adams and other Americans of the revolutionary era, employed principles drawn from it to imply that the Cromwellian regime had betrayed the cause of liberty.)

The Restoration in 1660 marked England's return to an unwritten constitution, and yet by the mid-eighteenth century we find Bolingbroke writing about Britain's Constitution as if it was something far more complicated than Aristotle's simple division of constitutions into monarchies, aristocracies, democracies, and mixed governments. "By constitution," says Bolingbroke, "we mean, whenever we speak with propriety and exactness, that assemblage of laws, institutions, and customs, derived from certain fixed principles of reason . . . that compose the general system according to which the community hath agreed to be governed." The constitution is "a noble and wise system, the essential parts of which are so proportioned, and so intimately connected, that a change in one begets a change in the whole." In other words, a constitution is something that could in principle be written down, that embodies rational relationships, and that all political agents ought to respect. Blackstone's *Commentaries on the Laws of England* (1765–9) continued this tradition of trying to analyze and define the British constitution as if were something established and long-lasting, but also quite specific and detailed.

For these commentators, one might say their task was to define a constitution that already existed as a set of practices. Their fundamental conviction was that a constitution involved interactions between institutions such that each part contributed to a larger whole. Bolingbroke pioneered the use of the word "system" to describe this interactive framework, and it is not surprising to find the proposed American constitution being described from the beginning as a "system." Benjamin Franklin, addressing the Federal Convention on September 17, 1787, said, "It therefore astonishes me, Sir, to find this System [the proposed constitution] approaching as near to Perfection as it does," and the word "system" occurs frequently in the *Federalist* (e.g., "popular systems of civil government" in Federalist 9) and in the anti-Federalists (for Richard Henry Lee, for example, the proposed constitution is "the new system").

The conceptual tools required to construct and analyze written constitutions thus existed when such constitutions (with the solitary exception of the ill-fated Instrument of Government) did not yet exist. The written Constitution as we now know it was the offspring of the Revolution of 1776, which rapidly resulted in royal charters being rewritten as the constitutions for independent states. These new constitutions (Pennsylvania's is the most striking example) tended to transfer the powers of the royal governor to representative assemblies whose power was virtually unlimited. Within a few years, however, the pendulum had begun to swing the other way. Massachusetts pioneered a new type of constitution when it established a constitutional convention, elected directly by the people, in 1779. John Adams wrote the bulk of the resulting constitutional proposal, which provided for a declaration of rights; the separation of powers; a bicameral legislature; an independent judiciary; and a powerful executive directly elected by the people, with control over the armed forces, extensive powers of appointment, an ample salary, and (at least in Adams' original proposal) an absolute veto over legislation. The Massachusetts Constitution, ratified by the people in 1780, provided a model for constitutional reform in the other states (Madison and Jefferson led the campaign in Virginia), both in its specific provisions and in the procedure adopted to compose and ratify it.

The Constitution of the United States can be seen as one in a long series of constitutions based on the model of the Massachusetts Constitution produced in a period running from 1780 to the early 1790s. Its most contentious elements were precisely those where it diverged from the Massachusetts model: its abandonment of the principle of annual elections, the absence of an elected council to advise the chief executive, and its failure to include a bill of rights.

The enterprise of writing and rewriting constitutions necessarily encouraged a comparative study of constitutions. Adams assembled much of the material relevant to such an enterprise in his three-volume *Defense of the Constitutions of the United States of America* (1787–8), the first volume of which appeared in time to be read by the delegates to the Constitutional Convention. Adams' purpose was to defend the Massachusetts model against the radical unicameralism and concentration of powers in the hands of the legislature advocated by French philosophes such as Turgot and Americans such as Thomas Paine, and embodied in the constitution of Pennsylvania. (In Pennsylvania, defenders of the Constitution such as Noah Webster had to argue at length in support of bicameralism, a proposal that was not contentious elsewhere.)

All those gathered at Philadelphia, therefore, were familiar with a range of models of constitutional design, and were agreed on the need to construct a constitution that drew on the best examples. When Noah Webster, in *An Examination into the Leading Principles of the American Constitution,* says, "It is worth our while to institute a brief comparison between our American forms of government, and the two *best constitutions* that ever existed in Europe, the *Roman* and the *British,*" or the authors of the *Federalist* (in Essay 69) embark on "a comparison between the president and the King of Great Britain on the one hand, and the Governor of New York on the other," their enterprise is simply a smaller, more modest version of that of Adams in his vast *Defense.* When James Wilson maintained that "the ancients, so enlightened on other subjects, were very uninformed with regard to this [the science of politics]," his evidence was that "they seem scarcely to have had any idea of any other kinds of governments than the three simple forms design[at]ed by the epithets, monarchical, aristocratical, and democratical," and he could safely assume that his listeners were better informed. Above all, his listeners, unlike the ancients, were familiar with the modern idea of the separation of powers into legislative, executive, and judiciary.

Representation and Party Politics

In Federalist 9, the authors of the *Federalist* provide a list of principles unknown (or, at best, imperfectly known) to the ancients, but whose importance, they assert, is now well understood: "the regular distribution of power into distinct departments—the introduction of legislative balances and checks—the institution of courts composed of judges, holding their offices during good behavior—the representation of the people in the legislature by deputies of their own election—these are . . . wholly new discoveries." In the next few pages I want to look at these new principles, together with a principle they present as the newest and most American of all discoveries—the advantages of sheer size. In exploring these principles, we will be exploring the theory of constitutional design as it was understood by the authors of the *Federalist* and their contemporaries.

We begin with representation because it now seems to us, living in societies where the principle of political representation is deeply entrenched, so obvious a principle as scarcely to need comment. Already in 1787, James Wilson expected to "excite some surprise" when he pointed out "that representation of the people is not, even at this day, the sole principle of any government in Europe," so natural did it seem to Americans. "One thing is very certain," says Wilson, and that is "that the doctrine of representation in government was altogether unknown to the ancients."[3] But it was also unknown, for example, in early modern France. The principle of the States General was that representatives were delegates sent with their instructions on how to act and what to demand— they were not free agents, able to do whatever they thought best either for their constituents or for the political community as a whole. "The representation of the people in the legislature by deputies of their own choosing," where the deputies are not bound by the instructions of those they represent, appears to be a peculiarly Anglo-Saxon invention, transported by the English colonists to North America, and then copied from America by the French in 1789.

That the people should choose their representatives seems a straightforward principle, but a good deal depends on the nature of the choice. Until the late seventeenth century, elections in England were rarely contested; instead, the elite in each constituency reached agreement among themselves as to who should stand, and those candidates who had previously been *selected* were elected by acclamation. Contested elections developed along with party conflict, and during the period of "the rage of party," 1688 to 1715, English politics was conducted on the basis of vigorous electioneering. For fifty years after 1715, the long Whig ascendancy muffled party conflict, and patronage once more played a crucial role in

---

3. Madison expresses himself more cautiously in Federalist 9, and the detailed discussion of the subject in Federalist 63 shows that he thought representation not so much unknown as imperfectly known.

Parliamentary selections. The fundamental assumption of American politics, that elections are *contested,* is an assumption that became generally
valid for representative politics only after 1776. Even then, there was considerable resistance to the logic of contest—none of the Founders could
reconcile themselves to the idea that it was appropriate for a political
leader to campaign openly for office.

A second assumption, that representative assemblies make decisions
through majority votes, also seems obvious, but is not. Until the outbreak
of the English Civil War, the tradition in Parliament was that decisions
were based on consensus; the counting of votes was rare, and reliance on a
mere majority was unseemly. In the Middle Ages, it is hard to find clear
statements of the principle that a decision should be determined by who
has the most votes; the normal convention was that votes must be
weighed rather than counted (i.e., the older, more important, and more
experienced voters expected their votes to count for more than those of
their juniors, their inferiors, and the inexperienced). In 1579 Buchanan
still held that votes should be reckoned "not by their number but by their
worth." In practice there were exceptions: the Magna Carta (1216) established a group of barons to defend its principles, and they were to make
decisions by simple majority vote. But requirements for unanimity (as in
jury decisions) were far more common.

The first author to argue bluntly that a collective body can make decisions only on the basis of simple majorities is Hobbes; the first use of the
word "majority" to refer to the winning side in a vote is in Locke's manu-
scripts in 1660; its first use in print is in his *Second Treatise.* ("Minority"
first appears in *Cato's Letters* [1721], the key text that developed the idea
that majorities need to be prevented from acting tyrannically.) The idea of
representation on which the Americans relied was therefore little more
than a century old, although it had already come to seem so natural that
Noah Webster could describe the doctrine that "the opinions of a *majority*
must give law to the *whole State*" as "a doctrine as universally received, as
an intuitive truth."

Since this idea depended on the concept of majority decision making,
it implied an electorate and a legislature divided into factions or parties.
To the old way of thinking, factions were anathema: There existed one
common good, on which all virtuous and rational people could agree. It
ought always, therefore, to be possible to establish near unanimity; to
stand in the minority was to face the charge of belonging to a selfish interest group, of putting factional interest ahead of the public interest.

It is quite astonishing to discover how few and far between defenses of
party are before the nineteenth century. Machiavelli had taken it for
granted that politics involved conflicting interests, and that the clash of

interests was an essential mark of political vitality. However, he had time only for the clash of distinct social groups, patricians and plebeians, rich and poor; he had nothing but contempt for the conflict between more narrowly defined factional groups (such as Guelfs and Ghibellines—the two great factions of the late medieval Italian city-states, one allied to the Pope, the other to the Emperor).

The first important defense of party (in English) occurs in the introduction to Edward Spelman's translation of Polybius (the ancient Greek historian) on balanced government. First published in 1743 and twice republished, Spelman was used by Adams in his *Defense.* Spelman argues that "in all free governments there ever were and ever will be parties," and that party conflict is not an effect but a precondition of liberty. The cities of ancient Greece were divided into supporters of aristocracy and democracy, but

> [I]t was not the existence of the two parties I have mentioned that destroyed the liberties of any of those cities, but the occasional extinction of one of them by the superiority the other had gained over it. And if ever we should be so unhappy as to have the balance between the three orders [King, House of Lords, House of Commons] destroyed; and that any one of the three should utterly extinguish the other two, the name of a party would, from that moment, be unknown in England, and we should unanimously agree in being slaves to the conqueror.

Party thus becomes a crucial mechanism for checking the power of government:

> [W]hatever may be the success of the opposer, the public reaps great benefit from the opposition; since this keeps ministers upon their guard, and, often, prevents them from pursuing bold measures which an uncontrolled power might, otherwise, tempt them to engage in. They must act with caution, as well as fidelity, when they consider the whole nation is attentive to every step they take, and that the errors they may commit will not only be exposed but aggravated.

Spelman thus saw party divisions as a fundamental sign of health in representative government.

In Federalist 10 (the most famous of all the essays in the *Federalist*), Madison argues that the anti-Federalists were wrong to adopt Montesquieu's conviction that republics must be small in size, and wrong to conclude that one could not unite America into one republic, but could at best gather a number of States into a loose confederacy. The principle of representation frees the people of the need to gather together in an assembly (as in ancient Athens or Rome, or Renaissance Florence) and enables them to organize themselves across an extensive territory. At the same time, it replaces a turbulent and contentious assembly by one that is (because it consists only of a limited number of the best of the citizens) wise and patriotic. Madison maintains that Montesquieu (whom he does not mention by name, but who is one of the "theoretic politicians" he has in mind) was wrong because he did not understand the significance of representation.

Moreover, the larger the republic, the greater the beneficial consequences. In the first place, where representatives have to be chosen by large numbers of people, only candidates who have outstanding qualities are likely to be successful. Madison means to say that representation in an enlarged republic will necessarily have an elitist character. How is one to interpret the elitism of the *Federalist*? There is no doubt that many of those who participated in constitutional reform in the years after 1780 were concerned that annual elections, unicameral legislatures, and small electoral districts made governments unduly responsive to the wishes of the poorest and least educated citizens. American politics was increasingly divided between those who wanted to preserve close popular control over government and those who wanted a more elitist political framework, and this division was reproduced in the division between Federalists and anti-Federalists.

For contemporaries—and for us—the debate was a confusing and unsatisfactory one, partly because the participants lacked an adequate vocabulary. They were trapped within the language they had inherited from ancient Greece, relying on words such as "democracy" and "aristocracy." They lacked the word "elite," which was not to come into general use until the mid-nineteenth century. They lacked the words "plutocracy" (the rule of the rich) and "meritocracy" (the rule of the able). If they lacked these words, it was because they believed that the only issue was whether it was appropriate for a small group to hold power, and for them this issue was embodied in the word "aristocracy." It is to Madison's credit that in Essay 57, which is his contribution to this debate, he manages to avoid this word completely. He successfully argues that the constitution is not going to establish an "oligarchy," but he has no name for what it will establish, which is a new ruling elite.

Others were less cautious. Thus, "Atticus," writing in Massachusetts, maintained there were "two parties, or factions, in the State." One, "that of the populace," was envious of the rich and tended to "general levelism, and democratic turbulence," while the other, "that of the rich," tended to "an alteration of the constitution of our State, and the subjection of the people to a rigid aristocracy." Atticus was a Federalist because he wanted an effective government, and he believed in this he spoke for "the rich, the wise, the brave, the industrious and enterprising," who "will not be content to lie at the mercy of the idle, and licentious; and be the prey of harpy speculators." Underlying the debates over constitutional reform was the belief of many of the participants that they could trace a social conflict between rich and poor: it is for this reason that Charles Beard's classic *An Economic Interpretation of the Constitution* (1913) is a text of enduring importance.

Much recent debate, however, has centered on the issue not of class, but of virtue. Two distinct intellectual traditions have drawn attention to this theme. On the one hand, John Pocock and his followers have identified virtue as a central theme in republican thinking from Machiavelli on; on the other, the followers of Leo Strauss have seen in the idea of the virtuous ruler a modern version of Plato's philosopher-king. On virtue Madison was much more explicit than he was on the subject of class. "The aim of every political constitution is, or ought to be . . . to obtain for rulers men who possess most wisdom to discern, and most virtue to pursue, the common good of the society." Elections should serve to identify these individuals, and self-government would be simply impossible if virtuous individuals did not exist. (In Hamilton's words, "The institution of delegated power implies that there is a portion of virtue and honor among mankind which may be a reasonable foundation of confidence.")

At the same time, though, the authors of the *Federalist* shared with their opponents a conviction that men are easily corrupted by power and office. Where the authors differed from their opponents was in their understanding of how those in power are to be restrained. The anti-Federalists wanted to concentrate authority in the hands of a representative assembly, so that the responsibility of that assembly's members for government policy was clear; and they wished to hold their representatives accountable by frequent elections. Madison (who did not deny the crucial role of elections) also relied on more indirect controls and checks: "Duty, gratitude, interest, ambition itself" were powerful motives that could induce representatives to concern themselves with the welfare of their electors. These were, however, motives that would best operate on those who saw themselves as separate from the great mass of society, men with responsibilities and opportunities denied to others. They would, in fact, be most effective in controlling the behavior of a ruling elite.

Madison wanted the wise and virtuous to rule and insisted one must take "the most effectual precautions for keeping them virtuous while they hold their public trust." These precautions involved taking advantage of interest and ambition, which were often thought to be incompatible with virtue. Clearly Madison did not imagine that even the most virtuous of rulers would be selfless and disinterested; he expected them to be competitive and ambitious, for how else would they have won their way to membership of the ruling elite? Men with the "most wisdom to discern and the most virtue to pursue the common good" (note that "virtue" here is used in something close to the sense with which Machiavelli uses *virtú*, meaning, not Christian virtue, but the ability to attain one's goals) were to be neither idealized republican citizens, prepared to sacrifice all for their community, nor philosopher-rulers, but effective politicians, seeking to maximize reputation and status in order to consolidate their position within the new elite.

The fundamental objection to this new elitism was that the interests of the elite would be different from those of the population at large. In Federalist 35 Hamilton directly rejects the central anti-Federalist argument that a true representation is not one that selects the wisest and most virtuous, but one that mirrors the community. For Melancton Smith and Richard Henry Lee, the assembly of representatives should closely resemble the people they represent: "a full and equal representation, is that which possesses the same interests, feelings, opinions, and views the people themselves would were they all assembled."

The authors of the *Federalist*, by contrast, wanted rule not by the most typical, but by the best citizens, such as merchants, landlords, and academics. Could one rely on them to legislate in the interests of laborers and tenant farmers? Yes, because they would recognize that the whole society had a common interest in the advancement of commerce, and that the interests of each trade and profession were inseparable from those of all the others (Essay 12). A proper understanding of political economy was thus to be the precondition for enlightened legislation by an intellectual and social elite. The new political economy was also a precondition for the *Federalist*'s conviction that the interests of the elite and the populace were not at odds (Madison had been an early reader of Adam Smith's *Wealth of Nations*, first published in 1776). In an enlarged political arena, as Madison emphasized, the best men were more likely to come to the fore than they were in small-town politics. But it was only in a society imbued by a commercial spirit that a common interest in economic growth could be identified by both the electors and their representatives.

Madison makes a second key argument in Federalist 10. An enlarged republic is necessarily going to be one with diverse interest groups, reflecting the society's increased geographical and economic diversity (the point is repeated in Essay 51). Here Madison was reversing what Montesquieu had believed to be the key argument against large republics. In a large republic, Montesquieu claimed, it will be hard for individuals to think of their private interests as indistinguishable from the common interest, both because it will be more difficult to identify with a more anonymous society and because there will be a greater diversity of interests. As a consequence, ambition and corruption will flourish. Madison, on the other hand, argued that, because there will be a greater diversity of interests, it will be difficult for a single interest group to capture a majority in the legislature; parties and factions will necessarily tend to represent minorities, and government will have to be by compromise and coalition. Enlargement thus had the great advantage of weakening parties and encouraging nonpartisan debate.

Madison is thus normally read (not unreasonably) as being hostile to party politics. However, two things are worth noting here. The first is that in Federalist 28 (which also deals with the consequences of enlarging the political society) Hamilton attributes to the states precisely the constitutional role that Spelman had attributed to the opposition. It is their job to "afford complete security against invasions of the public liberty by the national authority . . . The legislatures . . . can discover the danger at a distance; and . . . can at once adopt a regular plan of opposition." Indeed, the states will have considerable advantages over a political party in fulfilling this function, for they will possess "all the organs of civil power and the confidence of the people." The *Federalist,* therefore, does not so much deny the importance of an organized opposition, as displace organized opposition from the national legislature to the inevitable conflict ("power being almost always the rival of power") between the federal government and the government of the states. Far from rejecting Spelman's analysis, the *Federalist* merely modifies it to take into account the distinct nature of politics within a federal system.

Second, it is often overlooked that Madison (in Federalist 50) adopts a position identical to Spelman's on the healthiness of party divisions. He is discussing party conflict in Pennsylvania, a state "violently heated and distracted by the rage of party." (Webster concurred: "The whole state is split into parties.") Conventionally, such a condition was to be deplored. Madison, however, regards it as positively healthy: "Is it to be presumed that any other State, at the same or any other given period, will be exempt from them [parties]? Such an event ought to be neither presumed nor desired; because an extinction of parties necessarily implies either a universal alarm for the public safety, or an absolute extinction of liberty." This is so exact a summary of Spelman, who also held that the extinction of party must lead to the extinction of liberty, that one can reasonably suspect a direct influence.

The writings of the anti-Federalists contain no comparable defense of opposition in general, or party in particular, and it is thus important that the *Federalist* wholeheartedly embraces the principle of opposition (if not always the principle of party conflict). Opposition is a necessary consequence of representation, but it is not only inevitable, but also desirable. Federalist 10 argues that in an enlarged political society factional conflict will be moderated and modified, not eliminated.

Not all Federalists would have agreed with Madison. For Fisher Ames "faction and enthusiasm are the instruments by which popular governments are destroyed. . . . A democracy is a volcano, which conceals the fiery materials of its own destruction." Atticus, however, maintained that

> [F]or a professed politician, to turn pale at the rise of parties, while the laws are preserved, is as much out of character, as for a veteran soldier to tremble at the discharge of cannon. Parties are the materials of which the most perfect societies are formed. . . . *Parties give life to the moving powers of the State*, and when properly checked and balanced, are productive of much good. . . . *Parties always keep alive, an attention to public measures. . . . Parties produce great attendance and carefulness respecting elections. . . . Parties keep any one interest from swallowing up the rest. . . .*

The main danger is the extinction of party through the triumph of one party over its opponent, which "would introduce a most insupportable tyranny." (Atticus published this essay on October 18, 1787, so that his argument is independent of, and may have influenced, Federalist 50.)

Representation, though, for the authors of the *Federalist*, was only a good thing if the number of representatives was not too large. Where it was advantageous to have an extensive community carrying out the elections, it was pernicious to have a large representative assembly. Too small a legislature could easily fall victim to bribery and intimidation; too large a legislature must degenerate into a mob: "In all very numerous assemblies, of whatever characters composed, passion never fails to wrest the scepter from reason. Had every Athenian citizen been a Socrates; every Athenian assembly would still have been a mob," writes Madison. "Has it been found that bodies of men act with more rectitude or greater disinterestedness than individuals?" asks Hamilton, and replies, "The contrary of this has been inferred by all accurate observers of the conduct of mankind." Here the critique of a large legislature also implies, and develops out of, a critique of direct democracy.

For Madison, representation, at least if properly managed, was the defining characteristic of good government ("A Republic, by which I mean a Government in which the scheme of representation takes place . . ."). This definition plays on an ambiguity in the term *republic*. The Latin *res publica* means simply "public thing," often translated as commonwealth. Aristotle had argued that mixed constitutions were best at pursuing the public good, so that one could easily argue that a limited monarchy (such as that of Britain) was a true commonwealth or republic.

Montesquieu, on the other hand, had used republic and monarchy as mutually exclusive terms—no republic could have a king. Madison's definition is delicately ambiguous, bridging two competing definitions of a republic: the claim that representation ensures good government, and the claim that representation is incompatible with (hereditary) monarchy.

There is a reason for this ambiguity. The logic of polemical debate obliged the *Federalist* to reject—in the strongest terms—any suggestion that the proposed President could be compared to a monarch (Essay 69), but the goal of the Convention was to establish a constitution which would have all the advantages traditionally ascribed to a mixed constitution: it would govern in the interest of the people, it would draw on the wisest and most virtuous, and it would, by having a single executive authority, be capable of energy and dispatch in warfare and foreign policy. It would be democratic, aristocratic, and monarchical. But all three elements were to be supplied through the single device of elections. In James Wilson's words, "In THIS CONSTITUTION, *all authority is derived from the* PEOPLE."

Montesquieu and the Separation of Powers

One book dominated constitutional theorizing in the years before 1787 and the debate over the Constitution in 1787–8: Montesquieu's *Spirit of the Laws*, first published in French in 1748. Montesquieu was important as the founder of the science of comparative politics and as someone who had written at length on republicanism (arguing that it was a political system suited only to small states with a virtuous citizenry). Above all, he was important because he had given an account of a form of constitution under which liberty was maximized. For Montesquieu the nearest example, in practice, of such a constitution was Britain's ("The British Constitution was to Montesquieu what Homer has been to the didactic writers on epic poetry," said Madison), and discussing Montesquieu in part provided a way in which former colonists could discuss how far they wanted to model their constitution on that of the imperial power, without raising the awkward question of how far their own principles differed from those of their former rulers. "We detested the British name; and unfortunately refused to copy some things in the administration of justice and power, in the British government, which have made it the admiration and envy of the world," said Benjamin Rush, who was unusual in not taking shelter behind Montesquieu. (At the Convention, Hamilton had bluntly said that the "British constitution [is the] best form" of government, but he avoided making so impolitic a remark in the *Federalist*.)

The crucial importance of Montesquieu was that his was the classic formulation of the doctrine of the separation of powers. Although the vocabulary required to think about the three powers and early formulations of the need for their separation arose during the English Civil War, it was Montesquieu who welded the idea of liberty to the idea of the separation of powers. It was this that made him an "oracle," "always consulted and cited" during the debate on ratification.

The idea that legislature, executive, and judiciary should be separated was, as we have seen, already present in Locke. Fundamental to his argument in the Second Treatise is the claim that no government can be legitimate if it does not provide impartial adjudication of disputes—an argument that appeared to make an independent judiciary the key index of legitimacy. Montesquieu gave the argument a new centrality. In order to understand his discussion of the subject in the *Spirit of the Laws* three points need to be made. The first is that Montesquieu, like Polybius, saw in ancient Sparta and Rome examples of governments in which different institutions were balanced against each other, the result being a limited government providing security against tyranny. These ancient constitutions, however, provided no proper separation of powers: this separation was thus a more recent construction. Where powers were separated, a new type of liberty was born. The balance of powers in ancient republics protected the community as a whole from tyranny; the separation of powers protected every individual.

The second point is crucial to understanding why Montesquieu did not stress the modernity of the concept of separation of powers. Broadly speaking, he identified the executive with the monarchy and the legislature with Parliament; both of these were long-established institutions. In addition, he identified the independent judicial element in the English Constitution with the *jury*. It was the jury who judged the facts in criminal cases and determined the innocence or guilt of the accused. Since the jury, too, was a long-established institution, the separation of powers appeared to Montesquieu to be deeply entrenched in English history.

He would have come up with a very different account had he focused on the independence of judges. Judges had served during the King's pleasure until 1715—they could simply be dismissed if their judgments did not please the king.[4] It was the activities of royalist judges such as Judge Jeffries (conductor of the Bloody Assizes, when those who had supported Monmouth's rebellion against James II were condemned to

---

4. That judges should serve during good behavior was one of Parliament's demands in 1641–2. The principle was briefly conceded by Charles I, and Charles II appointed judges on this basis from 1660 until 1667; after that the old formula, that judges served at the king's pleasure, was restored. Even the Bill of Rights of 1689 provided no guarantee of judicial independence.

death wholesale), who made no secret of their political allegiances, and did not hesitate to intimidate juries, which partly explains Locke's preoccupation with judicial impartiality. An independent judiciary—defined in the eighteenth century as a judiciary who served during good behavior, rather than at the executive's pleasure (Federalist 78)—had thus existed in England for less than a century when the debate on the Constitution took place. (Noah Webster, who thought that English judges had been independent "for many centuries," was simply mistaken.)

For Montesquieu, the principle of jury trial was central to English liberty. This principle, along with the separation of powers, was entrenched in the Massachusetts Constitution of 1780. For the anti-Federalists, the absence of any guarantee of jury trial was a fundamental weakness of the proposed constitution, and Federalist 83 was devoted to rebutting their arguments. In their original discussion of the separation of powers (Essays 47–51), the authors of the *Federalist* saw no need to discuss juries, nor even the independence of the judiciary, although this was the alternative to the independence of the jury on which they (and the Constitution) relied. They clearly did not foresee, in the early stages of planning and then writing the *Federalist*, how central the arguments that would lead to calls for a Bill of Rights would prove in the debate over ratification. They also did not foresee—as others did, even in their contributions to the debates at the Convention—the role the Supreme Court might play in interpreting and defending the Constitution. A recognition of the importance of this topic was something they took *from* the debates, not something they brought *to* them. We can date their new grasp of the importance of the topic between January 2 and January 16, 1788 (compare pages 213 and 230 below).

Instead (and this is the third point), the *Federalist* seeks to play the doctrine of the separation of powers against the doctrine of the balance of powers. Perfectly reasonably, the authors interpreted Montesquieu's doctrine of the separation of powers by referring to the practices embodied in the British Constitution, where the King had a veto over legislation and the House of Lords had a judicial role. They argued that if Britain embodied a separation of powers, then Montesquieu must have intended not a complete separation, but merely that no one power should be allowed to gain control over any of the others. They went on to argue that interaction between the departments was essential if each power was not only to be independent, but also to assist in controlling the others. In other words, the overriding importance of having a balance of powers required that one could not have a full separation. (In simultaneously stressing independence and interaction they were recapitulating the arguments of Bolingbroke, from whom Montesquieu is sometimes said to have

derived his doctrine of the separation of powers.) The separation of powers was thus a secondary principle for the authors of the *Federalist*. The
central principle was that power must be used to control power, and the
partial separation of powers was merely a means to this end.

Although Montesquieu writes of the distribution rather than the separation of powers, it was an easy step to derive a doctrine of the separation of powers from his argument because he evidently thinks of them as
separate and, because he thinks of them as separate, he assumes that the
power of the executive to control the legislature will be exercised through
the use of an unlimited veto.[5] It is surely because the veto is central to
Montesquieu's argument that sophisticated statesmen kept trying to
build vetoes into constitutions: Adams and Hamilton wanted the executive to have a veto over legislation, and Madison wanted the federal
assembly to have a veto over the state assemblies. Vetoes, however, are bad
politics, and again and again they had to be abandoned in the course of
turning drafts into agreed texts: Even Montesquieu recognized that in
theory vetoes would give rise to frequent deadlock, and they also imply
subordination rather than autonomy (something unacceptable, for example, to the states in their relation to the federal government). The text of
the Constitution contained only one absolute veto: The ability of Senate
and House to veto each other's proposals for legislation. The *Federalist*,
therefore, had to give an account of how one of the three powers might
control another without relying on what had long seemed the obvious
and simplest mechanism for control, the veto.

Thus, what was new (at least in an American context) in the *Federalist*
was the bold way in which the authors generalized the fundamental principle that power should act as a control on power, while making only a
glancing reference to the missing mechanism of the veto. Federalist 51
(along with Federalist 10, the most commented on of all the essays) is the
classic statement of this principle, but it merely crystallizes a line of argument that runs through the whole work. For example, in Essay 15: "Power
controlled or abridged is almost always the rival and enemy of that power
by which it is controlled or abridged." In Essay 28: "Power being almost
always the rival of power; the General Government will at all times stand
ready to check the usurpations of the state governments; and these will

---

5. Montesquieu also expects the executive to control the legislature by determining when and for how long it sits. The Constitution, which gives Presidents a
limited veto over legislation, gives them no control over the assembly and dissolution of Congress. The legislature was assumed to have no need for a veto over the
actions of the executive because it had both the power of impeachment and the
power to refuse taxation.

have the same disposition toward the General Government." This principle, "the policy of supplying, by opposite and rival interests, the defect of better motives," the policy that "ambition must be made to counteract ambition" is the underlying principle of constitutional design in the *Federalist*. In order to understand this principle, we need to look briefly at the development of the new science of politics.

The Science of Politics

The Federalists were conscious of relying on a new science of government, one still in its infancy. They felt obliged to stress both its weakness ("the science even of government itself seems yet to be almost in its state of infancy," said James Wilson) and its newfound strength ("The science of politics, however, like most other sciences, has received great improvement," said Hamilton). The most important exponent of the science of politics as far as the authors of the *Federalist* were concerned seems unquestionably to be the philosopher and historian David Hume, who had published a series of essays on political topics between 1741 and 1752, including the essay "That Politics May Be Reduced to a Science." (Many of the best works analyzing the *Federalist* since Douglass Adair's pathbreaking dissertation of 1943 have concentrated on bringing out just how much the *Federalist* is indebted to Hume.)

Hume, however, was not the originator of the new science of politics. In some respects that honor belongs to Machiavelli, who had first grasped the essential truth: Conflict is an irreducible fact of political life. In mid-seventeenth-century England, Harrington, who saw himself as a disciple of Machiavelli and Hobbes, had sought to identify institutional arrangements that would ensure that decisions were made in the public interest rather than in order to foster sectional interests. Some of Harrington's recommendations, such as the secret ballot and term limits, have been widely adopted. Harrington also proved to be deeply influential (one can see his influence, for example, in Webster's *Examination*) in insisting that power always follows property, so the crucial precondition for political freedom is a relatively equal distribution of wealth.

An important revolution in the techniques of political analysis took place around the year 1700, in writings by authors who are now rarely read, such as Neville, Moyle, Trenchard, and Toland. These writers (who continued to be read in the 1780s—we find Webster quoting "the ingenious Mr. Moyle") pioneered a view of constitutions as involving interactions comparable to those one might find in a watch or any other piece of complex machinery. Initially "machine," "engine," and "mechanism" were their preferred terms of analysis (Hume continued to write of "the political machine" and "the machine of government," and to compare forms of government to different types of engines), but their successors, from Bolingbroke on, generally preferred the new word (at least new in this sense) "system." (The *Federalist* uses the words "machine" [Essays 22, 59] and "mechanical" [Essay 14], along with "engine" [e.g., Essays 38, 83 (quoting Blackstone)], and frequently uses the word "system" [e.g., Essays 1, 9, 14, 16], along with a whole range of words—such as "momentum," "equilibrium," and "balance"—that imply a mechanical model.) Characteristic of the new way of thinking was Bolingbroke's statement quoted earlier: A constitution is a "noble and wise system, the essential parts of which are so proportioned, and so intimately connected, that a change in one begets a change in the whole."

A classic exposition of this new method of political analysis is found in one of the political texts most widely read in newly independent America: Trenchard and Gordon's *Cato's Letters* (1720–3). At the heart of *Cato's Letters* was the conviction that ambition and interest ensure that power always corrupts and that it always seeks to become despotic. One could not simply entrust power to the people in order to ensure that the interests of the rulers and the ruled remained the same, for there will always be divergent interests within society, and majorities will always be tempted to tyrannize minorities (religious persecution provided the textbook example of this). As we have seen, Trenchard and Gordon were perhaps the first to use the word "minority."

What was essential therefore was not simply that rulers should be made accountable, but that their powers should be limited. The problem was that in English law there was nothing to limit the power of Parliament. The Bill of Rights, for example, was simply a statute; if one Parliament had introduced it, another could repeal it. The people, of course, could exercise some control over their representatives through election, but elections provided no protection for the rights of minorities. So in order to limit the power of the government, one power had to be set against another. Experience, they argued in *Cato's Letters*, had shown there was only one type of free government that could survive, one where

> [T]he power and sovereignty of magistrates in free countries was so qualified, and so divided into different channels, and committed to the discretion of so many different men, with different interests and views, that the majority of them could seldom or never find their account in betraying their trust in fundamental instances. Their emulation, envy, fear, or interest, always made them spies and checks upon one another. . . . The only secret therefore in forming a free government is to make the interests of the governors and the governed the same, as far as human policy can contrive. Liberty cannot be preserved any other way.

Power was to be limited by being distributed (in James Wilson's words) "in different directions, in different dimensions, and at different heights." Only by such means could government be made to control itself, setting one part of the political system against another.

If the words "machine," "engine," and "system" were the first set used in this new political analysis, the second set was "check," "balance," "control," "clog," and "bridle." For us, a single phrase now sums it up: "checks and balances." This phrase was coined by Adams in the *Defense* and was widely adopted during the debate on ratification; but the type of political analysis that it epitomizes goes back to *Cato's Letters* and before, to 1700.

There was a fundamental paradox in this new conception of politics: All authority ought to be derived from the people, and yet there must be numerous authorities sufficiently independent to act against each other. Traditional accounts of mixed or balanced constitutions had assumed that the key political powers had an independent and entrenched existence. King, aristocracy, and the people all controlled military and financial resources. The constitutional balance reflected a balance in society as a whole. Indeed, the tradition derived from Harrington insisted that there could be no real power independent of property. This understanding of the mixed constitution thus seemed to imply that it could function only within a hierarchical society.

For Thomas Paine and his successors, republicanism involved replacing this balance of power by a new concentration of power in an assembly representing the people. To such people, the Massachusetts Constitution of 1780 and the constitutional proposals of 1787 were either ill-concealed attempts to restore monarchy, hierarchy, and inequality, or radically incoherent attempts to give newly minted institutions a type of power that could be held only by those able to directly control substantial resources and employ them for their private purposes. They dismissed the intricate mechanisms by which the new constitutions set power against power as mere parchment barriers, checks on paper. Patrick Henry called the limits on power in the proposed federal constitution "specious imaginary balances, your rope-dancing, chain-rattling, ridiculous ideal checks and contrivances," and insisted that the new constitution was so complicated that no one could predict how it would work in practice. Even the advocates of the new science of politics had to acknowledge that it involved something of a leap in the dark. In the words of Federalist 1, "The important question, whether societies of men are really capable or not, of establishing good government from reflection and choice, or whether they are forever destined to depend, for their political constitutions, on accident and force" remained to be

decided, for there was a "defect of antecedent experience on this complicated and difficult subject." Supporters of the proposed constitution
were being asked to trust themselves to the untested theories of the new
science.

There were two further principles fundamental to the new science,
beyond the claim that power should be set against power in order to limit
government. The first, though never more than implied and always clum-
sily formulated, was an immensely powerful new idea: that of the feedback loop. We have seen that Spelman argued that oppositions, even if
they never acquired power, were beneficial to the public because they
exposed and even exaggerated the defects of government; by organizing
resistance they served to change the behavior of governments for the better. There was thus a feedback loop where government behavior provoked
opposition, the opposition appealed to the electorate, and fear of the electorate altered the behavior of the government. It was only where the feedback loop failed to operate that the opposition would find itself in power.
The same mechanism is described in Federalist 28: When the national
authority invades public liberty, the state governments will discover the
usurpation, organize opposition, and force a change in policy. It is only
where the feedback loop fails to operate that the states might have to
engage in armed resistance.

The central claim of arguments such as this is that political institutions can be devised in such a way that corrupt or selfish behavior, by pro-
voking opposition, creates an incentive to correct that very same behavior.
These systems are therefore self-correcting or self-regulating, although
the process of correction requires an amount of time sufficient for the
feedback mechanism to operate. When Federalist 51 argues that "The
provision for defense must . . . be made commensurate to the danger of
attack. Ambition must be made to counteract ambition," it is arguing that
there must be scope for such feedback mechanisms throughout the political system.

The new science did not devise a new language to describe the feedback process for the simple reason that feedback loops were rarely to be
found in existing machines. Such processes were being newly analyzed in
the economy by Hume (who invented the modern theory of the balance of
trade) and Smith (who showed how markets are self-correcting), but
Hume, Smith, and the authors of the *Federalist* had few concrete examples they could point to of such mechanisms at work. One cannot, after
all, see either a balance of trade or a market correction. Within a few
years, however, self-correcting mechanisms were to become common-
place—the fantail windmill is one example, but the most familiar is James
Watt's invention in 1788 of the centrifugal speed governor for steam

engines. As a result, self-correcting and self-regulating mechanisms were soon to become easy to describe and understand, but Hume, Smith, and the authors of the *Federalist* had to make do as best they could. Here it must be said that Hume, Smith, and the early economists were more successful than the authors of the *Federalist* and the theorists of the new politics: Federalist 51 acknowledges its own failure to provide "a full development of this important idea."

The second new principle was clearly formulated in Jean Louis de Lolme's *Constitution of England* (1771), a work admired by Adams and Hamilton. It would be difficult to overemphasize the extent to which the key ideas of the *Federalist* were already present in de Lolme. De Lolme was a former disciple of Rousseau's who had turned against him, in the process pioneering the critique of direct democracy and large, unchecked assemblies, which we later find recapitulated in the *Federalist* and in works by Noah Webster. For our immediate purposes, de Lolme's most important argument is that in modern political systems it is the power of the legislature, not the executive, that is the greatest threat to the liberty and security of individuals.[6] The classic Whig tradition had been largely preoccupied with devising methods for strengthening the legislature so that it could control and limit the executive. De Lolme, in direct opposition to this tradition, thought that the true excellence of the modern British Constitution lay in the fact that it would prevent a degeneration into the sort of totalitarian democracy described by Rousseau, not simply because it relied on representation rather than direct democracy, but also because the legislature was weakened by being divided into two, and the executive was strengthened by being united in the monarch.

It is precisely this analysis that is taken up in the *Federalist*. In Essay 48 Madison argues that it is against "the enterprising ambition" of the legislature that "the people ought to indulge all their jealousy and exhaust all their precautions." In Essay 51 he asserts "In republican government, the legislative authority, necessarily, predominates. The remedy for this inconveniency is, to divide the legislature into different branches. . . . the weakness of the executive may require, on the other

---

6. Hume, in "Of the Independency of Parliament," had maintained that "the executive power in every government is altogether subordinate to the legislative," and had stressed the need to limit the power of the legislature, but his solution to this problem had been extraconstitutional. Corruption, in his view, fulfilled a function that he assumed no constitutional mechanism could fulfill—it gave the executive a capacity to influence the decisions of the legislative. What was new in de Lolme was not so much the identification of the problem of legislative supremacy, as the conviction that there were constitutional solutions to this problem.

hand, that it should be fortified."[7] It is in the context of these essays (together with Federalist 49 and 71) that we need to read the reference in Federalist 9 to "legislative checks and balances." This is the reading of the second publication, and has become the accepted text, but when first published the text read "legislature checks and balances," and the error is as likely to be in the second as in the first version. In either version what is meant is not checks and balances employed by the legislative to control the executive (the classic Whig project), but rather checks and balances to limit the inordinate powers of the legislature (de Lolme's new foundation for liberty). The states had provided plenty of evidence of the danger of overpowerful legislatures in the years following the Revolution; but it was de Lolme who had first formulated a constitutional solution to the problem.

The Constitutional Convention and Ratification

I have tried to show that the Convention that gathered in Philadelphia faced practical, rather than intellectual, difficulties. Although Montesquieu had made it hard to think about an extensive republic, Harrington and Hume had shown that representation made nonsense of the idea that republics could only be city-states. The delegates had good examples of written constitutions, and, with the idea that power should be used to check power, a clear understanding of how to construct a limited government. Their problems lay elsewhere. How should they delimit the powers of the federal governments and the states? How could they create a strong executive that would not resemble a monarchy? How should they represent the states at the federal level, and construct a constitution where none of the key regional interest groups was likely to be dictated to by the others in the foreseeable future?

Fifty-five delegates from twelve states met on May 25, 1787. Four days later they had in front of them the Virginia Plan, drafted by Madison, which offered a solution to the first two of these dilemmas.

We can see at once that the Virginia Plan did not only fail the test of protecting the states and regional interest groups. It also gave too much power to the first branch of the Legislature: They were to choose the President and the second branch of the Legislature, they were to have a

---

7. One key respect in which the Constitution fortified the executive was that it concentrated all of the executive's power in the hands of the President, rather than (as in the various state constitutions) giving it to a committee or sharing it between a Governor and an elected Council. It was thus the first American constitution to follow de Lolme's advice and unify the executive.

conditional veto over the legislation of the state legislatures,[8] and there was no mechanism by which unconstitutional legislation could be set aside. In the following months, the interests of the states were protected by removing the conditional veto, by redesigning the Senate, by Congress' being curtailed to a list of enumerated powers, and by the specific protection of slavery for a limited period. In addition, the Senate and President were strengthened by giving each of them an independent claim to be representative of the nation. By taking the election of the Senate and President out of the hands of the first branch, the Convention brought the proposed constitution closer to the Massachusetts model. On one final issue, that of unconstitutional legislation, the Convention (having rejected the Virginia Plan's proposal for a Council of Revision) never reached a clear consensus, partly because previous written constitutions had also fudged the issue: The nature of the problem was to be clarified during the Ratification debate, but considerable uncertainty with regard to the powers of the Supreme Court remained long after the Constitution was adopted.

The Philadelphia Convention had done much more than had been expected of it. It had not simply proposed some additional powers for the Confederation Congress, but had created a new constitution establishing a unified national government (although one in which the states were guaranteed a continuing, if limited, role). This constitution was to be approved by specially elected state conventions and was to come into effect so long as nine states adopted it.

The publication of the proposed constitution led immediately to a struggle for ratification. Although it was presented as having the unanimous support of the Convention (so strong was the ideal of unanimity even in the new age of majority rule—in fact, three of the delegates present had refused to sign), and although ninety percent of the newspapers backed it, there was sustained opposition in the large states of Massachusetts, Virginia, and New York. To its opponents, the constitution seemed to undermine the states, to establish aristocracy, and to threaten the possibility of monarchy. If the Federalists won the debate (and the votes in the three key states were close—187 to 168 in Massachusetts, 30 to 27 in New York, 89 to 79 in Virginia), it was partly because they had the better arguments. It was also because they had achieved at Philadelphia something close to a coup d'état: They had decisively undermined the legitimacy of the existing Confederation and had deprived their opponents of any opportunity to formulate an alternative. On one issue they

---

8. The power of veto is sometimes described as if it were absolute, but it is clearly limited by the powers of the Council of Revision.

were required to change their minds: The proposed constitution contained no Bill of Rights, but ratification was achieved only by promising
that there would be no resistance to one being added.

Reading the Federalist

In each state the debate took a different form, for in each state the Constitution was measured against the state Constitution. The *Federalist* was
addressed specifically to the people of New York, with a view to influencing the outcome of the debate there. It presented itself as a disinterested
commentary on the new Constitution—there was nothing about it to suggest that it had more than one author, that one of its authors was not from
New York, and that two of its authors had been present at the Convention.
Crucially, it defended the constitutional proposal as it had been adopted,
although its two key authors had had tremendous misgivings in the final
days of the Convention. Madison had wanted the central government to
retain a veto on state legislation, and had told Jefferson in early September that "the plan, should it be adopted, will neither effectually answer its
national object, nor prevent the local mischiefs which everywhere excite
disgust against the state governments." Hamilton, on the last day of the
Convention, had declared that "no man's ideas were more remote from
the plan than his own were known to be." He had wanted an executive and
Senate appointed for life, an executive with an absolute veto over all legislation, and an explicit subordination of the states to the new central government. Yet there are few moments when these misgivings show in the
text of the *Federalist*.[9] Moreover, if Madison and Hamilton both wanted a
stronger central government than the compromise proposal embodied in
the Constitution, they were soon to find themselves on opposite sides in
the politics of the new nation. Their alliance in 1787–8 was one of convenience, not principle.

In order to read the *Federalist*, then, we need to bear in mind four basic
principles: It was written for a New York audience; it was written over a
period of more than seven months, during which time the debate evolved

---

9. It is sometimes said that the Constitution embodies a new theory of Federalism; but the new Federalism was essentially a compromise between those who
wanted to adapt the existing Confederation and those who wanted a consolidated
government. As consolidators, Madison and Hamilton were ill-prepared to produce a new Federalist theory, and their discomfort around this topic is evident in
the revisions to Federalist 39 in the McLean edition. The triumph of Federalism
was very much an achievement of the so-called anti-Federalists in the years after
the ratification of the Constitution, and it is to the anti-Federalists rather than the
Federalists that one should look for the principles of the new Federalism.

(the question of the powers of the Supreme Court coming to the fore) and the political situation changed (eight states had already ratified the Constitution by the time the final installment was published); it was written anonymously; and it was written not to defend theoretical principles in the abstract, but to win support for a specific (and in the view of its authors imperfect) proposal. Since we know with reasonable certainty who wrote each of the essays, it is natural for us to associate particular arguments with Madison and with Hamilton, and there can be no doubt that each brought to the enterprise his own preoccupations (in Madison's case, a commitment to pluralism; in Hamilton's, a particular concern with the powers of the executive). But if "Publius," the supposed author of the *Federalist,* was a pure fiction, it is important to remember that writing in the guise of Publius freed Madison and Hamilton from any obligation to defend their personal opinions and enabled them to turn themselves into a mouthpiece for the infant Constitution.

To speak on behalf of the Constitution was not to speak the language of liberty as that language had traditionally been understood. In the opening pages of the *Federalist,* Publius acknowledges that it is his opponents who have a "noble enthusiasm" for, perhaps even a "violent love . . . of liberty," and it was the anti-Federalists who spoke of liberty endangered by the concentration of power in the hands of a few. It is to them, not the Federalists, that we owe the Bill of Rights and the principles of modern Federalism. Hamilton, speaking to the New York assembly, made clear that good governance is every bit as important as (perhaps in Hamilton's view even more important than) liberty: For him, "good administration . . . is the true touchstone."

To defend the Constitution was not to appeal to principles that had been known to ancient Greece or Rome, or even to the modern republics of Venice, Switzerland, and Holland. Instead it was to speak of power checking power, of representation by election, of the necessity of opposition, of the counterbalancing of an overpowerful legislature, and of the independence of the judiciary. These were new political principles, the principles of a new science of politics that saw constitutions as interacting systems, as systems of "checks and balances." The new science became possible with the distinction between legislature, executive, and judiciary during the English Civil War, and its principles were expounded in Hume's *Essays* (1741–77). Its most sophisticated formulation, prior to the *Federalist,* had been de Lolme's *Constitution of England* (1771). The *Federalist* was the definitive reformulation of these principles for the new era that had opened in 1776, the era of the written constitution. As such, it is a work of more than merely historical importance. It will continue to be relevant as long as powers are separated, elections held, and constitutions written or amended.

More than two centuries later, however, our world is very different from that of 1787. The authors of the *Federalist* were concerned to show that America was too big to have the defects of a city-state, but not so big as to be ungovernable by a representative assembly. Theirs was a world of sailing ships and stagecoaches, of newspapers and books. The railway, the automobile, and the airplane have shrunk journeys that once took weeks so that they are now completed in hours. The telegraph, the wireless, the telephone, the television, and the World Wide Web have made distance increasingly irrelevant. It would be wrong to assume that *all* the arguments of the *Federalist* still hold good in this new world, but all modern political science derives from the eighteenth-century science of politics that the *Federalist* refined and perfected. It was according to the principles of this science (already expounded for Americans in the first volume of Adams' *Defense*) that the Constitution was designed. To understand the Constitution, we have to recognize the principles on which it is based. We may agree with Patrick Henry that liberty is "the greatest of all earthly blessings," and even that "liberty ought to be the direct end of your government." But the argument of the *Federalist* is straightforward: Such a "noble enthusiasm" for liberty is not enough, unless it is combined with a respect for the fundamental principles embodied in the Constitution.

Suggestions for Further Reading

The best brief introduction to the Constitution as the culminating moment of the American Revolution is Gordon S. Wood, *The American Revolution: A History* (New York: Modern Library, 2002). The classic text is the same author's *The Creation of the American Republic, 1776–1787* (Chapel Hill: University of North Carolina Press, 1969). For a critique of Wood, see Marc Kruman, *Between Authority and Liberty* (Chapel Hill: University of North Carolina Press, 1997).

On the intellectual origins of the revolution of 1776, there is Bernard Bailyn's *The Ideological Origins of the American Revolution* (Cambridge, Mass.: Harvard University Press, 1967). But there is nothing comparable on the intellectual origin of the Constitution. On republicanism, there is Paul A. Rahe, *Republics Ancient and Modern* (Chapel Hill: University of North Carolina Press, 1992); on the separation of powers there is M. J. C. Vile, *Constitutionalism and the Separation of Powers* (1st ed., 1967; 2nd ed., Indianapolis: Liberty Fund, 1998); and on the idea of a new science of politics, there is David Wootton, "Liberty, Metaphor, and Mechanism: 'Checks and Balances' and the Origins of Modern Constitutionalism" in David Womersley, ed., *Liberty and American Experience in the Eighteenth*

Century (Indianapolis: Liberty Fund, forthcoming). A helpful survey of recent debates is Alan Gibson, "Ancients, Moderns and Americans: The Republicanism-Liberalism Debate Revisited," *History of Political Thought* 21 (2000), 261–307.

The key documents of the Convention are collected in Max Farrand, *The Records of the Federal Convention of 1787* (4 vols., New Haven: Yale, 1911). Two books that study both the Convention and the *Federalist* are Lance Banning, *The Sacred Fire of Liberty: James Madison and the Founding of the Federal Republic* (Ithaca: Cornell University Press, 1995) and Jack N. Rakove, *Original Meanings: Politics and Ideas in the Making of the Constitution* (New York: Knopf, 1996). A valuable introduction to Madison is Richard K. Matthews, *If Men Were Angels: James Madison and the Heartless Empire of Reason* (Lawrence, Kans.: University Press of Kansas, 1995).

The standard edition of the *Federalist* (and the one most valuable to me in preparing the text published here) is that edited by Jacob E. Cooke (Middletown, Conn.: Wesleyan University Press, 1961). The best short introduction to the *Federalist* is Garry Wills, *Explaining America: "The Federalist"* (Garden City, N.Y.: Doubleday, 1981). For a close reading of the arguments see Morton White, *Philosophy, "The Federalist," and the Constitution* (New York: Oxford University Press, 1987). A number of important essays by Douglass Adair are collected in his *Fame and the Founding Fathers* (New York: Norton, 1974). Other texts in defense of the Constitution are collected in Colleen A. Sheehan and Gary L. McDowell, eds., *Friends of the Constitution: Writings of the "Other" Federalists, 1787–1788* (Indianapolis: Liberty Fund, 1998).

For surveys of the political thinking of the anti-Federalists see Herbert Storing, *What the Anti-Federalists Were For* (Chicago: University of Chicago Press, 1981) and Saul Cornell, *The Other Founders: Anti-Federalism and the Dissenting Tradition in America, 1788–1828* (Chapel Hill: University of North Carolina Press, 1999). Two valuable collections of anti-Federalist writings are W. B. Allen and Gordon Lloyd, eds., *The Essential Antifederalist* (Lanham, Md.: University Press of America, 1985) and Bruce Frohnen, ed., *The Anti-Federalists: Selected Speeches and Writings* (Washington, D.C.: Regnery Publishing, 1999).

Documents relative to the Bill of Rights are collected in Gordon Lloyd and Margie Lloyd, eds., *The Essential Bill of Rights: Original Arguments and Fundamental Documents* (Lanham, Md.: University Press of America, 1998). An older study is Robert A. Rutland, *The Birth of the Bill of Rights, 1776–1791* (Chapel Hill: University of North Carolina Press, 1955); a valuable recent discussion is Akhil Amar, *The Bill of Rights: Creation and Reconstruction* (New Haven: Yale University Press, 1998).

Notes on the Authors and Texts

There was an established convention in postrevolutionary America that political polemics were published anonymously, for anonymous authors could not be accused of trying to advance their own reputations or further their own prospects—hence the adoption of pseudonyms such as Cato, Centinel, Publius, and Brutus. George Mason's "Objections" deliberately flouts this convention. Mason (1725–92) wrote the Declaration of Rights in the Virginia Constitution of 1776 and was one of Virginia's delegates to the Constitutional Convention. He refused to sign the proposed constitution because it lacked a Bill of Rights, and he published a summary of his objections in November 1787; they were widely republished. Mason's objective was clearly to undermine the appearance that the proposed constitution had the unanimous support of delegates to the Convention.

"The Address and Reasons of Dissent of the Minority of the Convention of Pennsylvania to Their Constituents" was published in the *Pennsylvania Packet and Daily Advertiser* on December 18, 1787 and was widely reprinted. Samuel Bryan, though not himself a member of the Pennsylvania Convention, is thought to have been the author. He was the son of a leading Pennsylvania anti-Federalist.

Patrick Henry (1736–99), a Virginia politician, had participated in both Continental Congresses, and played a key role in drafting the Virginia Constitution of 1776, under which he was elected Governor five times. He had refused to represent Virginia at the Federal Convention in 1787 and opposed the proposed constitution from the beginning. His speeches were published in *Debates and Other Proceedings of the Convention of Virginia* (1788–9): The text here follows that edition, including the interpolations of the original editor, who was clearly working from an imperfect record.

The New York Ratifying Convention met on June 17, 1788. Although more than two-thirds of the delegates were believed to be opposed to ratification, by the time the Convention met, eight states had ratified; two more did so while it deliberated, which gave the supporters of the Constitution a tremendous advantage during the debates. Melancton Smith led the anti-Federalist opposition. He was a prominent businessman who had been a member of New York's first Provincial Congress and of the Continental Congress. His speeches were published in *The Debates and Proceedings of the Convention of the State of New York* (1788).

The "Letters of Cato" appeared in the *New York Journal* between September 1787 and January 1788; the first appeared in the issue that contained the proposed constitution. They are generally thought to have been written by the state governor, George Clinton.

The "Letters of Centinel" appeared in the Philadelphia *Independent Gazeteer* and *Freeman's Journal* between October 1787 and April 1788; several—especially the first two—were reprinted elsewhere. Their author is thought to have been Samuel Bryan (who is also believed to have written the Address of the Minority of the Pennsylvania Convention). "Centinel" is simply an eighteenth-century spelling of "sentinel": The author presents himself as a lookout who is raising the alarm.

The "Essays of Brutus" appeared between October 1787 and April 1788 in the *New York Journal*. They are generally thought to have been written by Robert Yates, a judge and a dissenting member of the Constitutional Convention, from which he had withdrawn in opposition to its proposals.

James Wilson (1742–98), a lawyer and speculator, was born and educated in Scotland and emigrated to Pennsylvania in 1766. He was a delegate to the Continental Congress (in 1775 he argued that an act of Parliament could be unconstitutional, a line of argument that leads directly to the idea of judicial review), and a signer of the Declaration of Independence. He opposed the Pennsylvania Constitution of 1776 and was an active and influential participant in the Constitutional Convention. He played a key role in persuading Pennsylvania to ratify the Constitution and in drafting the Pennsylvania Constitution of 1790. He was appointed an Associate Justice of the U.S. Supreme Court in 1789. A version of his speech to the ratifying convention quickly appeared in print; the text here is a later one produced by Thomas Lloyd, Secretary to the Pennsylvania Convention, and includes Lloyd's notes.

Noah Webster (1758–1843), who later became famous for his *American Dictionary of the English Language* (1828), was a publisher, editor of newspapers, and author of books on history, politics, and science. He was an early campaigner for copyright, a campaign that convinced him of the need for a strong federal government, since he was obliged to seek to persuade each state separately to introduce copyright legislation.

The *Federalist* was written under the pseudonym "Publius" by Alexander Hamilton, James Madison, and John Jay. The first essay appeared in the *Independent Journal*, October 27, 1787, and Essays 2 through 77 appeared in four New York newspapers: the *Independent Journal*, the *New York Packet*, the *Daily Advertiser*, and the *New York Journal*. The text that appeared in the newspapers is closest to the original manuscript, and had the greatest immediate impact on the ratification debate; therefore, this text is followed here. Essays 78 through 85 first appeared in the second volume of the first book edition, edited by John and Archibald McLean (May 28, 1788), and then in the *Independent Journal* and the *New York Packet*. In the McLean edition all the essays were corrected by

Hamilton, but mistakes were introduced as well as being corrected. McLean (or perhaps Hamilton) summarized the contents of each essay in the table of contents (reproduced here). McLean also altered the numbering of the essays and divided one essay into two; McLean's numbering is followed here. In 1802, a new edition, edited by George F. Hopkins, contained further revisions—largely stylistic in nature—approved by Hamilton. In 1818 a further edition, edited by Jacob Gideon, appeared with corrections by Madison, and with Madison's identification of the author of each essay. (The result has been considerable textual confusion: At least one modern edition that claims to follow McLean in fact incorporates some revisions from later editions; another faithfully follows Gideon but provides no indication of where the Gideon edition differs from its predecessors.) Because of some claims made by Hamilton, there has been some dispute over the authorship of a number of essays (18–20, 49–58, 62–3). The attributions that appear here are those of Madison, which are now generally accepted. The present text follows the first edition of each essay (with the correction of obvious errors) but records in the notes all significant variations in the McLean edition and in the later editions based on McLean, those of Gideon and Hopkins. In this approach it follows the principles of the first modern scholarly edition, that of Jacob E. Cooke (1961).

James Madison (1751–1836) was from a wealthy Virginia family and was educated at Princeton, where he read the philosophers of the Scottish Enlightenment. He was a delegate to the Virginia Convention that wrote a new state constitution in 1776 and was appointed to the Virginia Council of State in 1777, and then to the Continental Congress in 1779. In 1784 he was elected to the Virginia House of Delegates and began to campaign for a new national constitution. Madison played key roles in shaping the outcome of the Constitutional Convention in 1787, in the Virginia Ratifying Convention, and in persuading the first Congress to adopt a Bill of Rights (1789). With Thomas Jefferson he led the opposition to Hamilton's efforts to centralize government. He was Secretary of State under Jefferson. Madison was elected President in 1809 and 1812.

Alexander Hamilton (1757–1804) was born in the West Indies, came to America in 1773 (where he soon began reading Hume), and served during the War of Independence, becoming Washington's aide-de-camp. He represented New York at the Continental Congress in 1782–3 and at the Constitutional Convention in 1787: There his arguments for a strong national government were strongly opposed by New York's other two delegates, who went on to reject the proposed Constitution. Hamilton led the campaign for ratification in New York and was the architect of the *Federalist*. From 1789 to 1795 he was the first Secretary of the Treasury, and in 1801 he played a decisive role in securing the presidency for Jefferson (his political opponent) in Jefferson's tied race with Aaron Burr; in 1804 he fought a duel with Burr, which resulted in Hamilton's death.

John Jay (1745–1829), a New York attorney, helped draft New York's first constituton in 1777 and was the first Chief Justice of the New York Supreme Court. He was a member of both the first and second Continental Congresses and (with Benjamin Franklin and John Adams) negotiated the Treaty of Paris (1783), in which Britain recognized American independence. Jay's contribution to the *Federalist* was limited by a severe illness that began in November 1787. In 1789 he was appointed the first Chief Justice of the U.S. Supreme Court. He was governor of New York from 1795 to 1801.

It should be noted that the Bill of Rights was originally intended only to entrench certain rights against the federal government; only with the 14th Constitutional Amendment of 1868 did the process begin whereby the rights enumerated in the Bill of Rights became rights that could be claimed against the governments of the states. Previously, rights against the state governments depended on the Bills of Rights enacted in each state.

All the texts reproduced here have modernized spelling, though I have retained throughout the variant spelling of "case," when discussing legal cases, as "cause." The punctuation and capitalization remains close to that of the original, but minor changes have been made, including the systematic introduction of the serial comma. Notes in square brackets are my own. Other notes are attributed to their authors (e.g., "Publius" or "Lloyd").

I would like to thank Paul A. Rahe and Barry Shain for correcting some of my errors. Those that remain are mine alone.

The Anti-Federalists

GEORGE MASON, *OBJECTIONS TO THE CONSTITUTION*
OF GOVERNMENT FORMED BY THE CONVENTION

November 1787

There is no Declaration of Rights; and the Laws of the general Government being paramount to the Laws and Constitutions of the several States, the Declarations of Rights in the separate States are no Security. Nor are the people secured even in the Enjoyment of the Benefits of the common law: which stands here upon no other Foundation than its having been adopted by the respective Acts forming the Constitutions of the several States.

In the House of Representatives there is not the Substance, but the Shadow only of Representation; which can never produce proper Information in the Legislature, or inspire Confidence in the People: the Laws will therefore be generally made by Men little concerned in, and unacquainted with their Effects and Consequences.[1]

The Senate have the Power of altering all Money Bills and of originating Appropriations of Money and the Salaries of the Officers of their own Appointment in Conjunction with the President of the United States; although they are not the Representatives of the People, or amenable to them.

These with their other great Powers (viz. their Power in the Appointment of Ambassadors and all public Officers, in making Treaties, and in trying all Impeachments) their Influence upon and Connection with the supreme Executive from these Causes, their Duration of Office, and their being a constant existing Body almost continually sitting, joined with their being one complete Branch of the Legislature, will destroy any Balance in the Government, and enable them to accomplish what Usurpations they please upon the Rights and Liberties of the People.

The Judiciary of the United States is so constructed and extended, as to absorb and destroy the Judiciaries of the several States; thereby rendering

---

1. This Objection has been in some Degree lessened by an Amendment, often before refused, and at last made by an Erasure, after the Engrossment upon Parchment, of the word *forty*, and inserting *thirty*, in the Third Clause of the Second Section of the First Article. (Mason)

1

Law as tedious, intricate, and expensive, and Justice as unattainable, by a great part of the Community, as in England, and enabling the Rich to oppress and ruin the Poor.

The President of the United States has no constitutional Council (a thing unknown in any safe and regular Government): he will therefore be unsupported by proper Information and Advice; and will generally be directed by Minions and Favorites—or He will become a Tool to the Senate—or a Council of State will grow out of the principal Officers of the great Departments; the worst and most dangerous of all Ingredients for such a Council, in a free Country; for they may be induced to join in any dangerous or oppressive Measures, to shelter themselves, and prevent an Inquiry into their own Misconduct in Office; whereas had a constitutional Council been formed (as was proposed) of six Members; viz. two from the Eastern, two from the Middle, and two from the Southern States, to be appointed by Vote of the States in the House of Representatives, with the same Duration and Rotation of Office as the Senate, the Executive would always have had safe and proper Information and Advice, the President of such a Council might have acted as Vice President of the United States, pro tempore, upon any Vacancy or Disability of the chief Magistrate; and long continued Sessions of the Senate would in a great Measure have been prevented.

From this fatal Defect of a constitutional Council has arisen the improper Power of the Senate, in the Appointment of public Officers, and the alarming Dependence and Connection between that Branch of the Legislature, and the supreme Executive.

Hence also sprung that unnecessary and dangerous Officer, the Vice President; who for want of other Employment, is made President of the Senate; thereby dangerously blending the executive and legislative Powers; besides always giving to some one of the States an unnecessary and unjust Preeminence over the others.

The President of the United States has the unrestrained Power of granting Pardon for Treason; which may be sometimes exercised to screen from Punishment those whom he had secretly instigated to commit the Crime, and thereby prevent a Discovery of his own Guilt.

By declaring all Treaties supreme Laws of the Land, the Executive and the Senate have in many Cases, an exclusive Power of Legislation; which might have been avoided by proper Distinctions with Respect to Treaties, and requiring the Assent of the House of Representatives, where it could be done with Safety.

By requiring only a Majority to make all commercial and navigation Laws, the five Southern States (whose Produce and Circumstances are totally different from that of the eight Northern and Eastern States) will be ruined; for such rigid and premature Regulations may be made, as will enable the Merchants of the Northern and Eastern States not only to demand an exorbitant Freight, but to monopolize the Purchase of the Commodities at their own Price, for many years: to the great Injury of the landed Interest, and Impoverishment of the People: and the Danger is the greater, as the Gain on one Side will be in Proportion to the Loss on the other. Whereas requiring two-thirds of the members present in both Houses would have produced mutual moderation, promoted the general Interest, and removed an insuperable Objection to the Adoption of the Government.

Under their own Construction of the general Clause at the End of the enumerated powers the Congress may grant Monopolies in Trade and Commerce, constitute new Crimes, inflict unusual and severe Punishments, and extend their Power as far as they shall think proper; so that the State Legislatures have no Security for the Powers now presumed to remain to them; or the People for their Rights.

There is no Declaration of any kind for preserving the Liberty of the Press, the Trial by Jury in civil Causes; nor against the Danger of standing Armies in time of Peace.

The State Legislatures are restrained from laying Export Duties on their own Produce.

The general Legislature is restrained from prohibiting the further Importation of Slaves for twenty-odd Years; though such Importations render the United States weaker, more vulnerable, and less capable of Defense.

Both the general Legislature and the State Legislatures are expressly prohibited making ex post facto Laws; though there never was, or can be a Legislature but must and will make such Laws, when necessity and the public Safety require them; which will hereafter be a Breach of all the Constitutions in the Union, and afford precedents for other Innovations.

This Government will commence in a moderate Aristocracy; it is at present impossible to foresee whether it will, in its Operation, produce a Monarchy, or a corrupt oppressive Aristocracy; it will most probably vibrate some Years between the two, and then terminate in the one or the other.

THE ADDRESS AND REASONS OF DISSENT OF THE
MINORITY OF THE CONVENTION OF THE STATE OF
PENNSYLVANIA TO THEIR CONSTITUENTS

[December 18, 1787]

It was not until after the termination of the late glorious contest, which made the people of the United States an independent nation, that any defect was discovered in the present confederation. It was formed by some of the ablest patriots in America. It carried us successfully through the war; and the virtue and patriotism of the people, with their disposition to promote the common cause, supplied the want of power in Congress.

The requisition of Congress for the five *percent.* impost was made before the peace, so early as the first of February, 1781, but was prevented taking effect by the refusal of one state; yet it is probable every state in the union would have agreed to this measure at that period, had it not been for the extravagant terms in which it was demanded. The requisition was new molded in the year 1783, and accompanied with an additional demand of certain supplementary funds for twenty-five years. Peace had now taken place, and the United States found themselves laboring under a considerable foreign and domestic debt, incurred during the war. The requisition of 1783 was commensurate with the interest of the debt, as it was then calculated; but it has been more accurately ascertained since that time. The domestic debt has been found to fall several millions of dollars short of the calculation, and it has lately been considerably diminished by large sales of the western lands. The states have been called on by Congress annually for supplies until the general system of finance proposed in 1783 should take place.

It was at this time that the want of an efficient federal government was first complained of, and that the powers vested in Congress were found to be inadequate to the procuring of the benefits that should result from the union. The impost was granted by most of the states, but many refused the supplementary funds; the annual requisitions were set at naught by some of the states, while others complied with them by legislative acts, [but] were tardy in their payments, and Congress found themselves incapable of complying with their engagements, and supporting the federal government. It was found that our national character was sinking in the opinion of foreign nations. The Congress could make treaties of commerce, but could not enforce the observance of them. We were suffering from the restrictions of foreign nations, who had shackled our commerce, while we were unable to retaliate: and all now agreed that it would be advantageous to the union to enlarge the powers of Congress; that they should be enabled in the amplest manner to regulate commerce, and to lay and collect duties on the imports throughout the United States. With this view a convention was first proposed by Virginia, and finally recommended by Congress for the different states to appoint deputies to meet in convention, "for the purposes of revising and amending the present articles of confederation, so as to make them adequate to the exigencies of the union." This recommendation the legislatures of twelve states complied with so hastily as not to consult their constituents on the subject; and though the different legislatures had no authority from their constituents for the purpose, they probably apprehended the necessity would justify the measure; and none of them extended their ideas at that time further than "revising and amending the present articles of confederation." Pennsylvania by the act appointing deputies expressly confined their powers to this object; and though it is probable that some of the members of the assembly of this state had at that time in contemplation to annihilate the present confederation as well as the constitution of Pennsylvania, yet the plan was not sufficiently matured to communicate it to the public.

The majority of the legislature of this commonwealth, were at that time under the influence of the members from the city of Philadelphia. They agreed that the deputies sent by them to convention should have no compensation for their services, which determination was calculated to prevent the election of any member who resided at a distance from the city. It was in vain for the minority to attempt electing delegates to the convention, who understood the circumstances, and the feelings of the people, and had a common interest with them. They found a disposition in the leaders of the majority of the house to choose themselves and some of their dependants. The minority attempted to prevent this by agreeing to vote for some of the leading members, who they knew had influence enough to be appointed at any rate, in hopes of carrying with them some respectable citizens of Philadelphia, in whose principles and integrity they could have more confidence; but even in this they were disappointed, except in one member; the eighth member was added at a subsequent session of the assembly.

The Continental convention met in the city of Philadelphia at the time appointed. It was composed of some men of excellent characters; of others who were more remarkable for their ambition and cunning, than their patriotism; and of some who had been opponents to the independence of the United States. The delegates from Pennsylvania were, six of them, uniform and decided opponents to the constitution of this commonwealth. The convention sat upward of four months. The doors were kept shut, and the members brought under the most solemn engagements of secrecy.[2] Some of those who opposed their going so far beyond their powers, retired, hopeless, from the convention, others had the firmness to refuse signing the plan altogether; and many who did sign it, did it not as a system they wholly approved, but as the best that could be then obtained, and notwithstanding the time spent on this subject, it is agreed on all hands to be a work of haste and accommodation.

---

2. The Journals of the conclave are still concealed. (Minority)

While the gilded chains were forging in the secret conclave, the meaner instruments of despotism without, were busily employed in alarming the fears of the people with dangers which did not exist, and exciting their hopes of greater advantages from the expected plan than even the best government on earth could produce.

The proposed plan had not many hours issued forth from the womb of suspicious secrecy, until such as were prepared for the purpose, were carrying about petitions for people to sign, signifying their approbation of the system, and requesting the legislature to call a convention. While every measure was taken to intimidate the people against opposing it, the public papers seethed with the most violent threats against those who should dare to think for themselves, and *tar and feathers* were liberally promised to all those who would not immediately join in supporting the proposed government be it what it would. Under such circumstances petitions in favor of calling a convention were signed by great numbers in and about the city, before they had leisure to read and examine the system, many of whom, now they are better acquainted with it, and have had time to investigate its principles, are heartily opposed to it. The petitions were speedily handed into the legislature.

Affairs were in this situation when on the 28th of September last a resolution was proposed to the assembly by a member of the house who had been also a member of the federal convention, for calling a state convention, to be elected within *ten* days for the purpose of examining and adopting the proposed constitution of the United States, though at this time the house had not received it from Congress. This attempt was opposed by a minority, who after offering every argument in their power to prevent the precipitate measure, without effect, absented themselves from the house as the only alternative left them, to prevent the measure taking place previous to their constituents being acquainted with the business—That violence and outrage which had been so often threatened was now practiced; some of the members were seized the next day by a mob collected for the purpose, and forcibly dragged to the house, and there detained by force while the quorum of the legislature, *so formed*, completed their resolution. We shall dwell no longer on this subject, the people of Pennsylvania have been already acquainted therewith. We would only further observe that every member of the legislature, previously to taking his seat, by solemn oath or affirmation, declares, "that he will not do or consent to any act or thing whatever that shall have a tendency to lessen or abridge their rights and privileges, as declared in the constitution of this state." And that constitution which they are so solemnly sworn to support cannot legally be altered but by a recommendation of the council of censors, who alone are authorized to propose alterations and amendments, and even these must be published at least *six months*, for the consideration of the people.—The proposed system of government for the United States, if adopted, will [alter] and may annihilate the constitution of Pennsylvania; and therefore the legislature had no authority whatever to recommend the calling a convention for that purpose. This proceeding could not be considered as binding on the people of this commonwealth. The house was formed by violence, some of the members composing it were detained there by force, which alone would have vitiated any proceedings, to which they were otherwise competent; but had the legislature been legally formed, this business was absolutely without[3] their power.

In this situation of affairs were the subscribers elected members of the convention of Pennsylvania. A convention called by a legislature in direct violation of their duty, and composed in part of members, who were compelled to attend for that purpose, to consider of a constitution proposed by a convention of the United States, who were not appointed for the purpose of framing a new form of government, but whose powers were expressly confined to altering and amending the present articles of confederation.—Therefore the members of the continental convention in proposing the plan acted as individuals, and not as deputies from Pennsylvania.[4] The assembly who called the state convention acted as individuals, and not as the legislature of Pennsylvania; nor could they or the convention chosen on their recommendation have authority to do any [act] or thing, that can alter or annihilate the constitution of Pennsylvania (both of which will be done by the new constitution) nor are their proceedings in our opinion, at all binding on the people.

The election for members of the convention was held at so early a period and the want of information was so great, that some of us did not know of it until after it was over, and we have reason to believe that great numbers of the people of Pennsylvania have not yet had an opportunity of sufficiently examining the proposed constitution—We apprehend that no change can take place that will affect the internal government or constitution of this commonwealth, unless a majority of the people should

---

3. [I.e., outside.]

4. The continental convention in direct violation of the thirteenth article of the confederation, have declared, "that the ratification of nine states shall be sufficient for the establishment of this constitution, between the states so ratifying the same."—Thus has the plighted faith of the states been sported with! They had solemnly engaged that the confederation now subsisting should be inviolably preserved by each of them, and the union thereby formed, should be perpetual, unless the same should be altered by mutual consent. (Minority)

evidence a wish for such a change; but on examining the number of votes given for members of the present state convention, we find that of upward of *seventy thousand* freemen who are entitled to vote in Pennsylvania, the whole convention has been elected by about *thirteen thousand* voters, and though *two-thirds* of the members of the convention have thought proper to ratify the proposed constitution, yet those *two-thirds* were elected by the votes of only *six thousand and eight hundred* freemen.

In the city of Philadelphia and some of the eastern counties, the junto that took the lead in the business agreed to vote for none but such as would solemnly promise to adopt the system *in toto*, without exercising their judgment. In many of the counties the people did not attend the elections as they had not an opportunity of judging of the plan. Others did not consider themselves bound by the call of a set of men who assembled at the statehouse in Philadelphia, and assumed the name of the legislature of Pennsylvania; and some were prevented from voting by the violence of the party who were determined at all events to force down the measure. To such lengths did the tools of despotism carry their outrage, that in the night of the election for members of convention, in the city of Philadelphia, several of the subscribers (being then in the city to transact your business) were grossly abused, ill-treated, and insulted while they were quiet in their lodgings, though they did not interfere, nor had anything to do with the said election, but, as they apprehend, because they were supposed to be adverse to the proposed constitution, and would not tamely surrender those sacred rights, which you had committed to their charge.

The convention met, and the same disposition was soon manifested in considering the proposed constitution, that had been exhibited in every other stage of the business. We were prohibited by an express vote of the convention, from taking any question on the separate articles of the plan, and reduced to the necessity of adopting or rejecting *in toto*.—It is true the majority permitted us to debate on each article, but restrained us from proposing amendments.—They also determined not to permit us to enter on the minutes our reasons of dissent against any of the articles, nor even on the final question our reasons of dissent against the whole. Thus situated we entered on the examination of the proposed system of government, and found it to be such as we could not adopt, without, as we conceived, surrendering up your dearest rights. We offered our objections to the convention, and opposed those parts of the plan, which, in our opinion, would be injurious to you, in the best manner we were able; and closed our arguments by offering the following propositions to the convention.

1. The right of conscience shall be held inviolable; and neither the legislative, executive, nor judicial powers of the United States shall have

authority to alter, abrogate, or infringe any part of the constitution of the several states, which provide for the preservation of liberty in matters of religion.

2. That in controversies respecting property, and in suits between man and man, trial by jury shall remain as heretofore, as well in the federal courts, as in those of the several states.

3. That in all capital and criminal prosecutions, a man has a right to demand the cause and nature of his accusation, as well in the federal courts, as in those of the several states; to be heard by himself and his counsel; to be confronted with the accusers and witnesses; to call for evidence in his favor, and a speedy trial by an impartial jury of his vicinage, without whose unanimous consent, he cannot be found guilty, nor can he be compelled to give evidence against himself; and that no man be deprived of his liberty, except by the law of the land or the judgment of his peers.

4. That excessive bail ought not to be required, nor excessive fines imposed, nor cruel nor unusual punishments inflicted.

5. That warrants unsupported by evidence, whereby any officer or messenger may be commanded or required to search suspected places, or to seize any person or persons, his or their property, not particularly described, are grievous and oppressive, and shall not be granted either by the magistrates of the federal government or others.

6. That the people have a right to the freedom of speech, of writing and publishing their sentiments, therefore, the freedom of the press shall not be restrained by any law of the United States.

7. That the people have a right to bear arms for the defense of themselves and their own state, or the United States, or for the purpose of killing game; and no law shall be passed for disarming the people or any of them, unless for crimes committed, or real danger of public injury from individuals; and as standing armies in the time of peace are dangerous to liberty, they ought not to be kept up: and that the military shall be kept under strict subordination to and be governed by the civil powers.

8. The inhabitants of the several states shall have liberty to fowl and hunt in seasonable times, on the lands they hold, and on all other lands in the United States not enclosed, and in like manner to fish in all navigable waters, and others not private property, without being restrained therein by any laws to be passed by the legislature of the United States.

9. That no law shall be passed to restrain the legislatures of the several states from enacting laws for imposing taxes, except imposts and duties on goods imported or exported, and that no taxes, except imposts and duties upon goods imported and exported, and postage on letters shall be levied by the authority of Congress.

10. That the house of representatives be properly increased in number; that elections shall remain free; that the several states shall have power to regulate the elections for senators and representatives, without being controlled either directly or indirectly by any interference on the part of the Congress; and that elections of representatives be annual.

11. That the power of organizing, arming, and disciplining the militia (the manner of disciplining the militia to be prescribed by Congress) remain with the individual states, and that Congress shall not have authority to call or march any of the militia out of their own state, without the consent of such state, and for such length of time only as such state shall agree.

That the sovereignty, freedom, and independency of the several states shall be retained, and every power, jurisdiction, and right which is not by this constitution expressly delegated to the United States in Congress assembled.

12. That the legislative, executive, and judicial powers be kept separate; and to this end that a constitutional council be appointed, to advise and assist the president, who shall be responsible for the advice they give, hereby the senators would be relieved from almost constant attendance; and also that the judges be made completely independent.

13. That no treaty which shall be directly opposed to the existing laws of the United States in Congress assembled, shall be valid until such laws shall be repealed, or made conformable to such treaty; neither shall any treaties be valid which are in contradiction to the constitution of the United States, or the constitutions of the several states.

14. That the judiciary power of the United States shall be confined to cases affecting ambassadors, other public ministers, and consuls; to cases of admiralty and maritime jurisdiction; to controversies to which the United States shall be a party; to controversies between two or more states—between a state and citizens of different states—between citizens claiming lands under grants of different states; and between a state or the citizens thereof and foreign states, and in criminal cases, to such only as are expressly enumerated in the constitution, and that the United States in Congress assembled, shall not have power to enact laws, which shall alter the laws of descents and distribution of the effects of deceased persons, the titles of lands or goods, or the regulation of contracts in the individual states.

After reading these propositions, we declared our willingness to agree to the plan, provided it was so amended as to meet those propositions, or something similar to them: and finally moved the convention to adjourn, to give the people of Pennsylvania time to consider the subject, and determine for themselves; but these were all rejected, and the final vote was taken, when our duty to you induced us to vote against the proposed plan, and to decline signing the ratification of the same.

During the discussion we met with many insults, and some personal abuse; we were not even treated with decency, during the sitting of the convention, by the persons in the gallery of the house; however, we flatter ourselves that in contending for the preservation of those invaluable rights you have thought proper to commit to our charge, we acted with a spirit becoming freemen, and being desirous that you might know the principles which actuated our conduct, and being prohibited from inserting our reasons of dissent on the minutes of the convention, we have subjoined them for your consideration, as to you alone we are accountable. It remains with you whether you will think those inestimable privileges, which you have so ably contended for, should be sacrificed at the shrine of despotism, or whether you mean to contend for them with the same spirit that has so often baffled the attempts of an aristocratic faction, to rivet the shackles of slavery on you and your unborn posterity.

Our objections are comprised under three general heads of dissent, viz.

WE Dissent, first, because it is the opinion of the most celebrated writers on government, and confirmed by uniform experience, that a very extensive territory cannot be governed on the principles of freedom, otherwise than by a confederation of republics, possessing all the powers of internal government; but united in the management of their general, and foreign concerns.

If any doubt could have been entertained of the truth of the foregoing principle, it has been fully removed by the concession of *Mr. Wilson*, one of [the] majority on this question, and who was one of the deputies in the late general convention. In justice to him, we will give his own words; they are as follows, viz. "The extent of country for which the new constitution was required, produced another difficulty in the business of the federal convention. It is the opinion of some celebrated writers, that to a small territory, the democratical; to a middling territory (as Montesquieu has termed it) the monarchial; and to an extensive territory, the despotic form of government is best adapted. Regarding then the wide and almost unbounded jurisdiction of the United States, at first view, the hand of despotism seemed necessary to control, connect, and protect it; and hence the chief embarrassment rose. For, we know that, although our constituents would cheerily submit to the legislative restraints of a free government, they would spurn at every attempt to shackle them with despotic power."—And again in another part of his speech he continues.—"Is it probable that the dissolution of the state governments, and the establishment of one *consolidated empire* would be eligible in its nature, and satisfactory to the people in its administration? I think not, as I have given reasons to show that so extensive a territory could not be governed, connected, and preserved, but by the *supremacy of despotic power*. All the exertions of the most potent emperors of Rome were not capable of keeping that empire together, which in extent was far inferior to the dominion of America."

We dissent, secondly, because the powers vested in Congress by this constitution, must necessarily annihilate and absorb the legislative, executive, and judicial powers of the several states, and produce from their ruins one consolidated government, which from the nature of things will be *an iron-handed despotism*, as nothing short of the supremacy of despotic sway could connect and govern these United States under one government.

As the truth of this position is of such decisive importance, it ought to be fully investigated, and if it is founded to be clearly ascertained; for, should it be demonstrated, that the powers vested by this constitution in Congress will have such an effect as necessarily to produce one consolidated government, the question then will be reduced to this short issue, viz. whether satiated with the blessings of liberty; whether repenting of the folly of so recently asserting their inalienable rights, against foreign despots at the expense of so much blood and treasure, and such painful and arduous struggles, the people of America are now willing to resign every privilege of freemen, and submit to the dominion of an absolute government, that will embrace all America in one chain of despotism; or whether they will with virtuous indignation, spurn at the shackles prepared for them, and confirm their liberties by a conduct becoming freemen.

That the new government will not be a confederacy of states, as it ought, but one consolidated government, founded upon the destruction of the several governments of the states, we shall now show.

The powers of Congress under the new constitution, are complete and unlimited over the *purse* and the *sword*, and are perfectly independent of, and supreme over, the state governments; whose intervention in these great points is entirely destroyed. By virtue of their power of taxation, Congress may command the whole, or any part of the property of the people. They may impose what imposts upon commerce; they may impose what land taxes, poll taxes, excises, duties on all written instruments, and duties on every other article that they may judge proper; in short, every species of taxation, whether of an external or internal nature is comprised in section the 8th, of article the 1st, viz. "The Congress shall have power to lay and collect taxes, duties, imposts, and excises, to pay the debts, and provide for the common defense and general welfare of the United States."

As there is no one article of taxation reserved to the state governments, the Congress may monopolize every source of revenue, and thus indirectly demolish the state governments, for without funds they could not exist, the taxes, duties, and excises imposed by Congress may be so high as to render it impracticable to levy further sums on the same articles; but whether this should be the case or not, if the state governments should presume to impose taxes, duties, or excises, on the same articles with Congress, the latter may abrogate and repeal the laws whereby they are imposed, upon the allegation that they interfere with the due collection of their taxes, duties, or excises, by virtue of the following clause, part of section 8th, article 1st. viz. "To make all laws which shall be necessary and proper for carrying into execution the foregoing powers, and all other powers vested by this constitution in the government of the United States, or in any department or officer thereof."

The Congress might gloss over this conduct by construing every purpose for which the state legislatures now lay taxes, to be for the *general welfare,*" and therefore as of their jurisdiction.

And the supremacy of the laws of the United States is established by article 6th, viz. "That this constitution and the laws of the United States, which shall be made in pursuance thereof, and *all treaties* made, or which shall be made, under the authority of the United States, shall be the *supreme law of the land;* and *the judges in every state shall be bound thereby; anything in the constitution or laws of any state to the contrary notwithstanding."* It has been alleged that the words "pursuant to the constitution," are a restriction upon the authority of Congress; but when it is considered that by other sections they are invested with every efficient power of government, and which may be exercised to the absolute destruction of the state governments, without any violation of even the forms of the constitution, this seeming restriction, as well as every other restriction in it, appears to us to be nugatory and delusive; and only introduced as a blind upon the real nature of the government. In our opinion, "pursuant to the constitution," will be coextensive with the *will* and *pleasure* of Congress, which, indeed, will be the only limitation of their powers.

We apprehend that two coordinate sovereignties would be a solecism in politics. That therefore as there is no line of distinction drawn between the general, and state governments; as the sphere of their jurisdiction is undefined, it would be contrary to the nature of things, that both should exist together, one or the other would necessarily triumph in the fullness of dominion. However the contest could not be of long continuance, as the state governments are divested of every means of defense, and will be obliged by "the supreme law of the land" *to yield at discretion.*

It has been objected to this total destruction of the state governments, that the existence of their legislatures is made essential to the organization of Congress; that they must assemble for the appointment of the senators and president-general of the United States. True, the state legislatures may be continued for some years, as boards of appointment, merely, after they are divested of every other function, but the framers of the constitution foreseeing that the people will soon be disgusted with this solemn mockery of a government without power and usefulness, have made a provision for relieving them from the imposition, in section 4th, of article 1st, viz. "The times, places, and manner of holding elections for senators and representatives, shall be prescribed in each state by the legislature thereof; *but the Congress may at any time, by law make or alter such regulations; except as to the place of choosing senators.*"

As Congress have the control over the time of the appointment of the president-general, of the senators, and of the representatives of the United States, they may prolong their existence in office, for life, by postponing the time of their election and appointment, from period to period, under various pretenses, such as an apprehension of invasion, the factious disposition of the people, or any other plausible pretense that the occasion may suggest; and having thus obtained life-estates in the government, they may fill up the vacancies themselves, by their control over the mode of appointment; with this exception in regard to the senators, that as the place of appointment for them, must, by the constitution, be in the particular state, they may depute some body in the respective states, to fill up the vacancies in the senate, occasioned by death, until they can venture to assume it themselves. In this manner, may the only restriction in this clause be evaded. By virtue of the foregoing section, when the spirit of the people shall be gradually broken; when the general government shall be firmly established, and when a numerous standing army shall render opposition vain, the Congress may complete the system of despotism, in renouncing all dependence on the people, by continuing themselves and [their] children in the government.

The celebrated *Montesquieu*, in his Spirit of Laws, volume 1, page 12th, says, "That in a democracy there can be no exercise of sovereignty, but by the suffrages of the people, which are their will; now the sovereign's will is the sovereign himself; the laws therefore, which establish the right of suffrage, are fundamental to this government. In fact, it is as important to regulate in a republic in what manner, by whom, and concerning what suffrages are to be given, as it is in a monarchy to know who is the prince, and after what manner he ought to govern." The *time, mode,* and *place* of the election of representatives, senators and president-general of the United States, ought not to be under the control of Congress, but fundamentally ascertained and established.

The new constitution, consistently with the plan of consolidation, contains no reservation of the rights and privileges of the state governments, which was made in the confederation of the year 1778, by article the 2nd, viz. "That each state retains its sovereignty, freedom, and independence, and every power, jurisdiction, and right, which is not by this confederation expressly delegated to the United States in Congress assembled."

The legislative power vested in Congress by the foregoing recited sections, is so unlimited in its nature; may be so comprehensive and boundless [in] its exercise, that this alone would be amply sufficient to annihilate the state governments, and swallow them up in the grand vortex of general empire.

The judicial powers vested in Congress are also so various and extensive, that by legal ingenuity they may be extended to every case, and thus absorb the state judiciaries, and when we consider the decisive influence that a general judiciary would have over the civil polity of the several states, we do not hesitate to pronounce that this power, unaided by the legislative, would effect a consolidation of the states under one government.

The powers of a court of equity, vested by this constitution, in the tribunals of Congress; powers which do not exist in Pennsylvania, unless so far as they can be incorporated with jury trial, would, in this state, greatly contribute to this event. The rich and wealthy suitor would eagerly lay hold of the infinite makes,[5] perplexities, and delays, which a court of chancery, with the appellate powers of the supreme court in fact as well as law would furnish him with, and thus the poor man being plunged in the bottomless pit of legal discussion, would drop his demand in despair.

In short, consolidation pervades the whole constitution. It begins with an annunciation that such was the intention. The main pillars of the fabric correspond with it, and the concluding paragraph is a confirmation of it. The preamble begins with the words, "We the people of the United States," which is the style of a compact between individuals entering into a state of society, and not that of a confederation of states. The other features of consolidation, we have before noticed.

Thus we have fully established the position, that the powers vested by this constitution in Congress, will effect a consolidation of the states under one government, which even the advocates of this constitution admit, could not be done without the sacrifice of all liberty.

We dissent, Thirdly, Because if it were practicable to govern so extensive a territory as these United States includes, on the plan of a consolidated government, consistent with the principles of liberty and the happiness of the people, yet the construction of this constitution is not calculated to attain the object, for independent of the nature of the case, it

---

5. [*Make* can mean a fraud or a swindle.]

would of itself, necessarily, produce a despotism, and that not by the usual gradations, but with the celerity that has hitherto only attended revolutions effected by the sword.

To establish the truth of this position, a cursory investigation of the principles and form of this constitution will suffice.

The first consideration that this review suggests, is the omission of a BILL OF RIGHTS ascertaining and fundamentally establishing those inalienable and personal rights of men, without the full, free, and secure enjoyment of which there can be no liberty, and over which it is not necessary for a good government to have the control. The principal of which are the rights of conscience, personal liberty by the clear and unequivocal establishment of the writ of *habeas corpus,* jury trial in criminal and civil cases, by an impartial jury of the vicinage or county, with the common-law proceedings, for the safety of the accused in criminal prosecutions; and the liberty of the press, that scourge of tyrants, and the grand bulwark of every other liberty and privilege; the stipulations heretofore made in saving of them in the state constitutions, are entirely superseded by this constitution.

The legislature of a free country should be so formed as to have a competent knowledge of its constituents, and enjoy their confidence. To produce these essential requisites, the representation ought to be fair, equal, and sufficiently numerous, to possess the same interests, feelings, opinions, and views, which the people themselves would possess, were they all assembled; and so numerous as to prevent bribery and undue influence, and so responsible to the people, by frequent and fair elections, as to prevent their neglecting or sacrificing the views and interests of their constituents, to their own pursuits.

We will now bring the legislature under this constitution to the test of the foregoing principles, which will demonstrate, that it is deficient in every essential quality of a just and fair representation.

The house of representatives is to consist of sixty-five members; that is one for about every fifty-thousand inhabitants, to be chosen every two years. Thirty-three members will form a quorum for doing business, and seventeen of these, being the majority, determine the sense of the house.

The senate, the other constituent branch of the legislature, consists of twenty-six members, being *two* from each state, appointed by their legislatures every six years—fourteen senators make a quorum; the majority of whom, eight, determines the sense of the body; except in judging on impeachments, or in making treaties, or in expelling a member, when two-thirds of the senators present, must concur.

The president is to have the control over the enacting of laws, so far as to make the concurrence of *two*-thirds of the representatives and senators present necessary, if he should object to the laws.

Thus it appears that the liberties, happiness, interests, and great concerns of the whole United States, may be dependent upon the integrity, virtue, wisdom, and knowledge of twenty-five or twenty-six men.—How inadequate and unsafe a representation! Inadequate, because the sense and views of three or four millions of people diffused over so extensive a territory comprising such various climates, products, habits, interests, and opinions, cannot be collected in so small a body; and besides, it is not a fair and equal representation of the people even in proportion to its number, for the smallest state has as much weight in the senate as the largest, and from the smallness of the number to be chosen for both branches of the legislature; and from the mode of election and appointment, which is under the control of Congress; and from the nature of the thing, men of the most elevated rank in life will alone be chosen. The other orders in the society, such as farmers, traders, and mechanics, who all ought to have a competent number of their best-informed men in the legislature, will be totally unrepresented.

The representation is unsafe, because in the exercise of such great powers and trusts, it is so exposed to corruption and undue influence, by the gift of the numerous places of honor and emolument, at the disposal of the executive; by the arts and address of the great and designing; and by direct bribery.

The representation is moreover inadequate and unsafe, because of the long terms for which it is appointed, and the mode of its appointment, by which Congress may not only control the choice of the people, but may so manage as to divest the people of this fundamental right, and become self-elected.

The number of members in the house of representatives *may* be increased to one for every thirty-thousand inhabitants. But when we consider, that this cannot be done without the consent of the senate, who from their share in the legislative, in the executive, and judicial departments, and permanency of appointment, will be the great efficient body in this government, and whose weight and predominance would be abridged by an increase of the representatives, we are persuaded that this is a circumstance that cannot be expected. On the contrary, the number of representatives will probably be continued at sixty-five, although the population of the country may swell to treble what it now is; unless a revolution should effect a change.

We have before noticed the judicial power as it would effect a consolidation of the states into one government; we will now examine it, as it would affect the liberties and welfare of the people, supposing such a government were practicable and proper.

The judicial power, under the proposed constitution, is founded on the well-known principles of the *civil law*, by which the judge determines both on law and fact, and appeals are allowed from the inferior tribunals to the superior, upon the whole question; so that *facts* as well as *law*, would be reexamined, and even new facts brought forward in the court of appeals and to use the words of a very eminent Civilian—"The cause is many times another thing before the court of appeals, than what it was at the time of the first sentence."

That this mode of proceeding is the one which must be adopted under this constitution, is evident from the following circumstances:—First. That the trial by jury, which is the grand characteristic of the common law, is secured by the constitution, only in criminal cases.—Second. That the appeal from both *law* and *fact* is expressly established, which is utterly inconsistent with the principles of the common law, and trials by jury. The only mode in which an appeal from law and fact can be established, is, by adopting the principles and practice of the civil law; unless the United States should be drawn into the absurdity of calling and swearing juries, merely for the purpose of contradicting their verdicts, which would render juries contemptible and worse than useless.—Third. That the courts to be established would decide on all cases *of law and equity*, which is a well-known characteristic of the civil law, and these courts would have conusance[6] not only of the laws of the United States and of treaties, and of cases affecting ambassadors, but of all cases of *admiralty and maritime jurisdiction*, which last are matters belonging exclusively to the civil law, in every nation in Christendom.

Not to enlarge upon the loss of the invaluable right of trial by an unbiased jury, so dear to every friend of liberty, the monstrous expense and inconveniences of the mode of proceeding to be adopted, are such as will prove intolerable to the people of this country. The lengthy proceedings of the civil law courts in the chancery of England, and in the courts of Scotland and France, are such that few men of moderate fortune can endure the expense of; the poor man must therefore submit to the wealthy. Length of purse will too often prevail against right and justice. For instance, we are told by the learned judge *Blackstone*, that a question only on the property of an ox of the value of *three* guineas, originating under the civil law proceedings in Scotland, after many interlocutory orders and sentences below, was carried at length from the court of sessions, the highest court in that part of Great Britain, by way of *appeal* to the house of lords, where the question of law and fact was finally determined. He adds, that no pique or spirit could in the court of king's bench or common pleas at Westminster, have given continuance to such a cause

---

6. [I.e., cognizance.]

for a tenth part of the time, nor have cost a twentieth part of the expense. Yet the costs in the courts of king's bench and common pleas in England, are infinitely greater than those which the people of this country have ever experienced. We abhor the idea of losing the transcendent privilege of trial by jury, with the loss of which, it is remarked by the same learned author, that in Sweden, the liberties of the commons were extinguished by an aristocratic senate; and that *trial by jury* and the liberty of the people went out together. At the same time we regret the intolerable delay, the enormous expenses, and infinite vexation to which the people of this country will be exposed from the voluminous proceedings of the courts of civil law, and especially from the appellate jurisdiction, by means of which a man may be drawn from the utmost boundaries of this extensive country to the seat of the supreme court of the nation to contend, perhaps with a wealthy and powerful adversary. The consequence of this establishment will be an absolute confirmation of the power of aristocratical influence in the courts of justice; for the common people will not be able to contend or struggle against it.

Trial by jury in criminal cases may also be excluded by declaring that the libeller[7] for instance shall be liable to an action of debt for a specified sum thus evading the common-law prosecution by indictment and trial by jury. And the common course of proceeding against a ship for breach of revenue laws by information (which will be classed among civil causes) will at the civil law be within the resort of a court, where no jury intervenes. Besides, the benefit of jury trial, in cases of a criminal nature, which cannot be evaded, will be rendered of little value, by calling the accused to answer far from home; there being no provision that the trial be by a jury of the neighborhood or country. Thus an inhabitant of Pittsburgh, on a charge of crime committed on the banks of the Ohio, may be obliged to defend himself at the side of the Delaware, and so *vice versa:* To conclude this head: we observe that the judges of the courts of Congress would not be independent, as they are not debarred from holding other offices, during the pleasure of the president and senate, and as they may derive their support in part from fees, alterable by the legislature.

The next consideration that the constitution presents, is the undue and dangerous mixture of the powers of government: the same body possessing legislative, executive, and judicial powers. The senate is a constituent branch of the legislature, it has judicial power in judging on impeachments, and in this case unites in some measure the characters of judge and party as all the principal officers are appointed by the president-general

---

7. [I.e., one who libels another.]

with the concurrence of the senate and therefore they derive their offices in part from the senate. This may bias the judgments of the senators, and tend to screen great delinquents from punishment. And the senate has, moreover, various and great executive powers, viz. in concurrence with the president-general, they form treaties with foreign nations, that may control and abrogate the constitutions and laws of the several states. Indeed, there is no power, privilege, or liberty of the state governments, or of the people, but what may be affected by virtue of this power. For all treaties, made by them, are to be the "supreme law of the land: any thing in the constitution or laws of any state, to the contrary notwithstanding."

And this great power may be exercised by the president and ten senators (being two-thirds of fourteen, which is a quorum of that body). What an inducement would this offer to the ministers of foreign powers to compass by bribery *such concessions* as could not otherwise be obtained. It is the unvaried usage of all free states, whenever treaties interfere with the positive laws of the land, to make the intervention of the legislature necessary to give them operation. This became necessary, and was afforded by the parliament of Great Britain, in consequence of the late commercial treaty between that kingdom and France—As the senate judges on impeachments, who is to try the members of the senate for the abuse of this power! And none of the great appointments to office can be made without the consent of the senate.

Such various, extensive, and important powers combined in one body of men, are inconsistent with all freedom; the celebrated Montesquieu tells us, that "when the legislative and executive powers are united in the same person, or in the same body of magistrates, there can be no liberty, because apprehensions may arise, lest the same monarch or *senate* should enact tyrannical laws, to execute them in a tyrannical manner."

"Again, there is no liberty, if the power of judging be not separated from the legislative and executive powers. Were it joined with the legislative, the life and liberty of the subject would be exposed to arbitrary control; for the judge would then be legislator. Were it joined to the executive power, the judge might behave with all the violence of an oppressor. There would be an end of everything, were the same man, or the same body of the nobles, or of the people, to exercise those three powers; that of enacting laws; that of executing the public resolutions; and that of judging the crimes or differences of individuals."

The president-general is dangerously connected with the senate; his coincidence with the views of the ruling junto in that body, is made essential to his weight and importance in the government, which will destroy the independency and purity in the executive department, and having the power of pardoning without the concurrence of a council, he may screen from punishment the most [treasonable] attempts that may be made on the liberties of the people, when instigated by his enadjutors[8] in the senate. Instead of this dangerous and improper mixture of the executive with the legislative and judicial, the supreme executive powers ought to have been placed in the president, with a small independent council, made personally responsible for every appointment to office or other act, by having their opinions recorded; and that without the concurrence of the majority of the quorum of this council, the president should not be capable of taking any step.

The power of direct taxation applies to every individual, as congress, under this government, is expressly vested with the authority of laying a capitation or poll tax upon every person to any amount. This is a tax that, however oppressive in its nature, and unequal in its operation, is certain as to its produce and simple in its collection; it cannot be evaded like the objects of imposts or excise, and will be paid, because all that a man hath will he give for his head. This tax is so congenial to the nature of despotism, that it has ever been a favorite under such governments. Some of those who were in the late general convention from this state, have long labored to introduce a poll tax among us.

The power of direct taxation will further apply to every individual as congress may tax land, cattle, trades, occupations, etc. to any amount, and every object of internal taxation is of that nature that however oppressive, the people will have but this alternative, either to pay the tax, or let their property be taken, for all resistance will be vain. The standing army and select militia would enforce the collection,

For the moderate exercise of this power, there is no control left in the state governments, whose intervention is destroyed. No relief, or redress of grievances can be extended, as heretofore by them. There is not even a declaration of RIGHTS to which the people may appeal for the vindication of their wrongs in the court of justice. They must therefore, implicitly, obey the most arbitrary laws, as the worst of them will be pursuant to the principles and form of the constitution, and that strongest of all checks upon the conduct of administration, *responsibility to the people,* will not exist in this government. The permanency of the appointments of senators and representatives, and the control the congress have over their election, will place them independent of the sentiments and resentment of the people, and the administration having a greater interest in the government than in the community, there will be no consideration to

---

8. [Presumably "coconspirators," but the word is unknown to the dictionaries.]

restrain them from oppression and tyranny. In the government of this state, under the old confederation, the members of the legislature are taken from among the people, and their interests and welfare are so inseparably connected with those of their constituents, that they can derive no advantage from oppressive laws and taxes, for they would suffer in common with their fellow citizens; would participate in the burdens they impose on the community, as they must return to the common level, after a short period; and notwithstanding every exertion of influence, every means of corruption, a necessary rotation excludes them from permanency in the legislature.

This large state is to have but ten members in that Congress which is to have the liberty, property, and dearest concerns of every individual in this vast country at absolute command and even these ten persons, who are to be our only guardians; who are to supersede the legislature of Pennsylvania, will not be of the choice of the people, nor amenable to them. From the mode of their election and appointment they will consist of the lordly and high-minded; of men who will have no congenial feelings with the people, but a perfect indifference for, and contempt of them; they will consist of those harpies of power, that prey upon the very vitals; that riot on the miseries of the community. But we will suppose, although in all probability it may never be realized in fact, that our deputies in Congress have the welfare of their constituents at heart, and will exert themselves in their behalf, what security could even this afford; what relief could they extend to their oppressed constituents? To attain this, the majority of the deputies of the twelve other states in Congress must be alike well-disposed; must alike forego the sweets of power, and relinquish the pursuits of ambition which from the nature of things is not to be expected. If the people part with a responsible representation in the legislature, founded upon fair, certain, and frequent elections, they have nothing left they can call their own. Miserable is the lot of that people whose every concern depends on the WILL and PLEASURE of their rulers. Our soldiers will become Janissaries, and our officers of government Bashaws;[9] in short, the system of despotism will soon be completed.

From the foregoing investigation, it appears that the Congress under this constitution will not possess the confidence of the people, which is an essential requisite in a good government; for unless the laws command the confidence and respect of the great body of the people so as to induce them to support them, when called on by the civil magistrate, they must

---

9. [Janissaries were soldiers and Bashaws were governors of provinces in Turkey.]

be executed by the aid of a numerous standing army, which would be inconsistent with every idea of liberty; for the same force that may be employed to compel obedience to good laws, might and probably would be used to wrest from the people their constitutional liberties. The framers of this constitution appear to have been aware of this great deficiency; to have been sensible that no dependence could be placed on the people for their support; but on the contrary, that the government must be executed by force. They have therefore made a provision for this purpose in a permanent STANDING ARMY, and a MILITIA that may be subjected to as strict discipline and government.

A standing army in the hands of a government placed so independent of the people, may be made a fatal instrument to overturn the public liberties; it may be employed to enforce the collection of the most oppressive taxes, and to carry into execution the most arbitrary measures. An ambitious man who may have the army at his devotion, may step up into the throne, and seize upon absolute power.

The absolute unqualified command that Congress have over the militia may be made instrumental to the destruction of all liberty, both public and private; whether of a personal, civil, or religious nature.

First, the personal liberty of every man probably from sixteen to sixty years of age, may be destroyed by the power Congress have in organizing and governing of the militia. As militia they may be subjected to fines to any amount, levied in a military manner; they may be subjected to corporal punishments of the most disgraceful and humiliating kind, and to death itself, by the sentence of a court martial: To this our young men will be more immediately subjected, as a select militia, composed of them, will best answer the purposes of government.

Secondly, the rights of conscience may be violated, as there is no exemption of those persons who are conscientiously scrupulous of bearing arms. These compose a respectable proportion of the community in the state. This is the more remarkable, because even when the distresses of the late war, and the evident disaffection of many citizens of that description, inflamed our passions, and when every person, who was obliged to risk his own life, must have been exasperated against such as on any account kept back from the common danger, yet even then, when outrage and violence might have been expected, the rights of conscience were held sacred.

At this momentous crisis, the framers of our state constitution made the most express and decided declaration and stipulations in favor of the rights of conscience; but now when no necessity exists, those dearest rights of men are left insecure.

Thirdly, the absolute command of Congress over the militia may be destructive of public liberty; for under the guidance of an arbitrary government, they may be made the unwilling instruments of tyranny. The militia of Pennsylvania may be marched to New England or Virginia to quell an insurrection occasioned by the most galling oppression, and aided by the standing army, they will no doubt be successful in subduing their liberty and independency; but in so doing, although the magnanimity of their minds will be extinguished, yet the meaner passions of resentment and revenge will be increased, and these in turn will be the ready and obedient instruments of despotism to enslave the others; and that with an irritated vengeance. Thus, may the militia be made the instruments of crushing the last efforts of expiring liberty, of riveting the chains of despotism on their fellow citizens, and on one another. This power can be exercised not only without violating the constitution but in strict conformity with it; it is calculated for this express purpose, and will doubtless be executed accordingly.

As this government will not enjoy the confidence of the people, but be executed by force, it will be a very expensive and burdensome government. The standing army must be numerous, and as a further support, it will be the policy of this government to multiply officers in every department; judges, collectors, tax gatherers, excise men, and the whole host of revenue officers will swarm over the land, devouring the hard earnings of the industrious. Like the locusts of old, impoverishing and defoliating all before them.

We have not noticed the smaller, nor many of the considerable blemishes, but have confined our objections to the great and essential defects; the main pillars of the constitution; which we have shown to be inconsistent with the liberty and happiness of the people, as its establishment will annihilate the state governments, and produce one consolidated government, that will eventually and speedily issue in the supremacy of despotism.

In this investigation, we have not confined our views to the interests or welfare of this state, in preference to the others. We have overlooked all local circumstances—we have considered this subject on the broad scale of the general good: we have asserted the cause of the present and future ages; the cause of liberty and mankind.

NATHANIEL BREADING, JOHN SMILIE, RICHARD BAIRD, ADAM ORTH, JOHN A. HANNA, JOHN WHITEHILL, JOHN HARRIS, ROBERT WHITEHILL, JOHN REYNOLDS, JONATHAN HOGE, NICHOLAS LUTZ, JOHN LUDWIG, ABRAHAM LINCOLN, JOHN BISHOP, JOSEPH HEISTER, JOSEPH POWEL, JAMES MARTIN, WILLIAM FINDLEY, JOHN BAIRD, JAMES EDGAR, WILLIAM TODD

SPEECH OF PATRICK HENRY BEFORE THE
VIRGINIA RATIFYING CONVENTION

June 5, 1788

Mr. Chairman—I am much obliged to the very worthy Gentleman for his encomium. I wish I was possessed of talents, or possessed of anything, that might enable me to elucidate this great subject. I am not free from suspicion: I am apt to entertain doubts: I rose yesterday to ask a question, which arose in my own mind. When I asked that question, I thought the meaning of my interrogation was obvious: The fate of this question and America may depend on this: Have they said, we the States? Have they made a proposal of a compact between States? If they had, this would be a confederation: It is otherwise most clearly a consolidated government. The question turns, Sir, on that poor little thing—the expression, _We, the people,_ instead of the States of America. I need not take much pains to show, that the principles of this system, are extremely pernicious, impolitic, and dangerous. Is this a Monarchy, like England—a compact between Prince and people; with checks on the former, to secure the liberty of the latter? Is this a Confederacy, like Holland—an association of a number of independent States, each of which retain its individual sovereignty? It is not a democracy, wherein the people retain all their rights securely. Had these principles been adhered to, we should not have been brought to this alarming transition, from a Confederacy to a consolidated Government. We have no detail of those great considerations which, in my opinion, ought to have abounded before we should recur to a government of this kind. Here is a revolution as radical as that which separated us from Great Britain. It is as radical, if in this transition, our rights and privileges are endangered, and the sovereignty of the States be relinquished: And cannot we plainly see, that this is actually the case? The rights of conscience, trial by jury, liberty of the press, all your immunities and franchises, all pretensions to human rights and privileges, are rendered insecure, if not lost, by this change so loudly talked of by some, and inconsiderately by others. Is this tame relinquishment of rights worthy of freemen? Is it worthy of that manly fortitude that ought to characterize republicans: It is said eight States have adopted this plan. I declare that if twelve States and an half had adopted it, I would with manly firmness, and in spite of an erring world, reject it. You are not to inquire how your trade may be increased, nor how you are to become a great and powerful people, but how your liberties can be secured; for liberty ought to be the direct end of your Government. Having premised these things, I shall, with the aid of my judgment and information, which I confess are not extensive, go into the discussion of this system more minutely. Is it necessary for your liberty; that you should abandon those great rights by the adoption of this system? Is the relinquishment of the trial by jury, and the liberty of the press, necessary for your liberty? Will the abandonment of your most sacred rights tend to the security of your liberty? Liberty the greatest of all earthly blessings—give us that precious jewel, and you may take everything else: But I am fearful I have lived long enough to become an old-fashioned fellow: Perhaps an invincible attachment to the dearest rights of man, may, in these refined enlightened days, be deemed *old-fashioned:* If so, I am contented to be so: I say, the time has been, when every pore of my heart beat for American liberty, and which, I believe, had a counterpart in the breast of every true American: But suspicions have gone forth—suspicions of my integrity—publicly reported that my professions are not real—twenty-three years ago was I supposed a traitor to my country: I was then said to be a bane of sedition, because I supported the rights of my country: I may be thought suspicious when I say our privileges and rights are in danger: But, Sir, a number of the people of this country are weak enough to think these things are too true: I am happy to find that the Honorable Gentleman on the other side, declares they are groundless: But, Sir, suspicion is a virtue, as long as its object is the preservation of the public good, and as long as it stays within proper bounds: Should it fall on me, I am contented: Conscious rectitude is a powerful consolation: I trust, there are many who think my professions for the public good to be real. Let your suspicion look to both sides: There are many on the other side, who, possibly may have been persuaded of the necessity of these measures, which I conceive to be dangerous to your liberty. Guard with jealous attention the public liberty. Suspect everyone who approaches that jewel. Unfortunately, nothing will preserve it, but downright force: Whenever you give up that force, you are inevitably ruined. I am answered by Gentlemen, that though I might speak of terrors, yet the fact was, that we were surrounded by none of the dangers I apprehended. I conceive this new Government to be one of those dangers: It has produced those horrors, which distress many of our best citizens. We are come hither to preserve the poor Commonwealth of Virginia, if it can be possibly done: Something must be done to preserve your liberty and mine: The Confederation; this same despised Government, merits, in my opinion, the highest encomium: It carried us through a long and dangerous war: It rendered us victorious in that bloody conflict with a powerful nation: It has secured us a territory greater than any European Monarch possesses: And shall a Government which has been thus strong and vigorous, be accused of imbecility and abandoned for want of energy? Consider what you are about to do before you part with this Government. Take longer time in reckoning things: Revolutions like this have happened in almost every country in Europe: Similar examples are to be found in ancient Greece and ancient Rome: Instances of the people losing their liberty by their own carelessness and the ambition of a few. We are cautioned by the Honorable Gentleman who presides, against faction and turbulence: I acknowledge that licentiousness is dangerous, and that it ought to be provided against: I acknowledge also the new form of Government may effectually prevent it: Yet, there is another thing it will as effectually do; it will oppress and ruin the people. There are sufficient guards placed against sedition and licentiousness: For when power is given to this Government to suppress these, or, for any other purpose, the language it assumes is clear, express, and unequivocal; but when this Constitution speaks of privileges, there is an ambiguity, Sir, a fatal ambiguity;—an ambiguity which is very astonishing: In the clause under consideration, there is the strangest that I can conceive. I mean, when it says, that there shall not be more Representatives, than one for every thirty-thousand. Now, Sir, how easy is it to evade this privilege? "The number shall not exceed one for every thirty-thousand." This may be satisfied by one Representative from each State. Let our numbers be ever so great, this immense continent, may, by this artful expression, be reduced to have but thirteen Representatives: I confess this construction is not natural; but the ambiguity of the expression lays a good ground for a quarrel. Why was it not clearly and unequivocally expressed, that they *should* be entitled to have one for every thirty-thousand? This would have obviated all disputes; and was this difficult to be done? What is the inference? When population increases, and a State shall send Representatives in this proportion, Congress *may* remand them, because the right of having one for every thirty-thousand is not clearly expressed: This possibility of reducing the number to one for each State, approximates to probability by that other expression, "but each State shall at least have one Representative." Now is it not clear that from the first expression, the number might be reduced so much, that some States should have no Representative at all, were it not for the insertion of this last expression? And as this is the only restriction upon them, we may fairly conclude that they *may* restrain the number to one from each State: Perhaps the same horrors may hang over my mind again. I shall be told I am continually afraid: But, Sir, I have strong cause of apprehension: In some parts of the plan before you, the great rights of freemen are endangered, in other parts absolutely taken away. How does your trial by jury stand? In civil cases gone—not sufficiently secured in criminal—this best privilege is gone: But we are told that we need not fear, because those in power being our Representatives, will not abuse the powers we put in their hands: I am not well-versed in history, but I will submit to your recollection, whether liberty has been destroyed most often by the licentiousness of the people, or by the tyranny of rulers? I imagine, Sir, you will find the balance on the side of tyranny: Happy will you be if you miss the fate of those nations, who, omitting to resist their oppressors, or negligently suffering their liberty to be wrested from them, have groaned under intolerable despotism. Most of the human race are now in this deplorable condition: And those nations who have gone in search of grandeur, power, and splendor, have also fallen a sacrifice, and been the victims of their own folly: While they acquired those visionary blessings, they lost their freedom. My great objection to this Government is, that it does not leave us the means of defending our rights; or, of waging war against tyrants: It is urged by some Gentlemen, that this new plan will bring us an acquisition of strength, an army, and the militia of the States: This is an idea extremely ridiculous: Gentlemen cannot be in earnest. This acquisition will trample on your fallen liberty: Let my beloved Americans guard against that fatal lethargy that has pervaded the universe: Have we the means of resisting disciplined armies, when our only defense, the militia is put into the hands of Congress? The Honorable Gentleman said, that great danger would ensue if the Convention rose without adopting this system: I ask, where is that danger? I see none: Other Gentlemen have told us within these walls, that the Union is gone—or, that the Union will be gone: Is not this trifling with the judgment of their fellow citizens? Until they tell us the ground of their fears, I will consider them as imaginary: I rose to make inquiry where those dangers were; they could make no answer: I believe I never shall have that answer: Is there a disposition in the people of this country to revolt against the dominion of laws? Has there been a single tumult in Virginia? Have not the people of Virginia, when laboring under the severest pressure of accumulated distresses, manifested the most cordial acquiescence in the execution of the laws? What could be more awful than their unanimous acquiescence under general distresses? Is there any revolution in Virginia? Whither is the spirit of America gone? Whither is the genius of America fled? It was but yesterday, when our enemies marched in triumph through our country: Yet the people of this country could not be appalled by their pompous armaments: They stopped their career, and victoriously captured them: Where is the peril now compared to that? Some minds are agitated by foreign alarms: Happily for us, there is no real danger from Europe; that country is engaged in more arduous business; from that quarter there is no cause of fear: You may sleep in safety forever for them. Where is the danger? If, Sir, there was any, I would recur to the American spirit to defend us;—that spirit which has enabled us to surmount the greatest difficulties: To that illustrious spirit I address my most fervent prayer, to prevent our adopting a system destructive to liberty. Let not Gentlemen be told, that it is not safe to reject this Government. Wherefore is it not safe? We are told there are dangers; but those dangers are ideal;[10] they cannot be demonstrated: To encourage us to adopt it, they tell us, that there is a plain easy way of getting amendments: When I come to contemplate this part, I suppose that I am mad, or, that my countrymen are so: The way to amendment, is, in my conception, shut. Let us consider this plain easy way: "The Congress, whenever two-thirds of both Houses shall deem it necessary, shall propose amendments to this Constitution, or, on the application of the Legislatures of two-thirds of the several States, shall call a Convention for proposing amendments, which, in either case, shall be valid to all intents and purposes, as part of this Constitution, when ratified by the Legislatures of three-fourths of the several States, or by Conventions in three-fourths thereof, as the one or the other mode of ratification may be proposed by the Congress. Provided, that no amendment which may be made prior to the year 1808, shall in any manner affect the first and fourth clauses in the ninth section of the first article; and that no State, without its consent, shall be deprived of its equal suffrage in the Senate." Hence it appears that three-fourths of the States must ultimately agree to any amendments that may be necessary. Let us consider the consequences of this: However uncharitable it may appear, yet I must tell my opinion, that the most unworthy characters may get into power and prevent the introduction of amendments: Let us suppose (for the case is supposable, possible, and probable) that you happen to deal these powers to unworthy hands; will they relinquish powers already in their possession, or, agree to amendments? Two-thirds of the Congress, or, of the State Legislatures, are necessary even to propose amendments: If one-third of these be unworthy men, they may prevent the application for amendments; but what is destructive and mischievous is, that three-fourths of the State Legislatures, or of State Conventions, must concur in the amendments when proposed: In such numerous bodies, there must necessarily be some designing bad men: To suppose that so large a number as three-fourths of the States will concur, is to suppose that they will possess genius, intelligence, and integrity, approaching to miraculous. It would indeed be miraculous that they should concur in the same amendments, or, even in such as would bear some likeness to one another. For four of the smallest States, that do not collectively contain one-tenth part of the population of the United States, may obstruct the most salutary and necessary amendments: Nay, in these four States, six-tenths of the

10. [I.e., theoretical.]

people may reject these amendments; and suppose, that amendments shall be opposed to amendments (which is highly probable) is it possible, that three-fourths can ever agree to the same amendments? A bare majority in these four small States may hinder the adoption of amendments; so that we may fairly and justly conclude, that one-twentieth part of the American people, may prevent the removal of the most grievous inconveniences and oppression, by refusing to accede to amendments. A trifling minority may reject the most salutary amendments. Is this an easy mode of securing the public liberty? It is, Sir, a most fearful situation, when the most contemptible minority can prevent the alteration of the most oppressive Government; for it may in many respects prove to be such: Is this the spirit of republicanism? What, Sir, is the genius of democracy? Let me read that clause of the Bill of Rights of Virginia, which relates to this: third clause, "That Government is or ought to be instituted for the common benefit, protection, and security of the people, nation, or community: Of all the various modes and forms of Government, that is best which is capable of producing the greatest degree of happiness and safety, and is most effectually secured against the danger of maladministration, and *that whenever any Government shall be found inadequate, or contrary to these purposes, a majority of the community hath, an indubitable, inalienable and indefeasible right to reform, alter, or abolish it, in such manner as shall be judged most conducive to the public weal.*" This, Sir, is the language of democracy; that a majority of the community have a right to alter their Government when found to be oppressive: But how different is the genius of your new Constitution from this? How different from the sentiments of freemen, that a contemptible minority can prevent the good of the majority? If then Gentlemen standing on this ground, are come to that point, that they are willing to bind themselves and their posterity to be oppressed, I am amazed and inexpressibly astonished. If this be the opinion of the majority, I must submit; but to me, Sir, it appears perilous and destructive: I cannot help thinking so: Perhaps it may be the result of my age; these may be feelings natural to a man of my years, when the American spirit has left him, and his mental powers, like the members of the body, are decayed. If, Sir, amendments are left to the twentieth or the tenth part of the people of America, your liberty is gone forever. We have heard that there is a great deal of bribery practiced in the House of Commons in England; and that many of the members raised themselves to preferments, by selling the rights of the people: But, Sir, the tenth part of that body cannot continue oppressions on the rest of the people. English liberty is in this case, on a firmer foundation than American liberty. It will be easily contrived to procure the opposition of one-tenth of the people to any alteration, however judicious. The Honorable Gentleman who presides, told us, that to prevent abuses in our Government, we will assemble in Convention, recall our delegated powers, and punish our servants for abusing the trust reposed in them. Oh, Sir, we should have fine times indeed, if to punish tyrants, it were only sufficient to assemble the people. Your arms wherewith you could defend yourselves, are gone; and have no longer an aristocratical; no longer democratical spirit. Did you ever read of any revolution in any nation, brought about by the punishment of those in power, inflicted by those who had no power at all? You read of a riot act in a country which is called one of the freest in the world, where a few neighbors cannot assemble without the risk of being shot by a hired soldiery, the engines of despotism. We may see such an act in America. A standing army we shall have also, to execute the execrable commands of tyranny: And how are you to punish them? Will you order them to be punished? Who shall obey these orders? Will your Mace bearer be a match for a disciplined regiment? In what situation are we to be? The clause before you gives a power of direct taxation, unbounded and unlimited: Exclusive power of Legislation in all cases whatsoever, for ten miles square; and over all places purchased for the erection of forts, magazines, arsenals, dockyards, etc. What resistance could be made? The attempt would be madness. You will find all the strength of this country in the hands of your enemies: Those garrisons will naturally be the strongest places in the country. Your militia is given up to Congress also in another part of this plan: They will therefore act as they think proper: All power will be in their own possession: You cannot force them to receive their punishment: Of what service would militia be to you, when most probably you will not have a single musket in the State; for as arms are to be provided by Congress, they may or may not furnish them. Let me here call your attention to that part which gives the Congress power, "To provide for organizing, arming, and disciplining the militia, and for governing such part of them as may be employed in the service of the United States, reserving to the States respectively, the appointment of the officers, and the authority of training the militia, according to the discipline prescribed by Congress." By this, Sir, you see that their control over our last and best defense, is unlimited. If they neglect or refuse to discipline or arm our militia, they will be useless: The States can do neither, this power being exclusively given to Congress: The power of appointing officers over men not disciplined or armed, is ridiculous: So that this pretended little remains of power left to the States, may, at the pleasure of Congress, be rendered nugatory. Our situation will be deplorable indeed: Nor can we ever expect to get this government amended, since I have already shown, that a very small minority may prevent it; and that small minority interested in the continuance of the oppression: Will the oppressor let go the oppressed? Was there ever an instance? Can the annals of mankind exhibit one single example, where rulers overcharged with power, willingly let go the oppressed, though solicited and requested most earnestly? The application for amendments will therefore be fruitless. Sometimes the oppressed have got loose by one of those bloody struggles that desolate a country. A willing relinquishment of power is one of those things which human nature never was, nor ever will be capable of: The Honorable Gentleman's observations respecting the people's right of being the agents in the formation of this Government, are not accurate in my humble conception. The distinction between a National Government and a Confederacy is not sufficiently discerned. Had the delegates who were sent to Philadelphia a power to propose a Consolidated Government instead of a Confederacy? Were they not deputed by States, and not by the people? The assent of the people in their collective capacity is not necessary to the formation of a Federal Government. The people have no right to enter into leagues, alliances, or confederations: They are not the proper agents for this purpose: States and sovereign powers are the only proper agents for this kind of Government: Show me an instance where the people have exercised this business: Has it not always gone through the Legislatures? I refer you to the treaties with France, Holland, and other nations: How were they made? Were they not made by the States? Are the people therefore in their aggregate capacity, the proper persons to form a Confederacy? This, therefore, ought to depend on the consent of the Legislatures; the people having never sent delegates to make any proposition of changing the Government. Yet I must say, at the same time, that it was made on grounds the most pure, and perhaps I might have been brought to consent to it so far as to the change of Government; but there is one thing in it which I never would acquiesce in. I mean the changing it into a Consolidated Government; which is so abhorrent to my mind. The Honorable Gentleman then went on to the figure we make with foreign nations; the contemptible one we make in France and Holland; which, according to the system of my notes, he attributes to the present feeble Government. An opinion has gone forth, we find, that we are a contemptible people: The time has been when we were thought otherwise: Under this same despised Government, we commanded the respect of all Europe: Wherefore are we now reckoned otherwise? The American spirit has fled from hence: It has gone to regions, where it has never been expected: It has gone to the people of France in search of a splendid Government—a strong energetic Government. Shall we imitate the example of those nations who have gone from a simple to a splendid Government? Are those nations more worthy of our imitation? What can make an adequate satisfaction to them for the loss they suffered in attaining such a Government for the loss of their liberty?

If we admit this Consolidated Government it will be because we like a great splendid one. Some way or other we must be a great and mighty empire; we must have an army, and a navy, and a number of things: When the American spirit was in its youth, the language of America was different: Liberty, Sir, was then the primary object. We are descended from a people whose Government was founded on liberty: Our glorious forefathers of Great Britain, made liberty the foundation of everything. That country is become a great, mighty, and splendid nation; not because their Government is strong and energetic; but, Sir, because liberty is its direct end and foundation: We drew the spirit of liberty from our British ancestors; by that spirit we have triumphed over every difficulty: But now, Sir, the American spirit, assisted by the ropes and chains of consolidation, is about to convert this country to a powerful and mighty empire: If you make the citizens of this country agree to become the subjects of one great consolidated empire of America, your Government will not have sufficient energy to keep them together: Such a Government is incompatible with the genius of republicanism: There will be no checks, no real balances, in this Government: What can avail your specious imaginary balances, your rope-dancing, chain-rattling, ridiculous ideal checks and contrivances? But, Sir, we are not feared by foreigners; we do not make nations tremble: Would this, Sir, constitute happiness, or secure liberty? I trust, Sir, our political hemisphere will ever direct their operations to the security of those objects. Consider our situation, Sir: Go to the poor man, ask him what he does; he will inform you, that he enjoys the fruits of his labor, under his own fig tree with his wife and children around him, in peace and security. Go to every other member of the society, you will find the same tranquil ease and content; you will find no alarms or disturbances: Why then tell us of dangers to terrify us into an adoption of this new Government? and yet who knows the dangers that this new system may produce; they are out of the sight of the common people: They cannot foresee latent consequences: I dread the operation of it on the middling and lower class of people: It is for them I fear the adoption of this system. I fear I tire the patience of the Committee, but I beg to be indulged with a few more observations: When I thus profess myself an advocate for the liberty of the people, I shall be told, I am a designing man, that I am to be a great man, that I am to be a demagogue; and many similar illiberal insinuations will be thrown out; but, Sir, conscious rectitude, outweighs these things with me: I see great jeopardy in this new Government. I see none from our present one: I hope some Gentleman or other will bring forth, in full array, those dangers, if there be any, that we may see and touch them: I have said that I thought this a Consolidated Government: I will now prove it. Will the great rights of the people be secured by this Government? Suppose it should prove oppressive, how can it be altered? Our Bill of Rights declares, "That a majority of the community hath an *indubitable, inalienable,* and *indefeasible right* to reform, alter, or abolish it, in such manner as shall be judged most conducive to the public weal." I have just proved that one-tenth, or less, of the people of America, a most despicable minority may prevent this reform or alteration. Suppose the people of Virginia should wish to alter their Government, can a majority of them do it? No, because they are connected with other men; or, in other words, consolidated with other States: When the people of Virginia at a future day shall wish to alter their Government, though they should be unanimous in this desire, yet they may be prevented therefrom by a despicable minority at the extremity of the United States: The founders of your own Constitution made your Government changeable: But the power of changing it is gone from you! Whither is it gone? It is placed in the same hands that hold the rights of twelve other States; and those who hold those rights, have right and power to keep them: It is not the particular Government of Virginia: One of the leading features of that Government is, that a majority can alter it, when necessary for the public good. This Government is not a Virginian but an American Government. Is it not therefore a Consolidated Government? The sixth clause of your Bill of Rights tells you, "That elections of members to serve as Representatives of the people in Assembly, ought to be free, and that all men having sufficient evidence of permanent common interest with, and attachment to the community, have the right of suffrage, and *cannot* be *taxed* or *deprived* of *their property* for public uses, without their own consent, or that of their Representatives so elected, nor bound by any law to which they have not in like manner assented for the public good." But what does this Constitution say? The clause under consideration gives an unlimited and unbounded power of taxation: Suppose every delegate from Virginia opposes a law laying a tax, what will it avail? They are opposed by a majority: Eleven members can destroy their efforts: Those feeble ten cannot prevent the passing the most oppressive tax law. So that in direct opposition to the spirit and express language of your Declaration of Rights, you are taxed, not by your own consent, but by people who have no connection with you. The next clause of the Bill of Rights tells you, "That all power of suspending law, or the execution of laws, by any authority without the consent of the Representatives of the people, is injurious to their rights, and ought not to be exercised." This tells us that there can be no suspension of Government, or laws without our own consent: Yet this Constitution can counteract and suspend any of our laws, that contravene its oppressive operation; for they have the power of direct taxation; which suspends our Bill of Rights; and it is expressly provided, that they can make all laws necessary for carrying their powers into execution; and it is declared paramount to the laws and constitutions of the States. Consider how the only remaining defense we have left is destroyed in this manner: Besides the expenses of maintaining the Senate and other House in as much splendor as they please, there is to be a great and mighty President, with very extensive powers; the powers of a King: He is to be supported in extravagant magnificence: So that the whole of our property may be taken by this American Government, by laying what taxes they please, giving themselves what salaries they please, and suspending our laws at their pleasure: I might be thought too inquisitive, but I believe I should take up but very little of your time in enumerating the little power that is left to the Government of Virginia; for this power is reduced to little or nothing: Their garrisons, magazines, arsenals, and forts, which will be situated in the strongest places within the States: Their ten miles square, with all the fine ornaments of human life, added to their powers, and taken from the States, will reduce the power of the latter to nothing. The voice of tradition, I trust, will inform posterity of our struggles for freedom: If our descendants be worthy the name of Americans, they will preserve and hand down to their latest posterity, the transactions of the present times; and though, I confess, my exclamations are not worthy the hearing, they will see that I have done my utmost to preserve their liberty: For I never will give up the power of direct taxation, but for a scourge: I am willing to give it conditionally; that is, after noncompliance with requisitions: I will do more, Sir, and what I hope will convince the most skeptical man, that I am a lover of the American Union, that in case Virginia shall not make punctual payment, the control of our custom houses, and the whole regulation of trade, shall be given to Congress, and that Virginia shall depend on Congress even for passports, until Virginia shall have paid the last farthing; and furnished the last soldier: Nay, Sir, there is another alternative to which I would consent: Even that they should strike us out of the Union, and take away from us all federal privileges until we comply with federal requisitions; but let it depend upon our own pleasure to pay our money in the most easy manner for our people. Were all the States, more terrible than the mother country, to join against us, I hope Virginia could defend herself; but, Sir, the dissolution of the Union is most abhorrent to my mind: The first thing I have at heart is American *liberty;* the second thing is American Union; and I hope the people of Virginia will endeavor to preserve that Union: The increasing population of the southern States, is far greater than that of New England: Consequently, in a short time, they will be far more numerous than the people of that country: Consider this, and you will find this State more particularly interested to support American liberty, and not bind our posterity by an improvident relinquishment of our rights. I would give the best security for a punctual compliance with requisitions; but I beseech Gentlemen, at all hazards, not to give up this unlimited power of taxation: The Honorable Gentleman has told us these powers given to Congress, are accompanied by a Judiciary which will connect all: On examination you will find this very Judiciary oppressively constructed; your jury trial destroyed, and the Judges dependent on Congress. In this scheme of energetic Government, the people will find two sets of tax gatherers—the State and the Federal Sheriffs. This it seems to me will produce such dreadful oppression, as the people cannot possibly bear: The Federal Sheriff may commit what oppression, make what distresses he pleases, and ruin you with impunity: For how are you to tie his hands? Have you any sufficient decided means of preventing him from sucking your blood by speculations, commissions, and fees? Thus thousands of your people will be most shamefully robbed: Our State Sheriffs, those unfeeling bloodsuckers, have, under the watchful eye of our Legislature, committed the most horrid and barbarous ravages on our people: It has required the most constant vigilance of the Legislature to keep them from totally ruining the people: A repeated succession of laws has been made to suppress their iniquitous speculations and cruel extortions; and as often have their nefarious ingenuity devised methods of evading the force of those laws: In the struggle they have generally triumphed over the Legislature. It is a fact that lands have sold for five shillings, which were worth one hundred pounds: If Sheriffs thus immediately under the eye of our State Legislature and Judiciary, have dared to commit these outrages, what would they not have done if their masters had been at Philadelphia or New York? If they perpetrate the most unwarrantable outrage on your persons or property, you cannot get redress on this side of Philadelphia or New York: And how can you get it there? If your domestic avocations could permit you to go thither, there you must appeal to Judges sworn to support this Constitution, in opposition to that of any State, and who may also be inclined to favor their own officers: When these harpies are aided by excise men, who may search at any time your houses and most secret recesses, will the people bear it? If you think so you differ from me: Where I thought there was a possibility of such mischiefs, I would grant power with a niggardly hand; and here there is a strong probability that these oppressions shall actually happen. I may be told, that it is safe to err on that side; because such regulations *may* be made by Congress, as shall restrain these officers, and because laws are made by our Representatives, and judged by righteous Judges: But, Sir, as these regulations may be made, so they may not; and many reasons there are to induce a belief that they will not: I shall therefore be an infidel on that point until the day of my death.

This Constitution is said to have beautiful features; but when I come to examine these features, Sir, they appear to me horridly frightful: Among other deformities, it has an awful squinting; it squints toward monarchy: And does not this raise indignation in the breast of every American? Your President may easily become King: Your Senate is so imperfectly constructed that your dearest rights may be sacrificed by what may be a small minority; and a very small minority may continue forever unchangeably this Government, although horridly defective: Where are your checks in this Government? Your strongholds will be in the hands of your enemies: It is on a supposition that our American Governors shall be honest, that all the good qualities of this Government are founded: But its defective, and imperfect construction, puts it in their power to perpetrate the worst of mischiefs, should they be bad men: And, Sir, would not all the world, from the Eastern to the Western hemisphere, blame our distracted folly in resting our rights upon the contingency of our rulers being good or bad. Show me that age and country where the rights and liberties of the people were placed on the sole chance of their rulers being good men, without a consequent loss of liberty? I say that the loss of that dearest privilege has ever followed with absolute certainty, every such mad attempt. If your American chief, be a man of ambition, and abilities, how easy is it for him to render himself absolute: The army is in his hands, and, if he be a man of address, it will be attached to him; and it will be the subject of long meditation with him to seize the first auspicious moment to accomplish his design; and, Sir, will the American spirit solely relieve you when this happens? I would rather infinitely, and I am sure most of this Convention are of the same opinion, have a King, Lords, and Commons, than a Government so replete with such insupportable evils. If we make a King, we may prescribe the rules by which he shall rule his people, and interpose such checks as shall prevent him from infringing them: But the President, in the field, at the head of his army, can prescribe the terms on which he shall reign master, so far that it will puzzle any American ever to get his neck from under the galling yoke. I cannot with patience, think of this idea. If ever he violates the laws, one of two things will happen: He shall come at the head of his army to carry everything before him; or, he will give bail, or do what Mr. Chief Justice will order him. If he be guilty, will not the recollection of his crimes teach him to make one bold push for the American throne? Will not the immense difference between being master of everything, and being ignominiously tried and punished, powerfully excite him to make this bold push? But, Sir, where is the existing force to punish him? Can he not at the head of his army beat down every opposition? Away with your President, we shall have a King: The army will salute him Monarch; your militia will leave you and assist in making him King, and fight against you: And what have you to oppose this force? What will then become of you and your rights? Will not absolute despotism ensue? {Here Mr. Henry strongly and pathetically expatiated on the probability of the President's enslaving America, and the horrible consequences that must result.}[11] What can be more defective than the clause concerning the elections?—The control given to Congress over the time, place, and manner of holding elections, will totally destroy the end of suffrage. The elections may be held at one place, and the most inconvenient in the State; or they may be at remote distances from those who have a right of suffrage: Hence nine out of ten must either not vote at all, or vote for strangers: For the most influential characters will be applied to, to know who are the most proper to be chosen. I repeat that the control of Congress over the *manner*, etc., of electing, well warrants this idea. The natural consequence will be, that this democratic branch, will possess none of the public confidence: The people will be prejudiced against Representatives chosen in such an injudicious manner. The proceedings in the northern conclave will be hidden from the yeomanry of this country: We are told that the yeas and nays shall be taken and entered on the journals: This, Sir, will avail nothing: It may be locked up in their chests, and concealed forever from the people; for they are not to publish what parts they think require secrecy: They *may* think, and *will* think, the whole requires it. Another beautiful feature of this Constitution is, the publication from time to time of the receipts and expenditures of the public money. This expression, from time to time, is very indefinite and indeterminate: It may extend to a century. Grant that any of them are wicked, they may squander the public money so as to ruin you, and yet this expression will give you no redress. I say, they may ruin you;—for where, Sir, is the responsibility? The yeas and nays will show you nothing, unless they be fools as well as knaves: For after having wickedly trampled on the rights of the people, they would act like fools indeed, were they to publish and divulge their iniquity, when they have it equally in their power to suppress and conceal it.—Where is the responsibility—that leading principle in the British government? In that government a punishment, certain and inevitable, is provided: But in this, there is no real actual punishment for the grossest maladministration. They may go without punishment, though they commit the most outrageous violation on our immunities. That paper may tell me they will be punished. I ask, by

---

11. [Clearly the stenographer had difficulty keeping up with Henry and was occasionally reduced to recording a mere summary, not his actual words.]

what law? They must make the law—for there is no existing law to do it. What—will they make a law to punish themselves? This, Sir, is my great objection to the Constitution, that there is no true responsibility—and that the preservation of our liberty depends on the single chance of men being virtuous enough to make laws to punish themselves. In the country from which we are descended, they have real, and not imaginary, responsibility—for there, maladministration has cost their heads, to some of the most saucy geniuses that ever were. The Senate, by making treaties may destroy your liberty and laws for want of responsibility. Two-thirds of those that shall happen to be present, can, with the President, make treaties, that shall be the supreme law of the land: They may make the most ruinous treaties; and yet there is no punishment for them. Whoever shows me a punishment provided for them, will oblige me. So, Sir, notwithstanding there are eight pillars, they want another. Where will they make another? I trust, Sir, the exclusion of the evils wherewith this system is replete, in its present form, will be made a condition, precedent to its adoption, by this or any other State. The transition from a general unqualified admission to offices, to a consolidation of government, seems easy; for though the American States are dissimilar in their structure, this will assimilate them: This, Sir, is itself a strong consolidating feature, and is not one of the least dangerous in that system. Nine States are sufficient to establish this government over those nine: Imagine that nine have come into it. Virginia has certain scruples. Suppose she will consequently, refuse to join with those States:—May not they still continue in friendship and union with her? If she sends her annual requisitions in dollars, do you think their stomachs will be so squeamish that they will refuse her dollars? Will they not accept her regiments? They would intimidate you into an inconsiderate adoption, and frighten you with ideal evils, and that the Union shall be dissolved. It is a bugbear, Sir:—The fact is, Sir, that the eight adopting States can hardly stand on their own legs. Public fame tells us, that the adopting States have already heartburnings and animosity, and repent their precipitate hurry: This, Sir, may occasion exceeding great mischief. When I reflect on these and many other circumstances, I must think those States will be fond to be in confederacy with us. If we pay our quota of money annually, and furnish our ratable number of men, when necessary, I can see no danger from a rejection. The history of Switzerland clearly proves, we might be in amicable alliance with those States without adopting this Constitution. Switzerland is a Confederacy, consisting of dissimilar Governments. This is an example which proves that Governments of dissimilar structure may be Confederated; that Confederate Republic has stood upward of four hundred years; and although several of the individual republics are democratic, and the rest aristocratic, no evil has resulted from this dissimilarity, for they have braved all the power of France and Germany during that long period. The Swiss spirit, Sir, has kept them together: They have encountered and overcome immense difficulties with patience and fortitude. In this vicinity of powerful and ambitious monarchs, they have retained their independence, republican simplicity, and valor. {Here he makes a comparison of the people of that country, and those of France, and makes a quotation from Addison, illustrating the subject.} Look at the peasants of that country and of France, and mark the difference. You will find the condition of the former far more desirable and comfortable. No matter whether a people be great, splendid, and powerful, if they enjoy freedom. The Turkish Grand Seigneur, alongside of our President, would put us to disgrace: But we should be abundantly consoled for this disgrace, when our citizen should be put in contrast with the Turkish slave. The most valuable end of government, is the liberty of the inhabitants. No possible advantages can compensate for the loss of this privilege. Show me the reason why the American Union is to be dissolved. Who are those eight adopting States? Are they averse to give us a little time to consider, before we conclude? Would such a disposition render a junction with them eligible; or is it the genius of that kind of government, to precipitate people hastily into measures of the utmost importance, and grant no indulgence? If it be, Sir, is it for us to accede to such a government? We have a right to have time to consider—We shall therefore insist upon it. Unless the government be amended, we can never accept it. The adopting States will doubtless accept our money and our regiments—And what is to be the consequence, if we are disunited? I believe that it is yet doubtful, whether it is not proper to stand by a while, and see the effect of its adoption in other States. In forming a government, the utmost care should be taken to prevent its becoming oppressive; and this government is of such an intricate and complicated nature, that no man on this earth can know its real operation. The other States have no reason to think, from the antecedent conduct of Virginia, that she has any intention of seceding from the Union, or of being less active to support the general welfare: Would they not therefore acquiesce in our taking time to deliberate? Deliberate whether the measure be not perilous, not only for us, but the adopting States. Permit me, Sir, to say, that a great majority of the people even in the adopting States, are averse to this government. I believe I would be right to say, that they have been egregiously misled. Pennsylvania has *perhaps* been tricked into it. If the other States who have adopted it, have not been tricked, still they were too much hurried into its adoption. There were very respectable minorities in several of them; and if reports be true, a clear majority of the people are averse to it. If we also accede, and it should prove grievous, the peace and prosperity of our country, which we all love, will be destroyed. This government has not the affection of the people, at present. Should it be oppressive, their affection will be totally estranged from it—and, Sir, you know that a Government without their affections can neither be durable nor happy. I speak as one poor individual—but when I speak, I speak the language of thousands. But, Sir, I mean not to breathe the spirit nor utter the language of secession. I have trespassed so long on your patience, I am really concerned that I have something yet to say. The honorable member has said that we shall be properly represented: Remember, Sir, that the number of our Representatives is but ten, whereof six is a majority. Will these men be possessed of sufficient information? A particular knowledge of particular districts will not suffice. They must be well acquainted with agriculture, commerce, and a great variety of other matters throughout the Continent: They must know not only the actual state of nations in Europe, and America, the situation of their farmers, cottagers, and mechanics, but also the relative situation and intercourse of those nations. Virginia is as large as England. Our proportion of Representatives is but ten men. In England they have five hundred thirty. The House of Commons in England, numerous as they are, we are told, is bribed, and have bartered away the rights of their constituents: What then shall become of us? Will these few protect our rights? Will they be incorruptible? You say they will be better men than the English Commoners.[12] I say they will be infinitely worse men, because they are to be chosen blindfolded: Their election (the term, as applied to their appointment, is inaccurate) will be an involuntary nomination, and not a choice. I have, I fear, fatigued the Committee, yet I have not said the one-hundred-thousandth part of what I have on my mind, and wish to impart. On this occasion I conceived myself bound to attend strictly to the interest of the State; and I thought her dearest rights at stake: Having lived so long—been so much honored—my efforts, though small, are due to my country. I have found my mind hurried on from subject to subject, on this very great occasion. We have been all out of order from the Gentleman who opened today, to myself. I did not come prepared to speak on so multifarious a subject, in so general a manner. I trust you will indulge me another time.—Before you abandon the present system, I hope you will consider not only its defects, most maturely, but likewise those of that which you are to substitute to it. May you be fully apprised of the dangers of the latter, not by fatal experience, but by some abler advocate than me.

---

12. [I.e., members of Parliament.]

SPEECHES OF MELANCTON SMITH BEFORE THE NEW YORK
RATIFYING CONVENTION (JUNE 20, 21, 23, 1788)

June 20, 1788

Mr. *Smith* again rose—He most heartily concurred in sentiment with the
honorable gentleman who opened the debate yesterday,[13] that the discussion of the important question now before them ought to be entered on
with a spirit of patriotism; with minds open to conviction; with a determination to form opinions only on the merits of the question, from those
evidences which should appear in the course of the investigation.

How far the general observations made by the honorable gentleman
accorded with these principles, he left to the House to determine.

It was not, he said, his intention to follow that gentleman through all
his remarks—he should only observe, that what had been advanced did
not appear to him to apply to the subject under consideration.

He was as strongly impressed with the necessity of a Union, as any one
could be: He would seek it with as much ardor. In the discussion of this
subject, he was disposed to make every reasonable concession, and indeed
to sacrifice everything for a Union, except the liberties of his country,
than which he could contemplate no greater misfortune. But he hoped we
were not reduced to the necessity of sacrificing or even endangering our
liberties to preserve the Union. If that was the case, the alternative was
dreadful. But he would not now say that the adoption of the Constitution
would endanger our liberties; because that was the point to be debated,
and the premises should be laid down previously to the drawing of any
conclusion. He wished that all observations might be confined to this
point; and that declamation and appeals to the passions might be omitted.

Why, said he, are we told of our weaknesses? Of the defenseless condition of the southern parts of our state? Of the exposed situation of our
capital? Of Long Island surrounded by water, and exposed to the incur-
sions of our neighbors in Connecticut? Of Vermont having separated
from us and assumed the powers of a distinct government; And of the
Northwest part of our state being in the hands of a foreign enemy?—Why
are we to be alarmed with apprehensions that the Eastern states are inim-
ical, and disinclined to form alliances with us? He was sorry to find that
such suspicions were entertained. He believed that no such disposition
existed in the Eastern states. Surely it could not be supposed that those
states would make war upon us for exercising the rights of freemen, deliberating and judging for ourselves, on a subject the most interesting that

---

13. [Robert Livingston, the Chancellor of New York.]

ever came before any assembly. If a war with our neighbor was to be the result of not acceding, there was no use in debating here; we had better receive their dictates, if we were unable to resist them. The defects of the Old Confederation needed as little proof as the necessity of an Union: But there was no proof in all this, that the proposed Constitution was a good one. Defective as the Old Confederation is, he said, no one could deny but it was possible we might have a worse government. But the question was not whether the present Confederation be a bad one; but whether the proposed Constitution be a good one.

It had been observed, that no examples of Federal Republics had succeeded. It was true that the ancient confederated Republics were all destroyed—so were those which were not confederated; and all ancient Governments of every form had shared the same fate. Holland had undoubtedly experienced many evils from the defects in her government; but with all these defects, she yet existed; she had under her Confederacy made a principal figure among the nations of Europe, and he believed few countries had experienced a greater share of internal peace and prosperity.[14] The Germanic Confederacy was not the most pertinent example to produce on this occasion:—Among a number of absolute Princes who consider their subjects as their property, whose will is law, and to whose ambition there are no bounds, it was no difficult task to discover other causes from which the convulsions in that country rose, than the defects of their Confederation. Whether a Confederacy of States under any form be a practicable Government, was a question to be discussed in the course of investigating this Constitution.

He was pleased that thus early in the debate, the honorable gentleman had himself shown, that the intent of the Constitution was not a Confederacy, but a reduction of all the states into a consolidated government. He hoped the gentleman would be complaisant enough to exchange names with those who disliked the Constitution, as it appeared from his own concession that they were Federalists, and those who advocated it Anti-Federalists.[15] He begged leave, however, to remind the gentleman, that

---

14. [The United Provinces (Holland being merely one of the Provinces) had a constitution under which all the provinces had to agree before any action could be taken.]

15. [The term "Federalist" was profoundly ambiguous during the debates on ratification. Those who favored a more energetic government laid claim to the term, and said the new government, like the old, was to be a confederation; those who opposed the new government said that it was a consolidation of power into one new state, and that it was they who were upholding the principles of Federalism. In the changes made to Federalist 39 one can see a faint echo of these difficulties.]

Montesquieu, with all the examples of modern and ancient Republics in view, gives it as his opinion, that a confederated Republic has all the internal advantages of a Republic, with the external force of a Monarchical Government.[16] He was happy to find an officer of such high rank recommending to the other officers of Government, and to those who are members of the Legislature, to be unbiased by any motives of interest or state importance. Fortunately for himself, he was out of the verge of temptations of this kind, not having the honor to hold any office under the state. But then he was exposed, in common with other gentlemen of the Convention, to another temptation, against which he thought it necessary that we should be equally guarded:—If, said he, this constitution is adopted, there will be a number of honorable and lucrative offices to be filled, and we ought to be cautious lest an expectancy of some of them should influence us to adopt without due consideration.

We may wander, said he, in the fields of fancy without end, and gather flowers as we go: It may be entertaining—but it is of little service to the discovery of truth:—We may on one side compare the scheme advocated by our opponents to *golden images, with feet part of iron and part of clay;* and on the other, *to a beast dreadful and terrible, and strong exceedingly, having great iron teeth, which devours, breaks in pieces, and stamps the residue with his feet:* And after all, said he, we shall find that both these allusions are taken from the same *vision;* and their true meaning must be discovered by sober reasoning.

He would agree with the honorable gentleman, that perfection in any system of government was not to be looked for. If that was the object, the debates on the one before them might soon be closed.—But he would observe that this observation applied with equal force against changing any systems—especially against material and radical changes.—Fickleness and inconstancy, he said, was characteristic of a free people; and in framing a Constitution for them, it was, perhaps the most difficult thing to correct this spirit, and guard against the evil effects of it—he was persuaded it could not be altogether prevented without destroying their freedom—it would be like attempting to correct a small indisposition in the habit of the body, by fixing the patient in a confirmed consumption.— This fickle and inconstant spirit was the more dangerous in bringing about changes in the government. The instance that had been adduced by the gentleman from sacred history, was an example in point to prove this: The nation of Israel having received a form of civil government from Heaven, enjoyed it for a considerable period; but at length laboring under pressures, which were brought upon them by their own misconduct and

---

16. [*Spirit of the Laws,* book 9, chapter 1.]

imprudence, instead of imputing their misfortunes to their true causes, and making a proper improvement of their calamities, by a correction of their errors, they imputed them to a defect in their constitution; they rejected their Divine Ruler, and asked Samuel to make them a King to judge them, like other nations. Samuel was grieved at their folly; but still, by the command of God, he hearkened to their voice; though not until he had solemnly declared unto them the manner in which the King should reign over them. "This, (says Samuel) shall be the manner of the King that shall reign over you. He will take your sons and appoint them for himself, for his chariots, and for his horsemen, and some shall run before his chariots; and he will appoint him captains over thousands, and captains over fifties, and will set them to ear his ground, and to reap his harvest, and to make his instruments of war, and instruments of his chariots. And he will take your daughters to be confectioneries, and to be cooks, and to be bakers. And he will take your fields, and your vineyards, and your olive yards, even the best of them, and give them to his servants. And he will take the tenth of your seed, and of your vineyards, and give to his officers and to his servants. And he will take your men servants and your maid servants, and your goodliest young men, and your asses, and put them to his work. He will take the tenth of your sheep: And ye shall be his servants. And ye shall cry out in that day, because of your King which ye have chosen you; and the Lord will not hear you in that day."[17]—How far this was applicable to the subject he would not now say; it could be better judged of when they had gone through it.—On the whole he wished to take up this matter with candor and deliberation.

He would now proceed to state his objections to the clause just read (section 2 of article I, clause 3). His objections were comprised under three heads: First. the rule of apportionment is unjust; second. there is no precise number fixed on below which the house shall not be reduced; third. it is inadequate. In the first place the rule of apportionment of the representatives is to be according to the whole number of the white inhabitants, with three-fifths of all others; that is in plain English, each state is to send Representatives in proportion to the number of freemen, and three-fifths of the slaves it contains. He could not see any rule by which slaves are to be included in the ratio of representation: The principle of a representation, being that every free agent should be concerned in governing himself, it was absurd to give that power to a man who could not exercise it—slaves have no will of their own: The very operation of it was to give certain privileges to those people who were so wicked as to keep slaves. He knew it would be admitted that this rule of apportionment was

---

17. [I Samuel 8:11–18.]

founded on unjust principles, but that it was the result of accommodation; which he supposed we should be under the necessity of admitting, if we meant to be in union with the Southern States, though utterly repugnant to his feelings. In the second place, the number was not fixed by the Constitution, but left at the discretion of the Legislature; perhaps he was mistaken; it was his wish to be informed. He understood from the Constitution, that sixty-five Members were to compose the House of Representatives for three years; that after that time a census was to be taken, and the numbers to be ascertained by the Legislature on the following principles: First, they shall be apportioned to the respective States according to numbers; second, each State shall have one at least; third, they shall never exceed one to every thirty thousand. If this was the case, the first Congress that met might reduce the number below what it now is; a power inconsistent with every principle of a free government, to leave it to the discretion of the rulers to determine the number of the representatives of the people. There was no kind of security except in the integrity of the men who were entrusted; and if you have no other security, it is idle to contend about Constitutions. In the third place, supposing Congress should declare that there should be one representative for every thirty thousand of the people, in his opinion it would be incompetent to the great purposes of representation. It was, he said, the fundamental principle of a free government, that the people should make the laws by which they were to be governed: He who is controlled by another is a slave; and that government which is directed by the will of any one or a few, or any number less than is the will of the community, is a government for slaves.

The next point was, how was the will of the community to be expressed? It was not possible for them to come together; the multitude would be too great: In order, therefore to provide against this inconvenience, the scheme of representation had been adopted, by which the people deputed others to represent them. Individuals entering into society became one body, and that body ought to be animated by one mind; and he conceived that every form of government should have that complexion. It was true that notwithstanding all the experience we had from others, it had not appeared that the experiment of representation had been fairly tried: there was something like it in the ancient republics, in which, being of small extent, the people could easily meet together, though instead of deliberating, they only considered of those things which were submitted to them by their magistrates. In Great Britain representation had been carried much further than in any government we knew of, except our own; but in that country it now had only a name. America was the only country, in which the first fair opportunity had been offered. When we were Colonies, our representation was better than any that was then known: Since the revolution we had advanced still nearer to perfection. He considered it as an object, of all others the most important, to have it fixed on its true principle; yet he was convinced that it was impracticable to have such a representation in a consolidated government. However, said he, we may approach a great way toward perfection by increasing the representation and limiting the powers of Congress. He considered that the great interests and liberties of the people could only be secured by the State Governments. He admitted, that if the new government was only confined to great national objects, it would be less exceptionable; but it extended to every thing dear to human nature. That this was the case could be proved without any long chain of reasoning:—for that power which had both the purse and the sword, had the government of the whole country, and might extend its powers to any and to every object. He had already observed, that by the true doctrine of representation, this principle was established— that the representative must be chosen by the free will of the majority of his constituents: It therefore followed that the representative should be chosen from small districts. This being admitted, he would ask, could sixty-five men, for three million, or one for thirty thousand, be chosen in this manner? Would they be possessed of the requisite information to make happy the great number of souls that were spread over this extensive country?—There was another objection to the clause: If great affairs of government were trusted to a few men, they would be more liable to corruption. Corruption, he knew, was unfashionable among us, but he supposed that Americans were like other men; and though they had hitherto displayed great virtues, still they were men; and therefore such steps should be taken as to prevent the possibility of corruption. We were now in that stage of society, in which we could deliberate with freedom;—how long it might continue, God only knew! Twenty years hence, perhaps, these maxims might become unfashionable; we already hear, said he, in all parts of the country, gentlemen ridiculing that spirit of patriotism and love of liberty, which carried us through all our difficulties in times of danger.—When patriotism was already nearly hooted out of society, ought we not to take some precautions against the progress of corruption?

He had one more observation to make, to show that the representation was insufficient—Government, he said, must rest for its execution, on the good opinion of the people, for if it was made in heaven, and had not the confidence of the people, it could not be executed:[18] that this was proved,

18. [Hamilton replied saying, "It was remarked yesterday, that a numerous representation was necessary to obtain the confidence of the people. This is not generally true. The confidence of the people will easily be gained by a good administration. This is the true touchstone."]

by the example given by the gentleman, of the Jewish theocracy. It must have a good setting out, or the instant it takes place there is an end of liberty. He believed that the inefficacy of the old Confederation, had arisen from that want of confidence; and this caused in a great degree by the continual declamation of gentlemen of importance against it from one end of the continent to the other, who had frequently compared it to a rope of sand. It had pervaded every class of citizens, and their misfortunes, the consequences of idleness and extravagance, were attributed to the defects of that system. At the close of the war, our country had been left in distress; and it was impossible that any government on earth could immediately retrieve it; it must be time and industry alone that could effect it. He said he would pursue these observations no further at present,—And concluded with making the following motion:

"*Resolved*, That it is proper that the number of representatives be fixed at the rate of one for every twenty thousand inhabitants, to be ascertained on the principles mentioned in the second section of the first article of the Constitution, until they amount to three hundred; after which they shall be apportioned among the States, in proportion to the number of inhabitants of the States respectively: And that before the first enumeration shall be made, the several States shall be entitled to choose double the number of representatives for that purpose, mentioned in the Constitution."

June 21, 1788

Mr. *M. Smith.* I had the honor yesterday of submitting an amendment to the clause under consideration, with some observations in support of it. I hope I shall be indulged in making some additional remarks in reply to what has been offered by the honorable gentleman from New York [Alexander Hamilton].

He has taken up much time in endeavoring to prove that the great defect in the old confederation was, that it operated upon states instead of individuals. It is needless to dispute concerning points on which we do not disagree: It is admitted that the powers of the general government ought to operate upon individuals to a certain degree. How far the powers should extend, and in what cases to individuals is the question. As the different parts of the system will come into view in the course of our investigation, an opportunity will be afforded to consider this question; I wish at present to confine myself to the subject immediately under the consideration of the committee. I shall make no reply to the arguments offered by the honorable gentleman to justify the rule of apportionment fixed by this clause: For though I am confident they might be easily refuted, yet I am persuaded we must yield this point, in accommodation to the southern states. The amendment therefore proposes no alteration to the clause in this respect.

The honorable gentleman says, that the clause by obvious construction fixes the representation. I wish not to torture words or sentences. I perceive no such obvious construction. I see clearly, that on the one hand the representatives cannot exceed one for thirty thousand inhabitants; and on the other, that whatever larger number of inhabitants may be taken for the rule of apportionment, each state shall be entitled to send one representative. Everything else appears to me in the discretion of the legislature. If there be any other limitation, it is certainly implied. Matters of such moment should not be left to doubtful construction. It is urged that the number of representatives will be fixed at one for thirty thousand, because it will be the interest of the larger states to do it. I cannot discern the force of this argument.—To me it appears clear, that the relative weight of influence of the different states will be the same, with the number of representatives at sixty-five as at six hundred, and that of the individual members greater. For each member's share of power will decrease as the number of the house of representatives increases.—If therefore this maxim be true, that men are unwilling to relinquish powers which they once possess, we are not to expect that the house of representatives will be inclined to enlarge the numbers. The same motive will operate to influence the president and senate to oppose the increase of the number of representatives; for in proportion as the weight of the house of representatives is augmented, they will feel their own diminished: It is therefore of the highest importance that a suitable number of representatives should be established by the constitution.

It has been observed by an honorable member, that the eastern states insisted upon a small representation on the principles of economy.—This argument must have no weight in the mind of a considerate person. The difference of expense, between supporting a house of representatives sufficiently numerous, and the present proposed one would be about twenty or thirty thousand dollars per annum. The man who would seriously object to this expense, to secure his liberties, does not deserve to enjoy them. Besides, by increasing the number of representatives, we open a door for the admission of the substantial yeomanry of your country; who, being possessed of the habits of economy, will be cautious of imprudent expenditures, by which means a much greater saving will be made of public money than is sufficient to support them. A reduction of the number of the state legislatures might also be made, by which means there might be a saving of expense much more than sufficient for the purpose of supporting the general legislature.—For, as under this system all the powers of legislation relating to our general concerns, are vested in the general government, the powers of the state legislatures will be so curtailed, as to render it less necessary to have them so numerous as they now are.

But an honorable gentleman has observed that it is a problem that cannot be solved, what the proper number is which ought to compose the house of representatives, and calls upon me to fix the number. I admit this is a question that will not admit of a solution with mathematical certainty—few political questions will—yet we may determine with certainty that certain numbers are too small or too large. We may be sure that ten is too small and a thousand too large a number—everyone will allow that the first number is too small to possess the sentiments, be influenced by the interests of the people, or secure against corruption: A thousand would be too numerous to be capable of deliberating.

To determine whether the number of representatives proposed by this Constitution is sufficient, it is proper to examine the qualifications which this house ought to possess, in order to exercise their powers discreetly for the happiness of the people. The idea that naturally suggests itself to our minds, when we speak of representatives is, that they resemble those they represent; they should be a true picture of the people; possess the knowledge of their circumstances and their wants; sympathize in all their distresses, and be disposed to seek their true interests. The knowledge necessary for the representatives of a free people, not only comprehends extensive political and commercial information, such as is acquired by men of refined education, who have leisure to attain to high degrees of improvement, but it should also comprehend that kind of acquaintance with the common concerns and occupations of the people, which men of the middling class of life are in general much better competent to, than those of a superior class. To understand the true commercial interests of a country, not only requires just ideas of the general commerce of the world, but also, and principally, a knowledge of the productions of your own country and their value, what your soil is capable of producing, the nature of your manufactures, and the capacity of the country to increase both. To exercise the power of laying taxes, duties, and excises with discretion, requires something more than an acquaintance with the abstruse parts of the system of finance. It calls for a knowledge of the circumstances and ability of the people in general, a discernment how the burdens imposed will bear upon the different classes.

From these observations results this conclusion that the number of representatives should be so large, as that while it embraces men of the first class, it should admit those of the middling class of life. I am convinced that this Government is so constituted, that the representatives will generally be composed of the first class in the community, which I shall distinguish by the name of the natural aristocracy of the country. I do not mean to give offense by using this term. I am sensible this idea is treated by many gentlemen as chimerical. I shall be asked what is meant by the natural aristocracy—and told that no such distinction of classes of men exists among us.[19] It is true it is our singular felicity that we have no legal or hereditary distinctions of this kind; but still there are real differences: Every society naturally divides itself into classes. The author of nature has bestowed on some greater capacities than on others—birth, education, talents, and wealth, create distinctions among men as visible and of as much influence as titles, stars, and garters. In every society, men of this class will command a superior degree of respect—and if the government is so constituted as to admit but few to exercise the powers of it, it will, according to the natural course of things, be in their hands. Men in the middling class, who are qualified as representatives, will not be so anxious to be chosen as those of the first. When the number is so small the office will be highly elevated and distinguished—the style in which the members live will probably be high—circumstances of this kind, will render the place of a representative not a desirable one to sensible, substantial men, who have been used to walk in the plain and frugal paths of life.

Besides, the influence of the great will generally enable them to succeed in elections—it will be difficult to combine a district of country containing thirty or forty thousand inhabitants, frame your election laws as you please, in any one character; unless it be in one of conspicuous, military, popular, civil, or legal talents. The great easily form associations; the poor and middling class form them with difficulty. If the elections be by plurality, as probably will be the case in this state, it is almost certain, none but the great will be chosen—for they easily unite their interest—The common people will divide, and their divisions will be promoted by the others. There will be scarcely a chance of their uniting, in any other but some great man, unless in some popular demagogue, who will probably be destitute of principle. A substantial yeoman of sense and discernment, will hardly ever be chosen. From these remarks it appears that the government will fall into the hands of the few and the great. This will be a government of oppression. I do not mean to declaim against the great,

---

19. [Hamilton replied saying, "But who are the aristocracy among us? Where do we find men elevated to a perpetual rank above their fellow citizens, and possessing powers entirely independent of them? The arguments of the gentleman only go to prove that there are men who are rich, men who are poor, some who are wise, and others who are not; that, indeed, every distinguished man is an aristocrat."]

and charge them indiscriminately with want of principle and honesty.—
The same passions and prejudices govern all men. The circumstances in
which men are placed in a great measure give a cast to the human character. Those in middling circumstances, have less temptation—they are
inclined by habit and the company with whom they associate, to set
bounds to their passions and appetites—if this is not sufficient, the want
of means to gratify them will be a restraint—they are obliged to employ
their time in their respective callings—hence the substantial yeomanry of
the country are more temperate, of better morals, and less ambition than
the great.[20] The latter do not feel for the poor and middling class; the reasons are obvious—they are not obliged to use the pains and labor to procure property as the other.—They feel not the inconveniences arising
from the payment of small sums. The great consider themselves above the
common people—entitled to more respect—do not associate with
them—they fancy themselves to have a right of preeminence in everything. In short, they possess the same feelings, and are under the influence of the same motives, as a hereditary nobility. I know the idea that
such a distinction exists in this country is ridiculed by some—But I am
not the less apprehensive of danger from their influence on this
account—Such distinctions exist all the world over—have been taken
notice of by all writers on free government—and are founded in the
nature of things. It has been the principal care of free governments to
guard against the encroachments of the great. Common observation and
experience prove the existence of such distinctions. Will anyone say, that
there does not exist in this country the pride of family, of wealth, of talents; and that they do not command influence and respect among the
common people? Congress, in their address to the inhabitants of the
province of Quebec, in 1775, state this distinction in the following forcible
words quoted from the Marquis Beccaria. "In every human society, there
is an essay continually tending to confer on one part the height of power
and happiness, and to reduce the other to the extreme of weakness and
misery. The intent of good laws is to oppose this effort, and to diffuse

---

20. [Hamilton replied saying, "It is a harsh doctrine that men grow wicked in
proportion as they improve and enlighten their minds. Experience has by no
means justified us in the supposition that there is more virtue in one class of men
than in another. Look through the rich and the poor of the community, the
learned and the ignorant, where does virtue predominate? The difference indeed
consists, not in the quantity, but kind, of vices which are incident to various
classes; and here the advantage of character belongs to the wealthy. Their vices are
probably more favorable to the prosperity of the state than those of the indigent,
and partake less of moral depravity."]

their influence universally and equally."[21] We ought to guard against the government being placed in hands of this class—They cannot have that sympathy with their constituents which is necessary to connect them closely to their interest: Being in the habit of profuse living, they will be profuse in the public expenses. They find no difficulty in paying their taxes, and therefore do not feel the public burdens: Besides if they govern, they will enjoy the emoluments of the government. The middling class, from their frugal habits, and feeling themselves the public burdens, will be careful how they increase them.

But I may be asked, would you exclude the first class in the community, from any share in legislation? I answer by no means—they would be more dangerous out of power than in it—they would be factious—discontented and constantly disturbing the government—it would also be unjust—they have their liberties to protect as well as others—and the largest share of property. But my idea is, that the Constitution should be so framed as to admit this class, together with a sufficient number of the middling class to control them. You will then combine the abilities and honesty of the community—a proper degree of information, and a disposition to pursue the public good. A representative body, composed principally of respectable yeomanry is the best possible security to liberty.—When therefore this class in society pursue their own interest, they promote that of the public, for it is involved in it.

In so small a number of representatives, there is great danger from corruption and combination. A great politician has said that every man has his price.[22] I hope this is not true in all its extent—But I ask the gentlemen to inform, what government there is, in which it has not been practiced. Notwithstanding all that has been said of the defects in the Constitution of the ancient Confederacies of the Grecian Republics, their destruction is to be imputed more to this cause than to any imperfection in their forms of government. This was the deadly poison that effected their dissolution. This is an extensive country, increasing in population and growing in consequence. Very many lucrative offices will be in the grant of the government, which will be the object of avarice and ambition. How easy will it be to gain over a sufficient number, in the bestowment of these offices, to promote the views and purposes of those who grant them!

---

21. [From the introduction to Beccaria's *Essay on Crimes and Punishments* (first published in Italian in 1764). Beccaria stood for radical egalitarianism in the debates during the Revolution and Ratification. Paine, in *Common Sense,* quotes Beccaria's disciple Dragonetti.]

22. [Probably Sir Robert Walpole, who had perfected the art of using pensions and places to secure government majorities.]

Foreign corruption is also to be guarded against. A system of corruption is known to be the system of government in Europe. It is practiced without blushing. And we may lay it to our account it will be attempted among us. The most effectual as well as natural security against this, is a strong democratic branch in the legislature frequently chosen, including in it a number of the substantial, sensible yeomanry of the country. Does the house of representatives answer this description? I confess, to me they hardly wear the complexion of a democratic branch—they appear the mere shadow of representation. The whole number in both houses amounts to ninety-one—Of these forty-six make a quorum; and twenty-four of those being secured, may carry any point. Can the liberties of three million people be securely trusted in the hands of twenty-four men? Is it prudent to commit to so small a number the decision of the great questions which come before them? Reason revolts at the idea.

The honorable gentleman from New York has said that sixty-five members in the house of representatives are sufficient for the present situation of the country, and taking it for granted that they will increase as one for thirty thousand, in twenty-five years they will amount to two hundred. It is admitted by this observation that the number fixed in the Constitution, is not sufficient without it is augmented. It is not declared that an increase shall be made, but is left at the discretion of the legislature, by the gentleman's own concession; therefore the Constitution is imperfect. We certainly ought to fix in the Constitution those things which are essential to liberty. If anything falls under this description, it is the number of the legislature. To say, as this gentleman does, that our security is to depend upon the spirit of the people, who will be watchful of their liberties, and not suffer them to be infringed, is absurd. It would equally prove that we might adopt any form of government. I believe were we to create a despot, he would not immediately dare to act the tyrant; but it would not be long before he would destroy the spirit of the people, or the people would destroy him. If our people have a high sense of liberty, the government should be congenial to this spirit—calculated to cherish the love of liberty, while yet it had sufficient force to restrain licentiousness. Government operates upon the spirit of the people, as well as the spirit of the people operates upon it—and if they are not conformable to each other, the one or the other will prevail. In a less time than twenty-five years, the government will receive its tone. What the spirit of the country may be at the end of that period, it is impossible to foretell: Our duty is to frame a government friendly to liberty and the rights of mankind, which will tend to cherish and cultivate a love of liberty among our citizens. If this government becomes oppressive it will be by degrees: It will aim at its end by disseminating sentiments of government opposite to republicanism; and proceed from step to step in depriving the people of a share in the government. A recollection of the change that has taken place in the minds of many in this country in the course of a few years, ought to put us upon our guard. Many who are ardent advocates for the new system, reprobate republican principles as chimerical and such as ought to be expelled from society. Who would have thought ten years ago, that the very men who risked their lives and fortunes in support of republican principles, would now treat them as the fictions of fancy?—A few years ago we fought for liberty—We framed a general government on free principles—We placed the state legislatures, in whom the people have a full and fair representation, between Congress and the people. We were then, it is true, too cautious; and too much restricted the powers of the general government. But now it is proposed to go into the contrary, and a more dangerous extreme; to remove all barriers; to give the New Government free access to our pockets, and ample command of our persons; and that without providing for a genuine and fair representation of the people. No one can say what the progress of the change of sentiment may be in twenty-five years. The same men who now cry up the necessity of an energetic government, to induce a compliance with this system, may in much less time reprobate this in as severe terms as they now do the confederation, and may as strongly urge the necessity of going as far beyond this, as this is beyond the Confederation.—Men of this class are increasing—they have influence, talents, and industry—It is time to form a barrier against them. And while we are willing to establish a government adequate to the purposes of the union, let us be careful to establish it on the broad basis of equal liberty.

June 23, 1788

Honorable Mr. *Smith.* I did not intend to make any more observations on this article. Indeed, I have heard nothing today, which has not been suggested before, except the polite reprimand I have received for my declamation. I should not have risen again, but to examine who has proved himself the greatest declaimer. The gentleman wishes me to describe what I meant, by representing the feelings of the people.[23] If I recollect right, I said the

---

23. [Livingston had said: "As to the idea of representing the feelings of the people, I do not entirely understand it, unless by their feelings are meant their interests. They appear to me to be the same thing. But if they have feelings which do not rise out of their interests, I think they ought not to be represented. What! shall the unjust, the selfish, the unsocial feelings, be represented? Government, sir, would be a monster . . . the feelings of the people are so variable and inconstant,

representative ought to understand, and govern his conduct by the true interest of the people.—I believe I stated this idea precisely. When he attempts to explain my ideas, he explains them away to nothing; and instead of answering, he distorts, and then sports with them. But he may rest assured, that in the present spirit of the Convention, to irritate is not the way to conciliate. The gentleman, by the false gloss he has given to my argument, makes me an enemy to the rich: This is not true. All I said, was, that mankind were influenced, in a great degree, by interests and prejudices:—That men, in different ranks of life, were exposed to different temptations—and that ambition was more peculiarly the passion of the rich and great. The gentleman supposes the poor have less sympathy with the sufferings of their fellow creatures; for that those who feel most distress themselves, have the least regard to the misfortunes of others:—Whether this be reasoning or declamation, let all who hear us determine. I observed that the rich were more exposed to those temptations, which rank and power hold out to view; that they were more luxurious and intemperate, because they had more fully the means of enjoyment; that they were more ambitious, because more in the hope of success. The gentleman says my principle is not true; for that a poor man will be as ambitious to be a constable, as a rich man to be a governor:—But he will not injure his country so much by the party he creates to support his ambition.

The next object of the gentleman's ridicule is my idea of an aristocracy; and he indeed has done me the honor, to rank me in the order.[24] If then I am an aristocrat, and yet publicly caution my countrymen against the encroachments of the aristocrats, they will surely consider me as one of their most disinterested friends. My idea of aristocracy is not new:—It is embraced by many writers on government:—I would refer the gentleman

---

that our rulers should be chosen every day: people have one sort of feeling today, another tomorrow, and the voice of the representative must be incessantly changing in correspondence with these feelings. This would be making him a political weathercock."]

24. [Livingston: "We are told that, in every country, there is a natural aristocracy, and that this aristocracy consists of the rich and the great: nay, the gentleman goes further, and ranks in this class of men the wise, the learned, and those eminent for their talents or great virtues. Does a man possess the confidence of his fellow citizens for having done them important services? He is an *aristocrat*. Has he great integrity? Such a man will be greatly trusted: he is an aristocrat. Indeed, to determine that one is an aristocrat, we need only be assured that he is a man of merit. But I hope we have many such. I hope, sir, we are all aristocrats. So sensible am I of that gentleman's talents, integrity, and virtue, that we might at once hail him the first of the nobles, the very prince of the Senate."]

for a definition of it to the honorable *John Adams*, one of our natural aristocrats.[25] This writer will give him a description the most ample and satisfactory. But I by no means intended to carry my idea of it to such a ridiculous length as the gentleman would have me; nor will any of my expressions warrant the construction he imposes on them. My argument was, that in order to have a true and genuine representation, you must receive the middling class of people into your government—such as compose the body of this assembly. I observed, that a representation from the United States could not be so constituted, as to represent completely the feelings and interests of the people; but that we ought to come as near this object as possible. The gentlemen say, that the exactly proper number of representatives is so indeterminate and vague, that it is impossible for them to ascertain it with any precision. But surely, they are able to see the distinction between twenty and thirty. I acknowledged that a complete representation would make the legislature too numerous; and therefore, it is our duty to limit the powers, and form checks on the government, in proportion to the smallness of the number.

The honorable gentleman next animadverts on my apprehensions of corruption, and instances the present Congress, to prove an absurdity in my argument. But is this fair reasoning? There are many material checks to the operations of that body, which the future Congress will not have. In the first place, they are chosen annually:—What more powerful check! They are subject to recall: Nine states must agree to any important resolution, which will not be carried into execution, until it meets the approbation of the people in the state legislatures. Admitting what he says, that they have pledged their faith to support the acts of Congress; yet, if these be contrary to the essential interests of the people, they ought not to be acceded to; for they are not bound to obey any law, which tends to destroy them.

It appears to me, that had economy been a motive for making the representation small; it might have operated more properly in leaving out some of the offices which this constitution requires. I am sensible that a great many of the common people, who do not reflect, imagine that a numerous representation involves a great expense:—But they are not aware of the real security it gives to an economical management in all the departments of government.

The gentleman further declared, that as far his acquaintance extended, the people thought sixty-five a number fully large enough for our State

25. [John Adams, *Defense of the Constitutions of the United States*, volume 1, letter 25.]

Assembly; and hence inferred, that sixty-five is to two hundred and forty thousand, as sixty-five is to three million.—This is curious reasoning.

I feel that I have troubled the committee too long. I should not indeed have risen again upon this subject, had not my ideas been grossly misrepresented.

LETTERS OF CATO (4 AND 5)

No. 4   [November 8, 1787]

Admitting, however, that the vast extent of America, together with the various other reasons which I offered you in my last number, against the practicability of the just exercise of the new government are insufficient to convince you; still it is an undeniable truth, that its several parts are either possessed of principles, which you have heretofore considered as ruinous, and that others are omitted which you have established as fundamental to your political security, and must in their operation, I will venture to assert—fetter your tongues and minds, enchain your bodies, and ultimately extinguish all that is great and noble in man.

In pursuance of my plan, I shall begin with observations on the executive branch of this new system; and though it is not the first in order, as arranged therein, yet being the *chief* is perhaps entitled by the rules of rank to the first consideration. The executive power as described in the second article, consists of a president and vice president, who are to hold their offices *during* the term of four years; the same article has marked the manner and time of their election, and established the qualifications of the president; it also provides against the removal, death, or inability of the president and vice president—regulates the salary of the president, delineates his duties and powers; and lastly, declares the causes for which the president and vice president shall be removed from office.

Notwithstanding the great learning and abilities of the gentlemen who composed the convention, it may be here remarked with deference, that the construction of the first paragraph of the first section of the second article, is vague and inexplicit, and leaves the mind in doubt, as to the election of a president and vice president, after the expiration of the election for the first term of four years—in every other case, the election of these great officers is expressly provided for; but there is no explicit provision for their election in case of the expiration of their offices, subsequent to the election which is to set this political machine in motion—no certain and express terms as in your state constitution, that *statedly* once in every four years, and as often as these offices shall become vacant, by expiration or otherwise, as is therein expressed, an election shall be held as follows, etc.—this inexplicitness perhaps may lead to an establishment for life.

It is remarked by Montesquieu, in treating of republics, that *in all magistracies, the greatness of the power must be compensated by the brevity of the duration; and that a longer time than a year, would be dangerous.* It is therefore obvious to the least intelligent mind, to account why, great power in the hands of a magistrate, and that power connected, with a considerable duration, may be dangerous to the liberties of a republic—the deposit of vast trusts in the hands of a single magistrate, enables him in their exercise, to create a numerous train of dependents—this tempts his *ambition,* which in a republican magistrate is also remarked, *to be pernicious* and the duration of his office for any considerable time favors his views, gives him the means and time to perfect and execute his designs—*he therefore fancies that he may be great and glorious by oppressing his fellow citizens, and raising himself to permanent grandeur on the ruins of his country.*—And here it may be necessary to compare the vast and important powers of the president, together with his continuance in office with the foregoing doctrine—his eminent magisterial situation will attach many adherents to him, and he will be surrounded by expectants and courtiers—his power of nomination and influence on all appointments—the strong posts in each state comprised within his superintendence, and garrisoned by troops under his direction—his control over the army, militia, and navy—the unrestrained power of granting pardons for treason, which may be used to screen from punishment, those whom he had secretly instigated to commit the crime, and thereby prevent a discovery of his own guilt—his duration in office for four years: these, and various other principles evidently prove the truth of the position—that if the president is possessed of ambition, he has power and time sufficient to ruin his country.

Though the president, during the sitting of the legislature, is assisted by the senate, yet he is without a constitutional council in their recess—he will therefore be unsupported by proper information and advice, and will generally be directed by minions and favorites, or a council of state will grow out of the principal officers of the great departments, the most dangerous council in a free country.

The ten miles square, which is to become the seat of government, will of course be the place of residence for the president and the great officers of state—the same observations of a great man will apply to the court of a president possessing the powers of a monarch, that is observed of that of a monarch—*ambition with idleness—baseness with pride—the thirst of riches without labor—aversion to truth—flattery—treason—perfidy—violation of engagements—contempt of civil duties—hope from the magistrates' weakness;*

but above all, the perpetual ridicule of virtue—these, he remarks, are the characteristics by which the courts in all ages have been distinguished.

The language and the manners of this court will be what distinguishes them from the rest of the community, not what assimilates them to it, and in being remarked for a behavior that shows they are not *meanly born*, and in adulation to people of fortune and power.

The establishment of a vice president is as unnecessary as it is dangerous. This officer, for want of other employment, is made president of the senate, thereby blending the executive and legislative powers, besides always giving to some one state, from which he is to come, an unjust pre-eminence.

It is a maxim in republics, that the representative of the people should be of their immediate choice; but by the manner in which the president is chosen he arrives to this office at the fourth or fifth hand, nor does the highest votes, in the way he is elected, determine the choice—for it is only necessary that he should be taken from the highest of five, who may have a plurality of votes.

Compare your past opinions and sentiments with the present proposed establishment, and you will find, that if you adopt it, that it will lead you into a system which you heretofore reprobated as odious. Every American Whig, not long since, bore his emphatic testimony against a monarchical government, though limited, because of the dangerous inequality that it created among citizens as relative to their rights and property; and wherein does this president, invested with his powers and prerogatives, essentially differ from the king of Great Britain (save as to name, the creation of nobility, and some immaterial incidents, the offspring of absurdity and locality) the direct prerogatives of the president, as springing from his political character, are among the following:—It is necessary, in order to distinguish him from the rest of the community, and enable him to keep, and maintain his court, that the compensation for his services; or in other words, his revenue should be such as to enable him to appear with the splendor of a prince; he has the power of receiving ambassadors from, and a great influence on their appointments to foreign courts; as also to make treaties, leagues, and alliances with foreign states, assisted by the senate, which when made, become the supreme law of the land: he is a constituent part of the legislative power; for every bill which shall pass the house of representatives and senate, is to be presented to him for approbation; if he approves of it, he is to sign it, if he disapproves, he is to return it with objections, which in many cases will amount to a complete negative; and in this view he will have a great share in the power of making peace, coining money, etc. and all the various objects of legislation, expressed or implied in this Constitution: for though it may be asserted that the king of Great Britain has the express power of making peace or war, yet he never thinks it prudent so to do without the advice of his parliament from whom he is to derive his support, and therefore these powers, in both president and king, are substantially the same: he is the generalissimo of the nation, and of course, has the command and control of the army, navy, and militia; he is the general conservator of the peace of the union—he may pardon all offenses, except in cases of impeachment, and the principal fountain of all offices and employments. Will not the exercise of these powers therefore tend either to the establishment of a vile and arbitrary aristocracy, or monarchy? The safety of the people in a republic depends on the share or proportion they have in the government; but experience ought to teach you, that when a man is at the head of an elective government invested with great powers, and interested in his reelection, in what circle appointments will be made; by which means *an imperfect aristocracy* bordering on monarchy may be established.

You must, however, my countrymen, beware, that the advocates of this new system do not deceive you, by a fallacious resemblance between it and your own state government, which you so much prize; and if you examine, you will perceive that the chief magistrate of this state, is your immediate choice, controlled and checked by a just and full representation of the people, divested of the prerogative of influencing war and peace, making treaties, receiving and sending embassies, and commanding standing armies and navies, which belong to the power of the confederation, and will be convinced that this government is no more like a true picture of your own, than an Angel of darkness resembles an Angel of light.

No. 5   [November 22, 1787]

In my last number I endeavored to prove that the language of the article relative to the establishment of the executive of this new government was vague and inexplicit, that the great powers of the President, connected with his duration in office would lead to oppression and ruin. That he would be governed by favorites and flatterers, or that a dangerous council would be collected from the great officers of state;—that the ten miles square, if the remarks of one of the wisest men, drawn from the experience of mankind, may be credited, would be the asylum of the base, idle, avaricious, and ambitious, and that the court would possess a language and manners different from yours; that a vice president is as unnecessary, as he is dangerous in his influence—that the president cannot represent you, because he is not of your own immediate choice, that if you adopt this government, you will incline to an arbitrary and odious aristocracy or monarchy—that the president possessed of the power, given him by this frame of government differs but very immaterially from the establishment of monarchy in Great Britain, and I warned you to beware of the fallacious resemblance that is held out to you by the advocates of this new system between it and your own state governments. And here I cannot help remarking, that inexplicitness seems to pervade this whole political fabric: certainty in political compacts, which Mr. Coke[26] calls *the mother and nurse of repose and quietness*, the want of which induced men to engage in political society, has ever been held by a wise and free people as essential to their security; as on the one hand it fixes barriers which the ambitious and tyrannically disposed magistrate dare not overleap, and on the other, becomes a wall of safety to the community—otherwise stipulations between the governors and governed are nugatory; and you might as well deposit the important powers of legislation and execution in one or a few and permit them to govern according to their disposition and will; but the world is too full of examples, which prove that *to live by one man's will became the cause of all men's misery.* Before the existence of express political compacts it was reasonably implied that the magistrate should govern with wisdom and justice, but mere implication was too feeble to restrain the unbridled ambition of a bad man, or afford security against negligence, cruelty, or any other defect of mind. It is alleged that the opinions and manners of the people of America, are capable to resist and prevent an extension of prerogative or oppression; but you must recollect that opinion and manners are mutable, and may not always be a permanent obstruction against the encroachments of government; that the progress of a commercial society begets luxury, the parent of inequality, the foe to virtue, and the enemy to restraint; and that ambition and voluptuousness aided by flattery, will teach magistrates, where limits are not explicitly fixed, to have separate and distinct interests from the people, besides it will not be denied that government assimilates the manners and opinions of the community to it. Therefore, a general presumption that rulers will govern well is not a sufficient security.—You are then under a sacred obligation to provide for the safety of your posterity, and would you now basely desert their interests, when by a small share of prudence you may transmit to them a beautiful political patrimony, which will prevent the necessity of their traveling through seas of blood to obtain that, which your wisdom might have secured:—It is a duty you owe likewise to your own reputation, for you have a great name to lose; you are characterized as cautious, prudent, and jealous in politics; whence is it therefore, that you are about to precipitate yourselves into a sea of uncertainty, and adopt a

---

26. [Coke was a famous common lawyer under James I.]

system so vague, and which has discarded so many of your valuable rights:—Is it because you do not believe that an American can be a tyrant? If this be the case you rest on a weak basis, Americans are like other men in similar situations, when the manners and opinions of the community are changed by the causes I mentioned before, and your political compact inexplicit, your posterity will find that great power connected with ambition, luxury, and flattery, will as readily produce a Caesar, Caligula, Nero, and Domitian[27] in America, as the same causes did in the Roman empire.

But the next thing to be considered in conformity to my plan, is the first article of this new government, which comprises the erection of the house of representatives and senate, and prescribes their various powers and objects of legislation. The most general objections to the first article, are that biennial elections for representatives are a departure from the safe democratical principles of annual ones—that the number of representatives are too few; that the apportionment and principles of increase are unjust; that no attention has been paid to either the numbers or property in each state in forming the senate; that the mode in which they are appointed and their duration, will lead to the establishment of an aristocracy; that the senate and president are improperly connected, both as to appointments, and the making of treaties, which are to become the supreme law of the land; that the judicial in some measure, to wit, as to the trial of impeachments is placed in the senate a branch of the legislative, and sometimes a branch of the executive: that Congress have the improper power of making or altering the regulations prescribed by the different legislatures, respecting the time, place, and manner of holding elections for representatives; and the time and manner of choosing senators; that standing armies may be established, and appropriation of money made for their support, for two years; that the militia of the most remote state may be marched into those states situated at the opposite extreme of this continent; that the slave trade, is to all intents and purposes permanently established; and a slavish capitation, or poll tax,[28] may at any time be levied—these are some of the many evils that will attend the adoption of this government.

But with respect to the first objection, it may be remarked that a well-digested democracy has this advantage over all others, to wit; that it affords to many the opportunity to be advanced to the supreme command, and the honors they thereby enjoy fills them with a desire of rendering

---

27. [Caesar destroyed the republic of Rome, and Caligula, Nero, and Domitian were emperors notorious for their cruelty.]

28. [I.e., a tax paid by every adult. Poll taxes, since the amount paid by the poor is the same as the amount paid by the rich, are regressive.]

themselves worthy of them; hence this desire becomes part of their education, is matured in manhood, and produces an ardent affection for their country, and it is the opinion of the great Sidney,[29] and Montesquieu that this is in a great measure produced by annual election of magistrates.

If annual elections were to exist in this government, and learning and information to become more prevalent, you never will want men to execute whatever you could design—Sidney observes *that a well-governed state it as fruitful to all good purposes as the seven-headed serpent is said to have been in evil; when one head is cut off, many rise up in the place of it.* He remarks further, that *it was also thought, that free cities by frequent elections of magistrates became nurseries of great and able men, every man endeavoring to excel others, that he might be advanced to the honor he had no other title to, than what might arise from his merit, or reputation,* but the framers of this *perfect government,* as it is called, have departed from this democratical principle, and established biennial elections; for the house of representatives, who are to be chosen by the people, and sextennial for the senate, who are to be chosen by the legislatures of the different states, and have given to the executive the unprecedented power of making temporary senators, in case of vacancies, by resignation or otherwise, and so far forth establishing a precedent for virtual representation (though in fact, their original appointment is virtual) thereby influencing the choice of the legislatures, or if they should not be so complaisant as to conform to his appointment—offense will be given to the executive and the temporary members, will appear ridiculous by rejection; this temporary member, during his time of appointment, will of course act by a power derived from the executive, and for, and under his immediate influence.

It is a very important objection to this government, that the representation consists of so few; too few to resist the influence of corruption, and the temptation to treachery, against which all governments ought to take precautions—how guarded you have been on this head, in your own state constitution, and yet the number of senators and representatives proposed for this vast continent, does not equal those of your own state; how great the disparity, if you compare them with the aggregate numbers in the United States. The history of representation in England, from which we have taken our model of legislation, is briefly this, before the institution of legislating by deputies, the whole free part of the community usually met for that purpose; when this became impossible, by the increase of numbers the community was divided into districts, from each of which

---

29. [Algernon Sidney, who had opposed the accession of James II, and was executed in 1683. His posthumous *Discourses of Government* was widely read in America.]

was sent such a number of deputies as was a complete representation of the various numbers and orders of citizens within them; but can it be asserted with truth, that six men can be a complete and full representation of the numbers and various orders of the people in this state? Another thing may be suggested against the small number of representatives is, that but few of you will have the chance of sharing even in this branch of the legislature; and that the choice will be confined to a very few; the more complete it is, the better will your interests be preserved, and the greater the opportunity you will have to participate in government, one of the principal securities of a free people; but this subject has been so ably and fully treated by a writer under the signature of Brutus, that I shall content myself with referring you to him thereon, reserving further observations on the other objections I have mentioned, for my future numbers.

LETTERS OF CENTINEL (1)

No. 1   [October 5, 1787]

Friends, Countrymen, and *Fellow Citizens,*

Permit one of yourselves to put you in mind of certain *liberties* and *privileges* secured to you by the constitution of this commonwealth, and to beg your serious attention to his uninterested[30] opinion upon the plan of federal government submitted to your consideration, before you surrender these great and valuable privileges up forever. Your present frame of government, secures to you a right to hold yourselves, houses, papers, and possessions free from search and seizure, and therefore warrants granted without oaths or affirmations first made, affording sufficient foundation for them, whereby any officer or messenger may be commanded or required to search your houses or seize your persons or property, not particularly described in such warrant, shall not be granted. Your constitution further provides "that in controversies respecting property, and in suits between man and man, the parties have a right *to trial by jury, which ought to be held sacred.*" It also provides and declares, *"that the people have a right* of FREEDOM OF SPEECH, and of WRITING and PUBLISHING *their sentiments, therefore* THE FREEDOM OF THE PRESS OUGHT NOT TO BE RESTRAINED." The constitution of Pennsylvania is *yet* in existence, *as yet* you have the right to *freedom of speech,* and of *publishing your sentiments.*

---

30. [I.e., disinterested.]

How long those rights will appertain to you, you yourselves are called upon to say, whether your *houses* shall continue to be your *castles;* whether your *papers*, your *persons*, and your *property*, are to be held sacred and free from *general warrants*, you are now to determine. Whether the *trial by jury* is to continue as your birthright, the freemen of Pennsylvania, nay, of all America, are now called upon to declare.

Without presuming upon my own judgment, I cannot think it an unwarrantable presumption to offer my private opinion, and call upon others for theirs; and if I use my pen with the boldness of a freeman, it is because I know that *the liberty of the press yet remains unviolated*, and *juries yet are judges.*

The late Convention have submitted to your consideration on a plan of a new, federal government—The subject is highly interesting to your future welfare—Whether it be calculated to promote the great ends of civil society, *viz.* the happiness and prosperity of the community; it behooves you well to consider, uninfluenced by the authority of names. Instead of that frenzy of enthusiasm, that has actuated the citizens of Philadelphia, in their approbation of the proposed plan, before it was possible that it could be the result of a rational investigation into its principles; it ought to be dispassionately and deliberately examined, and its own intrinsic merit the only criterion of your patronage. If ever free and unbiased discussion was proper or necessary, it is on such an occasion.—All the blessings of liberty and the dearest privileges of freemen, are now at stake and dependent on your present conduct. Those who are competent to the task of developing the principles of government, ought to be encouraged to come forward, and thereby the better enable the people to make a proper judgment; for the science of government is so abstruse, that few are able to judge for themselves; without such assistance the people are too apt to yield an implicit assent to the opinions of those characters, whose abilities are held in the highest esteem, and to those in whose integrity and patriotism they can confide; not considering that the love of domination is generally in proportion to talents, abilities, and superior acquirements; and that the men of the greatest purity of intention may be made instruments of despotism in the hands of the *artful and designing.* If it were not for the stability and attachment which time and habit gives to forms of government, it would be in the power of the enlightened and aspiring few, if they should combine, at any time to destroy the best establishments, and even make the people the instruments of their own subjugation.

The late revolution having effaced in a great measure all former habits, and the present institutions are so recent, that there exists not that great reluctance to innovation, so remarkable in old communities, and which accords with reason, for the most comprehensive mind cannot foresee the full operation of material changes on civil polity; it is the genius of the common law to resist innovation.

The wealthy and ambitious, who in every community think they have a right to lord it over their fellow creatures, have availed themselves, very successfully, of this favorable disposition; for the people thus unsettled in their sentiments, have been prepared to accede to any extreme of government; all the distresses and difficulties they experience, proceeding from various causes, have been ascribed to the impotency of the present confederation, and thence they have been led to expect full relief from the adoption of the proposed system of government; and in the other event, immediately ruin and annihilation as a nation. These characters flatter themselves that they have lulled all distrust and jealousy of their new plan, by gaining the concurrence of the two men in whom America has the highest confidence,[31] and now triumphantly exult in the completion of their long meditated schemes of power and aggrandizement. I would be very far from insinuating that the two illustrious personages alluded to, have not the welfare of their country at heart; but that the unsuspecting goodness and zeal of the one, has been imposed on, in a subject of which he must be necessarily inexperienced, from his other arduous engagements; and that the weakness and indecision attendant on old age, has been practiced on in the other.

I am fearful that the principles of government inculcated in Mr. Adams' treatise,[32] and enforced in the numerous essays and paragraphs in the newspapers, have misled some well-designing members of the late Convention.—But it will appear in the sequel, that the construction of the proposed plan of government is infinitely more extravagant.

I have been anxiously expecting that some enlightened patriot would, ere this, have taken up the pen to expose the futility, and counteract the baneful tendency of such principles. Mr. Adams' *sine qua non* of a good government is three balancing powers, whose repelling qualities are to produce an equilibrium of interests, and thereby promote the happiness of the whole community. He asserts that the administrators of every government, will ever be actuated by views of private interest and ambition, to the prejudice of the public good; that therefore the only effectual method to secure the rights of the people and promote their welfare, is to create an opposition of interests between the members of two distinct bodies, in the exercise of the powers of government, and balanced by those of a third. This hypothesis supposes human wisdom competent to

31. [I.e., Washington and Franklin.]

32. [I.e., John Adams, *Defense of the Constitutions of the United States of America* (1787–8).]

the task of instituting three coequal orders in government, and a corresponding weight in the community to enable them respectively to exercise their several parts, and whose views and interests should be so distinct as to prevent a coalition of any two of them for the destruction of the third. Mr. Adams, although he has traced the constitution of every form of government that ever existed, as far as history affords materials, has not been able to adduce a single instance of such a government; he indeed says that the British constitution is such in theory, but this is rather a confirmation that his principles are chimerical and not to be reduced to practice. If such an organization of power were practicable, how long would it continue? not a day—for there is so great a disparity in the talents, wisdom, and industry of mankind, that the scale would presently preponderate to one or the other body, and with every accession of power the means of further increase would be greatly extended. The state of society in England is much more favorable to such a scheme of government than that of America. There they have a powerful hereditary nobility, and real distinctions of rank and interests; but even there, for want of that perfect equality of power and distinction of interests, in the three orders of government, they exist but in name; the only operative and efficient check, upon the conduct of administration, is the sense of the people at large.

Suppose a government could be formed and supported on such principles, would it answer the great purposes of civil society? If the administrators of every government are actuated by views of private interest and ambition, how is the welfare and happiness of the community to be the result of such jarring adverse interests?

Therefore, as different orders in government will not produce the good of the whole, we must recur to other principles. I believe it will be found that the form of government, which holds those entrusted with power, in the greatest responsibility to their constituents, [is] the best calculated for freemen. A republican, or free government, can only exist where the body of the people are virtuous, and where property is pretty equally divided, in such a government the people are the sovereign and their sense or opinion is the criterion of every public measure; for when this ceases to be the case, the nature of the government is changed, and an aristocracy, monarchy, or despotism will rise on its ruin. The highest responsibility is to be attained, in a simple construction of government, for the great body of the people never steadily attend to the operations of government, and for want of due information are liable to be imposed on.—If you complicate the plan by various orders, the people will be perplexed and divided in their sentiments about the source of abuses or misconduct, some will impute it to the senate, others to the house of representatives, and so on, that the interposition of the people may be rendered imperfect or perhaps wholly abortive. But if, imitating the constitution of Pennsylvania, you vest all the legislative power in one body of men (separating the executive and judicial) elected for a short period, and necessarily excluded by rotation from permanency, and guarded from precipitancy and surprise by delays imposed on its proceedings, you will create the most perfect responsibility, for then, whenever the people feel a grievance they cannot mistake the authors, and will apply the remedy with certainty and effect, discarding them at the next election. This tie of responsibility will obviate all the dangers apprehended from a single legislature, and will the best secure the rights of the people.

Having promised thus much, I shall now proceed to the examination of the proposed plan of government, and I trust, shall make it appear to the meanest capacity, that it has none of the essential requisites of a free government, that it is neither founded on those balancing restraining powers, recommended by Mr. Adams and attempted in the British constitution, or possessed of that responsibility to its constituents, which, in my opinion, is the only effectual security for the liberties and happiness of the people; but on the contrary, that it is a most daring attempt to establish a despotic aristocracy among freemen, that the world has ever witnessed.

I shall previously[33] consider the extent of the powers intended to be vested in Congress, before I examine the construction of the general government.

It will not be controverted that the legislative is the highest delegated power in government, and that all others are subordinate to it. The celebrated *Montesquieu* establishes it as a maxim, that legislation necessarily follows the power of taxation. By section 8, of the first article of the proposed plan of government, "the Congress are to have power to lay and collect taxes, duties, imposts and excises, to pay the debts and provide for the common defense and *general welfare* of the United States; but all duties, imposts and excises, shall be uniform throughout the United States." Now what can be more comprehensive than these words; not content by other sections of this plan, to grant all the great executive powers of a confederation, and, a STANDING ARMY IN TIME OF PEACE, that grand engine of oppression, and moreover the absolute control over the commerce of the United States and all external objects of revenue, such as unlimited imposts upon imports, etc.—they are to be vested with every species of *internal* taxation;—whatever taxes, duties, and excises that they may deem requisite for the *general welfare*, may be imposed on the citizens of these states, levied by the officers of Congress, distributed through every district in America; and the collection would be enforced

---

33. [I.e., first.]

by the standing army, however grievous or improper they may be. The Congress may construe every purpose for which the state legislatures now lay taxes, to be for the *general welfare*, and thereby seize upon every object of revenue.

The judicial power by first[34] section of article 3 ["]shall extend to all cases, in law and equity, arising under this constitution, the laws of the United States, and treaties made or which shall be made under their authority; to all cases affecting ambassadors, other public ministers and consuls; to all cases of admiralty and maritime jurisdiction, to controversies to which the United States shall be a party, to controversies between two or more states, between a state and citizens of another state, between citizens of different states, between citizens of the same state claiming lands under grants of different states, and between a state, or the citizens thereof, and foreign states, citizens, or subjects."

The judicial power to be vested in one Supreme Court, and in such Inferior Courts as the Congress may from time to time ordain and establish.

The objects of jurisdiction recited above, are so numerous, and the shades of distinction between civil causes[35] are oftentimes so slight, that it is more than probable that the state judicatories would be wholly superseded, for in contests about jurisdiction, the federal court, as the most powerful, would ever prevail. Every person acquainted with the history of the courts in England, knows by what ingenious sophisms they have, at different periods, extended the sphere of their jurisdiction over objects out of the line of their institution, and contrary to their very nature; courts of a criminal jurisdiction obtaining cognizance in civil causes.

To put the omnipotency of Congress over the state government and judicatories out of all doubt, the sixth article ordains that "this constitution and the laws of the United States which shall be made in pursuance thereof, and all treaties made, or which shall be made under the authority of the United States, shall be the *Supreme law of the land,* and the judges in every state shall be bound thereby, anything in the constitution or laws of any state to the contrary notwithstanding."

By these sections the all-prevailing power of taxation, and such extensive legislative and judicial powers are vested in the general government, as must in their operation, necessarily absorb the state legislatures and judicatories; and that such was in the contemplation of the framers of it, will appear from the provision made for such event, in another part of it;

---

34. [Read "second."]
35. [I.e., cases.]

(but that, fearful of alarming the people by so great an innovation, they have suffered the forms of the separate governments to remain, as a blind). By section four of the first article, "the times, places, and manner of holding elections for senators and representatives, shall be prescribed in each state by the legislature thereof; *but the Congress may at any time, by law, make or alter such regulations, except as to the place of choosing senators.*" The plain construction of which is, that when the state legislatures drop out of sight, from the necessary operation of this government, then Congress are to provide for the election and appointment of representatives and senators.

If the foregoing be a just comment—if the United States are to be melted down into one empire, it becomes you to consider, whether such a government, however constructed, would be eligible[36] in so extended a territory; and whether it would be practicable, consistent with freedom? It is the opinion of the greatest writers, that a very extensive country cannot be governed on democratical principles, on any other plan, than a confederation of a number of small republics, possessing all the powers of internal government, but united in the management of their foreign and general concerns.

It would not be difficult to prove, that anything short of despotism, could not bind so great a country under one government; and that whatever plan you might, at the first setting out, establish, it would issue in a despotism.

If one general government could be instituted and maintained on principles of freedom, it would not be so competent to attend to the various local concerns and wants, of every particular district; as well as the peculiar governments, who are nearer the scene, and possessed of superior means of information, besides, if the business of the *whole* union is to be managed by one government, there would not be time. Do we not already see, that the inhabitants in a number of larger states, who are remote from the seat of government, are loudly complaining of the inconveniences and disadvantages they are subjected to on this account, and that, to enjoy the comforts of local government, they are separating into smaller divisions.

Having taken a review of the powers, I shall now examine the construction of the proposed general government.

Article 1 section 1. "All legislative powers herein granted shall be vested in a Congress of the United States, which shall consist of a senate and house of representatives." By another section, the president (the principal executive officer) has a conditional control over their proceedings.

---

36. [I.e., would be one that one would choose.]

Section 2. "The house of representatives shall be composed of members chosen every second year, by the people of the several states. The number of representatives shall not exceed one for every thirty thousand inhabitants."

The senate, the other constituent branch of the legislature, is formed by the legislature of each state appointing two senators, for the term of six years.

The executive power by Article 2, Section 1. is to be vested in a president of the United States of America, elected for four years: Section 2. gives him power, by and with the consent of the senate to make treaties, provided two-thirds of the senators present concur; and he shall nominate, and by and with the advice and consent of the senate, shall appoint ambassadors, other public ministers and consuls, judges of the Supreme Court, and all other officers of the United States, whose appointments are not herein otherwise provided for, and which shall be established by law, etc. And by another section he has the absolute power of granting reprieves and pardons for treason and all other high crimes and misdemeanors, except in case of impeachment.

The foregoing are the outlines of the plan.

Thus we see, the house of representatives, are on the part of the people to balance the senate, who I suppose will be composed of the *better sort*, the *wellborn*, etc. The number of the representatives (being only one for every thirty-thousand inhabitants) appears to be too few, either to communicate the requisite information, of the wants, local circumstances, and sentiments of so extensive an empire, or to prevent corruption and undue influence, in the exercise of such great powers; the term for which they are to be chosen, too long to preserve a due dependence and accountability to their constituents; and the mode and places of their election not sufficiently ascertained, for as Congress have the control over both, they may govern the choice, by ordering the *representatives* of a *whole* state, to be *elected* in *one* place, and that too may be the most *inconvenient*.

The senate, the great efficient body in this plan of government, is constituted on the most unequal principles. The smallest state in the union has equal weight with the great States of Virginia, Massachusetts, or Pennsylvania.—The Senate, besides its legislative functions, has a very considerable share in the Executive; none of the principal appointments to office can be made without its advice and consent. The term and mode of its appointment, will lead to permanency; the members are chosen for six years, the mode is under the control of Congress, and as there is no exclusion by rotation, they may be continued for life, which, from their extensive means of influence, would follow of course. The President, who

would be a mere pageant of state,[37] unless he coincides with the views of
the Senate, would either become the head of the aristocratic junto[38] in
that body, or its minion;[39] besides, their influence[,] being the most predominant, could the best secure his reelection to office. And from his
power of granting pardons, he might screen from punishment the most
[t]reasonable attempts on the liberties of the people, when instigated by
the Senate.

From this investigation into the organization of this government, it
appears that it is devoid of all responsibility or accountability to the great
body of the people, and that so far from being a regular balanced government, it would be in practice a *permanent* ARISTOCRACY.

The framers of it; actuated by the true spirit of such a government,
which ever abominates and suppresses all free inquiry and discussion,
have made no provision for the *liberty of the press*, that grand *palladium of
freedom, and scourge of tyrants;* but observed a total silence on that head. It
is the opinion of some great writers, that if the liberty of the press, by an
institution of religion, or otherwise, could be rendered *sacred*, even in
Turkey, that despotism would fly before it. And it is worthy of remark,
that there is no declaration of personal rights, premised in most free constitutions; and that trial by *jury* in *civil* cases is taken away; for what other
construction can be put on the following, viz. Article III Section 2nd. "In
all cases affecting ambassadors, other public ministers and consuls, and
those in which a State shall be party, the Supreme Court shall have *original* jurisdiction. In all the other cases above mentioned, the Supreme
Court shall have *appellate* jurisdiction, both as to *law and fact*"? It would
be a novelty in jurisprudence, as well as evidently improper to allow an
appeal from the verdict of a jury, on the matter of fact; therefore, it
implies and allows of a dismission of the jury in civil cases, and especially
when it is considered, that jury trial in criminal cases is expressly stipu-
lated for, but not in civil cases.

But our situation is represented to be so *critically* dreadful, that,
however reprehensible and exceptionable the proposed plan of government may be, there is no alternative, between the adoption of it and
absolute ruin.—My fellow citizens, things are not at that crisis, it is the
argument of tyrants; the present distracted state of Europe secures us
from injury on that quarter, and as to domestic dissensions, we have
not so much to fear from them, as to precipitate us into this form of

37. [I.e., a mere figurehead.]
38. [A clique or cabal.]
39. [Its creature or dependent.]

_mment, without[40] it is a safe and a proper one. For remember, of all _possible_ evils, that of _despotism_ is the _worst_ and the most to be _dreaded._

Besides, it cannot be supposed, that the first essay on so difficult a subject, is so well digested, as it ought to be;—if the proposed plan, after a mature deliberation, should meet the approbation of the respective States, the matter will end; but if it should be found to be fraught with dangers and inconveniences, a future general Convention being in possession of the objections, will be the better enabled to plan a suitable government.

"WHO'S HERE SO BASE, THAT WOULD A BOND MAN BE?
IF ANY, SPEAK, FOR HIM HAVE I OFFENDED.
WHO'S HERE SO VILE THAT WILL NOT LOVE HIS COUNTRY?
IF ANY SPEAK; FOR HIM HAVE I OFFENDED."

CENTINEL

ESSAYS OF BRUTUS (6, 11, 12, 15)

No. 6   [December 27, 1787]

It is an important question, whether the general government of the United States should be so framed, as to absorb and swallow up the state governments? or whether, on the contrary, the former ought not to be confined to certain defined national objects, while the latter should retain all the powers which concern the internal police of the states?

I have, in my former papers, offered a variety of arguments to prove, that a simple free government could not be exercised over this whole continent and that therefore we must either give up our liberties and submit to an arbitrary one, or frame a constitution on the plan of confederation. Further reasons might be urged to prove this point—but it seems unnecessary, because the principal advocates of the new constitution admit of the position. The question therefore between us, this being admitted, is, whether or not this system is so formed as either directly to annihilate the state governments, or that in its operation it will certainly effect it. If this is answered in the affirmative, then the system ought not to be adopted, without such amendments as will avoid this consequence. If on the contrary it can be shown, that the state governments are secured in their rights to manage the internal police of the respective states, we must confine ourselves in our inquiries to the organization of the government and

---

40. [I.e., unless.]

the guards and provisions it contains to prevent a misuse or abuse of power. To determine this question, it is requisite, that we fully investigate the nature, and the extent of the powers intended to be granted by this constitution to the rulers.

In my last number I called your attention to this subject, and proved, as I think, uncontrovertibly, that the powers given the legislature under the eighth section of the first article, had no other limitation than the discretion of the Congress. It was shown, that even if the most favorable construction was given to this paragraph, that the advocates for the new constitution could wish, it will convey a power to lay and collect taxes, imposts, duties, and excises, according to the discretion of the legislature, and to make all laws which they shall judge proper and necessary to carry this power into execution. This I showed would totally destroy all the power of the state governments. To confirm this, it is worthwhile to trace the operation of the government in some particular instances.

The general government is to be vested with authority to levy and collect taxes, duties, and excises; the separate states have also power to impose taxes, duties, and excises, except that they cannot lay duties on exports and imports without the consent of Congress. Here then the two governments have concurrent jurisdiction; both may lay impositions of this kind. But then the general government have superadded to this power, authority to make all laws which shall be necessary and proper for carrying the foregoing power into execution. Suppose then that both governments should lay taxes, duties, and excises, and it should fall so heavy on the people that they would be unable, or be so burdensome that they would refuse to pay them both—would it not be necessary that the general legislature should suspend the collection of the state tax? It certainly would. For, if the people could not, or would not pay both, they must be discharged from the tax to the state, or the tax to the general government could not be collected.—The conclusion therefore is inevitable, that the respective state governments will not have the power to raise one shilling in any way, but by the permission of the Congress. I presume no one will pretend, that the states can exercise legislative authority, or administer justice among their citizens for any length of time, without being able to raise a sufficiency to pay those who administer their governments.

If this be true, and if the states can raise money only by permission of the general government, it follows that the state governments will be dependent on the will of the general government for their existence.

What will render this power in Congress effectual and sure in its operation is, that the government will have complete judicial and executive authority to carry all their laws into effect, which will be paramount to the judicial and executive authority of the individual states: in vain therefore will be all interference of the legislatures, courts, or magistrates of any of the states on the subject; for they will be subordinate to the general government, and engaged by oath to support it, and will be constitutionally bound to submit to their decisions.

The general legislature will be empowered to lay any tax they choose, to annex any penalties they please to the breach of their revenue laws; and to appoint as many officers as they may think proper to collect the taxes. They will have authority to farm the revenues and to vest the farmer general, with his subalterns, with plenary powers to collect them, in any way which to them may appear eligible. And the courts of law, which they will be authorized to institute, will have cognizance of every case arising under the revenue laws, the conduct of all the officers employed in collecting them; and the officers of these courts will execute their judgments. There is no way, therefore, of avoiding the destruction of the state governments, whenever the Congress please to do it, unless the people rise up, and, with a strong hand, resist and prevent the execution of constitutional laws. The fear of this, will, it is presumed, restrain the general government, for some time, within proper bounds; but it will not be many years before they will have a revenue, and force, at their command, which will place them above any apprehensions on that score.

How far the power to lay and collect duties and excises, may operate to dissolve the state governments, and oppress the people, it is impossible to say. It would assist us much in forming a just opinion on this head, to consider the various objects to which this kind of taxes extend, in European nations, and the infinity of laws they have passed respecting them. Perhaps, if leisure will permit, this may be essayed in some future paper.

It was observed in my last number, that the power to lay and collect duties and excises, would invest the Congress with authority to impose a duty and excise on every necessary and convenience of life. As the principal object of the government, in laying a duty or excise, will be, to raise money, it is obvious, that they will fix on such articles as are of the most general use and consumption; because, unless great quantities of the article, on which the duty is laid, is used, the revenue cannot be considerable. We may therefore presume, that the articles which will be the object of this species of taxes will be either the real necessaries of life; or if not these, such as from custom and habit are esteemed so. I will single out a few of the productions of our own country, which may, and probably will, be of the number.

Cider is an article that most probably will be one of those on which an excise will be laid, because it is one, which this country produces in great abundance, which is in very general use, is consumed in great quantities, and which may be said too not to be a real necessary of life. An excise on this would raise a large sum of money in the United States. How would the power, to lay and collect an excise on cider, and to pass all laws proper and necessary to carry it into execution, operate in its exercise? It might be necessary, in order to collect the excise on cider, to grant to one man, in each county, an exclusive right of building and keeping cider mills, and oblige him to give bonds and security for payment of the excise; or, if this was not done, it might be necessary to license the mills, which are to make this liquor, and to take from them security, to account for the excise; or, if otherwise, a great number of officers must be employed, to take account of the cider made, and to collect the duties on it.

Porter, ale, and all kinds of malt liquors, are articles that would probably be subject also to an excise. It would be necessary, in order to collect such an excise, to regulate the manufactory of these, that the quantity made might be ascertained, or otherwise security could not be had for the payment of the excise. Every brewery must then be licensed, and officers appointed, to take account of its product, and to secure the payment of the duty, or excise, before it is sold. Many other articles might be named, which would be objects of this species of taxation, but I refrain from enumerating them. It will probably be said, by those who advocate this system, that the observations already made on this head, are calculated only to inflame the minds of the people, with the apprehension of dangers merely imaginary. That there is not the least reason to apprehend, the general legislature will exercise their power in this manner. To this I would only say, that these kinds of taxes exist in Great Britain, and are severely felt. The excise on cider and perry, was imposed in that nation a few years ago, and it is in the memory of everyone, who read the history of the transaction, what great tumults it occasioned.

This power, exercised without limitation, will introduce itself into every corner of the city, and country—It will wait upon the ladies at their toilette, and will not leave them in any of their domestic concerns; it will accompany them to the ball, the play, and the assembly; it will go with them when they visit, and will, on all occasions, sit beside them in their carriages, nor will it defect[41] them even at church; it will enter the house of every gentleman, watch over his cellar, wait upon his cook in the kitchen, follow the servants into the parlor, preside over the table, and note down all he eats or drinks; it will attend him to his bedchamber, and watch him while he sleeps; it will take cognizance of the professional mail in his office, or his study; it will watch the merchant in the counting house, or in his store; it will follow the mechanic to his shop, and in his work, and will haunt him in his family, and in his bed; it will be a constant

---

41. [I.e., leave.]

companion of the industrious farmer in all his labor, it will be with him
in the house, and in the field, observe the toil of his hands, and the sweat
of his brow; it will penetrate into the most obscure cottage; and finally, it
will light upon the head of every person in the United States. To all
these different classes of people, and in all these circumstances, in which
it will attend them, the language in which it will address them, will be
GIVE! GIVE!

A power that has such latitude, which reaches every person in the
community to every conceivable circumstance, and lays hold of every species of property they possess and which has no bounds set to it but the
discretion of those who exercise it. I say, such a power must necessarily,
from its very nature, swallow up all the power of the state governments.

I shall add but one other observation on this head, which is this—It
appears to me a solecism, for two men, or bodies of men, to have unlimited power respecting the same object. It contradicts the scripture maxim,
which saith, "no man can serve two masters," the one power or the other
must prevail, or else they will destroy each other, and neither of them
effect their purpose. It may be compared to two mechanic powers, acting
upon the same body in opposite directions, the consequence would be, if
the powers were equal, the body would remain in a state of rest, or if the
force of the one was superior to that of the other, the stronger would prevail, and overcome the resistance of the weaker.

But it is said, by some of the advocates of this system, "That the idea
that Congress can levy taxes at pleasure, is false, and the suggestion
wholly unsupported: that the preamble to the constitution is declaratory
of the purposes of the union, and the assumption of any power not necessary to establish justice, etc. to provide for the common defense, etc. will
be unconstitutional. Besides, in the very clause which gives the power of
levying duties and taxes, the purposes to which the money shall be appropriated, are specified, viz. to pay the debts, and provide for the common
defense and general welfare."[42] I would ask those, who reason thus, to
define what ideas are included under the terms, to provide for the common defense and general welfare? Are these terms definite, and will they
be understood in the same manner, and to apply to the same cases by
everyone? No one will pretend they will. It will then be matter of opinion,
what tends to the general welfare; and the Congress will be the only
judges in the matter. To provide for the general welfare, is an abstract
proposition, which mankind differ in the explanation of, as much as they
do on any political or moral proposition that can be proposed; the most

---

42. Vide an examination into the leading principles of the federal constitution,
printed in Philadelphia, Page 34. (Brutus)

opposite measures may be pursued by different parties, and both may profess, that they have in view the general welfare; and both sides may be honest in their professions, or both may have sinister views. Those who advocate this new constitution declare, they are influenced by a regard to the general welfare; those who oppose it, declare they are moved by the same principle; and I have no doubt but a number on both sides are honest in their professions; and yet nothing is more certain than this, that to adopt this constitution, and not to adopt it, cannot both of them be promotive of the general welfare.

It is as absurd to say, that the power of Congress is limited by these general expressions, "to provide for the common safety, and general welfare," as it would be to say, that it would be limited, had the constitution said they should have power to lay taxes, etc. at will and pleasure. Were this authority given, it might be said, that under it the legislature could not do injustice, or pursue any measures, but such as were calculated to promote the public good, and happiness. For every man, rulers as well as others, are bound by the immutable laws of God and reason, always to will what is right. It is certainly right and fit, that the governors of every people should provide for the common defense and general welfare; every government, therefore, in the world, even the greatest despot, is limited in the exercise of his power. But however just this reasoning may be, it would be found, in practice, a most pitiful restriction. The government would always say, their measures were designed and calculated to promote the public good; and there being no judge between them and the people, the rulers themselves must, and would always, judge for themselves.

There are others of the favorers of this system, who admit, that the power of the Congress under it, with respect to revenue, will exist without limitation, and contend, that so is ought to be.

It is said, "The power to raise armies, to build and equip fleets, and to provide for their support ought to exist without limitation, because it is impossible to foresee, or to define, the extent and variety of national exigencies, or the correspondent extent and variety of the means which may be necessary to satisfy them."

This, it is said, "is one of those truths which, to correct and unprejudiced minds, carries its own evidence along with it. It rests upon axioms as simple as they are universal: the means ought to be proportioned to the end; the person, from whose agency the attainment of any end is expected, ought to possess the means by which it is to be attained."[43]

This same writer insinuates, that the opponents to the plan promulgated by the convention, manifest a want of candor, in objecting to the

---

43. Vide the Federalist, No. 23. (Brutus) [See below, p. 195.]

extent of the powers proposed to be vested in this government; because
he asserts, with an air of confidence, that the powers ought to be unlimited as to the object to which they extend; and that this position, if not
self-evident, is at least clearly demonstrated by the foregoing mode of
reasoning. But with submission to this author's better judgment, I hum-
bly conceive his reasoning will appear, upon examination, more specious
than solid. The means, says the gentleman, ought to be proportioned to
the end; admit the proposition to be true it is then necessary to inquire,
what is the end of the government of the United States, in order to draw
any just conclusions from it. Is this end simply to preserve the general
government, and to provide for the common defense and general welfare
of the union only? certainly not[;] for beside this, the state governments
are to be supported, and provision made for the managing such of their
internal concerns as are allotted to them. It is admitted, "that the circumstances of our country are such, as to demand a compound, instead of a
simple, a confederate, instead of a sole government," that the objects of
each ought to be pointed out, and that each ought to possess ample
authority to execute the powers committed to them. The government
then, being complex in its nature, the end it has in view is so also; and it is
as necessary, that the state governments should possess the means to
attain the ends expected from them, as for the general government. Neither the general government, nor the state governments, ought to be
vested with all the powers proper to be exercised for promoting the ends
of government. The powers are divided between them—certain ends are
to be attained by the one, and other certain ends by the other; and these,
taken together, include all the ends of good government. This being the
case, the conclusion follows, that each should be furnished with the
means, to attain the ends, to which they are designed.

To apply this reasoning to the case of revenue; the general government
is charged with the case of providing for the payment of the debts of the
United States; supporting the general government, and providing for the
defense of the union. To obtain these ends, they should be furnished with
means. But does it hence follow, that they should command all the revenues of the United States! Most certainly it does not. For if so, it will follow, that no means will be left to attain other ends, as necessary to the
happiness of the country, as those committed to their care. The individual
states have debts to discharge; their legislatures and executives are to be
supported, and provision is to be made for the administration of justice in
the respective states. For those objects the general government has no
authority to provide; nor is it proper it should. It is clear then, that the
states should have the command of such revenues, as to answer the ends
they have to obtain. To say, "that the circumstances that endanger the

safety of nations are infinite," and from hence to infer, that all the sources of revenue in the states should be yielded to the general government, is not conclusive reasoning: for the Congress are authorized only to control in general concerns, and not regulate local and internal ones; and these are as essentially requisite to be provided for as those. The peace and happiness of a community is as intimately connected with the prudent direction of their domestic affairs, and the due administration of justice among themselves, as with a competent provision for their defense against foreign invaders, and indeed more so.

Upon the whole, I conceive, that there cannot be a clearer position than this, that the state governments ought to have an uncontrollable power to raise a revenue, adequate to the exigencies of their governments; and, I presume, no such power is left them by this constitution.

No. 11   [January 31, 1788]

The nature and extent of the judicial power of the United States, proposed to be granted by this constitution, claims our particular attention.

Much has been said and written upon the subject of this new system on both sides, but I have not met with any writer, who has discussed the judicial powers with any degree of accuracy. And yet it is obvious, that we can form but very imperfect ideas of the manner in which this government will work, or the effect it will have in changing the internal police and mode of distributing justice at present subsisting in the respective states, without a thorough investigation of the powers of the judiciary and of the manner in which they will operate. This government is a complete system, not only for making, but for executing laws. And the courts of law, which will be constituted by it, are not only to decide upon the constitution and the laws made in pursuance of it, but by officers subordinate to them to execute all their decisions. The real effect of this system of government, will therefore be brought home to the feelings of the people, through the medium of the judicial power. It is, moreover, of great importance, to examine with care the nature and extent of the judicial power; because those who are to be vested with it, are to be placed in a situation altogether unprecedented in a free country. They are to be rendered totally independent, both of the people and the legislature, both with respect to their offices and salaries. No errors they may commit can be corrected by any power above them, if any such power there be, nor can they be removed from office for making ever so many erroneous adjudications.

The only cause for which they can be displaced, is conviction of treason, bribery, and high crimes and misdemeanors.

This part of the plan is so modeled, as to authorize the courts, not only to carry into execution the powers expressly given, but where these are wanting or ambiguously expressed, to supply what is wanting by their own decisions.

That we may be enabled to form a just opinion on this subject, I shall, in considering it,

First. Examine the nature and extent of the judicial powers—and

Second. Inquire, whether the courts who are to exercise them, are so constituted as to afford reasonable ground of confidence, that they will exercise them for the general good.

With a regard to the nature and extent of the judicial powers, I have to regret my want of capacity to give that full and minute explanation of them that the subject merits. To be able to do this, a man should be possessed of a degree of law knowledge far beyond what I pretend to. A number of hard words and technical phrases are used in this part of the system, about the meaning of which gentlemen learned in the law differ.

Its advocates know how to avail themselves of these phrases. In a number of instances, where objections are made to the powers given to the judicial,[44] they give such an explanation to the technical terms as to avoid them.

Though I am not competent to give a perfect explanation of the powers granted to this department of the government, I shall yet attempt to trace some of the leading features of it, from which I presume it will appear, that they will operate to a total subversion of the state judiciaries, if not, to the legislative authority of the states.

In article third, section 2nd, it is said, "The judicial power shall extend to all cases in law and equity arising under this constitution, the laws of the United States, and treaties made, or which shall be made, under their authority, etc."

The first article to which this power extends, is, all cases in law and equity arising under this constitution.

What latitude of construction this clause should receive, it is not easy to say. At first view, one would suppose, that it meant no more than this, that the courts under the general government should exercise, not only the powers of courts of law, but also that of courts of equity, in the manner in which those powers are usually exercised in the different states. But this cannot be the meaning, because the next clause authorizes the courts to take cognizance of all cases in law and equity arising under the laws of the United States; this last article, I conceive, conveys as much power to the general judicial as any of the state courts possess.

---

44. [Here and on several subsequent occasions Brutus uses "judicial" in a sense not recognized by the *Oxford English Dictionary*, to mean "judiciary."]

The cases arising under the constitution must be different from those arising under the laws, or else the two clauses mean exactly the same thing.

The cases arising under the constitution must include such, as bring into question its meaning, and will require an explanation of the nature and extent of the powers of the different departments under it.

This article, therefore, vests the judicial with a power to resolve all questions that may arise on any case on the construction of the constitution, either in law or in equity.

First. They are authorized to determine all questions that may arise upon the meaning of the constitution in law. This article vests the courts with authority to give the constitution a legal construction, or to explain it according to the rules laid down for construing a law.—These rules give a certain degree of latitude of explanation. According to this mode of construction, the courts are to give such meaning to the constitution as comports best with the common, and generally received acceptation of the words in which it is expressed, regarding their ordinary and popular use, rather than their grammatical propriety. Where words are dubious, they will be explained by the context. The end of the clause will be attended to, and the words will be understood, as having a view to it; and the words will not be so understood as to bear no meaning or a very absurd one.

Second. The judicial are not only to decide questions arising upon the meaning of the constitution in law, but also in equity.

By this they are empowered, to explain the constitution according to the reasoning spirit of it, without being confined to the words or letter.

"From this method of interpreting laws (says Blackstone) by the reason of them, arises what we call equity"; which is thus defined by Grotius, "the correction of that, wherein the law, by reason of its universality, is deficient; for since in laws all cases cannot be foreseen, or expressed, it is necessary, that when the decrees of the law cannot be applied to particular cases, there should somewhere be a power vested of [adapting the law to] those circumstances, which had they been foreseen the legislator would have expressed; and these are the cases, which according to Grotius, lex non exacte definit, sed arbitrio boni viri permittet."[45]

The same learned author observes, "That equity, thus depending essentially upon each individual case, there can be no established rules and fixed principles of equity laid down, without destroying its very essence, and reducing it to a positive law."

---

45. [Which the law does not adequately define, but which in the opinion of a good man are to be permitted.]

From these remarks, the authority and business of the courts of law, under this clause, may be understood.

They will give the sense of every article of the constitution, that may from time to time come before them. And in their decisions they will not confine themselves to any fixed or established rules, but will determine, according to what appears to them, the reason and spirit of the constitution. The opinions of the supreme court, whatever they may be, will have the force of law; because there is no power provided in the constitution, that can correct their errors, or control their adjudications. From this court there is no appeal. And I conceive the legislature themselves, cannot set aside a judgment of this court, because they are authorized by the constitution to decide in the last resort. The legislature must be controlled by the constitution, and not the constitution by them. They have therefore no more right to set aside any judgment pronounced upon the construction of the constitution, than they have to take from the president, the chief command of the army and navy, and commit it to some other person. The reason is plain; the judicial and executive derive their authority from the same source, that the legislature do theirs; and therefore in all cases, where the constitution does not make the one responsible to, or controllable by the other, they are altogether independent of each other.

The judicial power will operate to effect, in the most certain, but yet silent and imperceptible manner, what is evidently the tendency of the constitution:—I mean, an entire subversion of the legislative, executive, and judicial powers of the individual states. Every adjudication of the supreme court, on any question that may arise upon the nature and extent of the general government, will affect the limits of the state jurisdiction. In proportion as the former enlarge the exercise of their powers, will that of the latter be restricted.

That the judicial power of the United States, will lean strongly in favor of the general government, and will give such an explanation to the constitution, as will favor an extension of its jurisdiction, is very evident from a variety of considerations.

First. The constitution itself strongly countenances such a mode of construction. Most of the articles in this system, which convey powers of any considerable importance, are conceived in general and indefinite terms, which are either equivocal, ambiguous, or which require long definitions to unfold the extent of their meaning. The two most important powers committed to any government, those of raising money, and of raising and keeping up troops, have already been considered, and shown to be [unlimited] by anything but the discretion of the legislature. The clause which vests the power to pass all laws which are proper and necessary, to carry the powers given into execution, it has been shown, leaves the legislature at liberty, to do everything, which in their judgment is best. It is said, I know, that this clause confers no power on the legislature, which they would not have had without it—though I believe this is not the fact, yet, admitting it to be, it implies that the constitution is not to receive an explanation strictly, according to its letter; but more power is implied than is expressed. And this clause, if it is to be considered, as explanatory of the extent of the powers given, rather than giving a new power, is to be understood as declaring, that in construing any of the articles conveying power, the spirit, intent, and design of the clause, should be attended to, as well as the words in their common acceptation.

This constitution gives sufficient color for adopting an equitable construction, if we consider the great end and design it professedly has in view—these appear from its preamble to be, "to form a more perfect union, establish justice, insure domestic tranquillity, provide for the common defense, promote the general welfare, and secure the blessings of liberty to ourselves and posterity." The design of this system is here expressed, and it is proper to give such a meaning to the various parts, as will best promote the accomplishment of the end; this idea suggests itself naturally upon reading the preamble, and will countenance the court in giving the several articles such a sense, as will the most effectually promote the ends the constitution had in view—how this manner of explaining the constitution will operate in practice, shall be the subject of future inquiry.

Second. Not only will the constitution justify the courts in inclining to this mode of explaining it, but they will be interested in using this latitude of interpretation. Every body of men invested with office are tenacious of power; they feel interested, and hence it has become a kind of maxim, to hand down their offices, with all its rights and privileges, unimpaired to their successors; the same principle will influence them to extend their power, and increase their rights; this of itself will operate strongly upon the courts to give such a meaning to the constitution in all cases where it can possibly be done, as will enlarge the sphere of their own authority. Every extension of the power of the general legislature, as well as of the judicial powers, will increase the powers of the courts; and the dignity and importance of the judges, will be in proportion to the extent and magnitude of the powers they exercise. I add, it is highly probable the emolument of the judges will be increased, with the increase of the business they will have to transact and its importance. From these considerations the judges will be interested to extend the powers of the courts, and to construe the constitution as much as possible, in such a way as to favor it; and that they will do it, appears probable.

Third. Because they will have precedent to plead, to justify them in it. It is well-known, that the courts in England, have by their own authority, extended their jurisdiction far beyond the limits set them in their original institution, and by the laws of the land.

The court of exchequer is a remarkable instance of this. It was originally intended principally to recover the king's debts, and to order the revenues of the crown. It had a common law jurisdiction, which was established merely for the benefit of the king's accountants. We learn from Blackstone, that the proceedings in this court are grounded on a writ called quo minus, in which the plaintiff suggests, that he is the king's farmer or debtor, and that the defendant hath done him the damage complained of, by which he is less able to pay the king. These suits, by the statute of Rutland, are expressly directed to be confined to such matters as specially concern the king, or his ministers in the exchequer. And by the articuli super cartas, it is enacted, that no common pleas be thenceforth held in the exchequer contrary to the form of the great charter: but now any person may sue in the exchequer. The surmise of being debtor to the king being matter of form, and mere words of course; and the court is open to all the nation.

When the courts will have a precedent before them of a court which extended its jurisdiction in opposition to an act of the legislature, is it not to be expected that they will extend theirs, especially when there is nothing in the constitution expressly against it? and they are authorized to construe its meaning, and are not under any control?

This power in the judicial, will enable them to mold the government, into almost any shape they please.—The manner in which this may be effected we will hereafter examine.

No. 12   [February 7 and 14, 1788]

In my last, I showed, that the judicial power of the United States under the first clause of the second section of article eight, would be authorized to explain the constitution, not only according to its letter, but according to its spirit and intention; and having this power, they would strongly incline to give it such a construction as to extend the powers of the general government, as much as possible, to the diminution, and finally to the destruction, of that of the respective states.

I shall now proceed to show how this power will operate in its exercise to effect these purposes. In order to perceive the extent of its influence, I shall consider,

First. How it will tend to extend the legislative authority.

Second. In what manner it will increase the jurisdiction of the courts, and

Third. The way in which it will diminish, and destroy, both the legislative and judicial authority of the United States.

First. Let us inquire how the judicial power will effect an extension of the legislative authority.

Perhaps the judicial power will not be able, by direct and positive decrees, ever to direct the legislature, because it is not easy to conceive how a question can be brought before them in a course of legal discussion, in which they can give a decision, declaring, that the legislature have certain powers which they have not exercised, and which, in consequence of the determination of the judges, they will be bound to exercise. But it is easy to see, that in their adjudications they may establish certain principles, which being received by the legislature, will enlarge the sphere of their power beyond all bounds.

It is to be observed, that the supreme court has the power, in the last resort, to determine all questions that may arise in the course of legal discussion, on the meaning and construction of the constitution. This power they will hold under the constitution, and independent of [the] legislature. The latter can no more deprive the former of this right, than either of them, or both of them together, can take from the president, with the advice of the senate, the power of making treaties, or appointing ambassadors.

In determining these questions, the court must and will assume certain principles, from which they will reason, in forming their decisions. These principles, whatever they may be, when they become fixed, by a course of decisions, will be adopted by the legislature, and will be the rule by which they will explain their own powers. This appears evident from this consideration, that if the legislature pass laws, which, in the judgment of the court, they are not authorized to do by the constitution, the court will not take notice of them; for it will not be denied, that the constitution is the highest or supreme law. And the courts are vested with the supreme and uncontrollable power, to determine, in all cases that come before them, what the constitution means; they cannot, therefore, execute a law, which, in their judgment, opposes the constitution, unless we can suppose they can make a superior law give way to an inferior. The legislature, therefore, will not go over the limits by which the courts may adjudge they are confined. And there is little room to doubt but that they will come up to those bounds, as often as occasion and opportunity may offer, and they may judge it proper to do it. For as on the one hand, they will not readily pass laws which they know the courts will not execute, so on the other, we may be sure they will not scruple to pass such as they know they will give effect, as often as they may judge it proper.

From these observations it appears, that the judgment of the judicial, on the constitution, will become the rule to guide the legislature in their construction of their powers.

What the principles are, which the courts will adopt, it is impossible for us to say; but taking up the powers as I have explained them in my last number, which they will possess under this clause, it is not difficult to see, that they may, and probably will, be very liberal ones.

We have seen, that they will be authorized to give the constitution a construction according to its spirit and reason, and not to confine themselves to its letter.

To discover the spirit of the constitution, it is of the first importance to attend to the principal ends and designs it has in view. These are expressed in the preamble, in the following words, viz. "We, the people of the United States, in order to form a more perfect union, establish justice, insure domestic tranquillity, provide for the common defense, promote the general welfare, and secure the blessings of liberty to ourselves and our posterity, do ordain and establish this constitution," etc. If the end of the government is to be learned from these words, which are clearly designed to declare it, it is obvious it has in view every object which is embraced by any government. The preservation of internal peace—the due administration of justice—and to provide for the defense of the community, seems to include all the objects of government; but if they do not, they are certainly comprehended in the words, "to provide for the general welfare." If it be further considered, that this constitution, if it is ratified, will not be a compact entered into by states, in their corporate capacities, but an agreement of the people of the United States, as one great body politic, no doubt can remain, but that the great end of the constitution, if it is to be collected from the preamble, in which its end is declared, is to constitute a government which is to extend to every case for which any government is instituted, whether external or internal. The courts, therefore, will establish this as a principle in expounding the constitution, and will give every part of it such an explanation, as will give latitude to every department under it, to take cognizance of every matter, not only that affects the general and national concerns of the union, but also of such as relate to the administration of private justice, and to regulating the internal and local affairs of the different parts.

Such a rule of exposition is not only consistent with the general spirit of the preamble, but it will stand confirmed by considering more minutely the different clauses of it.

The first object declared to be in view is, "To form a perfect union." It is to be observed, it is not an union of states or bodies corporate; had this been the case the existence of the state governments, might have been secured. But it is a union of the people of the United States considered as one body, who are to ratify this constitution, if it is adopted. Now to make a union of this kind perfect, it is necessary to abolish all inferior governments, and to give the general one complete legislative, executive, and judicial powers to every purpose. The courts therefore will establish it as a rule in explaining the constitution: To give it such a construction as will best tend to perfect the union or take from the state government every power of either making or executing laws. The second object is "to establish justice." This must include not only the idea of instituting the rule of justice, or of making laws which shall be the measure or rule of right, but also of providing for the application of this rule or of administering justice under it. And under this the courts will in their decisions extend the power of the government to all cases they possibly can, or otherwise they will be restricted in doing what appears to be the intent of the constitution they should do, to wit, pass laws and provide for the execution of them, for the general distribution of justice between man and man. Another end declared is "to insure domestic tranquillity." This comprehends a provision against all private breaches of the peace, as well as against all public commotions or general insurrections; and to attain the object of this clause fully, the government must exercise the power of passing laws on these subjects, as well as of appointing magistrates with authority to execute them. And the courts will adopt these ideas in their expositions. I might proceed to the other clauses, in the preamble, and it would appear by a consideration of all of them separately, as it does by taking them together, that if the spirit of this system is to be known from its declared end and design in the preamble, its spirit is to subvert and abolish all the powers of the state government, and to embrace every object to which any government extends.

As it sets out in the preamble with this declared intention, so it proceeds in the different parts with the same idea. Any person, who will peruse the eighth section with attention, in which most of the powers are enumerated, will perceive that they either expressly or by implication extend to almost everything about which any legislative power can be employed. But if this equitable mode of construction is applied to this part of the constitution; nothing can stand before it.

This will certainly give the first clause in that article a construction which I confess I think the most natural and grammatical one, to authorize the Congress to do anything which in their judgment will tend to provide for the general welfare, and this amounts to the same thing as general and unlimited powers of legislation in all cases.

This same manner of explaining the constitution, will fix a meaning, and a very important one too, to the twelfth clause of the same section, which authorizes the Congress to make all laws which shall be proper and necessary for carrying into effect the foregoing powers, etc. A voluminous writer in favor of this system, has taken great pains to convince the public, that this clause means nothing: for that the same powers expressed in this, are implied in other parts of the constitution. Perhaps it is so, but still this will undoubtedly be an excellent auxiliary to assist the courts to discover the spirit and reason of the constitution, and when applied to any and every of the other clauses granting power, will operate powerfully in extracting the spirit from them.

I might instance a number of clauses in the constitution, which, if explained in an *equitable* manner, would extend the powers of the government to every case, and reduce the state legislatures to nothing; but, I should draw out my remarks to an undue length, and I presume enough has been said to show, that the courts have sufficient ground in the exercise of this power, to determine, that the legislature have no bounds set to them by this constitution, by any supposed right the legislatures of the respective states may have, to regulate any of their local concerns.

I proceed, second, To inquire, in what manner this power will increase the jurisdiction of the courts.

I would here observe, that the judicial power extends, expressly, to all civil cases that may arise save such as arise between citizens of the same state, with this exception to those of that description, that the judicial of the United States have cognizance of cases between citizens of the same state, claiming lands under grants of different states. Nothing more, therefore, is necessary to give the courts of law, under this constitution, complete jurisdiction of all civil causes, but to comprehend cases between citizens of the same state not included in the foregoing exception.

I presume there will be no difficulty in accomplishing this. Nothing more is necessary than to set forth, in the process, that the party who brings the suit is a citizen of a different state from the one against whom the suit is brought, and there can be little doubt but that the court will take cognizance of the matter, and if they do, who is to restrain them? Indeed, I will freely confess, that it is my decided opinion, that the courts ought to take cognizance of such causes, under the powers of the constitution. For one of the great ends of the constitution is, "to establish justice." This supposes that this cannot be done under the existing governments of the states; and there is certainly as good reason why individuals, living in the same state, should have justice, as those who live in different states. Moreover, the constitution expressly declares, that "the citizens of each state shall be entitled to all the privileges and immunities of citizens in the several states." It will therefore be no fiction, for a citizen of one state to set forth, in a suit, that he is a citizen of another; for he that is entitled to all the privileges and immunities of a country, is a citizen of that country. And in truth, the citizen of one state will, under this constitution, be a citizen of every state.

But supposing that the party, who alleges that he is a citizen of another state, has recourse to fiction in bringing in his suit; it is well-known, that the courts have high authority to plead, to justify them in suffering actions to be brought before them by such fictions. In my last number I stated, that the court of exchequer tried all causes in virtue of such a fiction. The court of king's bench, in England, extended their jurisdiction in the same way. Originally, this court held pleas, in civil cases, only of trespasses and other injuries alleged to be committed *vi et armis*.[46] They might likewise, says Blackstone, upon the division of the *aula regia*, have originally held pleas of any other civil action whatsoever (except in real actions[47] which are now very seldom in use) provided the defendant was an officer of the court, or in the custody of the marshall or prison keeper of this court, for breach of the peace, etc. In process of time, by a fiction, this court began to hold pleas of any personal action whatsoever; it being surmised, that the defendant has been arrested for a supposed trespass that "he has never committed, and being thus in the custody of the marshall of the court, the plaintiff is at liberty to proceed against him, for any other personal injury: which surmise of being in the marshall's custody, the defendant is not at liberty to dispute." By a much less [elaborate] fiction, may the pleas of the courts of the United States extend to cases between citizens of the same state. I shall add no more on this head, but proceed briefly to remark, in what way this power will diminish, and destroy both the legislative and judicial authority of the states.

It is obvious that these courts will have authority to decide upon the validity of the laws of any of the states, in all cases where they come in question before them. Where the constitution gives the general government exclusive jurisdiction, they will adjudge all laws made by the state, in such cases, *void ab [initio]*.[48] Where the constitution gives them concurrent jurisdiction, the laws of the United States must prevail, because they are the supreme law. In such cases, therefore, the laws of the state legislatures must be repealed, restricted, or so construed, as to give full effect to the laws of the union on the same subject. From these remarks it is easy to see, that in proportion as the general government acquires power and jurisdiction, by the liberal construction which the judges may give the constitution, will those of the states lose their rights, until they become so trifling

---

46. [By force and with weapons.]
47. [Actions related to landed property, rather than persons or movable goods.]
48. [Void from the beginning.]

and unimportant, as not to be worth having. I am much mistaken, if this system will not operate to effect this with as much celerity, as those who have the administration of it will think prudent to suffer it. The remaining objections to the judicial power shall be considered in a future paper.

No. 15   [March 20, 1788]

I said in my last number,[49] that the supreme court under this constitution would be exalted above all other power in the government, and subject to no control. The business of this paper will be to illustrate this, and to show the danger that will result from it. I question whether the world ever saw, in any period of it, a court of justice invested with such immense powers, and yet placed in a situation so little responsible. Certain it is, that in England, and in the several states, where we have been taught to believe, the courts of law are put upon the most prudent establishment, they are on a very different footing.

The judges in England, it is true, hold their offices during their good behavior, but then their determinations are subject to correction by the house of lords; and their power is by no means so extensive as that of the proposed supreme court of the union.—I believe they in no instance assume the authority to set aside an act of parliament under the idea that it is inconsistent with their constitution. They consider themselves bound to decide according to the existing laws of the land, and never undertake to control them by adjudging that they are inconsistent with the constitution—much less are they vested with the power of giving an *equitable* construction to the constitution.

The judges in England are under the control of the legislature, for they are bound to determine according to the laws passed by them. But the judges under this constitution will control the legislature, for the supreme court are authorized in the last resort, to determine what is the extent of the powers of the Congress; they are to give the constitution an explanation, and there is no power above them to set aside their judgment. The framers of this constitution appear to have followed that of the British, in rendering the judges independent, by granting them their offices during good behavior, without following the constitution of England, in instituting a tribunal in which their errors may be corrected; and without adverting to this, that the judicial under this system have a power which is above the legislative, and which indeed transcends any power before given to a judicial by any free government under heaven.

---

49. [Essay 14, not included in this selection.]

I do not object to the judges holding their commissions during good behavior. I suppose it a proper provision provided they were made properly responsible. But I say, this system has followed the English government in this, while it has departed from almost every other principle of their jurisprudence, under the idea, of rendering the judges independent; which, in the British constitution, means no more than that they hold their places during good behavior, and have fixed salaries, they have made the judges *independent*, in the fullest sense of the word. There is no power above them, to control any of their decisions. There is no authority that can remove them, and they cannot be controlled by the laws of the legislature. In short, they are independent of the people, of the legislature, and of every power under heaven. Men placed in this situation will generally soon feel themselves independent of heaven itself. Before I proceed to illustrate the truth of these assertions, I beg liberty to make one remark—Though in my opinion the judges ought to hold their offices during good behavior, yet I think it is clear, that the reasons in favor of this establishment of the judges in England, do by no means apply to this country.

The great reason assigned, why the judges in Britain ought to be commissioned during good behavior, is this, that they may be placed in a situation, not to be influenced by the crown, to give such decisions, as would tend to increase its powers and prerogatives. While the judges held their places at the will and pleasure of the king, on whom they depended not only for their offices, but also for their salaries, they were subject to every undue influence. If the crown wished to carry a favorite point, to accomplish which the aid of the courts of law was necessary, the pleasure of the king would be signified to the judges. And it required the spirit of a martyr, for the judges to determine contrary to the king's will.—They were absolutely dependent upon him both for their offices and livings. The king, holding his office during life, and transmitting it to his posterity as an inheritance, has much stronger inducements to increase the prerogatives of his office than those who hold their offices for stated periods, or even for life. Hence the English nation gained a great point, in favor of liberty. When they obtained the appointment of the judges, during good behavior, they got from the crown a concession, which deprived it of one of the most powerful engines with which it might enlarge the boundaries of the royal prerogative and encroach on the liberties of the people. But these reasons do not apply to this country, we have no hereditary monarch; those who appoint the judges do not hold their offices for life, nor do they descend to their children. The same arguments, therefore, which will conclude in favor of the tenor of the judge's offices for good behavior, lose a considerable part of their weight when applied to the state and condition of America. But much less can it be shown, that the nature of our government requires that the courts should be placed beyond all account more independent, so much so as to be above control.

I have said that the judges under this system will be *independent* in the strict sense of the word: To prove this I will show—That there is no power above them that can control their decisions, or correct their errors. There is no authority that can remove them from office for any errors or want of capacity, or lower their salaries, and in many cases their power is superior to that of the legislature.

First. There is no power above them that can correct their errors or control their decisions—The adjudications of this court are final and irreversible, for there is no court above them to which appeals can lie, either in error or on the merits. In this respect it differs from the courts in England, for there the house of lords is the highest court, to whom appeals, in error, are carried from the highest of the courts of law.—

Second. They cannot be removed from office or suffer a diminution of their salaries, for any error in judgment or want of capacity.

It is expressly declared by the constitution,—"That they shall at stated times receive a compensation for their services which shall not be diminished during their continuance in office."

The only clause in the constitution which provides for the removal of the judges from offices, is that which declares, that "the president, vice president, and all civil officers of the United States, shall be removed from office, on impeachment for, and conviction of treason, bribery, or other high crimes and misdemeanors." By this paragraph, civil officers, in which the judges are included, are removable only for crimes. Treason and bribery are named, and the rest are included under the general terms of high crimes and misdemeanors.—Errors in judgment, or want of capacity to discharge the duties of the office, can never be supposed to be included in these words, *high crimes and misdemeanors.* A man may mistake a case in giving judgment, or manifest that he is incompetent to the discharge of the duties of a judge, and yet give no evidence of corruption or want of [integrity]. To support the charge, it will be necessary to give in evidence some facts that will show, that the judges committed the error from wicked and corrupt motives.

Third. The power of this court is in many cases superior to that of the legislature. I have showed, in a former paper,[50] that this court will be authorized to decide upon the meaning of the constitution, and that, not only according to the natural and obvious meaning of the words, but also according to the spirit and intention of it. In the exercise of this power they will not be subordinate to, but above the legislature. For all the

---

50. [I.e., Essay 11, above.]

departments of this government will receive their powers, so far as they are expressed in the constitution, from the people immediately, who are the source of power. The legislature can only exercise such powers as are given them by the constitution, they cannot assume any of the rights annexed to the judicial, for this plain reason, that the same authority which vested the legislature with their powers, vested the judicial with theirs—both are derived from the same source, both therefore are equally valid, and the judicial hold their powers independently of the legislature, as the legislature do of the judicial—The supreme court then have a right, independent of the legislature, to give a construction to the constitution and every part of it, and there is no power provided in this system to correct their construction or do it away. If, therefore, the legislature pass any laws, inconsistent with the sense the judges put upon the constitution, they will declare it void; and therefore in this respect their power is superior to that of the legislature. In England the judges are not only subject to have their decisions set aside by the house of lords, for error, but in cases where they give an explanation to the laws or constitution of the country, contrary to the sense of the parliament, though the parliament will not set aside the judgment of the court, yet, they have authority, by a new law, to explain a former one, and by this means to prevent a reception of such decisions. But no such power is in the legislature. The judges are supreme—and no law, explanatory of the constitution, will be binding on them.

From the preceding remarks, which have been made on the judicial powers proposed in this system, the policy of it may be fully developed.

I have, in the course of my observations on this constitution, affirmed and endeavored to show, that it was calculated to abolish entirely the state governments, and to melt down the states into one entire government, for every purpose as well internal and local, as external and national. In this opinion the opposers of the system have generally agreed—and this has been uniformly denied by its advocates in public. Some individuals indeed, among them, will confess, that it has this tendency, and scruple not to say, it is what they wish; and I will venture to predict, without the spirit of prophecy, that if it is adopted without amendments, or some such precautions as will ensure amendments immediately after its adoption, that the same gentlemen who have employed their talents and abilities with such success to influence the public mind to adopt this plan, will employ the same to persuade the people, that it will be for their good to abolish the state governments as useless and burdensome.

Perhaps nothing could have been better conceived to facilitate the abolition of the state governments than the constitution of the judicial. They will be able to extend the limits of the general government gradually, and by insensible degrees, and to accommodate themselves to the temper of the people. Their decisions on the meaning of the constitution will commonly take place in cases which arise between individuals, with which the public will not be generally acquainted; one adjudication will form a precedent to the next; and this to a following one. These cases will immediately affect individuals only; so that a series of determinations will probably take place before even the people will be informed of them. In the meantime all the art and address of those who wish for the change will be employed to make converts to their opinion. The people will be told, that their state officers, and state legislatures are a burden and expense without affording any solid advantage, for that all the laws passed by them, might be equally well made by the general legislature. If to those who will be interested in the change, be added, those who will be under their influence, and such who will submit to almost any change of government, which they can be persuaded to believe will ease them of taxes, it is easy to see, the party who will favor the abolition of the state governments would be far from being inconsiderable.—In this situation, the general legislature, might pass one law after another, extending the general and abridging the state jurisdictions, and to sanction their proceedings would have a course of decisions of the judicial to whom the constitution has committed the power of explaining the constitution.—If the states remonstrated, the constitutional mode of deciding upon the validity of the law, is with the supreme court, and neither people, nor state legislatures, nor the general legislature can remove them or reverse their decrees.

Had the construction of the constitution been left with the legislature, they would have explained it at their peril; if they exceed their powers, or sought to find, in the spirit of the constitution, more than was expressed in the letter, the people from whom they derived their power could remove them, and do themselves right; and indeed I can see no other remedy that the people can have against their rulers for encroachments of this nature. A constitution is a compact of a people with their rulers; if the rulers break the compact, the people have a right and ought to remove them and do themselves justice; but in order to enable them to do this with the greater facility, those whom the people choose at stated periods, should have the power in the last resort to determine the sense of the compact; if they determine contrary to the understanding of the people, an appeal will lie to the people at the period when the rulers are to be elected, and they will have it in their power to remedy the evil; but when this power is lodged in the hands of men independent of the people, and of their representatives, and who are not, constitutionally, accountable for their opinions, no way is left to control them but *with a high hand and an outstretched arm.*

The Constitution Defended

SPEECH OF JAMES WILSON BEFORE THE PENNSYLVANIA CONVENTION

November 24, 1787

The system proposed, by the late Convention, for the government of the United States is now before you. Of that Convention I had the honor to be a member. As I am the only member of that body, who has the honor to be also a member of this, it may be expected that I should prepare the way for the deliberations of this assembly by unfolding the difficulties which the late Convention were obliged to encounter, by pointing out the end which they proposed to accomplish, and by tracing the general principles which they have adopted for the accomplishment of that end.

To form a good system of government for a single city or state, however limited as to territory or inconsiderable as to numbers, has been thought to require the strongest efforts of human genius. With what conscious diffidence, then, must the members of the Convention have revolved in their minds the immense undertaking, which was before them. Their views could not be confined to a small or a single community, but were expanded to a great number of states; several of which contain an extent of territory; and resources of population, equal to those of some of the most respectable kingdoms on the other side of the Atlantic. Nor were even these the only objects to be comprehended within their deliberations. Numerous states yet unformed, myriads of the human race, who will inhabit regions hitherto uncultivated, were to be affected by the result of their proceedings. It was necessary; therefore, to form their calculations on a scale commensurate to a large portion of the globe.

For my own part, I have been often lost in astonishment at the vastness of the prospect before us. To open the navigation of a single river was lately thought in Europe, an enterprise adequate to imperial glory. But could the commercial scenes of the Schelde be compared with those, that, under a good government, will be exhibited on the Hudson, the Delaware, the Potomac, and the numerous other rivers, that water and are intended to enrich the dominions of the United States?

The difficulty of the business was equal to its magnitude. No small share of wisdom and address is requisite to combine and reconcile the jarring interests, that prevail, or seem to prevail, in a single community. The United States contain already thirteen governments mutually independent.

Those governments present to the Atlantic a front of fifteen hundred miles in extent. Their soil, their climates, their productions, their dimensions, their numbers are different. In many instances a difference and even an opposition subsists among their interests. And a difference and even an opposition is imagined to subsist in many more. An apparent interest produces the same attachment as a real one; and is often pursued with no less perseverance and vigor. When all these circumstances are seen and attentively considered, will any member of this honorable body be surprised, that such a diversity of things produced a proportioned diversity of sentiment? Will he be surprised that such a diversity of sentiment rendered a spirit of mutual forbearance and conciliation indispensably necessary to the success of the great work, and will he be surprised that mutual concessions and sacrifices were the consequences of mutual forbearance and conciliation? When the springs of opposition were so numerous and strong, and poured forth their waters in courses so varying, need we be surprised that the stream formed by their conjunction was impelled in a direction somewhat different from that, which each of them would have taken separately?

I have reason to think that a difficulty arose in the minds of some members of Convention from another consideration—their ideas of the temper and disposition of the people for whom the Constitution is proposed. The citizens of the United States, however different in some other respects, are well-known to agree in one strongly marked feature of their character—a warm and keen sense of freedom and independence. This sense has been heightened by the glorious result of their late struggle against all the efforts of one of the most powerful nations of Europe. It was apprehended, I believe, by some, that a people so highly spirited, would ill brook the restraints of an efficient government. I confess that this consideration did not influence my conduct. I knew my constituents to be high-spirited, but I knew them also to possess sound sense. I knew that, in the event, they would be best pleased with that system of government, which would best promote their freedom and happiness. I have often revolved this subject in my mind. I have supposed one of my constituents to ask me, why I gave such a vote on a particular question? I have always thought it would be a satisfactory answer to say, "because I judged, upon the best consideration I could give, that such a vote was right." I have thought that it would be but a very poor compliment to my constituents to say—"that, in my opinion, such a vote would have been proper, but that I supposed a contrary one would be more agreeable to those who sent me to the Convention." I could not, even in idea, expose myself to such a retort, as, upon the last answer, might have been justly made to me. "Pray, sir, what reasons have you for supposing that a right vote would displease your constituents? Is this the proper return for the high confidence they have placed in you?" If they have given cause for such a surmise, it was by choosing a representative, who could entertain such an opinion of them. I was under no apprehension that the good people of this state would behold with displeasure the brightness of the rays of delegated power, when it only proved the superior splendor of the luminary, of which those rays were only the reflection.

A very important difficulty arose from comparing the extent of the country to be governed with the kind of government which it would be proper to establish in it. It has been an opinion, countenanced by high authority, "that the natural property of small states is to be governed as a republic; of middling ones, to be subject to a monarch; and of large empires, to be swayed by a despotic prince; and that the consequence is, that, in order to preserve the principles of the established government, the state must be supported in the extent it has acquired; and that the spirit of the state will alter in proportion as it extends or contracts its limits."[1] This opinion seems to be supported, rather than contradicted, by the history of the governments in the Old World. Here then the difficulty appeared in full view. On one hand, the United States contain an immense extent of territory, and, according to the foregoing opinion, a despotic government is best adapted to that extent. On the other hand, it was well-known, that, however the citizens of the United States might, with pleasure, submit to the legitimate restraints of a republican constitution, they would reject, with indignation, the fetters of despotism. What then was to be done? The idea of a confederate republic presented itself. This kind of constitution has been thought to have "all the internal advantages of a republican, together with the external force of a monarchical government."[2] Its description is, "a convention, by which several states agree to become members of a larger one, which they intend to establish. It is a kind of assemblage of societies, that constitute a *new one*, capable of increasing by means of further association."[3] The *expanding* quality of such a government is peculiarly fitted for the United States, the greatest part of whose territory is yet uncultivated.

But while this form of government enabled us to surmount the difficulty last mentioned, it conducted us to another, of which I am now to take notice. It left us almost without precedent or guide; and consequently, without the benefit of that instruction, which, in many cases, may

---

1. Montesquieu, book 8, chapter 20. (Lloyd)

2. Montesquieu, book 9, chapters 1, 2. Paley 199, 202. (Lloyd) [William Paley, *The Principles of Moral and Political Philosophy* (1785).]

3. Montesquieu, book 9, chapter 1. (Lloyd)

be derived from the constitution, and history and experience of other nations. Several associations have frequently been called by the name of confederate states, which have not, in propriety of language, deserved it. The Swiss cantons are connected only by alliances. The United Netherlands are indeed an assemblage of societies; but this assemblage constitutes *no new one;* and, therefore, it does not correspond with the full definition of a confederate republic. The Germanic body is composed of such disproportioned and discordant materials, and its structure is so intricate and complex, that little useful knowledge can be drawn from it. Ancient history discloses, and barely discloses to our view, some confederate republics—the Achaean League, the Lycian Confederacy, and the Amphyctyonic Council. But the facts recorded concerning their constitutions are so few and general, and their histories are so unmarked and defective, that no satisfactory information can be collected from them concerning many particular circumstances, from an accurate discernment and comparison, of which alone legitimate and practical inferences can be made from one constitution to another. Besides, the situation and dimensions of those confederacies, and the state of society, manners, and habits in them, were so different from those of the United States, that the most correct descriptions could have supplied but a very small fund of applicable remarks. Thus, in forming this system, we were deprived of many advantages, which the history and experience of other ages and other countries would, in other cases, have afforded us.

Permit me to add, in this place, that the science even of government itself seems yet to be almost in its state of infancy. Governments, in general, have been the result of force, of fraud, and of accident. After a period of six thousand years has elapsed since the Creation, the United States exhibit to the world, the first instance, as far as we can learn, of a nation, unattacked by external force, unconvulsed by domestic insurrections, assembling voluntarily, deliberating fully, and deciding calmly, concerning that system of government, under which they would wish that they and their posterity should live. The ancients, so enlightened on other subjects, were very uninformed with regard to this. They seem scarcely to have had any idea of any other kinds of governments than the three simple forms designed[4] by the epithets, monarchical, aristocratical, and democratical. I know that much and pleasing ingenuity has been exerted, in modern times, in drawing entertaining parallels between some of the ancient constitutions and some of the mixed governments that have since existed in Europe. But I much suspect that, on strict examination, the instances of resemblance will be found to be few and weak; to be suggested by the

---

4. ["Designed" is used here in the now obsolete sense of "designated."]

improvements, which, in subsequent ages, have been made in government, and not to be drawn immediately from the ancient constitutions themselves, as they were intended and understood by those who framed them. To illustrate this, a similar observation may be made on another subject. Admiring critics have fancied that they have discovered in their favorite, Homer, the seeds of all the improvements in philosophy and in the sciences made since his time. What induces me to be of this opinion is that Tacitus—the profound politician Tacitus—who lived toward the latter end of those ages, which are now denominated ancient, who undoubtedly had studied the constitutions of all the states and kingdoms known before and in his time; and who certainly was qualified in an uncommon degree for understanding the full force and operation of each of them, considers, after all he had known and read, a mixed government, composed of the three simple forms, as a thing rather to be wished than expected. And he thinks, that if such a government could even be instituted, its duration could not be long. One thing is very certain, that the doctrine of representation in government was altogether unknown to the ancients. Now the knowledge and practice of this doctrine is, in my opinion, essential to every system that can possess the qualities of freedom, wisdom, and energy.

It is worthy of remark, and the remark may, perhaps, excite some surprise, that representation of the people is not, even at this day, the sole principle of any government in Europe. Great Britain boasts, and she may well boast, of the improvement she has made in politics by the admission of representation. For the improvement is important as far as it goes, but it by no means goes far enough. Is the executive power of Great Britain founded on representation? This is not pretended. Before the Revolution[5] many of the kings claimed to reign by divine right, and others by hereditary right; and even at the Revolution nothing further was effected or attempted than the recognition of certain parts of an original contract[6] supposed, at some former remote period, to have been made between the king and the people. A contract seems to exclude, rather than to imply, delegated power. The judges of Great Britain are appointed by the Crown. The judicial authority, therefore, does not depend upon representation, even in its most remote degree. Does representation prevail in the legislative department of the British government? Even here it does not predominate; though it may serve as a check. The legislature consists of three branches, the King, the Lords, and the Commons. Of these only the latter are supposed by the constitution to represent the authority of the people.

---

5. [The overthrow of the Catholic James II and his replacement by William and Mary in 1688.]

6. Blackstone, 233. (Lloyd)

This short analysis clearly shows to what a narrow corner of the British constitution the principle of representation is confined. I believe it does not extend further, if so far, in any other government in Europe. For the American states were reserved the glory and the happiness of diffusing this vital principle throughout the constituent parts of government. Representation is the chain of communication between the people and those to whom they have committed the exercise of the powers of government. This chain may consist of one or more links; but in all cases it should be sufficiently strong and discernible.

To be left without guide or precedent was not the only difficulty, in which the Convention were involved, by proposing to their constituents a plan of a confederate republic. They found themselves embarrassed with another of peculiar delicacy and importance; I mean that of drawing a proper line between the national government and the governments of the several states. It was easy to discover a proper and satisfactory principle on the subject. Whatever object of government is confined in its operation and effects within the bounds of a particular state should be considered as belonging to the government of that state; whatever object of government extends in its operation or effects beyond the bounds of a particular state should be considered as belonging to the government of the United States. But though this principle be sound and satisfactory, its application to particular cases would be accompanied with much difficulty; because in its application, room must be allowed for great discretionary latitude of construction of the principle. In order to lessen or remove the difficulty arising from discretionary construction on this subject, an enumeration of particular instances, in which the application of the principle ought to take place, has been attempted with much industry and care. It is only in mathematical science that a line can be described with mathematical precision. But I flatter myself that upon the strictest investigation, the enumeration will be found to be safe and unexceptionable; and accurate too in as great a degree as accuracy can be expected in a subject of this nature. Particulars under this head will be more properly explained, when we descend to the minute view of the enumeration, which is made in the proposed Constitution.

After all, it will be necessary, that, on a subject so peculiarly delicate as this, much prudence, much candor, much moderation, and much liberality should be exercised and displayed both by the federal government and by the governments of the several states. It is to be hoped, that those virtues in government will be exercised and displayed, when we consider, that the powers of the federal government and those of the state governments are drawn from sources equally pure. If a difference can be discovered between them, it is in favor of the federal government, because that government is founded on a representation of the *whole* Union; whereas the government of any particular state is founded only on the representation of a part, inconsiderable when compared with the whole. Is it not more reasonable to suppose, that the counsels of the whole will embrace the interest of every part, than that the counsels of any part will embrace the interests of the whole?

I intend not, sir, by this description of the difficulties with which the Convention were surrounded to magnify their skill or their merit in surmounting them, or to insinuate that any predicament in which the Convention stood should prevent the closest and most cautious scrutiny into the performance, which they have exhibited to their constituents and to the world. My intention is of far other and higher aim—to evince by the conflicts and difficulties which must arise from the many and powerful causes which I have enumerated, that it is hopeless and impracticable to form a constitution, which, in every part, will be acceptable to every citizen, or even to every government in the United States; and that all which can be expected is to form such a constitution, as upon the whole, is the best that can possibly be obtained. Man and perfection!—a state and perfection!—an assemblage of states and perfection!—can we reasonably expect, however ardently we may wish, to behold the glorious union?

I can well recollect, though I believe I cannot convey to others the impression, which, on many occasions, was made by the difficulties which surrounded and pressed the Convention. The great undertaking, at some times, seemed to be at a stand; at other times, its motion seemed to be retrograde. At the conclusion, however, of our work, many of the members expressed their astonishment at the success with which it terminated.

Having enumerated some of the difficulties, which the Convention were obliged to encounter in the course of their proceedings, I shall next point out the end, which they proposed to accomplish. Our wants, our talents, our affections, our passions, all tell us that we were made for a state of society. But a state of society could not be supported long or happily without some civil restraint. It is true, that in a state of nature, any one individual may act uncontrolled by others; but it is equally true, that in such a state, every other individual may act uncontrolled by him. Amid this universal independence, the dissensions and animosities between interfering members of the society would be numerous and ungovernable. The consequence would be, that each member, in such a natural state, would enjoy less liberty, and suffer more interruption, than he would in a regulated society. Hence the universal introduction of governments of some kind or other into the social state. The liberty of every member is increased by this introduction; for each gains more by the limitation of the freedom of every other member, than he loses by the limitation of his own. The result is, that civil government is necessary to the perfection and happiness of man. In forming this government, and carrying it into execution, it is *essential* that the *interest* and *authority* of the whole community should be binding in every part of it.

The foregoing principles and conclusions are generally admitted to be just and sound with regard to the nature and formation of single governments, and the duty of submission to them. In some cases they will apply, with much propriety and force, to states already formed. The advantages and necessity of civil government among individuals in society are not greater or stronger than, in some situations and circumstances, are the advantages and necessity of a federal government among states. A natural and a very important question now presents itself—is such the situation—are such the circumstances of the United States? A proper answer to this question will unfold some very interesting truths.

The United States may adopt any one of four different systems. They may become consolidated into one government, in which the separate existence of the states shall be entirely absorbed. They may reject any plan of union or association and act as separate and unconnected states. They may form two or more confederacies. They may unite in one federal republic. Which of these systems ought to have been formed by the Convention? To support, with vigor, a single government over the whole extent of the United States would demand a system of the most unqualified and the most unremitted despotism. Such a number of separate states, contiguous in situation, unconnected and disunited in government, would be, at one time, the prey of foreign force, foreign influence, and foreign intrigue; at another, the victim of mutual rage, rancor, and revenge. Neither of these systems found advocates in the late Convention. I presume they will not find advocates in this. Would it be proper to divide the United States into two or more confederacies? It will not be unadvisable to take a more minute survey of this subject. Some aspects, under which it may be viewed, are far from being, at first sight, uninviting. Two or more confederacies would be each more compact and more manageable than a single one extending over the same territory. By dividing the United States into two or more confederacies, the great collision of interests, apparently or really different and contrary, in the *whole extent* of their dominion, would be broken, and, in a great measure, disappear in the several parts. But these advantages which are discovered from certain points of view, are greatly overbalanced by inconveniences that will appear on a more accurate examination. Animosities, and perhaps wars, would arise from assigning the extent, the limits, and the rights of the different confederacies. The expenses of governing would be multiplied by the number of federal governments. The danger resulting from foreign influence and mutual dissensions would not, perhaps, be less great and alarming in the instance of different confederacies, than in the instance of different though more numerous unassociated states. These observations, and many others that might be made on the subject, will be sufficient to evince, that a division of the United States into a number of separate confederacies would probably be an unsatisfactory and an unsuccessful experiment. The remaining system which the American states may adopt is a union of them under one confederate republic. It will not be necessary to employ much time or many arguments to show, that this is the most eligible system that can be proposed. By adopting this system, the vigor and decision of a wide-spreading monarchy may be joined to the freedom and beneficence of a contracted republic. The extent of territory, the diversity of climate and soil, the number, and greatness, and connection of lakes and rivers, with which the United States are intersected and almost surrounded, all indicate an enlarged government to be fit and advantageous for them. The principles and dispositions of their citizens indicate that in this government, liberty shall reign triumphant. Such indeed have been the general opinions and wishes entertained since the era of independence. If those opinions and wishes are as well-founded as they have been general, the late Convention were justified in proposing to their constituents, *one* confederate republic as the best system of a national government for the United States.

In forming this system, it was proper to give minute attention to the interest of all the parts; but there was a duty of still higher import—to feel and to show a predominating regard to the superior interests of the whole. If this great principle had not prevailed, the plan before us would never have made its appearance. The same principle that was so necessary in forming it is equally necessary in our deliberations, whether we should reject or ratify it.

I make these observations with a design to prove and illustrate this great and important truth—that in our decisions on the work of the late Convention, we should not limit our views and regards to the State of Pennsylvania. The aim of the Convention was to form a system of good and efficient government on the more extensive scale of the United States. In this, and in every other instance, the work should be judged with the same spirit with which it was performed. A principle of duty as well as candor demands this.

We have remarked, that civil government is necessary to the perfection of society. We now remark that civil liberty is necessary to the perfection of civil government. Civil liberty is natural liberty itself, divested only of that part, which, placed in the government, produces more good and happiness to the community than if it had remained in the individual. Hence it follows, that civil liberty, while it resigns a part of natural liberty, retains the free and generous exercise of all the human faculties, so far as it is compatible with the public welfare.

In considering and developing the nature and end of the system before us, it is necessary to mention another kind of liberty, which has not yet, as far as I know, received a name. I shall distinguish it by the appellation of *"federal liberty."* When a single government is instituted, the individuals, of which it is composed, surrender to it a part of their natural independence, which they before enjoyed as men. When a confederate republic is instituted, the communities, of which it is composed, surrender to it a part of their political independence, which they before enjoyed as states. The principles, which directed, in the former case, what part of the natural liberty of the man ought to be given up and what part ought to be retained, will give similar directions in the latter case. The states should resign, to the national government, that part, and that part only, of their political liberty, which placed in that government will produce more good to the whole than if it had remained in the several states. While they resign this part of their political liberty, they retain the free and generous exercise of all their other faculties as states, so far as it is compatible with the welfare of the general and superintending confederacy.

Since *states* as well as *citizens* are represented in the Constitution before us, and form the objects on which that Constitution is proposed to operate, it was necessary to notice and define *federal* as well as *civil* liberty.

These general reflections have been made in order to introduce, with more propriety and advantage, a practical illustration of the end proposed to be accomplished by the late Convention.

It has been too well-known—it has been too severely felt—that the present Confederation is inadequate to the government and to the exigencies of the United States. The great struggle for liberty in this country, should it be unsuccessful, will probably be the last one which she[7] will have for her existence and prosperity, in any part of the globe. And it must be confessed, that this struggle has, in some of the stages of its progress, been attended with symptoms, that foreboded no fortunate issue. To the iron hand of tyranny, which was lifted up against her, she manifested, indeed, an intrepid superiority. She broke in pieces the fetters, which were forged for her, and showed that she was unassailable by force. But she was environed with dangers of another kind, and springing from a very different source. While she kept her eye steadily fixed on the efforts of oppression, licentiousness was secretly undermining the rock on which she stood.

Need I call to your remembrance the *contrasted* scenes of which we have been witnesses? On the glorious conclusion of our conflict with Britain,

---

7. [I.e., liberty.]

what high expectations were formed concerning us by others! What high expectations did we form concerning ourselves! Have those expectations been realized? No. What has been the cause? Did our citizens lose their perseverance and magnanimity? Did they become insensible of resentment and indignation at any high-handed attempt that might have been made to injure or enslave them? No. What then has been the cause? The truth is, we dreaded danger only on one side. This we manfully repelled. But on another side, danger not less formidable, but more insidious, stole in upon us; and our unsuspicious tempers were not sufficiently attentive either to its approach or to its operations. Those, whom foreign strength could not overpower, have well-nigh become the victims of internal anarchy.

If we become a little more particular, we shall find that the foregoing representation is by no means exaggerated. When we had baffled all the menaces of foreign power, we neglected to establish among ourselves a government, that would ensure domestic vigor and stability. What was the consequence? The commencement of peace was the commencement of every disgrace and distress, that could befall a people in a peaceful state. Devoid of national power, we could not prohibit the extravagance of our importations, nor could we derive a revenue from their excess. Devoid of national importance, we could not procure, for our exports, a tolerable sale at foreign markets. Devoid of national credit, we saw our public securities[8] melt in the hands of the holders, like snow before the sun. Devoid of national dignity, we could not, in some instances, perform our treaties, on our parts; and, in other instances, we could neither obtain nor compel the performance of them on the part of others. Devoid of national energy, we could not carry into execution our own resolutions, decisions, or laws.

Shall I become more particular still? The tedious detail would disgust me. Nor is it now necessary. The years of languor are passed. We have felt the dishonor with which we have been covered. We have seen the destruction with which we have been threatened. We have penetrated to the causes of both, and when we have once discovered them, we have begun to search for the means of removing them. For the confirmation of these remarks, I need not appeal to an enumeration of facts. The proceedings of Congress, and of the several states, are replete with them. They all point out the weakness and insufficiency as the cause, and an *efficient* general government as the only cure of our political distempers.

Under these impressions, and with these views, was the late Convention appointed; and under these impressions, and with these views, the late Convention met.

---

8. [I.e., our government bonds.]

We now see the great end which they propose to accomplish. It was to frame, for the consideration of their constituents, one federal and national constitution—a constitution, that would produce the advantages of good, and prevent the inconveniences of bad government—a constitution whose beneficence and energy would pervade the whole Union; and bind and embrace the interests of every part—a constitution that would ensure peace, freedom, and happiness, to the states and people of America.

We are now naturally led to examine the means by which they proposed to accomplish this end. This opens more particularly to our view the important discussion before us. But previously to our entering upon it, it will not be improper to state some general and leading principles of government, which will receive particular applications in the course of our investigations.

There necessarily exists in every government a power from which there is no appeal; and which, for that reason, may be termed supreme, absolute, and uncontrollable. Where does this power reside? To this question, writers on different governments will give different answers. Sir William Blackstone will tell you, that in Britain the power is lodged in the British Parliament, that the Parliament may alter the form of the government; and that its power is absolute without control. The idea of a constitution, limiting and superintending the operations of legislative authority, seems not to have been accurately understood in Britain. There are, at least, no traces of practice conformable to such a principle. The British constitution is just what the British Parliament pleases. When the Parliament transferred legislative authority to Henry VIII, the act transferring could not in the strict acceptation of the term be called unconstitutional.

To control the power and conduct of the legislature by an overruling constitution was an improvement in the science and practice of government reserved to the American states.

Perhaps some politician, who has not considered, with sufficient accuracy, our political systems, would answer, that in our governments, the supreme power was vested in the constitutions. This opinion approaches a step nearer to the truth; but does not reach it. The truth is, that, in our governments, the supreme, absolute, and uncontrollable power *remains* in the people. As our constitutions are superior to our legislatures; so the people are superior to our constitutions. Indeed the superiority, in this last instance, is much greater; for the people possess, over our constitutions, control in *act*, as well as in right.

The consequence is, that the people may change the constitutions whenever and however they please. This is a right, of which no positive institution can ever deprive them.

These important truths, sir, are far from being merely speculative. We, at this moment, speak and deliberate under their immediate and benign influence. To the operation of these truths, we are to ascribe the scene, hitherto unparalleled, which America now exhibits to the world—a gentle, a peaceful, a voluntary, and a deliberate transition from one constitution of government to another. In other parts of the world, the idea of revolutions in government is, by a mournful and an indissoluble association, connected with the idea of wars and all the calamities attendant on wars. But happy experience teaches us to view such revolutions in a very different light—to consider them only as progressive steps in improving the knowledge of government, and increasing the happiness of society and mankind.

Oft have I viewed, with silent pleasure and admiration, the force and prevalence of this principle through the United States, that the supreme power resides in the people; and that they never part with it. It may be called the *panacea* in politics. There can be no disorder in the community but may here receive a radical cure. If the error be in the legislature, it may be corrected by the constitution. If in the constitution, it may be corrected by the people. There is a remedy, therefore, for every distemper in government, if the people are not wanting to themselves. For a people wanting to themselves, there is no remedy. From their power, as we have seen, there is no appeal. To their error, there is no superior principle of correction.

There are three simple species of government—monarchy, where the supreme power is in a single person; aristocracy, where the supreme power is in a select assembly, the members of which either fill up, by election, the vacancies in their own body, or succeed to their places in it by inheritance, property, or in respect of some *personal* right or qualification; a republic or democracy, where the people at large *retain* the supreme power, and act either collectively or by representation.

Each of these species of government has its advantages and disadvantages.

The advantages of a monarchy are strength, dispatch, secrecy, unity of counsel. Its disadvantages are tyranny, expense, ignorance of the situation and wants of the people, insecurity, unnecessary wars, evils attending elections or successions.

The advantages of aristocracy are wisdom, arising from experience and education. Its disadvantages are dissensions among themselves, oppression to the lower orders.

The advantages of democracy are liberty, equal, cautious, and salutary laws, public spirit, frugality, peace, opportunities of exciting and producing abilities of the best citizens. Its disadvantages are dissensions, the delay and disclosure of public counsels, the imbecility of public measures retarded by the necessity of a numerous consent.

A government may be composed of two or more of the simple forms above mentioned. Such is the British government. It would be an improper government for the United States; because it is inadequate to such an extent of territory; and because it is suited to an establishment of different orders of men. A more minute comparison between some parts of the British constitution and some parts of the plan before us may perhaps find a proper place in a subsequent period of our business.

What is the nature and kind of that government which has been proposed for the United States by the late Convention? In its principle, it is purely democratical. But that principle is applied in different forms, in order to obtain the advantages and exclude the inconveniences of the simple modes of government.

If we take an extended and accurate view of it, we shall find the streams of power running in different directions, in different dimensions, and at different heights watering, adorning, and fertilizing the fields and meadows through which their courses are led; but if we trace them, we shall discover, that they all originally flow from one abundant fountain.

In THIS CONSTITUTION, *all authority is derived from the* PEOPLE.

Fit occasions will hereafter offer for particular remarks on the different parts of the plan. I have now to ask pardon of the house for detaining them so long.

A CITIZEN OF AMERICA [NOAH WEBSTER], *AN EXAMINATION INTO
THE LEADING PRINCIPLES OF THE FEDERAL CONSTITUTION*

October 17, 1787

Of all the memorable eras that have marked the progress of men from the savage state to the refinements of luxury, that which has combined them into society, under a wise system of government, and given form to a nation, has ever been recorded and celebrated as the most important. Legislators have ever been deemed the greatest benefactors of mankind—respected when living, and often deified after their death. Hence the fame of Fohi and Confucius—of Moses, Solon, and Lycurgus—of Romulus and Numa—of Alfred, Peter the Great, and Mango Capac; whose names will be celebrated through all ages, for framing and improving constitutions of government, which introduced order into society and secured the benefits of law to millions of the human race.

This western world now beholds an era important beyond conception, and which posterity will number with the age of Czar of Muscovy, and with the promulgation of the Jewish laws at Mount Sinai. The names of those men who have digested a system of constitutions for the American empire, will be enrolled with those of Zamolxis and Odin, and celebrated by posterity with the honors which less enlightened nations have paid to the fabled demigods of antiquity.

But the origin of the AMERICAN REPUBLIC is distinguished by peculiar circumstances. Other nations have been driven together by fear and necessity—the governments have generally been the result of a single man's observations; or the offspring of particular interests. In the formation of our constitution, the wisdom of all ages is collected—the legislators of antiquity are consulted—as well as the opinions and interests of the millions who are concerned. In short, it is *an empire of reason.*

In the formation of such a government, it is not only the *right,* but the indispensable *duty* of every citizen to examine the principles of it, to compare them with the principles of other governments, with a constant eye to our particular situation and circumstances, and thus endeavor to foresee the future operations of our own system, and its effects upon human happiness.

Convinced of this truth, I have no apology to offer for the following remarks, but[9] an earnest desire to be useful to my country.

In attending to the proposed Federal Constitution, the first thing that presents itself to our consideration, is the division of the legislative into two branches. This article has so many advocates in America, that it needs not any vindication.[10]—But it has its opposers, among whom are some respectable characters, especially in Pennsylvania; for which reason, I will state some of the arguments and facts which incline me to favor the proposed division.

On the first view of men in society, we should suppose that no man would be bound by a law to which he had not given his consent. Such would be our first idea of political obligation. But experience, from time immemorial, has proved it to be impossible to unite the opinions of all the members of a community, in every case; and hence the doctrine, that the opinions of *a majority* must give law to the *whole State:* a doctrine as universally received as any intuitive truth.

Another idea that naturally presents itself to our minds, on a slight consideration of the subject, is, that in a perfect government, all the members of a society should be present, and each give his suffrage in acts of legislation, by which he is to be bound. This is impracticable in large states; and even were it not, it is very questionable whether it would be

---

9. [I.e., other than.]

10. A division of the legislature has been adopted in the constitution of every state except Pennsylvania and Georgia. (Webster)

the *best* mode of legislation. It was however practiced in the free states of antiquity; and was the cause of innumerable evils. To avoid these evils, the moderns have invented the doctrine of *representation,* which seems to be the perfection of human government.

Another idea, which is very natural, is, that to complete the mode of legislation, all the representatives should be collected into *one body,* for the purpose of debating questions and enacting laws. Speculation would suggest the idea; and the desire of improving upon the systems of government in the old world, would operate powerfully in its favor.

But men are ever running into extremes. The passions, after a violent constraint, are apt to run into licentiousness; and even the reason of men, who have experienced evils from the *defects* of a government, will sometimes coolly condemn the *whole system.*

Every person, moderately acquainted with human nature, knows that public bodies, as well as individuals, are liable to the influence of sudden and violent passions, under the operation of which, the voice of reason is silenced. Instances of such influence are not so frequent, as in individuals; but its effects are extensive in proportion to the numbers that compose the public body. This fact suggests the expediency of dividing the powers of legislation between the two bodies of men, whose debates shall be separate and not dependent on each other: that, if at any time, one part should appear to be under any undue influence, either from passion, obstinacy, jealousy of particular men, attachment to a popular speaker, or other extraordinary causes, there might be a power in the legislature sufficient to check every pernicious measure. Even in a small republic, composed of men, equal in property and abilities, and all meeting for the purpose of making laws, like the old Romans in the field of Mars, a division of the body into two independent branches, would be a necessary step to prevent the disorders, which arise from the pride, irritability, and stubbornness of mankind. This will ever be the case, while men possess passions, easily inflamed, which may bias their reason and lead them to erroneous conclusions.

Another consideration has weight: A single body of men may be led astray by one person of abilities and address, who, on the first starting a proposition, may throw a plausible appearance on one side of the question, and give a lead to the whole debate. To prevent any ill consequence from such a circumstance, a separate discussion, before a different body of men, and taken up on new grounds, is a very eligible expedient.

Besides, the design of a senate is not merely to check the legislative assembly, but to collect wisdom and experience. In most of our constitutions, and particularly in the proposed federal system, greater age and longer residence are required to qualify for the senate, than for the house of representatives. This is a wise provision. The house of representatives may be composed of new and inexperienced members—strangers to the forms of proceeding, and the science of legislation. But either positive institutions, or customs, which may supply their place, fill the senate with men venerable for age and respectability, experienced in the ways of men, and in the art of governing, and who are not liable to the bias of passions that govern the young. If the senate of Rhode Island is an exception to this observation, it is a proof that the mass of the people are corrupted, and that the senate should be elected less frequently than the other house: Had the old senate in Rhode Island held their seats for three years; had they not been chosen, amidst a popular rage for paper money, the honor of that state would probably have been saved. The old senate would have stopped the measure for a year or two, until the people could have had time to deliberate upon its consequences. I consider it as a capital excellence of the proposed constitution, that the senate can be wholly renewed but once in six years.

Experience is the best instructor—it is better than a thousand theories. The history of every government on earth affords proof of the utility of different branches in a legislature. But I appeal only to our own experience in America. To what cause can we ascribe the absurd measures of Congress, in times past, and the speedy recision[11] of whole measures, but to the want of some check? I feel the most profound deference for that honorable body, and perfect respect for their opinions; but some of their steps betray a great want of consideration—a defect, which perhaps nothing can remedy, but a division of their deliberations. I will instance only their *resolution* to build a *Federal Town*. When we were involved in a debt, of which we could hardly pay the interest, and when Congress could not command a shilling, the very proposition was extremely absurd. Congress themselves became ashamed of the resolution, and rescinded it with as much silence as possible. Many other acts of that body are equally reprehensible—but respect forbids me to mention them.

Several states, since the war, have experienced the necessity of a division of the legislature. Maryland was saved from a most pernicious measure, by her senate. A rage for paper money, bordering on madness, prevailed in their house of delegates—an emission of £500,000 was proposed; a sum equal to the circulating medium of the State.[12] Had the sum

---

11. [I.e., rescinding.]

12. [The decimal system of coinage and the dollar were formally adopted by the Continental Congress in 1785, but the new currency did not come into use until 1794; prior to that dollars were Spanish pieces of eight. In 1767 a dollar was worth eight shillings in paper money of New York, at which rate of exchange £500,000 would be $1,250,000.]

been emitted, every shilling of specie would have been driven from circulation, and most of it from the state. Such a loss would not have been repaired in seven years—not to mention the whole catalog of frauds which would have followed the measure. The senate, like honest, judicious men, and the protectors of the interests of the state, firmly resisted the rage, and gave the people time to cool and to think. Their resistance was effectual—the people acquiesced, and the honor and interest of the state were secured.

The house of representatives in Connecticut, soon after the war, had taken offense at a certain act of Congress. The upper house, who understood the necessity and expediency of the measure, better than the people, refused to concur in a remonstrance to Congress. Several other circumstances gave umbrage to the lower house; and to weaken or destroy the influence of the senate, the representatives, among other violent proceedings, resolved, not merely to remove the seat of government, but to make every county town in the state the seat of government, by rotation. This foolish resolution would have disgraced schoolboys—the senate saved the honor of the state, by rejecting it with disdain—and within two months, every representative was ashamed of the conduct of the house. All public bodies have these fits of passion, when their conduct seems to be perfectly boyish;[13] and in these paroxysms, a check is highly necessary.

Pennsylvania exhibits many instances of this hasty conduct. At one session of the legislature, an armed force is ordered, by a precipitate resolution, to expel the settlers at Wyoming from their possessions—at a succeeding session, the same people are confirmed in their possessions. At one session, a charter is wrested from a corporation—at another, restored. The whole state is split into parties—everything is decided by party—any proposition from one side of the house, is sure to be damned by the other—and when one party perceives the other has the advantage, they play truant—and an officer or a mob hunt the absconding members in all the streets and alleys in town. Such farces have been repeated in Philadelphia—and *there alone*. Had the legislature been framed with some check upon rash proceedings, the honor of the state would have been saved—the party spirit would have died with the measures proposed in the legislature. But now, any measure may be carried by party in the house; it then becomes a law, and sows the seeds of dissension throughout the state.[14]

---

13. [I.e., childish.]

14. I cannot help remarking the singular jealousy of the constitution of Pennsylvania, which requires that a bill shall be published for the consideration of the people, before it is enacted into a law, except in extraordinary cases. This annihilates the legislature, and reduces it to an advisory body. It almost wholly supersedes the

A thousand examples similar to the foregoing may be produced, both in ancient and modern history. Many plausible things may be said in favor of pure democracy—many in favor of uniting the representatives of the people in one single house—but uniform experience proves both to be inconsistent with the peace of society, and the rights of freemen.

The state of Georgia has already discovered such inconveniences in its constitution, that a proposition has been made for altering it; and there is a prospect that a revisal will take place.

People who have heard and read of the European governments, founded on the different ranks *of monarch, nobility, and people,* seem to view the *senate* in America, where there is no difference of ranks and titles, as a useless branch—or as a servile imitation of foreign constitutions of government, without the same reasons. This is a capital mistake. Our senates, it is true, are not composed of a different order of men; but the same reasons, the same necessity for distinct branches of the legislature exists in all governments. But in most of our American constitutions, we have all the advantages of checks and balance, without the danger which may arise from a superior and independent order of men.

It is worth our while to institute a brief comparison between our American forms of government, and the two *best constitutions* that ever existed in Europe, the *Roman* and the *British.*

In England, the king or supreme executive officer, is hereditary. In America, the president of the United States, is elective. That this is an advantage will hardly be disputed.

In ancient Rome, the king was elective, and so were the consuls, who were the executive officers in the republic. But they were elected by the body of the people, in their public assemblies; and this circumstance paved the way for such excessive bribery and corruption as are wholly unknown in modern times. The president of the United States is also elective; but by a few men—chosen by the several legislatures—under their inspection—separated at a vast distance—and holding no office under the United States. Such a mode of election almost precludes the

---

uses of *representation,* the most excellent improvement in modern governments. Besides the absurdity of constituting a legislature, without supreme power, such a system will keep the state perpetually embroiled. It carries the spirit of discussion into all quarters, without the means of reconciling the opinions of men, who are not assembled to hear each others' arguments. They debate with themselves—form their own opinions, without the reasons which influence others, and without the means of information. Thus the warmth of different opinions, which, in other states, dies in the legislature, is diffused through the state of Pennsylvania, and becomes personal and permanent. The seeds of dissension are sown in the constitution, and no state, except Rhode Island, is so distracted by factions. (Webster)

possibility of corruption. Besides, no state however large, has the power of choosing a president in that state; for each elector must choose at least one man, who is not an inhabitant of that State to which he belongs.

The crown of England is hereditary—the consuls of Rome were chosen annually—both these extremes are guarded against in our proposed constitution. The president is not dismissed from his office, as soon as he is acquainted with business—he continues four years, and is reeligible, if the people approve his conduct. Nor can he canvass for his office, by reason of the distance of the electors; and the pride and jealousy of the states will prevent his continuing too long in office.

The age requisite to qualify for this office is thirty-five years. The age requisite for admittance to the Roman consulship was forty-three years.[15] For this difference, good reasons may be assigned—the improvements in science, and particularly in government, render it practicable for a man to qualify himself for an important office, much earlier in life, than he could among the Romans; especially in the early part of their commonwealth, when the office was instituted. Besides it is very questionable whether any inconvenience would have attended admission to the consulship at an earlier age.

The powers vested in the president resemble the powers of the supreme magistrates in Rome. They are not so extensive as those of the British king; but in one instance, the president, with concurrence of the senate, has powers exceeding those of the Roman consuls; I mean in the appointment of judges and other subordinate executive officers. The praetors or judges in Rome were chosen annually by the people. This was a defect in the Roman government. One half the evils in a state arise from a lax execution of the laws; and it is impossible that an executive officer can act with vigor and impartiality, when his office depends on the popular voice. An annual popular election of executive officers is the sure source of a negligent, partial, and corrupt administration. The independence of the judges in England has produced a course of the most just, impartial, and energetic judicial decisions, for many centuries, that can be exhibited in any nation on earth. In this point therefore I conceive the plan proposed in America to be an improvement on the Roman constitution. In all free governments, that is, in all countries, where *laws govern,* and not *men,* the supreme magistrate should have it in his power to execute any law, however unpopular, without hazarding his person or office. The laws are the sole *guardians* of right, and when the magistrate dares not act, every person is insecure.

---

15. In the decline of the republic, bribery or military force obtained this office for persons who had not attained this age—Augustus was chosen at the age of twenty; or rather obtained it with his sword. (Webster)

Let us now attend to the constitution and the powers of the senate.

The house of lords in England is wholly independent of the people. The lords spiritual hold their seats by office; and the people at large have no voice in disposing of the ecclesiastical dignities. The temporal lords hold their seats by hereditary right or by grant from the king: And it is a branch of the king's prerogative to make what peers he pleases.

The senate in Rome was elective; but a senator held his seat for life.[16]

The proposed senate in America is constituted on principles more favor-

---

16. I say the senate was *elective*—but this must be understood with some exceptions; or rather qualifications. The constitution of the Roman senate has been a subject of inquiry, with the first men in modern ages. Lord Chesterfield requested the opinion of the learned Vertot, upon the manner of choosing senators in Rome; and it was a subject of discussion between Lord Harvey and Dr. Middleton. The most probable account of the manner of forming the senate, and filling up vacancies, which I have collected from the best writers on this subject, is here abridged for the consideration of the reader.

Romulus chose one hundred persons, from the principal families in Rome, to form a council or senate; and reserved to himself the right of nominating their successors; that is of filling vacancies. "Mais comme Romulus avoit lui même choisi les premiers senateurs il se reserva le droit de nommer a son gre, leurs successeurs."—Mably, *sur les Romains.* Other well-informed historians intimate that Romulus retained the right of nominating the president only. After the union of the Sabines with the Romans, Romulus added another hundred members to the senate, but by *consent of the people.* Tarquin, the *ancient,* added another hundred; but historians are silent as to the manner.

On the destruction of Alba by Hostilius, some of the principal Alban families were added to the senate, *by consent of the senate and people.*

After the demolition of the monarchy, Appius Claudius was admitted into the senate by *order of the people.*

Cicero testifies that, from the extinction of the monarchy, all the members of the senate were admitted by *command of the people.*

It is observable that the first creation of the senators was the act of the monarch; and the first patrician families claimed the sole right of admission into the senate. "Les familles qui descendoient des deux cent senateurs que Romulus avoit créés,—se crurent seules en droit d'entrer dans le senat."—Mably.

This right however was not granted in its utmost extent; for many of the senators in the Roman commonwealth, were taken from plebian families. For sixty years before the institution of the *censorship,* which was A. U. C. [years since from the foundation of Rome] 311, we are not informed how vacancies in the senate were supplied. The most probable method was this; to enroll, in the list of senators, the different magistrates; viz., the consuls, praetors, the two quaestors of patrician families, the five tribunes (afterward ten), and the two aediles of plebeian families: The office of quaestor gave an immediate admission into the senate. The tribunes were admitted two years after their creation. This enrollment seems

able to liberty: The members are elective, and by the separate legislatures: They hold their seats for six years—they are thus rendered sufficiently dependent on their constituents; and yet are not dismissed from their office as soon as they become acquainted with the forms of proceeding.

It may be objected by the larger states, that the representation is not equal; the smallest states having the privilege of sending the same number of senators as the largest. To obviate this objection, I would suggest but two or three ideas.

1. If each state had a representation and a right in deciding questions, proportional to its property, three states would almost command the whole. Such a constitution would gradually annihilate the small states; and finally melt down the whole United States into one undivided sovereignty. The free states of Spain and the heptarchy[17] in England, afford striking examples of this.

---

to have been a matter of course; and likewise the confirmation by the people in their comitia or assemblies.

On extraordinary occasions, when the vacancies of the senate were numerous, the consuls used to nominate some of the most respectable of the equestrian order to be chosen by the people.

On the institution of the censorship, the censors were invested with full powers to inspect the manners of the citizens,—enroll them in their proper ranks according to their property,—make out lists of the senators and leave out the names of such as had rendered themselves unworthy of their dignity by any scandalous vices. This power they several times exercised; but the disgraced senators had an appeal to the people.

After the senate had lost half its members in the war with Hannibal, the dictator, M. Fabius Buteo, filled up the number with the magistrates, with those who had been honored with a civic crown, or others who were respectable for age and character. One hundred and seventy new members were added at once, with *the approbation of the people.* The vacancies occasioned by Sylla's proscriptions amounted to three hundred, which were supplied by persons nominated by Sylla and *chosen by the people.*

Before the time of the Gracchi, the number of senators did not exceed three hundred. But in Sylla's time, so far as we can collect from direct testimonies, it amounted to about five hundred. The age necessary to qualify for a seat in the senate is not exactly ascertained; but several circumstances prove it to have been about thirty years.

See Vertot, Mably, and Middleton on this subject.

In the last ages of Roman splendor, the property requisite to qualify a person for a senator, was settled by Augustus at eight hundred sestertia—more than six thousand pounds sterling. (Webster)

17. [The seven kingdoms that were supposed to have existed in Anglo-Saxon England.]

Should it be said that such an event is desirable, I answer; the states are all entitled to their respective sovereignties, and while they claim independence in international jurisdiction, the federal constitution ought to guarantee their sovereignty.

2. Another consideration has weight—There is, in all nations, a tendency toward an accumulation of power in some point. It is the business of the legislator to establish some barriers to check the tendency. In small societies, a man worth £100,000 has but one vote, when his neighbors, who are worth but fifty pounds, have each one vote likewise. To make property the sole basis of authority, would expose many of the best citizens to violence and oppression. To make the number of inhabitants in a state, the rule of apportioning power, is more equitable; and were the United States one indivisible interest, would be a perfect rule for representation. But the detached situation of the states has created some separate interests—some local institutions,[18] which they will not resign nor throw into the hands of other states. For these peculiar interests, the states have an *equal* attachment—for the preservation and enjoyment of these, an *equal* sovereignty is necessary; and the sovereignty of each state would not be secure, had each state, in both branches of the legislature an authority in passing laws, proportioned to its inhabitants.

3. But the senate should be considered as representing the confederacy in a body. It is a false principle in the vulgar idea of representation, that a man delegated by a particular district in a state, is the representative of that district only; whereas in truth a member of the legislature from any town or county, is the representative of the whole state. In passing laws, he is to view the whole collective interest of the state, and act from that view; not from a partial regard to the interest of the town or county where he is chosen.

The same principle extends to the Congress of the United States. A delegate is bound to represent the true local interest of his constituents—to state it in its true light to the whole body—but when each provincial interest is thus stated, every member should act for the *aggregate interest* of the whole confederacy. The design of representation is to bring the collective interest into view—a delegate is not the legislator of a single state—he is as much the legislator of the whole confederacy as of the particular state where he is chosen; and if he gives his vote for a law which he believes to be beneficial to his own state only; and pernicious to the rest, he betrays his trust and violates his oath. It is indeed difficult for a man to divest himself of local attachments and act from an impartial regard to the general good; but he who cannot for the most part do this, is not a good legislator.

---

18. [I.e., slavery.]

These considerations suggest the propriety of continuing the senators in office, for a longer period, than the representatives. They gradually lose their partiality, generalize their views, and consider themselves as acting for the whole confederacy. Hence in the senate we may expect union and firmness—here we may find the *general good* the object of legislation, and a check upon the more partial and interested acts of the other branch.

These considerations obviate the complaint, that the representation in the senate is not equal; for the senators represent the whole confederacy; and all that is wanted of the members is information of the true situation and interest of each state. As they act under the direction of the several legislatures, two men may as fully and completely represent a state, as twenty; and when the true interest of each state is known, if the senators perform the part of good legislators, and act impartially for the whole collective body of the United States, it is totally immaterial where they are chosen.[19]

The house of representatives is the more immediate voice of the separate states—here the states are represented in proportion to their number

---

19. It is a capital defect of most of the state constitutions, that the senators, like the representatives, are chosen in particular districts. They are thus inspired with local views, and however wrong it may be to entertain them, yet such is the constitution of human nature, that men are almost involuntarily attached to the interest of the district which has reposed confidence in their abilities and integrity. Some partiality therefore for constituents is always expectable. To destroy it as much as possible, a political constitution should remove the grounds of local attachment. Connecticut and Maryland have wisely destroyed this attachment in their senates, by ordaining that the members shall be chosen in the *state at large*. The senators hold their seats by the suffrages of the state, *not of a district;* hence they have no particular number of men to fear or to oblige.—They represent *the state;* hence that union and firmness which the senates of those states have manifested on the most trying occasions, and by which they have prevented the most rash and iniquitous measures.

It may be objected, that when the election of senators is vested in the people, they must choose men in their own neighborhood, or else those with whom they are unacquainted. With respect to representatives, this objection does not lie; for they are chosen in small districts; and as to senators, there is, in every state, a small number of men, whose reputation for abilities, integrity, and good conduct will lead the people to a very just choice. Old experienced statesmen should compose the senate; and people are generally, in this free country, acquainted with their characters. Were it possible, as it is in small states, it would be an improvement in the doctrine of representation, to give every freeman the right of voting for every member of the legislature, and the privilege of choosing the men in any part of the state. This would totally exclude bribery and undue influence; for no man can bribe a state; and it would almost annihilate partial views in legislation. But in large states it may be impracticable. (Webster)

of inhabitants—here the separate interests will operate with their full force, and the violence of parties and the jealousies produced by interfering interests, can be restrained and quieted only by a body of men, less local and dependent.[20]

It may be objected that no separate interests should exist in a state; and a division of the legislature has a tendency to create them. But this objection is founded on mere jealousy, or a very imperfect comparison of the Roman and British governments, with the proposed federal constitution.

The house of peers in England is a body originally and totally independent of the people—the senate in Rome was mostly composed of patrician or noble families, and after the first election of a senator, he was no longer dependent on the people—he held his seat for life. But the senate of the United States can have no separate interests from the body of the people; for they live among them—they are chosen by them—they *must* be dismissed from their place once in six years and *may* at any time be impeached for malpractices—their property is situated among the people, and with their persons, subject to the same laws. No title can be granted, but the temporary titles of office, bestowed by the voluntary election of the people; and no preeminence can be acquired but by the same means.

The separation of the legislature divides the power—checks—restrains—amends the proceedings—at the same time, it creates no division of interest, that can tempt either branch to encroach upon the other, or upon the people. In turbulent times, such restraint is our greatest safety—in calm times, and in measures obviously calculated for the general good, both branches must always be unanimous.

A man must be thirty years of age before he can be admitted into the senate—which was likewise a requisite in the Roman government. What property was requisite for a senator in the early ages of Rome, I cannot inform myself; but Augustus fixed it at six hundred sestertia—between six and seven thousand pounds sterling. In the federal constitution, money is not made a requisite—the places of senators are wisely left open to all persons of suitable age and merit, and who have been citizens of the United States for nine years; a term in which foreigners may acquire the feelings and acquaint themselves with the interests, of the native Americans.[21]

The house of representatives is formed on very equitable principles; and is calculated to guard the privileges of the people. The English house of commons is chosen by a small part of the people of England,

---

20. [Federalist 10 is a rejection of this claim that the violence of parties will operate with "full force" in the House of Representatives.]

21. ["Native Americans" here means those born in America, not the peoples resident before the arrival of the European settlers.]

and continues for seven years. The Romans never discovered the secret of representation—the whole body of citizens assembled for the purposes of legislation—a circumstance that exposed their government to frequent convulsions, and to capricious measures. The federal house of representatives is chosen by the people qualified to vote for state representatives,[22] and continues two years.

Some may object to their continuance in power *two years*. But I cannot see any danger arising from this quarter. On the contrary, it creates less

---

22. It is said by some, that no property should be required as a qualification for an elector. I shall not enter into a discussion of the subject; but remark that in most free governments, some property has been thought requisite, to prevent corruption and secure government from the influence of an unprincipled multitude.

In ancient Rome none but the free citizens had the right of a suffrage in the *comitia* or legislative assemblies. But in Sylla's time the Italian cities demanded the rights of the Roman citizens; alleging that they furnished two-thirds of the armies, in all their wars, and yet were despised as foreigners. Velleuis, *Patercules*, lib. 2. cap.15. This produced the *Marsic* or *social* war, which lasted two years, and carried off three hundred thousand men. Ibidem. It was conducted and concluded by Pompey, father of Pompey the Great, with his lieutenants Sylla and Marius. But most of the cities eventually obtained *the freedom of Rome;* and were of course entitled to the rights of suffrage in the comitia. "Paulatim deinde recipiendo in civitatem, qui arma aut non ceperant aut deposuerant maturiùs, vires refectae sunt." Velleuis, *Patercules*, lib. 2. cap. 16.

But Rome had cause to deplore this event, for however reasonable it might appear to admit the allies to a participation of the rights of citizens, yet the concession destroyed all freedom of election. It enabled an ambitious demagogue to engage and bring into the assemblies, whole towns of people, slaves and foreigners;—and everything was decided by faction and violence. This Montesquieu numbers among the causes of the decline of the Roman greatness. *De la grandeur des Romains,* chapter 9.

Representation would have, in some measure, prevented the consequences; but the admission of every man to a suffrage will ever open the door to corruption. In such a state as Connecticut, where there is no conflux of foreigners, no introduction of seamen, servants, etc., and scarcely a hundred persons in the state who are not natives, and very few whose education and connections do not attach them to the government; at the same time few men have property to furnish the means of corruption, very little danger could spring from admitting every man of age and discretion to the privilege of voting for rulers. But in the large towns of America there is more danger. A master of a vessel may put votes in the hands of his crew, for the purpose of carrying an election for a party. Such things have actually taken place in America. Besides, the middle states are receiving emigrations of poor people, who are not at once judges of the characters of men, and who cannot be safely trusted with the choice of legislators. (Webster)

trouble for the representatives, who by such choice are taken from their professions and obliged to attend Congress, some of them at the distance of at least seven hundred miles. While men are chosen by the people, and responsible to them, there is but little danger from ambition or corruption.

If it should be said that Congress may in time become triennial, and even septennial, like the English parliaments, I answer, this is not in their power. The English parliament had power to prolong the period of their existence—but Congress will be restrained by the different legislatures, without whose constitutional concurrence, no alteration can be made in the proposed system.

The fourth section, article I, of the new constitution declares that "The times, places, and manner of holding elections for senators and representatives, shall be prescribed in each state by the legislature thereof; *but the Congress may at any time by law make or alter such regulations, except as to the places of choosing senators.*" Here let us pause—What did the convention mean by giving Congress power to *make regulations*, prescribed by the legislatures? Is this expression accurate or intelligible? But the word *alter* is very intelligible, and the clause puts the election of representatives *wholly*, and the senators *almost wholly*, in the power of Congress.

The views of the convention I believe to be perfectly upright—They might mean to place the election of representatives and senators beyond the reach of faction—They doubtless had good reasons, in *their* minds, for the clause—But I see no occasion for any power in Congress to interfere with the choice of their own body—They will have power to suppress insurrections, as they ought to have; but the clause in *Italics* gives *needless* and *dangerous* powers—I hope the states will reject it with decency, and adopt the whole system, without altering another syllable.

The method of passing laws in Congress is much preferable to that of ancient Rome or modern Britain. Not to mention other defects in Rome, it lay in the power of a single tribune to obstruct the passing of a law. As the tribunes were popular magistrates, the right was often exercised in favor of liberty; but it was also abused, and the best regulations were prevented, to gratify the spleen, the ambition, or the resentment of an individual.

The king of Great Britain has the same power, but seldom exercises it. It is however a dangerous power—it is absurd and hazardous to lodge in *one man* the right of controlling the will of a state.

Every bill that passes a majority of both houses of Congress, must be sent to the president for his approbation; but it must be returned in ten days, whether approved by him or not; and the concurrence of two-thirds of both houses passes the bill into a law, notwithstanding any objections of the president. The constitution therefore gives the supreme executive a check but no negative, upon the sense of Congress.

The powers lodged in Congress are extensive; but it is presumed that they are not too extensive. The first object of the constitution is to *unite* the states into one *compact society*, for the purpose of government. If such *union* must exist, or the states be exposed to foreign invasions, internal discord, reciprocal encroachments upon each other's property—to weakness and infamy, which no person will dispute; what powers must be collected and lodged in the supreme head or legislature of these states? The answer is easy: This legislature must have exclusive jurisdiction in all matters in which the states have a mutual interest. There are some regulations in which all the states are equally concerned—there are others, which in their operation, are limited to one state. The first belongs to Congress—the last to the respective legislatures. No one state has a right to supreme control, in any affair in which the other states have an interest, nor should Congress interfere in any affair which respects one state only. This is the general line of division, which the convention have endeavored to draw, between the powers of Congress and the rights of the individual states. The only question therefore is, whether the new constitution delegates to Congress any powers which do not respect the general interest and welfare of the United States. If these powers entrench upon the present sovereignty of any *state*, without having for an object the *collective interest* of the whole, the powers are too extensive. But if they do not extend to all concerns, in which the states have a mutual interest, they are too limited. If in any instance, the powers necessary for protecting the *general* interest, interfere with the constitutional rights of an *individual state*, such state has assumed powers that are inconsistent with the safety of the United States, and which ought instantly to be resigned. Considering the states as individuals, on equal terms, entering into a social compact, no state has a right to any power which may prejudice its neighbors. If therefore the federal constitution has collected into the federal legislature no more power than is necessary for the *common defense and interest*, it should be recognized by the states, however particular clauses may supersede the exercise of certain powers by the individual states.

This question is of vast magnitude. The states have very high ideas of their separate sovereignty; although it is certain, that while each exists in its full latitude, we can have no *Federal sovereignty*. However flattered each state may be by its independent sovereignty, we can have no union, no respectability, no national character, and what is more, no national justice, until the states resign to one *supreme head* the exclusive power of *legislating, judging, and executing*, in all matters of a general nature. Everything of a private or provincial nature, must still rest on the ground of the respective state constitutions.

After examining the limits of the proposed congressional powers, I confess I do not think them too extensive—I firmly believe that the life, liberty, and property of every man, and the peace and independence of each state, will be more fully secured under such a constitution of federal government, than they will under a constitution with more limited powers; and infinitely more safe than under our boasted distinct sovereignties. It appears to me that Congress will have no more power than will be necessary for our union and general welfare; and such power they must have or we are in a wretched state. On the adoption of this constitution, I should value real estate twenty percent higher than I do at this moment.

I will not examine into the extent of the powers proposed to be lodged in the supreme federal head; the subject would be extensive and require more time than I could bestow upon it. But I will take up some objections, that have been made to particular points of the new constitution.

Most of the objections I have yet heard to the constitution, consist in mere insinuations unsupported by reasoning or fact. They are thrown out to instill groundless jealousies into the minds of the people, and probably with a view to prevent all government; for there are, in every society, some turbulent geniuses whose importance depends solely on faction. To seek the insidious and detestable nature of these insinuations, it is necessary to mention, and to remark on a few particulars.

1. The first objection against the constitution is, that the legislature will be more expensive than our present confederation. This is so far from being true, that the money we actually lose by our present weakness, disunion, and *want of government* would support the civil government of every state in the confederacy. Our public poverty does not proceed from the expensiveness of Congress, nor of the civil list; but from want of power to command our own advantages. We pay more money to foreign nations, in the course of business, and merely for *want of government*, than would, under an efficient government, pay the annual interest of our domestic debt. Every man in business knows this to be *truth;* and the objection can be designed only to delude the ignorant.

2. Another objection to the constitution, is the division of the legislature into two branches. Luckily this objection has no advocates but in Pennsylvania; and even here their number is dwindling. The factions that reign in this state, the internal discord and passions that disturb the government and the peace of the inhabitants, have detected the errors of the constitution, and will some time or other produce a reformation. The division of the legislature has been the subject of discussion in the beginning of this essay; and will be deemed, by nineteen-twentieths of the Americans, one of the principal excellencies of the constitution.

3. A third insinuation, is that the proposed federal government will annihilate the several legislatures. This is extremely disingenuous. Every person, capable of reading, must discover, that the convention have labored to draw the line between the federal and provincial powers—to define the powers of Congress, and limit them to those general concerns which *must* come under federal jurisdiction, and which *cannot be* managed in the separate legislatures—that in all internal regulations, whether of civil or criminal nature, the states retain their sovereignty, and have it guaranteed to them by this very constitution. Such a groundless insinuation, or rather mere surmise, must proceed from dark designs or extreme ignorance, and deserves the severest reprobation.

4. It is alleged that the liberty of the press is not guaranteed by the new constitution. But this objection is wholly unfounded. The liberty of the press does not come within the jurisdiction of federal government. It is firmly established in all the states either by law, or positive declarations in *bills of right;* and not being mentioned in the federal constitution, is not—and cannot be abridged by Congress. It stands on the basis of the respective state constitutions. Should any state resign to Congress the exclusive jurisdiction of a certain district, which should include any town where presses are already established, it is in the power of the state to reserve the liberty of the press, or any other fundamental privilege, and make it an immutable condition of the grant, that such rights shall never be violated. All objections therefore on this score are *"baseless visions."*

5. It is insinuated that the constitution gives Congress the power of levying internal taxes at pleasure. This insinuation seems founded on the eighth section of the first article, which declares, that "Congress shall have power to lay and collect taxes, duties, imposts, and excises, to pay the debts and provide for the common defense and general welfare of the United States."

That Congress should have power to collect duties, imposts, and excises, in order to render them uniform throughout the United States will hardly be controverted. The whole objection is to the right of levying internal taxes.

But it will be conceded that the supreme head of the states must have power, competent to the purposes of our union, or it will be, as it now is, *a useless body,* a mere expense, without any advantage. To pay our public debt, to support foreign ministers and our own civil government, money must be raised; and if the duties and imposts are not adequate to these purposes, where shall the money be obtained? It will be answered, let Congress apportion the sum to be raised, and leave the legislatures to collect the money. Well this is all that is intended by the clause under consideration; with the addition of a federal power that shall be sufficient to oblige a delinquent state to comply with the requisition. Such power must exist somewhere, or the debts of the United States can never be paid. For want of such power, our credit is lost and our national faith is a byword.

For want of such power, one state now complies fully with a requisition, another partially, and a third absolutely refuses or neglects to grant a shilling. Thus the honest and punctual are doubly loaded—and the knave triumphs in his negligence. In short, no honest man will dread a power that shall enforce an equitable system of taxation. The dishonest are ever apprehensive of a power that shall oblige them to do what honest men are ready to do voluntarily.

Permit me to ask those who object to this power of taxation, how shall money be raised to discharge our honest debts which are universally acknowledged to be just? Have we not already experienced the inefficacy of a system without power? Has it not been proved to demonstration, that a voluntary compliance with the demands of the union can never be expected? To what expedient shall we have recourse? What is the resort of all governments in cases of delinquency? Do not the states vest in the legislature, or even in the governor and council, a power to enforce laws, even with the militia of the states? And how rarely does there exist the necessity of exerting such a power? Why should such a power be more dangerous in Congress than in a legislature? Why should more confidence be reposed in a member of one legislature than of another? Why should we choose the best men in the state to represent us in Congress, and the moment they are elected arm ourselves against them as against tyrants and robbers? Do we not, in this conduct, act the part of a man, who, as soon as he has married a woman of unsuspected chastity, locks her up in a dungeon? Is there any spell or charm, that instantly changes a delegate to Congress from an honest man into a knave—a tyrant? I confess freely that I am willing to trust Congress with any powers that I should dare lodge in a state legislature. I believe life, liberty, and property is as safe in the hands of a federal legislature, organized in the manner proposed by the convention, as in the hands of any legislature, that has ever been or ever will be chosen in any particular state.

But the idea that Congress can levy taxes *at pleasure* is false, and the suggestion wholly unsupported. The preamble to the constitution is declaratory of the purposes of our union, and the assumption of any powers not necessary to *establish justice, insure domestic tranquillity, provide for the common defense, promote the general welfare, and secure the blessings of liberty to ourselves and our posterity,* will be unconstitutional, and endanger the existence of Congress. Besides, in the very clause which gives the power of levying duties and taxes, the purposes to which the money shall be appropriated are specified, viz. *to pay the debts and provide for the common defense and general welfare of the United States.*[23] For these purposes money must be collected, and the power of collection must be lodged, sooner or later, in a federal head; or the common defense and general welfare must be neglected.

The states in their separate capacity, cannot provide for the *common* defense; nay in case of a civil war, a state cannot secure its own existence. The only question therefore is, whether it is necessary to unite, and provide for our *common defense and general welfare.* For this question being once decided in the affirmative, leaves no room to controvert the propriety of constituting a power over the whole United States, adequate to these general purposes.

The states, by granting such power, do not throw it out of their own hands—they only throw, each its proportion, into a common stock—they merely combine the powers of the several states into one point, where they *must* be collected, before they *can* be exerted. But the powers are still in their own hands; and cannot be alienated, until they create a body independent of themselves, with a force at their command, superior to the whole yeomanry of the country.

6. It is said there is no provision made in the new constitution against a standing army in time of peace. Why do not people object that no provision is made against the introduction of a body of Turkish Janissaries; or against making the Koran the rule of faith and practice, instead of the Bible? The answer to such objections is simply this—*no such provision is necessary.* The people in this country cannot forget their apprehensions from a British standing army, quartered in America; and they turn their fears and jealousies against themselves. Why do not the people of most of the states apprehend danger from standing armies from their own legislatures? Pennsylvania and North Carolina, I believe, are the only states that have provided against this danger at all events. Other states have declared

---

23. The clause may at first appear ambiguous. It may be uncertain whether we should read and understand it thus—"The Congress shall have power to lay and collect taxes, duties, imposts, and excises *in order to pay the debts,*" etc. or whether the meaning is—"The Congress shall have power to lay and collect taxes, duties, imposts, and excises, and *shall have power to pay the debts,*" etc. On considering the construction of the clause, and comparing it with the preamble, the last sense seems to be improbable and absurd. But it is not very material; for no powers are vested in Congress but what are included under the general expressions, *of providing for the common defense and general welfare of the United States.* Any powers not promotive of these purposes, will be unconstitutional;—consequently any appropriations of money to any other purpose will expose the Congress to the resentment of the states, and the members to impeachment and loss of their seats. (Webster)

that "no standing armies shall be kept up without the consent of the legislature." But this leaves the power entirely in the hands of the legislature. Many of the states however have made *no provision* against this evil. What hazards these states suffer! Why does not a man pass a law in his family, that no armed soldier shall be quartered in his house by his consent? The reason is very plain: no man will suffer his liberty to be abridged, or endangered—his disposition and his power are uniformly opposed to any infringement of his rights. In the same manner, the principles and habits, as well as the power of the Americans are directly opposed to standing armies; and there is as little necessity to guard against them by positive constitutions, as to prohibit the establishment of the Mohammedan religion. But the constitution provides for our safety; and while it gives Congress power to raise armies, it declares that no appropriation of money to their support shall be for a longer term than two years.

Congress likewise are to have power to provide for organizing, arming, and disciplining the militia, but have no other command of them, except when in actual service. Nor are they at liberty to call out the militia at pleasure—but only, to execute the laws of the union, suppress insurrections, and repel invasions. For these purposes, government must always be armed with a military force, if the occasion should require it; otherwise laws are nugatory, and life and property insecure.

7. Some persons have ventured to publish an intimation, that by the proposed constitution, the trial by jury is abolished in all *civil cases*. Others very modestly insinuate, that it is in *some cases* only. The fact is, that trial by jury is not affected in *any* case, by the constitution; except in cases of impeachment, which are to be tried by the senate. None but persons in office in or under Congress can be impeached; and even after a judgment upon an impeachment, the offender is liable to a prosecution, before a common jury, in a regular course of law. The insinuation therefore that trials by jury are to be abolished, is groundless, and beyond conception, wicked. It must be wicked, because the circulation of a barefaced falsehood, respecting a privilege, dear to freemen, can proceed only from a depraved heart and the worst intentions.

8. It is also intimated as a probable event, that the federal courts will absorb the judiciaries of the federal states. This is a mere suspicion, without the least foundation. The jurisdiction of the federal states is very accurately defined and easily understood. It extends to the cases mentioned in the constitution, and to the execution of the laws of Congress, respecting commerce, revenue, and other general concerns.

With respect to other civil and criminal actions, the powers and jurisdiction of the several judiciaries of each state, remain unimpaired. Nor is there anything novel in allowing appeals to the supreme court. Actions are mostly to be tried in the state where the crimes are committed—But appeals are allowed under our present confederation, and no person complains; nay, were there no appeal, every man would have reason to complain, especially when a final judgment, in an inferior court, should affect property to a large amount. But why is an objection raised against an appellate jurisdiction in the supreme court, respecting *fact* as well as *law?* Is it less safe to have the opinions of two juries than of one? I suspect many people will think this is no defect in the constitution. But perhaps it will destroy a material requisite of a good jury, viz. their vicinity to the cause of action. I have no doubt, that when causes were tried, in periods prior to the Christian era, before twelve men, seated upon twelve stones, arranged in a circular form, under a huge oak, there was great propriety in submitting causes to men *in the vicinity.* The difficulty of collecting evidence, in those rude times, rendered it necessary that juries should judge mostly from their own knowledge of facts or from information obtained out of court. But in these polished ages, when juries depend almost wholly on the testimony of witnesses; and when a complication of interests, introduced by commerce and other causes, renders it almost impossible to collect men, in the vicinity of the parties, who are wholly disinterested, it is no disadvantage to have a cause tried by a jury of strangers. Indeed the latter is generally the most eligible.

But the truth is, the creation of all inferior courts is in the power of Congress; and the constitution provides that Congress may make such exceptions from the right of appeals as they shall judge proper. When these courts are erected, their jurisdictions will be ascertained, and in small actions, Congress will doubtless direct that a sentence in a subordinate court shall, to a certain amount, be definite and final. All objections therefore to the judicial powers of the federal courts appear to me as trifling as any of the preceding.

9. But, say the enemies of slavery, Negroes may be imported for twenty-one years. This exception is addressed to the Quakers; and a very pitiful exception it is.

The truth is, Congress cannot prohibit the importation of slaves during that period; but the laws against the importation into particular states, stand unrepealed. An immediate abolition of slavery would bring ruin upon the whites, and misery upon the blacks, in the southern states. The constitution has therefore wisely left each state to pursue its own measures, with respect to this article of legislation, during the period of twenty-one years.

Such are the principal objections that have yet been made by the enemies of the new constitution. They are mostly frivolous, or founded on false constructions, and a misrepresentation of the true state of facts.

They are evidently designed to raise groundless jealousies in the minds of well-meaning people, who have little leisure and opportunity to examine into the principles of government. But a little time and reflection will enable most people to detect such mischievous intentions; and the spirit and firmness which have distinguished the conduct of the Americans, during the conflict for independence, will eventually triumph over the enemies of union, and bury them in disgrace or oblivion.

But I cannot quit this subject without attempting to correct some of the erroneous opinions respecting *freedom and tyranny*, and the principles by which they are supported. Many people seem to entertain an idea, that liberty consists in *a power to act without any control*. This is more liberty than even the savages enjoy. But in civil society, political liberty consists in *acting conformably to a sense of a majority of the society*. In a free government every man binds himself to obey the *public voice*, or the opinions of a majority; and the *whole society* engages to *protect each individual*. In such a government a man is *free* and safe. But reverse the case; suppose every man to act without control or fear of punishment—every man would be free, but no man would be sure of his freedom one moment. Each would have the power of taking his neighbor's life, liberty, or property; and no man would command more than his own strength to repel the invasion.[24] The case is the same with states. If the states should not unite into one compact society, every state may trespass upon its neighbor, and the injured state has no means of redress but its own military force.

The present situation of our American states is very little better than a state of nature—Our boasted state sovereignties are so far from securing our liberty and property, that they, every moment, expose us to the loss of both. That state which commands the heaviest purse and longest sword, may at any moment, lay its weaker neighbor under tribute; and there is no superior power now existing, that can regularly oppose the invasion or redress the injury. From such liberty, O Lord, deliver us!

But what is tyranny? Or how can a free people be deprived of their liberties? Tyranny is the exercise of some power over a man, which is not warranted by law, or necessary for the public safety. A people can never be deprived of their liberties, while they retain in their own hands, a power sufficient to any other power in the state. This position leads me directly to inquire, in what consists the power of a nation or of an order of men?

In some nations, legislators have derived much of their power from the influence of religion, or from that implicit belief which an ignorant and superstitious people entertain of the gods, and their interposition in every transaction of life. The Roman senate sometimes availed themselves of

---

24. [This argument is clearly derived directly from Hobbes.]

this engine to carry their decrees and maintain their authority. This was particularly the case, under the aristocracy which succeeded the abolition of the monarchy. The augurs and priests were taken wholly from patrician families.[25] They constituted a distinct order of men—had power to negative any law of the people, by declaring that it was passed during the taking of the auspices.[26] This influence derived from the authority of opinion, was less perceptible, but as tyrannical as a military force. The same influence constitutes, at this day, a principal support of federal governments on the Eastern continent, and perhaps in South America. But in North America, by a singular concurrence of circumstances, the possibility of establishing this influence, as a pillar of government, is totally precluded.

Another source of power in government is a military force. But this, to be efficient, must be superior to any force that exists among the people, or which they can command: for otherwise this force would be annihilated, on the first exercise of acts of oppression. Before a standing army can rule, the people must be disarmed; as they are in almost every kingdom in Europe. The supreme power in America cannot enforce unjust laws by the sword; because the whole body of the people are armed, and constitute a force superior to any band of regular troops that can be, on any pretense, raised in the United States. A military force, at the command of Congress, can execute no laws, but such as the people perceive to be just and constitutional; for they will possess the *power,* and jealousy will instantly inspire the *inclination,* to resist the execution of a law which appears to them unjust and oppressive. In spite of all the nominal powers, vested in Congress by the constitution, were the system once adopted in its fullest latitude, still the actual exercise of them would be frequently interrupted by popular jealousy. I am bold to say, that *ten* just and constitutional measures would be resisted, where *one* unjust or oppressive law would be enforced. The powers vested in Congress are little more than *nominal;* nay *real* power cannot be vested in them, nor in any body, but in the *people.* The source of power is in the *people* of this country, and cannot for ages, and probably never will, be removed.

In what then does *real* power consist? The answer is short and plain— in *property.* Could we want any proofs of this, which are not exhibited in

---

25. "Quod nemo plebeius auspicia haberet, ideoque decemviros connubium diremisse, ne incerta prole auspicia turbarentur." Titus Livius lib. 4. cap. 6. (Webster)

26. "Auguriis certe sacerdotisque augurum tantus honos accessit, ut nihil belli domique postea, nisi auspicato, gereretur: concilia populi, exercitus vocati, summa rerum, ubi aves non admisissent, dirimerentur." Livius lib. 1. cap. 37. (Webster)

this country, the uniform testimony of history will furnish us with multitudes. But I will go no further for proof, than the two governments already mentioned, the Roman and the British.

Rome exhibited a demonstrative proof of the inseparable connection between property and dominion. The first form of its government was an elective monarchy—its second, an aristocracy; but these forms could not be permanent, because they were not supported by property. The kings at first and afterward the patricians had nominally most of the power; but the people, possessing most of the lands, never ceased to assert their privileges, until they established a commonwealth. And the kings and senate could not have held the reins of government in their hands so long as they did, had they not artfully contrived to manage the established religion, and play off the superstitious credulity of the people against their own power. "Thus this weak constitution of government," says the ingenious Mr. Moyle, speaking of the aristocracy of Rome, "not founded on the true *center of dominion, land,* nor on any standing foundation of authority, nor riveted in the esteem and affections of the people; and being attacked by strong passion, general interest, and the joint forces of the people, moldered away of course, and pined of a lingering consumption, until it was totally swallowed up by the prevailing faction, and the nobility were molded into the mass of the people."[27] The people, notwithstanding the nominal authority of the patricians, proceeded regularly in enlarging their own powers. They first extorted from the senate, the right of electing *tribunes,* with a negative upon the proceedings of the senate.[28] They obtained the right of proposing and debating laws; which before had been vested in the senate; and finally advanced to the power of enacting laws, without the authority of the senate.[29] They regained the rights of election in their comitia, of which they had been deprived by Servius Tullius.[30] They procured a permanent body of laws, collected from the Grecian institutions. They destroyed the influence of augurs, or diviners, by establishing the *tributa comitia,* in which they were not allowed to consult the gods. They increased their power by large accessions of conquered lands. They procured a repeal of the law which prohibited marriages

---

27. *Essay on the Roman government.* (Webster) [Walter Moyle wrote the *Essay* in the 1690s, but it was published posthumously in 1727. Moyle followed Harrington in his emphasis on property.]

28. Livy, 2.33. (Webster)

29. Livy, 3.54. (Webster)

30. Livy, 3.33. (Webster)

between the patricians and plebeians.[31] The Licinian law limited all possessions to five hundred acres of land; which, had it been fully executed, would have secured the commonwealth.[32]

The Romans proceeded thus step by step to triumph over the aristocracy, and to crown their privileges, they procured the right of being elected to the highest offices of the state. By acquiring *the property* of the plebeians, the nobility, several times, held most of the power of the state; but the people, by reducing the interest of money, abolishing debts, or by forcing other advantages from the patricians, generally held the power of governing in their own hands.

In America, we begin our empire with more popular privileges than the Romans ever enjoyed. We have not to struggle against a monarch or an aristocracy—power is lodged in the mass of the people.

On reviewing the English history, we observe a progress similar to that in Rome—an incessant struggle for liberty from the date of Magna Carta, in John's reign, to the revolution. The struggle has been successful, by abridging the enormous power of the nobility. But we observe that the power of the people has increased in an exact proportion to their acquisitions of property. Wherever the right of primogeniture is established, property must accumulate and remain in families. Thus the landed property in England will never be sufficiently distributed, to give the powers of government wholly into the hands of the people. But to assist the struggle for liberty, commerce has interposed, and in conjunction with manufactures, thrown a vast weight of property into the democratic scale. Wherever we cast our eyes, we see this truth, that *property* is the basis *of power;* and this, being established as a cardinal point, directs us to the means of preserving our freedom. Make laws, irrevocable laws in every state, destroying and barring entailments; leave real estates to revolve from hand to hand, as time and accident may direct; and no family influence can be acquired and established for a series of generations—no man can obtain dominion over a large territory—the laborious and saving, who are generally the best citizens, will possess each his share of property and power, and thus the balance of wealth and power will continue where it is, in the *body of the people.*[33]

A general and tolerably equal distribution of landed property is the whole basis of national freedom: The system of the great Montesquieu will ever be erroneous, until the words *property or lands in fee simple* are substituted for *virtue,* throughout his *Spirit of Laws.*

---

31. Livy, 4.6. (Webster)

32. Livy, 6.35, 42. "Ne quis plus quingenta jugera agri possideret." (Webster)

33. [Legislation limiting the size of inherited estates was a fundamental plank of the Harringtonian program.]

Virtue, patriotism, or love of country, never was and never will be, until men's natures are changed, a fixed, permanent principle and support of government. But in an agricultural country, a general possession of land in fee simple, may be rendered perpetual, and the inequalities introduced by commerce, are too fluctuating to endanger government. An equality of property, with a necessity of alienation, constantly operating to destroy combinations of powerful families, is the very *soul of a republic*—While this continues, the people will inevitably possess both *power* and *freedom;* when this is lost, power departs, liberty expires, and a commonwealth will inevitably assume some other form.

The liberty of the press, trial by jury, the Habeas Corpus writ, even Magna Carta itself, although justly deemed the palladia of freedom, are all inferior considerations, when compared with a general distribution of real property among every class of people.[34] The power of entailing estates is

---

34. Montesquieu supposed *virtue* to be the principle of a republic. He derived his notions of this form of government, from the astonishing firmness, courage, and patriotism which distinguished the republics of Greece and Rome. But this *virtue* consisted in pride, contempt of strangers, and a martial enthusiasm which sometimes displayed itself in defense of their country. These principles are never permanent—they decay with refinement, intercourse with other nations, and increase of wealth. No wonder then that these republics declined, for they were not founded on fixed principles; and hence authors imagine that republics cannot be durable. None of the celebrated writers on government seems to have laid sufficient stress on a general possession of real property in fee simple. Even the author of the *Political Sketches,* in the *Museum* for the month of September, seems to have passed it over in silence; although he combats Montesquieu's system, and to prove it false, enumerates some of the principles which distinguish our governments from others, and which he supposes constitutes the support of republics.

The English writers on law and government consider Magna Carta, trial by juries, the Habeas Corpus act, and the liberty of the press, as the bulwarks of freedom. All this is well. But in no government of consequence in Europe, is freedom established on its true and immovable foundation. The property is too much accumulated, and the accumulations too well guarded, to admit the *true principle of republics.* But few centuries have elapsed, since the body of the people were vassals. To such men, the smallest extension of popular privileges, was deemed an invaluable blessing. Hence the encomiums upon trial by juries, and the articles just mentioned. But these people have never been able to mount to the source of *liberty, estates in fee,* or at least but partially; they are yet obliged to drink at the streams. Hence the English jealousy of certain rights, which are guaranteed by acts of parliament. But in America, and here alone, we have gone at once to the *fountain of liberty,* and raised the people to their true dignity. Let the lands be possessed by the people in fee simple, let the fountain be kept pure, and the streams will be pure of course. Our jealousy of *trial by jury, the liberty of the press,* etc., is

more dangerous to liberty and republican government, than all the constitutions that can be written on paper, or even than a standing army.[35] Let the people have property, and they *will* have power—a power that will forever be exerted to prevent a restriction of the press, and abolition of trial by jury, or the abridgment of any other privilege. The liberties of America, therefore, and her forms of government, stand on the broadest basis. Removed from the fears of a foreign invasion and conquest, they are not exposed to the convulsions that shake other governments; and the principles of freedom are so general and energetic, as to exclude the possibility of a change in our republican constitutions.

But while *property* is considered as the *basis* of the freedom of the American yeomanry, there are other auxiliary supports; among which is the *information of the people.* In no country, is education so general—in no country, have the body of the people such a knowledge of the rights of men and the principles of government. This knowledge, joined with a keen sense of liberty and a watchful jealousy, will guard our constitutions, and awaken the people to an instantaneous resistance of encroachments.

But a principal bulwark of freedom is the *right of election.* An equal distribution of property is the *foundation* of a republic; but *popular elections* form the *great barrier,* which defends it from assault, and guards it from the slow and imperceptible approaches of corruption. Americans! never resign that right. It is not very material whether your representatives are elected for one year or two—but the *right* is the Magna Carta of your governments. For this reason, expunge that clause of the new constitution before mentioned, which gives Congress an influence in the election of their own body. The *time, places,* and *manner* of choosing senators or representatives are of little or no consequence to Congress. The number of members and time of meeting in Congress are fixed; but the *choice* should rest with the several states. *I* repeat it—reject the clause with decency, but with unanimity and firmness.

Excepting that clause the constitution is good—it guarantees the *fundamental principles* of our several constitutions—it guards our rights—and while it vests extensive powers in Congress, it vests no more than are necessary for our union. Without powers lodged somewhere in a single body, fully competent to lay and collect equal taxes and duties—to adjust

---

totally groundless. Such rights are inseparably connected with the *power* and *dignity* of the people, which rest on their *property.* They cannot be abridged. All *other* nations have wrested *property* and *freedom* from *barons* and *tyrants; we* begin our empire with full possession of property and all its attending rights. (Webster)

35. [An entail meant that an estate could not be sold or broken up, but had to be preserved intact from generation to generation.]

controversies between different states—to silence contending interests—to suppress insurrections—to regulate commerce—to treat with foreign nations, our confederation is a cobweb—liable to be blown asunder by every blast of faction that is raised in the remotest corner of the United States.

Every motive that can possibly influence men ever to unite under civil government, now urges the unanimous adoption of the new constitution. But in America we are urged to it by a singular necessity. By the local situation of the several states *a few* command *all* the advantages of commerce. Those states which have no advantages, made equal exertions for independence, loaded themselves with immense debts, and now are utterly unable to discharge them; while their richer neighbors are taxing them for their own benefit, merely because they *can*. I can prove to a demonstration that Connecticut, which has the heaviest internal or state debt, in proportion to its number of inhabitants, of any in the union, cannot discharge its debt, on any principles of taxation ever yet practiced. Yet the state pays in duties, at least $100,000 annually, on goods consumed by its own people, but imported by[36] New York. This sum, could it be saved to the state by an equal system of revenue, would enable that state to gradually sink[37] its debt.[38]

New Jersey and some other states are in the same situation, except that their debts are not so large, in proportion to their wealth and population.

The boundaries of the several states were not drawn with a view to independence; and while this country was subject to Great Britain, they produced no commercial or political inconveniences. But the revolution has placed things on a different footing. The advantages of some states, and the disadvantages of others are so great—and so materially affect the business and interest of each, that nothing but an equalizing system of revenue, that shall reduce the advantages to some equitable proportion, can prevent a civil war and save the national debt. Such a system of revenue is the *sine qua non* of public justice and tranquillity.

It is absurd for a man to oppose the adoption of the constitution, because *he* thinks some part of it defective or exceptionable. Let every man be at liberty to expunge what *he* judges to be exceptionable, and not a syllable of the constitution will survive the scrutiny. A painter, after executing a masterly piece, requested every spectator to draw a pencil mark

---

36. [I.e., from.]

37. [I.e., pay off.]

38. The state debt of Connecticut is about $3,500,000, its proportion of the federal debt about the same sum. The annual interest of the whole $420,000. (Webster)

over the part that did not please him; but to his surprise, he soon found the *whole piece* defaced. Let every man examine the most perfect building by his *own* taste, and like some microscopic critics, condemn the *whole* for small deviations from the rules of architecture, and not a part of the *best* constructed fabric would escape. But let *any* man take a *comprehensive view* of the whole, and he will be pleased with the general beauty and proportions, and admire the structure. The same remarks apply to the new constitution. I have no doubt that *every* member of the late convention has exceptions to *some part* of the system proposed. Their constituents have the same, and if *every* objection must be removed, before we have a national government, the Lord have mercy on us.

Perfection is not the lot of humanity. Instead of censuring the small faults of the constitution, I am astonished that so many clashing interests have been reconciled—and so many sacrifices made to the *general interest!* The mutual concessions made by the gentlemen of the convention, reflect the highest honor on their candor and liberality; at the same time, they prove that their minds were deeply impressed with a conviction, that such mutual sacrifices are *essential to our union.* They *must* be made sooner or later by every state; or jealousies, local interests, and prejudices will unsheathe the sword, and some Caesar or Cromwell will avail himself of our divisions, and wade to a throne through streams of blood.

It is not our duty as freemen, to receive the opinions of any men however great and respectable, without an examination. But when we reflect that some of the greatest men in America, with the venerable FRANKLIN and the illustrious WASHINGTON at their head; *some* of them the *fathers* and *saviors* of their country, men who have labored at the helm during a long and violent tempest, and guided us to the haven of peace—and *all* of them distinguished for their abilities [and] their acquaintance with ancient and modern governments, as well as with the temper, the passions, the interests, and the wishes of the Americans;—when we reflect on these circumstances, it is impossible to resist impressions of respect, and we are almost impelled to suspect our own judgments, when we call in question any part of the system, which they have recommended for adoption. Not having the same means of information, we are more liable to mistake the nature and tendency of particular articles of the constitution, or the reasons on which they were admitted. Great confidence therefore should be reposed in the abilities, the zeal, and integrity of that respectable body. But after all, if the constitution should, in its future operation, be found defective or inconvenient, two-thirds of both houses of Congress or the application of two-thirds of the legislatures, may open the door for amendments. Such improvements may then be made, as experience shall dictate.

Let us then consider the *New Federal Constitution*, as it really is, an *improvement* on the *best* constitutions that the world ever saw. In the house of representatives, the people of America have an equal voice and suffrage. The choice of men is placed in the freemen or electors at large; and the frequency of elections, and the responsibility of the members, will render them sufficiently dependent on their constituents. The senate will be composed of older men; and while their regular dismission from office, once in six years, will preserve their dependence on their constituents, the duration of their existence will give firmness to their decisions, and temper the factions which must necessarily prevail in the other branch. The president of the United States is elective, and what is a capital improvement on the best governments, the mode of choosing him excludes the danger of faction and corruption. As the supreme executive, he is invested with power to enforce the laws of the union and give energy to the federal government.

The constitution defines the powers of Congress; and every power not expressly delegated to that body, remains in the several state legislatures. The sovereignty and the republican form of government of each state is guaranteed by the constitution; and the bounds of jurisdiction between the federal and respective state governments, are marked with precision. In theory, it has all the energy and freedom of the British and Roman governments, without their defects. In short, the privileges of freemen are interwoven into the feelings and habits of the Americans; *liberty* stands on the immovable basis of a general distribution of property and diffusion of knowledge; but the Americans must cease to contend, to fear, and to hate, before they can realize the benefits of independence and government, or enjoy the blessings, which heaven has lavished, in rich profusion, upon this western world.

The *Federalist*

No. 1 [Hamilton]

INTRODUCTION

After an unequivocal experience of the inefficacy of the subsisting Federal
Government, you are called upon to deliberate on a new Constitution for
the United States of America. The subject speaks its own importance;
comprehending in its consequences, nothing less than the existence of the
UNION, the safety and welfare of the parts of which it is composed, the
fate of an empire, in many respects, the most interesting in the world. It
has been frequently remarked, that it seems to have been reserved to the
people of this country, by their conduct and example, to decide the
important question, whether societies of men are really capable or not, of
establishing good government from reflection and choice, or whether they
are forever destined to depend, for their political constitutions, on accident and force. If there be any truth in the remark, the crisis, at which we
are arrived, may with propriety be regarded as the era in which that decision is to be made; and a wrong election of the part we shall act, may, in
this view, deserve to be considered as the general misfortune of mankind.

This idea will add the inducements of philanthropy to those of patriotism to heighten the solicitude, which all considerate and good men must
feel for the event. Happy will it be if our choice should be decided[1] by a
judicious estimate of our true interests, unperplexed and unbiased by
considerations not connected with the public good. But this is a thing
more ardently to be wished, than seriously to be expected. The plan
offered to our deliberations, affects too many particular interests, inno-
vates upon too many local institutions, not to involve in its discussion a
variety of objects foreign to its merits, and of views, passions, and prejudices little favorable to the discovery of truth.

Among the most formidable of the obstacles which the new Constitution will have to encounter, may readily be distinguished the obvious
interest of a certain class of men in every State to resist all changes which
may hazard a diminution of the power, emolument, and consequence of
the offices they hold under the State establishments—and the perverted
ambition of another class of men, who will either hope to aggrandize

---

1. [McLean substitutes "directed."]

themselves by the confusions of their country, or will flatter themselves with fairer prospects of elevation from the subdivision of the empire into several partial confederacies, than from its union under one government.

It is not, however, my design to dwell upon observations of this nature. I am well aware that it would be disingenuous to resolve indiscriminately the opposition of any set of men (merely because their situations might subject them to suspicion) into interested or ambitious views: Candor will oblige us to admit, that even such men may be actuated by upright intentions; and it cannot be doubted that much of the opposition which has made its appearance, or may hereafter make its appearance, will spring from sources, blameless at least, if not respectable, the honest errors of minds led astray by preconceived jealousies and fears. So numerous indeed and so powerful are the causes, which serve to give a false bias to the judgment, that we upon many occasions, see wise and good men on the wrong as well as on the right side of questions, of the first magnitude to society. This circumstance, if duly attended to, would furnish a lesson of moderation to those, who are ever so much persuaded of their being in the right, in any controversy. And a further reason for caution, in this respect, might be drawn from the reflection, that we are not always sure, that those who advocate the truth are influenced by purer principles than their antagonists. Ambition, avarice, personal animosity, party opposition, and many other motives, not more laudable than these, are apt to operate as well upon those who support as upon those who oppose the right side of a question. Were there not even these inducements to moderation, nothing could be more ill-judged than that intolerant spirit, which has, at all times, characterized political parties. For, in politics as in religion, it is equally absurd to aim at making proselytes by fire and sword. Heresies in either can rarely be cured by persecution.

And yet however just these sentiments will be allowed to be, we have already sufficient indications, that it will happen in this as in all former cases of great national discussion. A torrent of angry and malignant passions will be let loose. To judge from the conduct of the opposite parties, we shall be led to conclude, that they will mutually hope to evince the justness of their opinions, and to increase the number of their converts by the loudness of their declamations, and by the bitterness of their invectives. An enlightened zeal for the energy and efficiency of government will be stigmatized, as the offspring of a temper fond of despotic power and hostile to the principles of liberty. An over-scrupulous jealousy of danger to the rights of the people, which is more commonly the fault of the head than of the heart, will be represented as mere pretense and artifice; the bait[2] for popularity at the expense of public good. It will

---

2. [McLean and later editions have "stale bait."]

be forgotten, on the one hand, that jealousy is the usual concomitant of violent love, and that the noble enthusiasm of liberty is too apt to be infected with a spirit of narrow and illiberal distrust. On the other hand, it will be equally forgotten, that the vigor of government is essential to the security of liberty; that, in the contemplation of a sound and well-informed judgment, their interests can never be separated; and that a dangerous ambition more often lurks behind the specious mask of zeal for the rights of the people, than under the forbidding appearance of zeal for the firmness and efficiency of government. History will teach us, that the former has been found a much more certain road to the introduction of despotism, than the latter, and that of those men who have overturned the liberties of republics the greatest number have begun their career, by paying an obsequious court to the people, commencing Demagogues and ending Tyrants.

In the course of the preceding observations I have had an eye, my Fellow Citizens, to putting you upon your guard against all attempts, from whatever quarter, to influence your decision in a matter of the utmost moment to your welfare by any impressions other than those which may result from the evidence of truth. You will, no doubt, at the same time, have collected from the general scope of them that they proceed from a source not unfriendly to the new Constitution. Yes, my Countrymen, I own to you, that, after having given it an attentive consideration, I am clearly of opinion, it is your interest to adopt it. I am convinced, that this is the safest course for your liberty, your dignity, and your happiness. I affect not reserves, which I do not feel. I will not amuse you with an appearance of deliberation, when I have decided. I frankly acknowledge to you my convictions, and I will freely lay before you the reasons on which they are founded. The consciousness of good intentions disdains ambiguity. I shall not however multiply professions on this head. My motives must remain in the depository of my own breast: My arguments will be open to all, and may be judged of by all. They shall at least be offered in a spirit, which will not disgrace the cause of truth.

I propose in a series of papers to discuss the following interesting particulars—The utility of the UNION to your political prosperity—The insufficiency of the present Confederation to preserve that Union—The necessity of a government at least equally energetic with the one proposed to the attainment of this object—The conformity of the proposed constitution to the true principles of republican government—Its analogy to your own state constitution—and lastly, The additional security, which its adoption will afford to the preservation of that species of government, to liberty and to property.

In the progress of this discussion I shall endeavor to give a satisfactory answer to all the objections which shall have made their appearance that may seem to have any claim to your attention.

It may perhaps be thought superfluous to offer arguments to prove the utility of the UNION, a point, no doubt, deeply engraved on the hearts of the great body of the people in every state, and one, which it may be imagined has no adversaries. But the fact is, that we already hear it whispered in the private circles of those who oppose the new constitution, that the Thirteen States are of too great extent for any general system, and that we must of necessity resort to separate confederacies of distinct portions of the whole.[3] This doctrine will, in all probability, be gradually propagated, until it has votaries enough to countenance an open avowal of it. For nothing can be more evident, to those who are able to take an enlarged view of the subject, than the alternative of an adoption of the new Constitution, or a dismemberment of the Union. It will therefore be of use to begin by examining the advantages of that Union, the certain evils and the probable dangers, to which every State will be exposed from its dissolution. This shall accordingly constitute the subject of my next address.

[October 27, 1787]

No. 2   [Jay]

CONCERNING THE DANGERS FROM FOREIGN FORCE AND INFLUENCE

When the people of America reflect that they are now called upon to decide a question, which, in its consequences, must prove one of the most important, that ever engaged their attention, the propriety of their taking a very comprehensive, as well as a very serious view of it, will be evident.

Nothing is more certain than the indispensable necessity of Government, and it is equally undeniable, that whenever and however it is instituted, the people must cede to it some of their natural rights, in order to vest it with requisite powers. It is well worthy of consideration therefore, whether it would conduce more to the interest of the people of America, that they should, to all general purposes, be one nation, under one federal Government, than that they should divide themselves into separate confederacies, and give to the head of each, the same kind of powers which they are advised to place in one national Government.

---

3. The same idea, tracing the arguments to their consequences, is held out in several of the late publications against the New Constitution. (Publius)

It has until lately been a received and uncontradicted opinion, that the prosperity of the people of America depended on their continuing firmly united, and the wishes, prayers, and efforts of our best and wisest Citizens have been constantly directed to that object. But Politicians now appear, who insist that this opinion is erroneous, and that instead of looking for safety and happiness in union, we ought to seek it in a division of the States into distinct confederacies or sovereignties. However extraordinary this new doctrine may appear, it nevertheless has its advocates; and certain characters who were much opposed to it formerly, are at present of the number. Whatever may be the arguments or inducements, which have wrought this change in the sentiments and declarations of these Gentlemen, it certainly would not be wise in the people at large to adopt these new political tenets without being fully convinced that they are founded in truth and sound Policy.

It has often given me pleasure to observe, that Independent America was not composed of detached and distant territories, but that one connected, fertile, wide-spreading country was the portion of our western sons of liberty. Providence has in a particular manner blessed it with a variety of soils and productions, and watered it with innumerable streams, for the delight and accommodation of its inhabitants. A succession of navigable waters forms a kind of chain round its borders, as if to bind it together; while the most noble rivers in the world, running at convenient distances, present them with highways for the easy communication of friendly aids, and the mutual transportation and exchange of their various commodities.

With equal pleasure I have as often taken notice, that Providence has been pleased to give this one connected country, to one united people, a people descended from the same ancestors, speaking the same language, professing the same religion, attached to the same principles of government, very similar in their manners and customs, and who, by their joint counsels, arms, and efforts, fighting side by side throughout a long and bloody war, have nobly established their general Liberty and Independence.

This country and this people seem to have been made for each other, and it appears as if it was the design of Providence, that an inheritance so proper and convenient for a band of brethren, united to each other by the strongest ties, should never be split into a number of unsocial, jealous, and alien sovereignties.

Similar sentiments have hitherto prevailed among all orders and denominations of men among us. To all general purposes we have uniformly been one people—each individual citizen everywhere enjoying the same national rights, privileges, and protection. As a nation we have made peace and war—as a nation we have vanquished our common enemies—

as a nation we have formed alliances and made treaties, and entered into various compacts and conventions with foreign States.

A strong sense of the value and blessings of Union induced the people, at a very early period, to institute a Federal Government to preserve and perpetuate it. They formed it almost as soon as they had a political existence; nay at a time, when their habitations were in flames, when many of their Citizens were bleeding, and when the progress of hostility and desolation left little room for those calm and mature inquiries and reflections, which must ever precede the formation of a wise and well balanced government for a free people. It is not to be wondered at that a Government instituted in times so inauspicious, should on experiment be found greatly deficient and inadequate to the purpose it was intended to answer.

This intelligent people perceived and regretted these defects. Still continuing no less attached to union, than enamored of liberty, they observed the danger, which immediately threatened the former and more remotely the latter; and being persuaded that ample security for both, could only be found in a national Government more wisely framed, they, as with one voice, convened the late Convention at Philadelphia, to take that important subject under consideration.

This Convention, composed of men, who possessed the confidence of the people, and many of whom had become highly distinguished by their patriotism, virtue, and wisdom, in times which tried the minds and hearts of men, undertook the arduous task. In the mild season of peace, with minds unoccupied by other subjects, they passed many months in cool, uninterrupted, and daily consultations: and finally, without having been awed by power, or influenced by any passions except love for their Country, they presented and recommended to the people the plan produced by their joint and very unanimous counsels.

Admit, for so is the fact, that this plan is only *recommended*, not imposed, yet let it be remembered, that it is neither recommended to *blind* approbation, nor to *blind* reprobation; but to that sedate and candid consideration, which the magnitude and importance of the subject demand, and which it certainly ought to receive. But this, (as was remarked in the foregoing number of this Paper,)[4] is more to be wished than expected that it may be so considered and examined. Experience on a former occasion teaches us not to be too sanguine in such hopes. It is not yet forgotten, that well-grounded apprehensions of imminent danger induced the people of America to form the Memorable Congress of 1774. That Body recommended certain measures to their Constituents, and the event proved their wisdom; yet it is fresh in our memories how soon the Press began to

---

4. [Replaced in McLean and later editions to avoid the reference to a "Paper."]

teem with Pamphlets and weekly Papers against those very measures. Not only many of the Officers of Government who obeyed the dictates of personal interest, but others from a mistaken estimate of consequences, or the undue influence of former attachments,[5] or whose ambition aimed at objects which did not correspond with the public good, were indefatigable in their endeavors to persuade the people to reject the advice of that Patriotic Congress. Many indeed were deceived and deluded, but the great majority of the people reasoned and decided judiciously; and happy they are in reflecting that they did so.

They considered that the Congress was composed of many wise and experienced men. That being convened from different parts of the country, they brought with them and communicated to each other a variety of useful information. That in the course of the time they passed together in inquiring into and discussing the true interests of their country, they must have acquired very accurate knowledge on that head. That they were individually interested in the public liberty and prosperity, and therefore that it was not less their inclination, than their duty, to recommend only such measures, as after the most mature deliberation they really thought prudent and advisable.

These and similar considerations then induced the people to rely greatly on the judgment and integrity of the Congress; and they took their advice, notwithstanding the various arts and endeavors used to deter and dissuade them from it. But if the people at large had reason to confide in the men of that Congress, few of whom had then been fully tried or generally known, still greater reason have they now to respect the judgment and advice of the Convention, for it is well-known that some of the most distinguished members of that Congress, who have been since tried and justly approved for patriotism and abilities, and who have grown old in acquiring political information, were also members of this Convention and carried into it their accumulated knowledge and experience.

It is worthy of remark that not only the first, but every succeeding Congress, as well as the late Convention, have invariably joined with the people in thinking that the prosperity of America depended on its Union. To preserve and perpetuate it, was the great object of the people in forming that Convention, and it is also the great object of the plan which the Convention has advised them to adopt. With what propriety therefore, or for what good purposes, are attempts at this particular period, made by some men, to depreciate the importance of the Union? or why is it suggested that three or four confederacies would be better than one? I am persuaded in my own mind, that the people have always thought right on

---

5. ["From . . . ancient attachments" in McLean and later editions.]

this subject, and that their universal and uniform attachment to the cause of the Union, rests on great and weighty reasons, which I shall endeavor to develop and explain in some ensuing papers. They who promote the idea of substituting a number of distinct confederacies in the room of the plan of the Convention, seem clearly to foresee that the rejection of it would put the continuance of the Union in the utmost jeopardy. That certainly would be the case, and I certainly wish that it may be as clearly foreseen by every good Citizen, that whenever the dissolution of the Union arrives, America will have reason to exclaim in the words of the Poet, "FAREWELL, A LONG FAREWELL, TO ALL MY GREATNESS."

[October 31, 1787]

No. 6   [Hamilton]

CONCERNING THE DANGERS FROM WAR BETWEEN THE STATES

The three last numbers of this Paper have been dedicated to an enumeration of the dangers to which we should be exposed, in a state of disunion, from the arms and arts of foreign nations. I shall now proceed to delineate dangers of a different, and, perhaps, still more alarming kind, those which will in all probability flow from dissensions between the States themselves, and from domestic factions and convulsions. These have been already in some instances slightly anticipated, but they deserve a more particular and more full investigation.

A man must be far gone in Utopian speculations who can seriously doubt, that if these States should either be wholly disunited, or only united in partial confederacies, the subdivisions into which they might be thrown would have frequent and violent contests with each other. To presume a want of motives for such contests, as an argument against their existence, would be to forget that men are ambitious, vindictive, and rapacious. To look for a continuation of harmony between a number of independent unconnected sovereignties, situated in the same neighborhood, would be to disregard the uniform course of human events, and to set at defiance the accumulated experience of ages.

The causes of hostility among nations are innumerable. There are some which have a general and almost constant operation upon the collective bodies of society: Of this description are the love of power or the desire of preeminence and dominion—the jealousy of power, or the desire of equality and safety. There are others which have a more circumscribed, though an equally operative influence, within their spheres. Such are the rivalships and competitions of commerce between commercial nations. And there are others, not less numerous than either of the former, which take their origin entirely in private passions; in the attachments, enmities, interests, hopes, and fears of leading individuals in the communities of which they are members. Men of this class, whether the favorites of a king or of a people, have in too many instances abused the confidence they possessed; and assuming the pretext of some public motive, have not scrupled to sacrifice the national tranquillity to personal advantage, or personal gratification.

The celebrated Pericles, in compliance with the resentments of a prostitute,[6] at the expense of much of the blood and treasure of his countrymen, attacked, vanquished, and destroyed, the city of the *Samnians*. The same man, stimulated by private pique against the *Megarensians*,[7] another nation of Greece, or to avoid a prosecution with which he was threatened as an accomplice in a supposed theft of the statuary[8] *Phidias*,[9] or to get rid of the accusations prepared to be brought against him for dissipating the funds of the State in the purchase of popularity,[10] or from a combination of all these causes, was the primitive author of that famous and fatal war, distinguished in the Grecian annals by the name of the *Peloponnesian* war; which, after various vicissitudes, intermissions, and renewals, terminated in the ruin of the Athenian commonwealth.

The ambitious Cardinal,[11] who was Prime Minister to Henry VIIIth, permitting his vanity to aspire to the Triple Crown,[12] entertained hopes of succeeding in the acquisition of that splendid prize by the influence of the Emperor Charles Vth. To secure the favor and interest of this enterprising and powerful Monarch, he precipitated England into a war with France, contrary to the plainest dictates of Policy, and at the hazard of the safety and independence, as well of the Kingdom over which he presided by his counsels, as of Europe in general. For if there ever was a Sovereign who bid fair to realize the project of universal monarchy it was the Emperor Charles Vth, of whose intrigues Wolsey was at once the instrument and the dupe.

---

6. ASPASIA, vide PLUTARCH'S life of Pericles. (Publius)

7. —Idem. (Publius)

8. [I.e., someone who makes statues.]

9. —Idem. Phidias was supposed to have stolen some public gold with the connivance of Pericles for the embellishment of the statue of Minerva. (Publius)

10. Idem. (Publius)

11. [Cardinal Wolsey.]

12. Worn by the Popes. (Publius)

The influence which the bigotry of one female,[13] the petulancies of another,[14] and the cabals of a third,[15] had in the contemporary policy, ferments, and pacifications of a considerable part of Europe are topics that have been too often descanted upon not to be generally known.

To multiply examples of the agency of personal considerations in the production of great national events, either foreign or domestic, according to their direction would be an unnecessary waste of time. Those who have but a superficial acquaintance with the sources from which they are to be drawn will themselves recollect a variety of instances; and those who have a tolerable knowledge of human nature will not stand in need of such lights, to form their opinion either of the reality or extent of that agency. Perhaps however a reference, tending to illustrate the general principle, may with propriety be made to a case which has lately happened among ourselves. If SHAYS had not been a *desperate debtor* it is much to be doubted whether Massachusetts would have been plunged into a civil war.[16]

But notwithstanding the concurring testimony of experience, in this particular, there are still to be found visionary, or designing men, who stand ready to advocate the paradox of perpetual peace between the States, though dismembered and alienated from each other. The genius of republics (say they) is pacific; the spirit of commerce has a tendency to soften the manners of men and to extinguish those inflammable humors which have so often kindled into wars. Commercial republics, like ours, will never be disposed to waste themselves in ruinous contentions with each other. They will be governed by mutual interest, and will cultivate a spirit of mutual amity and concord.

Is it not (we may ask these projectors in politics) the true interest of all nations to cultivate the same benevolent and philosophic spirit? If this be their true interest, have they in fact pursued it? Has it not, on the contrary, invariably been found, that momentary passions and immediate interests have a more active and imperious control over human conduct than general or remote considerations of policy, utility, or justice? Have republics in practice been less addicted to war than monarchies? Are not the former administered by *men* as well as the latter? Are there not aversions, predilections, rivalships, and desires of unjust acquisition that

---

13. Madame De Maintenon. (Publius) [Responsible for persuading Louis XIV to persecute the Huguenots.]

14. Duchess of Marlborough. (Publius) [Influential at the court of Queen Anne.]

15. Madame De Pompadour. (Publius) [Mistress to Louis XV.]

16. [Daniel Shays led a rebellion in Massachusetts in 1786 and early 1787.]

affect nations as well as kings? Are not popular assemblies frequently subject to the impulses of rage, resentment, jealousy, avarice, and of other
irregular and violent propensities? Is it not well-known that their determinations are often governed by a few individuals, in whom they place
confidence, and are of course liable to be tinctured by the passions and
views of those individuals? Has commerce hitherto done anything more
than change the objects of war? Is not the love of wealth as domineering
and enterprising a passion as that of power or glory? Have there not been
as many wars founded upon commercial motives, since that has become
the prevailing system of nations, as were before occasioned by the cupid-
ity of territory or domination? Has not the spirit of commerce in many
instances administered new incentives to the appetite both for the one and
for the other? Let experience the least fallible guide of human opinions be
appealed to for an answer to these inquiries.

Sparta, Athens, Rome, and Carthage were all Republics, two of them,
Athens and Carthage, of the commercial kind. Yet were they as often
engaged in wars, offensive and defensive, as the neighboring Monarchies
of the same times. Sparta was little better than a well-regulated camp; and
Rome was never sated of carnage and conquest.

Carthage, though a commercial Republic, was the aggressor in the very
war that ended in her destruction. Hannibal had carried her arms into the
heart of Italy and to the gates of Rome, before Scipio, in turn, gave him an
overthrow in the territories of Carthage and made a conquest of the Commonwealth.

Venice in latter times figured more than once in wars of ambition; until
becoming an object of terror to the other Italian States, Pope Julius the
Second found means to accomplish that formidable league,[17] which gave a
deadly blow to the power and pride of this haughty Republic.

The Provinces of Holland, until they were overwhelmed in debts and
taxes, took a leading and conspicuous part in the wars of Europe. They
had furious contests with England for the dominion of the sea; and were
among the most persevering and most implacable of the opponents of
Louis XIV.

In the government of Britain the representatives of the people compose one branch of the national legislature. Commerce has been for ages
the predominant pursuit of that country. Few nations, nevertheless, have
been more frequently engaged in war; and the wars, in which that kingdom has been engaged, have in numerous instances proceeded from the
people.

---

17. The League of Cambray, comprehending the Emperor, the King of France,
the King of Aragon, and most of the Italian Princes and States. (Publius)

There have been, if I may so express it, almost as many popular as royal wars. The cries of the nation and the importunities of their representatives have, upon various occasions, dragged their monarchs into war, or continued them in it contrary to their inclinations, and, sometimes, contrary to the real interests of the State. In that memorable struggle for superiority, between the rival Houses of *Austria* and *Bourbon* which so long kept Europe in a flame, it is well-known that the antipathies of the English against the French, seconding the ambition, or rather the avarice of a favorite leader,[18] protracted the war beyond the limits marked out by sound policy and for a considerable time in opposition to the views of the Court.

The wars of these two last mentioned nations have in a great measure grown out of commercial considerations—The desire of supplanting and the fear of being supplanted either in particular branches of traffic or in the general advantages of trade and navigation; and sometimes even the more culpable desire of sharing in the commerce of other nations, without their consent.

The last war but two between Britain and Spain sprang from the attempts of the English merchants, to prosecute an illicit trade with the Spanish main.[19] These unjustifiable practices on their part produced severities on the part of the Spaniards, toward the subjects of Great Britain, which were not more justifiable; because they exceeded the bounds of a just retaliation, and were chargeable with inhumanity and cruelty. Many of the English who were taken on the Spanish coasts were sent to dig in the mines of Potosi; and by the usual progress of a spirit of resentment, the innocent were after a while confounded with the guilty in indiscriminate punishment. The complaints of the merchants kindled a violent flame throughout the nation, which soon after broke out in the house of commons, and was communicated from that body to the ministry. Letters of reprisal were granted and a war ensued, which in its consequences overthrew all the alliances that but twenty years before had been formed, with sanguine expectations of the most beneficial fruits.[20]

From this summary of what has taken place in other countries, whose situations have borne the nearest resemblance to our own, what reason can we have to confide in those reveries, which would seduce us into an expectation of peace and cordiality between the members of the present

---

18. The Duke of Marlborough. (Publius)

19. [The War of Jenkins' Ear (1739).]

20. [The whole of this paragraph, and the end of the preceding one (from "and sometimes") were added in the McLean edition.]

confederacy, in a state of separation? Have we not already seen enough of the fallacy and extravagance of those idle theories which have amused us with promises of an exemption from the imperfections, weaknesses, and evils incident to society in every shape?[21] Is it not time to awake from the deceitful dream of a golden age, and to adopt as a practical maxim for the direction of our political conduct, that we, as well as the other inhabitants of the globe, are yet remote from the happy empire of perfect wisdom and perfect virtue?

Let the point of extreme depression to which our national dignity and credit have sunk—let the inconveniences felt everywhere from a lax and ill administration of government—let the revolt of a part of the State of North Carolina[22]—the late menacing disturbances in Pennsylvania,[23] and the actual insurrections and rebellions in Massachusetts declare!

So far is the general sense of mankind from corresponding with the tenets of those, who endeavor to lull asleep our apprehensions of discord and hostility between the States, in the event of disunion, that it has from long observation of the progress of society become a sort of axiom in politics, that vicinity, or nearness of situation, constitutes nations natural enemies. An intelligent writer expresses himself on this subject to this effect—"NEIGHBORING NATIONS (says he) are naturally ENEMIES of each other, unless their common weakness forces them to league in a CONFEDERATE REPUBLIC, and their constitution prevents the differences that neighborhood occasions, extinguishing that secret jealousy, which disposes all States to aggrandize themselves at the expense of their neighbors."[24] This passage, at the same time points out the EVIL and suggests the REMEDY.

[November 14, 1787]

No. 7   [Hamilton]

THE SUBJECT CONTINUED AND PARTICULAR CAUSES ENUMERATED

It is sometimes asked, with an air of seeming triumph, what inducements could the States have, if disunited, to make war upon each other? It would be a full answer to this question to say—precisely the same inducements,

---

21. ["The weakness . . . the evils" in McLean and later editions.]
22. [1784–7.]
23. [The inhabitants of the Wyoming Valley were threatening to secede.]
24. Vide *Principes des Negotiations* par L'Abbé de Mably. (Publius)

which have, at different times, deluged in blood all the nations in the world. But unfortunately for us, the question admits of a more particular answer. There are causes of difference within our immediate contemplation, of the tendency of which, even under the restraints of a Federal Constitution, we have had sufficient experience, to enable us to form a judgment of what might be expected, if those restraints were removed.

Territorial disputes have at all times been found one of the most fertile sources of hostility among nations. Perhaps the greatest proportion of the wars that have desolated the earth have sprung from this origin. This cause would exist, among us, in full force. We have a vast tract of unsettled territory within the boundaries of the United States. There still are discordant and undecided claims between several of them; and the dissolution of the Union would lay a foundation for similar claims between them all. It is well-known, that they have heretofore had serious and animated discussions concerning the right to the lands which were ungranted at the time of the revolution, and which usually went under the name of crown lands. The States within the limits of whose colonial governments they were comprised have claimed them as their property; the others have contended that the rights of the crown in this article devolved upon the Union; especially as to all that part of the Western territory which either by actual possession or through the submission of the Indian proprietors was subjected to the jurisdiction of the King of Great Britain, until it was relinquished in the treaty of peace. This, it has been said, was at all events an acquisition to the confederacy by compact with a foreign power. It has been the prudent policy of Congress to appease this controversy, by prevailing upon the States to make cessions to the United States for the benefit of the whole. This has been so far accomplished, as under a continuation of the Union, to afford a decided prospect of an amicable termination of the dispute. A dismemberment of the confederacy however would revive this dispute, and would create others on the same subject. At present, a large part of the vacant Western territory is by cession at least, if not by any anterior right, the common property of the Union. If that were at an end, the States which made the cession[25] on a principle of Federal compromise, would be apt, when the motive of the grant had ceased, to reclaim the lands as a reversion. The other States would no doubt insist on a proportion, by right of representation. Their argument would be that a grant, once made, could not be revoked, and that the justice of their participating in territory acquired, or secured by the joint efforts of the confederacy remained undiminished. If contrary to probability it should be admitted by all the States, that each had a right to a

---

25. ["Have made cession" in McLean and subsequent editions.]

share of this common stock, there would still be a difficulty to be surmounted, as to a proper rule of apportionment. Different principles
would be set up by different States for this purpose; and as they would
affect the opposite interests of the parties, they might not easily be susceptible of a pacific adjustment.

In the wide field of Western territory, therefore, we perceive an ample
theater for hostile pretensions, without any umpire or common judge to
interpose between the contending parties. To reason from the past to the
future we shall have good ground to apprehend, that the sword would
sometimes be appealed to as the arbiter of their differences. The circumstances of the dispute between Connecticut and Pennsylvania, respecting
the lands at Wyoming admonish us, not to be sanguine in expecting an
easy accommodation of such differences. The articles of confederation
obliged the parties to submit the matter to the decision of a Federal
Court. The submission was made, and the Court decided in favor of
Pennsylvania. But Connecticut gave strong indications of dissatisfaction
with that determination; nor did she appear to be entirely resigned to it,
until by negotiation and management something like an equivalent was
found for the loss she supposed herself to have sustained.[26] Nothing here
said is intended to convey the slightest censure on the conduct of that
State. She no doubt sincerely believed herself to have been injured by the
decision; and States like individuals acquiesce with great reluctance in
determinations to their disadvantage.

Those, who had an opportunity of seeing the inside of the transactions, which attended the progress of the controversy between this State
and the district of Vermont,[27] can vouch the opposition we experienced, as
well from States not interested as from those which were interested in the
claim; and can attest the danger, to which the peace of the Confederacy
might have been exposed, had this State[28] attempted to assert its rights by
force. Two motives preponderated in that opposition—one a jealousy
entertained of our future power—and the other, the interest of certain
individuals of influence in the neighboring States, who had obtained
grants of lands under the actual government of that district. Even the
States which brought forward claims, in contradiction to ours, seemed
more solicitous to dismember this State, than to establish their own pretensions. These were New Hampshire, Massachusetts, and Connecticut.

---

26. [This was the Western Reserve, some 3,500,000 acres adjoining Lake Erie.]

27. [New York, New Hampshire, and Massachusetts all laid claim to Vermont;
in 1777 Vermont declared independence, but its legal status remained in doubt
until it was admitted to the Union as the fourteenth state in 1791.]

28. [I.e., New York.]

New Jersey and Rhode Island upon all occasions discovered a warm zeal
for the independence of Vermont; and Maryland, until alarmed by the
appearance of a connection between Canada and that place, entered
deeply into the same views. These, being small States, saw with an
unfriendly eye the perspective of our growing greatness. In a review of
these transactions we may trace some of the causes, which would be likely
to embroil the States with each other, if it should be their unpropitious
destiny to become disunited.

The competitions of commerce would be another fruitful source of
contention. The States less favorably circumstanced would be desirous of
escaping from the disadvantages of local situation, and of sharing in the
advantages of their more fortunate neighbors. Each State, or separate confederacy, would pursue a system of commercial polity peculiar to itself.
This would occasion distinctions, preferences, and exclusions, which
would beget discontent. The habits of intercourse, on the basis of equal
privileges, to which we have been accustomed from the earliest settlement
of the country, would give a keener edge to those causes of discontent,
than they would naturally have, independent of this circumstance. *We
should be ready to denominate injuries those things which were in reality the
justifiable acts of independent sovereignties consulting a distinct interest.* The
spirit of enterprise, which characterizes the commercial part of America,
has left no occasion of displaying itself unimproved. It is not at all probable that this unbridled spirit would pay much respect to those regulations
of trade, by which particular States might endeavor to secure exclusive
benefits to their own citizens. The infractions of these regulations on one
side, the efforts to prevent and repel them on the other, would naturally
lead to outrages, and these to reprisals and wars.

The opportunities, which some States would have of rendering others
tributary to them, by commercial regulations, would be impatiently submitted to by the tributary States. The relative situation of New York, Connecticut, and New Jersey, would afford an example of this kind. New
York, from the necessities of revenue, must lay duties on her importations. A great part of these duties must be paid by the inhabitants of the
two other States in the capacity of consumers of what we import. New
York would neither be willing nor able to forego this advantage. Her citizens would not consent that a duty paid by them should be remitted in
favor of the citizens of her neighbors; nor would it be practicable, if there
were not this impediment in the way, to distinguish the customers in our
own markets. Would Connecticut and New Jersey long submit to be taxed
by New York for her exclusive benefit? Should we be long permitted to
remain in the quiet and undisturbed enjoyment of a metropolis, from the
possession of which we derived an advantage so odious to our neighbors,

and, in their opinion, so oppressive? Should we be able to preserve it against the incumbent weight of Connecticut on the one side, and the cooperating pressure of New Jersey on the other? These are questions that temerity alone will answer in the affirmative.

The public debt of the Union would be a further cause of collision between the separate States or confederacies. The apportionment, in the first instance, and the progressive extinguishment, afterward, would be alike productive of ill humor and animosity. How would it be possible to agree upon a rule of apportionment satisfactory to all? There is scarcely any, that can be proposed, which is entirely free from real objections. These, as usual, would be exaggerated by the adverse interests of the parties. There are even dissimilar views among the States, as to the general principle of discharging the public debt. Some of them, either less impressed with the importance of national credit, or because their citizens have little, if any, immediate interest in the question, feel an indifference, if not a repugnance to the payment of the domestic debt, at any rate. These would be inclined to magnify the difficulties of a distribution. Others of them, a numerous body of whose citizens are creditors to the public, beyond the proportion of the State in the total amount of the national debt, would be strenuous for some equitable and effectual provision. The procrastinations of the former would excite the resentments of the latter. The settlement of a rule would in the meantime be postponed, by real differences of opinion and affected delays. The citizens of the States interested, would clamor, foreign powers would urge, for the satisfaction of their just demands; and the peace of the States would be hazarded to the double contingency of external invasion and internal contention.

Suppose the difficulties of agreeing upon a rule surmounted, and the apportionment made. Still there is great room to suppose, that the rule agreed upon would, upon experiment, be found to bear harder upon some States than upon others. Those which were sufferers by it would naturally seek for a mitigation of the burden. The others would as naturally be disinclined to a revision, which was likely to end in an increase of their own encumbrances. Their refusal would be too plausible a pretext to the complaining States to withhold their contributions, not to be embraced with avidity; and the noncompliance of these States with their engagements would be a ground of bitter dissension and altercation. If even the rule adopted should in practice justify the equality of its principle, still delinquencies in payment, on the part of some of the States, would result from a diversity of other causes—the real deficiency of resources—the mismanagement of their finances, accidental disorders in the administration of the government—and in addition to the rest the reluctance with which men commonly part with money for purposes, that have outlived the exigencies which produced them, and interfere with the supply of immediate wants. Delinquencies from whatever causes would be productive of complaints, recriminations, and quarrels. There is perhaps nothing more likely to disturb the tranquillity of nations, than their being bound to mutual contributions for any common object, which does not yield an equal and coincident benefit. For it is an observation as true, as it is trite, that there is nothing men differ so readily about as the payment of money.

Laws in violation of private contracts as they amount to aggressions on the rights of those States, whose citizens are injured by them, may be considered as another probable source of hostility. We are not authorized to expect, that a more liberal or more equitable spirit would preside over the legislations of the individual States hereafter, if unrestrained by any additional checks, than we have heretofore seen, in too many instances, disgracing their several codes. We have observed the disposition to retaliation excited in Connecticut, in consequence of the enormities perpetrated by the legislature of Rhode Island;[29] and we may reasonably infer, that in similar cases, under other circumstances, a war not of *parchment* but of the sword would chastise such atrocious breaches of moral obligation and social justice.

The probability of incompatible alliances between the different States, or confederacies, and different foreign nations, and the effects of this situation upon the peace of the whole, have been sufficiently unfolded in some preceding papers. From the view they have exhibited, of this part of the subject, this conclusion is to be drawn, that America, if not connected at all, or only by the feeble tie of a simple league offensive and defensive, would by the operation of such opposite and jarring alliances be gradually entangled in all the pernicious labyrinths of European politics and wars; and by the destructive contentions of the parts, into which she was divided would be likely to become a prey to the artifices and machinations of powers equally the enemies of them all. *Divide et impera*[30] must be the motto of every nation, that either hates, or fears us.

[November 17, 1787]

---

29. [Rhode Island had introduced legislation unfavorable to creditors; in retaliation Connecticut passed a law forbidding its courts to uphold the claims of Rhode Island creditors against Connecticut debtors; in 1787 Connecticut protested to Congress that the Rhode Island legislation was a violation of the Articles of Confederation.]

30. *Divide and command.* (Publius)

No. 8 [Hamilton]

THE EFFECTS OF INTERNAL WAR IN PRODUCING STANDING ARMIES
AND OTHER INSTITUTIONS UNFRIENDLY TO LIBERTY

Assuming it therefore as an established truth that the several States, in
case of disunion, or such combinations of them as might happen to be
formed out of the wreck of the general confederacy, would be subject to
those vicissitudes of peace and war, of friendship and enmity with each
other, which have fallen to the lot of all neighboring nations not united
under one government, let us enter into a concise detail of some of the
consequences, that would attend such a situation.

War between the States, in the first periods of their separate existence,
would be accompanied with much greater distresses than it commonly is in
those countries, where regular military establishments have long obtained.
The disciplined armies always kept on foot on the continent of Europe,
though they bear a malignant aspect to liberty and economy, have notwithstanding been productive of this signal advantage, of rendering sudden
conquests impracticable, and of preventing that rapid desolation, which
used to mark the progress of war, prior to their introduction. The art of
fortification has contributed to the same ends. The nations of Europe are
encircled with chains of fortified places, which mutually obstruct invasion.
Campaigns are wasted in reducing two or three frontier garrisons, to gain
admittance into an enemy's country. Similar impediments occur at every
step, to exhaust the strength and delay the progress of an invader. Formerly
an invading army would penetrate into the heart of a neighboring country,
almost as soon as intelligence of its approach could be received; but now a
comparatively small force of disciplined troops, acting on the defensive
with the aid of posts, is able to impede and finally to frustrate the enterprises of one much more considerable. The history of war, in that quarter
of the globe, is no longer a history of nations subdued and empires overturned, but of towns taken and retaken, of battles that decide nothing, of
retreats more beneficial than victories, of much effort and little acquisition.

In this country the scene would be altogether reversed. The jealousy of
military establishments, would postpone them as long as possible. The
want of fortifications leaving the frontiers of one State open to another,
would facilitate inroads. The populous States would with little difficulty
overrun their less populous neighbors. Conquests would be as easy to be
made, as difficult to be retained. War therefore would be desultory and
predatory. PLUNDER and devastation ever march in the train of irregu-
lars. The calamities of individuals would make the principal figure in the
events, which would characterize our military exploits.

This picture is not too highly wrought, though I confess, it would not long remain a just one. Safety from external danger is the most powerful director of national conduct. Even the ardent love of liberty will, after a time, give way to its dictates. The violent destruction of life and property incident to war—the continual effort and alarm attendant on a state of continual danger, will compel nations the most attached to liberty, to resort for repose and security, to institutions, which have a tendency to destroy their civil and political rights. To be more safe they, at length, become willing to run the risk of being less free.

The institutions alluded to are STANDING ARMIES, and the correspondent appendages of military establishments. Standing armies it is said are not provided against in the new constitution; and it is therefore inferred, that they may exist under it.[31] Their existence however from the very terms of the proposition, is, at most, problematical and uncertain.[32] But standing armies, it may be replied, must inevitably result from a dissolution of the confederacy. Frequent war and constant apprehension, which require a state of as constant preparation, will infallibly produce them. The weaker States or confederacies, would first have recourse to them, to put themselves upon an equality with their more potent neighbors. They would endeavor to supply the inferiority of population and resources, by a more regular and effective system of defense, by disciplined troops and by fortifications. They would, at the same time, be necessitated to strengthen the executive arm of government; in doing which, their constitutions would acquire a progressive direction toward monarchy. It is of the nature of war to increase the executive at the expense of the legislative authority.

The expedients which have been mentioned, would soon give the States or confederacies that made use of them, a superiority over their neighbors. Small States, or States of less natural strength, under vigorous governments, and with the assistance of disciplined armies, have often triumphed over larger States, or States of greater natural strength, which have been destitute of these advantages. Neither the pride, nor the safety of the more important States, or confederacies, would permit them long to submit to this mortifying and adventitious inferiority. They would

---

31. This objection will be fully examined in its proper place, and it will be shown that the only natural ["rational" in McLean] precaution which could have been taken on this subject has been taken; and a much better one than is to be found in any constitution that has been heretofore framed in America, most of which contain no guard at all on this subject. (Publius) [See Essay 24, below.]

32. ["This inference, from the very form of the proposition, is, at best" in McLean and later editions, which—somewhat inconsistently—replace "may" with "would" in the previous sentence.]

quickly resort to means similar to those by which it had been effected, to reinstate themselves in their lost preeminence. Thus we should in a little time see established in every part of this country, the same engines of despotism, which have been the scourge of the old world. This at least would be the natural course of things, and our reasonings will be the more likely to be just, in proportion as they are accommodated to this standard.

These are not vague inferences drawn from supposed or speculative defects in a constitution, the whole power of which is lodged in the hands of the people, or their representatives and delegates, but they are solid conclusions drawn from the natural and necessary progress of human affairs.

It may perhaps be asked, by way of objection to this, why did not standing armies spring up out of the contentions which so often distracted the ancient republics of Greece? Different answers equally satisfactory may be given to this question. The industrious habits of the people of the present day, absorbed in the pursuits of gain, and devoted to the improvements of agriculture and commerce are incompatible with the condition of a nation of soldiers, which was the true condition of the people of those republics. The means of revenue, which have been so greatly multiplied by the increase of gold and silver, and of the arts of industry, and the science of finance, which is the offspring of modern times, concurring with the habits of nations, have produced an entire revolution in the system of war, and have rendered disciplined armies, distinct from the body of the citizens, the inseparable companion of frequent hostility.

There is a wide difference also, between military establishments in a country, seldom exposed by its situation to internal invasions, and in one which is often subject to them, and always apprehensive of them. The rulers of the former can have no good pretext, if they are even so inclined, to keep on foot armies so numerous as must of necessity be maintained in the latter. These armies being, in the first case, rarely, if at all, called into activity for interior defense, the people are in no danger of being broken to military subordination. The laws are not accustomed to relaxations, in favor of military exigencies—the civil state remains in full vigor, neither corrupted nor confounded with the principles or propensities of the other state. The smallness of the army renders the natural strength of the community an overmatch for it; and the citizens, not habituated to look up to the military power for perfection,[33] or to submit to its oppressions, neither love nor fear the soldiery: They view them with a spirit of jealous acquiescence in a necessary evil, and stand ready to resist a power which they suppose may be exerted to the prejudice of their rights. The army

---

33. ["Protection" substituted in McLean.]

under such circumstances, may usefully aid the magistrate to suppress a small faction, or an occasional mob, or insurrection; but it will be unable to enforce encroachments against the united efforts of the great body of the people.

In a country, in the predicament last described, the contrary of all this happens. The perpetual menacings of danger oblige the government to be always prepared to repel it—its armies must be numerous enough for instant defense. The continual necessity for their services enhances the importance of the soldier, and proportionably degrades the condition of the citizen. The military state becomes elevated above the civil. The inhabitants of territories, often the theater of war, are unavoidably subjected to frequent infringements on their rights, which serve to weaken their sense of those rights; and by degrees, the people are brought to consider the soldiery not only as their protectors, but as their superiors. The transition from this disposition to that of considering them as masters, is neither remote, nor difficult. But it is very difficult to prevail upon a people under such impressions, to make a bold, or effectual resistance, to usurpations, supported by the military power.

The kingdom of Great Britain falls within the first description. An insular situation, and a powerful marine, guarding it in a great measure against the possibility of foreign invasion, supersede the necessity of a numerous army within the kingdom. A sufficient force to make head against a sudden descent, until the militia could have time to rally and embody, is all that has been deemed requisite. No motive of national policy has demanded, nor would public opinion have tolerated a larger number of troops upon its domestic establishment. There has been, for a long time past, little room for the operation of the other causes, which have been enumerated as the consequences of internal war. This peculiar felicity of situation has, in a great degree, contributed to preserve the liberty, which that country to this day enjoys, in spite of the prevalent venality and corruption. If, on the contrary, Britain had been situated on the continent, and had been compelled, as she would have been, by that situation, to make her military establishments at home coextensive with those of the other great powers of Europe, she, like them, would in all probability, be at this day a victim to the absolute power of a single man. It is possible, though not easy, that the people of that island may be enslaved from other causes, but it cannot be by the powers of an army so inconsiderable as that which has been usually kept up in that kingdom.

If we are wise enough to preserve the Union, we may for ages enjoy an advantage similar to that of an insulated situation. Europe is at a great distance from us. Her colonies in our vicinity, will be likely to continue too much disproportioned in strength, to be able to give us any dangerous annoyance. Extensive military establishments cannot, in this position, be necessary to our security. But if we should be disunited, and the integral parts should either remain separated, or which is most probable, should be thrown together into two or three confederacies, we should be in a short course of time, in the predicament of the continental powers of Europe—our liberties would be a prey to the means of defending ourselves against the ambition and jealousy of each other.

This is an idea not superficial or futile, but solid and weighty. It deserves the most serious and mature consideration of every prudent and honest man of whatever party. If such men will make a firm and solemn pause, and meditate dispassionately on the importance of this interesting idea, if they will contemplate it, in all its attitudes, and trace it to all its consequences, they will not hesitate to part with trivial objections to a constitution, the rejection of which would in all probability put a final period to the Union. The airy phantoms that flit before the distempered imaginations of some of its adversaries, would quickly give place to the more substantial forms[34] of dangers real, certain, and formidable.

[November 20, 1787]

No. 9   [Hamilton]

THE UTILITY OF THE UNION AS A SAFEGUARD AGAINST
DOMESTIC FACTION AND INSURRECTION

A Firm Union will be of the utmost moment to the peace and liberty of the States as a barrier against domestic faction and insurrection. It is impossible to read the history of the petty Republics of Greece and Italy, without feeling sensations of horror and disgust at the distractions with which they were continually agitated, and at the rapid succession of revolutions, by which they were kept in a state of perpetual vibration, between the extremes of tyranny and anarchy. If they exhibit occasional calms, these only serve as short-lived contrasts to the furious storms that are to succeed. If now and then intervals of felicity open themselves to view, we behold them with a mixture of regret arising from the reflection that the pleasing scenes before us are soon to be overwhelmed by the tempestuous waves of sedition and party rage. If momentary rays of glory break forth from the gloom, while they dazzle us with a transient and fleeting brilliancy, they at the same time admonish us to lament that the

---

34. ["Prospects" in McLean and later editions.]

vices of government should pervert the direction and tarnish the luster of those bright talents and exalted endowments for which the favored soils, that produced them, have been so justly celebrated.

From the disorders that disfigure the annals of those republics, the advocates of despotism have drawn arguments, not only against the forms of republican government, but against the very principles of civil liberty. They have decried all free government, as inconsistent with the order of society, and have indulged themselves in malicious exultation over its friends and partisans. Happily for mankind, stupendous fabrics reared on the basis of liberty, which have flourished for ages, have in a few glorious instances refuted their gloomy sophisms. And, I trust, America will be the broad and solid foundation of other edifices not less magnificent, which will be equally permanent monuments of their errors.

But it is not to be denied that the portraits, they have sketched of republican government, were too just copies of the originals from which they were taken. If it had been found impracticable, to have devised models of a more perfect structure, the enlightened friends to liberty would have been obliged to abandon the cause of that species of government as indefensible. The science of politics, however, like most other sciences has received great improvement. The efficacy of various principles is now well understood, which were either not known at all, or imperfectly known to the ancients. The regular distribution of power into distinct departments—the introduction of legislature[35] balances and checks—the institutions of courts composed of judges, holding their offices during good behavior—the representation of the people in the legislature by deputies of their own election—these are either wholly new discoveries or have made their principal progress toward perfection in modern times. They are means, and powerful means, by which the excellencies of republican government may be retained and its imperfections lessened or avoided. To this catalog of circumstances, that tend to the amelioration of popular systems of civil government, I shall venture, however novel it may appear to some, to add one more on a principle, which has been made the foundation of an objection to the New Constitution, I mean the ENLARGEMENT of the ORBIT within which such systems are to revolve either in respect to the dimensions of a single State, or to the consolidation of several smaller States into one great confederacy.[36] The latter is that which immediately

---

35. [Changed to "legislative" in McLean and later editions.]

36. [Compare Hume, "Idea of a Perfect Commonwealth" (*Political Discourses*, 1752): "We shall conclude this subject, with observing the falsehood of the common opinion, that no large state, such as France or Great Britain, could ever be modeled into a commonwealth, but that such a form of government can only take

concerns the object under consideration. It will however be of use to examine the principle in its application to a single State which shall be attended to in another place.[37]

The utility of a confederacy, as well to suppress faction and to guard the internal tranquillity of States, as to increase their external force and security, is in reality not a new idea. It has been practiced upon in different countries and ages, and has received the sanction of the most applauded writers, on the subjects of politics. The opponents of the PLAN proposed have with great assiduity cited and circulated the observations of Montesquieu on the necessity of a contracted territory for a republican government.[38] But they seem not to have been apprised of the sentiments of that great man expressed in another part of his work, nor to have adverted to the consequences of the principle to which they subscribe, with such ready acquiescence.

When Montesquieu recommends a small extent for republics, the standards he had in view were of dimensions, far short of the limits of almost every one of these States. Neither Virginia, Massachusetts, Pennsylvania, New York, North Carolina, nor Georgia, can by any means be compared with the models, from which he reasoned and to which the terms of his description apply. If we therefore take his ideas on this point, as the criterion of truth, we shall be driven to the alternative, either of taking refuge at once in the arms of monarchy, or of splitting ourselves into an infinity of little jealous, clashing, tumultuous commonwealths, the wretched nurseries of unceasing discord and the miserable objects of universal pity or contempt. Some of the writers, who have come forward on the other side of the question, seem to have been aware of the dilemma; and have even been bold enough to hint at the division of the larger States, as a desirable thing. Such an infatuated policy, such a desperate expedient, might, by the multiplication of petty offices, answer the views

---

place in a city or small territory. The contrary seems probable. Though it is more difficult to form a republican government in an extensive country than in a city; there is more facility, when once it is formed, of preserving it steady and uniform, without tumult and faction. . . . In a large government, which is modeled with masterly skill, there is compass and room enough to refine the democracy, from the lower people, who may be admitted into the first elections or first concoctions of the commonwealth, to the higher magistrates, who direct all the movements. At the same time, the parts are so distant and remote, that it is very difficult, either by intrigue, prejudice, or passion, to hurry them into any measures against the public interest."]

37. [See Essays 10 and 14, below.]

38. [Montesquieu, *Spirit of the Laws*, vol. 1, book 8, chapter 16.]

of men, who possess not qualifications to extend their influence beyond the narrow circles of personal intrigue, but it could never promote the greatness or happiness of the people of America.

Referring the examination of the principle itself to another place, as has been already mentioned, it will be sufficient to remark here, that in the sense of the author who has been most emphatically quoted upon the occasion, it would only dictate a reduction of the SIZE of the more considerable MEMBERS of the Union; but would not militate against their being all comprehended in one Confederate Government. And this is the true question, in the discussion of which we are at present interested.

So far are the suggestions of Montesquieu from standing in opposition to a general Union of the States, that he explicitly treats of a CONFEDERATE REPUBLIC as the expedient for extending the sphere of popular government and reconciling the advantages of monarchy with those of republicanism.

"It is very probable (says he[39]) that mankind would have been obliged, at length, to live constantly under the government of a SINGLE PERSON, had they not contrived a kind of constitution, that has all the internal advantages of a republican, together with the external force of a monarchical government. I mean a CONFEDERATE REPUBLIC.

"This form of Government is a Convention, by which several smaller *States* agree to become members of a larger *one*, which they intend to form. It is a kind of assemblage of societies, that constitute a new one, capable of increasing by means of new associations, until they arrive to such a degree of power as to be able to provide for the security of the united body.

"A republic of this kind, able to withstand an external force, may support itself without any internal corruption. The form of this society prevents all manner of inconveniences.

"If a single member should attempt to usurp the supreme authority, he could not be supposed to have an equal authority and credit, in all the confederate states. Were he to have too great influence over one, this would alarm the rest. Were he to subdue a part, that which would still remain free might oppose him with forces, independent of those which he had usurped, and overpower him before he could be settled in his usurpation.

"Should a popular insurrection happen, in one of the confederate States, the others are able to quell it. Should abuses creep into one part, they are reformed by those that remain sound. The State may be destroyed on one side, and not on the other; the confederacy may be dissolved, and the confederates preserve their sovereignty.

---

39. *Spirit of Laws,* Volume I. Book IX. Chapter I. (Publius)

"As this government is composed of small republics it enjoys the internal happiness of each, and with respect to its external situation it is possessed, by means of the association of all the advantages of large monarchies."

I have thought it proper to quote at length these interesting passages, because they contain a luminous abridgment of the principal arguments in favor of the Union, and must effectually remove the false impressions, which a misapplication of other parts of the work was calculated to produce. They have at the same time an intimate connection with the more immediate design of this Paper; which is to illustrate the tendency of the Union to repress domestic faction and insurrection.

A distinction, more subtle than accurate has been raised between a *confederacy* and a *consolidation* of the States. The essential characteristic of the first is said to be, the restriction of its authority to the members in their collective capacities, without reaching to the individuals of whom they are composed. It is contended that the national council ought to have no concern with any object of internal administration. An exact equality of suffrage between the members has also been insisted upon as a leading feature of a Confederate Government. These positions are in the main arbitrary; they are supported neither by principle nor precedent. It has indeed happened that governments of this kind have generally operated in the manner, which the distinction, taken notice of, supposes to be inherent in their nature—but there have been in most of them extensive exceptions to the practice, which serve to prove as far as example will go, that there is no absolute rule on the subject. And it will be clearly shown, in the course of this investigation, that as far as the principle contended for has prevailed, it has been the cause of incurable disorder and imbecility in the government.

The definition of a *Confederate Republic* seems simply to be, "an assemblage of societies" or an association of two or more States into one State. The extent, modifications, and objects of the Federal authority are mere matters of discretion. So long as the separate organization of the members be not abolished, so long as it exists by a constitutional necessity for local purposes, though it should be in perfect subordination to the general authority of the Union, it would still be, in fact and in theory, an association of States, or a confederacy. The proposed Constitution, so far from implying an abolition of the State Governments, makes them constituent parts of the national sovereignty by allowing them a direct representation in the Senate, and leaves in their possession certain exclusive and very important portions of sovereign power. This fully corresponds, in every rational import of the terms, with the idea of a Federal Government.

In the Lycian confederacy, which consisted of twenty-three CITIES or republics, the largest were entitled to *three* votes in the COMMON COUNCIL, those of the middle class to *two* and the smallest to *one*. The COMMON COUNCIL had the appointment of all the judges and magistrates of the respective CITIES. This was certainly the most delicate species of interference in their internal administration; for if there be anything, that seems exclusively appropriated to the local jurisdictions, it is the appointment of their own officers. Yet Montesquieu, speaking of this association, says "Were I to give a model of an excellent confederate republic, it would be that of Lycia." Thus we perceive that the distinctions insisted upon were not within the contemplation of this enlightened civilian,[40] and we shall be led to conclude that they are the novel refinements of an erroneous theory.

[November 21, 1787]

No. 10   [Madison]

THE SAME SUBJECT CONTINUED

Among the numerous advantages promised by a well-constructed Union, none deserves to be more accurately developed than its tendency to break and control the violence of faction. The friend of popular governments, never finds himself so much alarmed for their character and fate, as when he contemplates their propensity to this dangerous vice. He will not fail therefore to set a due value on any plan which, without violating the principles to which he is attached, provides a proper cure for it. The instability, injustice, and confusion introduced into the public councils, have in truth been the mortal diseases under which popular governments have everywhere perished; as they continue to be the favorite and fruitful topics from which the adversaries to liberty derive their most specious declamations. The valuable improvements made by the American Constitutions on the popular models, both ancient and modern, cannot certainly be too much admired; but it would be an unwarrantable partiality, to contend that they have as effectually obviated the danger on this side as was wished and expected. Complaints are everywhere heard from our most considerate and virtuous citizens, equally the friends of public and private faith, and of public and personal liberty; that our governments

---

40. ["Civilian" here has the technical sense of a student of the law. The Hopkins edition substitutes "writer."]

are too unstable; that the public good is disregarded in the conflicts of rival parties; and that measures are too often decided, not according to the rules of justice, and the rights of the minor party; but by the superior force of an interested and overbearing majority. However anxiously we may wish that these complaints had no foundation, the evidence of known facts will not permit us to deny that they are in some degree true. It will be found indeed, on a candid review of our situation, that some of the distresses under which we labor, have been erroneously charged on the operation of our governments; but it will be found, at the same time, that other causes will not alone account for many of our heaviest misfortunes; and particularly, for that prevailing and increasing distrust of public engagements, and alarm for private rights, which are echoed from one end of the continent to the other. These must be chiefly, if not wholly, effects of the unsteadiness and injustice, with which a factious spirit has tainted our public administration.

By a faction I understand a number of citizens, whether amounting to a majority or minority of the whole, who are united and actuated by some common impulse of passion, or of interest, adverse to the rights of other citizens, or to the permanent and aggregate interests of the community.

There are two methods of curing the mischiefs of faction: The one, by removing its causes; the other, by controlling its effects.

There are again two methods of removing the causes of faction: The one by destroying the liberty which is essential to its existence; the other, by giving to every citizen the same opinions, the same passions, and the same interests.

It could never be more truly said than of the first remedy, that it is worse than the disease. Liberty is to faction, what air is to fire, an aliment without which it instantly expires. But it could not be a less folly to abolish liberty, which is essential to political life, because it nourishes faction, than it would be to wish the annihilation of air, which is essential to animal life, because it imparts to fire its destructive agency.

The second expedient is as impracticable, as the first would be unwise. As long as the reason of man continues fallible, and he is at liberty to exercise it, different opinions will be formed. As long as the connection subsists between his reason and his self-love, his opinions and his passions will have a reciprocal influence on each other; and the former will be objects to which the latter will attach themselves. The diversity in the faculties of men from which the rights of property originate, is not less an insuperable obstacle to a uniformity of interests. The protection of these faculties is the first object of Government. From the protection of different and unequal faculties of acquiring property, the possession of different degrees and kinds of property immediately results: and from the influence of these on the sentiments and views of the respective proprietors, ensues a division of the society into different interests and parties.

The latent causes of faction are thus sown in the nature of man; and we see them everywhere brought into different degrees of activity, according to the different circumstances of civil society. A zeal for different opinions concerning religion, concerning Government and many other points, as well of speculation as of practice; an attachment to different leaders ambitiously contending for preeminence and power; or to persons of other descriptions whose fortunes have been interesting to the human passions, have in turn divided mankind into parties, inflamed them with mutual animosity, and rendered them much more disposed to vex and oppress each other, than to cooperate for their common good. So strong is this propensity of mankind to fall into mutual animosities, that where no substantial occasion presents itself, the most frivolous and fanciful distinctions have been sufficient to kindle their unfriendly passions, and excite their most violent conflicts.[41] But the most common and durable source of factions, has been the various and unequal distribution of property. Those who hold, and those who are without property, have ever formed distinct interests in society. Those who are creditors, and those who are debtors, fall under a like discrimination. A landed interest, a manufacturing interest, a mercantile interest, a moneyed interest, with many lesser interests, grow up of necessity in civilized nations, and divide them into different classes, actuated by different sentiments and views. The regulation of these various and interfering interests forms the principal task of modern Legislation, and involves the spirit of party and faction in the necessary and ordinary operations of Government.

No man is allowed to be a judge in his own cause; because his interest would certainly bias his judgment, and, not improbably, corrupt his integrity. With equal, nay with greater reason, a body of men, are unfit to be both judges and parties, at the same time; yet, what are many of the most important acts of legislation, but so many judicial determinations, not indeed concerning the rights of single persons, but concerning the rights of large bodies of citizens; and what are the different classes of legislators, but advocates and parties to the causes which they

---

41. [Compare Hume, "Of Parties in General," *Essays, Moral and Political* (1741): "Men have such a propensity to divide into personal factions, that the smallest appearance of real difference will produce them. What can be imagined more trivial than the difference between one color of livery and another in horse races? Yet this difference begat two most inveterate factions in the GREEK empire, the PRASINI and VENETI, who never suspended their animosities, until they ruined that unhappy government."]

determine? Is a law proposed concerning private debts? It is a question to which the creditors are parties on one side, and the debtors on the other. Justice ought to hold the balance between them. Yet the parties are and must be themselves the judges; and the most numerous party, or, in other words, the most powerful faction must be expected to prevail. Shall domestic manufactures be encouraged, and in what degree, by restrictions on foreign manufactures? are questions which would be differently decided by the landed and the manufacturing classes; and probably by neither, with a sole regard to justice and the public good. The apportionment of taxes on the various descriptions of property, is an act which seems to require the most exact impartiality; yet, there is perhaps no legislative act in which greater opportunity and temptation are given to a predominant party, to trample on the rules of justice. Every shilling with which they overburden the inferior number, is a shilling saved to their own pockets.

It is in vain to say, that enlightened statesmen will be able to adjust these clashing interests, and render them all subservient to the public good. Enlightened statesmen will not always be at the helm: Nor, in many cases, can such an adjustment be made at all, without taking into view indirect and remote considerations, which will rarely prevail over the immediate interest which one party may find in disregarding the rights of another, or the good of the whole.

The inference to which we are brought, is, that the *causes* of faction cannot be removed; and that relief is only to be sought in the means of controlling its *effects*.

If a faction consists of less than a majority, relief is supplied by the republican principle, which enables the majority to defeat its sinister views by regular vote: It may clog the administration, it may convulse the society; but it will be unable to execute and mask its violence under the forms of the Constitution. When a majority is included in a faction, the form of popular government on the other hand enables it to sacrifice to its ruling passion or interest, both the public good and the rights of other citizens. To secure the public good, and private rights, against the danger of such a faction, and at the same time to preserve the spirit and the form of popular government, is then the great object to which our inquiries are directed: Let me add that it is the great desideratum, by which alone this form of government can be rescued from the opprobrium under which it has so long labored, and be recommended to the esteem and adoption of mankind.

By what means is this object attainable? Evidently by one of two only. Either the existence of the same passion or interest in a majority at the same time, must be prevented; or the majority, having such coexistent passion or interest, must be rendered, by their number and local situation, unable to concert and carry into effect schemes of oppression. If the impulse and the opportunity be suffered to coincide, we well know that neither moral nor religious motives can be relied on as an adequate control. They are not found to be such on the injustice and violence of individuals, and lose their efficacy in proportion to the number combined together; that is, in proportion as their efficacy becomes needful.[42]

From this view of the subject, it may be concluded that a pure Democracy, by which I mean, a Society, consisting of a small number of citizens, who assemble and administer the Government in person, can admit of no cure for the mischiefs of faction. A common passion or interest will, in almost every case, be felt by a majority of the whole; a communication and concert results from the form of Government itself; and there is nothing to check the inducements to sacrifice the weaker party, or an obnoxious[43] individual. Hence it is, that such Democracies have ever been spectacles of turbulence and contention; have ever been found incompatible with personal security, or the rights of property; and have in general been as short in their lives, as they have been violent in their deaths. Theoretic politicians, who patronized this species of government, have erroneously supposed, that by reducing mankind to a perfect equality in their political rights, they would, at the same time, be perfectly equalized and assimilated in their possessions, their opinions, and their passions.

A Republic, by which I mean a Government in which the scheme of representation takes place, opens a different prospect, and promises the cure for which we are seeking. Let us examine the points in which it varies from pure Democracy, and we shall comprehend both the nature of the cure, and the efficacy which it must derive from the Union.

The two great points of difference between a Democracy and a Republic are, first, the delegation of the Government, in the latter, to a small number of citizens elected by the rest: secondly, the greater number of citizens, and greater sphere of country, over which the latter may be extended.

---

42. [Compare Hume, "Of the Independency of Parliament" (*Essays, Moral and Political*, 1741): "Honour is a great check upon mankind: But where a considerable body of men act together, this check is, in a great measure, removed; since a man is sure to be approved of by his own party, for what promotes the common interest; and he soon learns to despise the clamour of adversaries."]

43. [There is either an ambiguity or (more likely) a pun here. The original meaning of *obnoxious* is "liable to injury" (e.g., below, p. 280), in which sense *obnoxious* is a synonym for *weaker;* but Madison probably also had in mind the modern sense of *obnoxious*, referring to someone who is disliked.]

The effect of the first difference is, on the one hand, to refine and enlarge the public views, by passing them through the medium of a chosen body of citizens, whose wisdom may best discern the true interest of their country, and whose patriotism and love of justice, will be least likely to sacrifice it to temporary or partial considerations. Under such a regulation, it may well happen that the public voice pronounced by the representatives of the people, will be more consonant to the public good, than if pronounced by the people themselves convened for the purpose. On the other hand, the effect may be inverted. Men of factious tempers, of local prejudices, or of sinister designs, may by intrigue, by corruption, or by other means, first obtain the suffrages, and then betray the interests of the people. The question resulting is, whether small or extensive Republics are most favorable to the election of proper guardians of the public weal: and it is clearly decided in favor of the latter by two obvious considerations.

In the first place it is to be remarked, that however small the Republic may be, the Representatives must be raised to a certain number, in order to guard against the cabals of a few; and that however large it may be, they must be limited to a certain number, in order to guard against the confusion of a multitude. Hence the number of Representatives in the two cases, not being in proportion to that of the Constituents, and being proportionally greatest in the small Republic, it follows, that if the proportion of fit characters, be not less, in the large than in the small Republic, the former will present a greater option, and consequently a greater probability of a fit choice.

In the next place, as each Representative will be chosen by a greater number of citizens in the large than in the small Republic, it will be more difficult for unworthy candidates to practice with success the vicious arts, by which elections are too often carried; and the suffrages of the people being more free, will be more likely to center on men who possess the most attractive merit, and the most diffusive and established characters.

It must be confessed, that in this, as in most other cases, there is a mean, on both sides of which inconveniences will be found to lie. By enlarging too much the number of electors, you render the representative too little acquainted with all their local circumstances and lesser interests; as by reducing it too much, you render him unduly attached to these, and too little fit to comprehend and pursue great and national objects. The Federal Constitution forms a happy combination in this respect; the great and aggregate interests being referred to the national, and local and particular to the state legislatures.

The other point of difference is, the greater number of citizens and extent of territory which may be brought within the compass of Republican, than of Democratic Government; and it is this circumstance principally which renders factious combinations less to be dreaded in the former, than in the latter. The smaller the society, the fewer probably will be the distinct parties and interests composing it; the fewer the distinct parties and interests, the more frequently will a majority be found of the same party; and the smaller the number of individuals composing a majority, and the smaller the compass within which they are placed, the more easily will they concert and execute their plans of oppression. Extend the sphere, and you take in a greater variety of parties and interests; you make it less probable that a majority of the whole will have a common motive to invade the rights of other citizens; or if such a common motive exists, it will be more difficult for all who feel it to discover their own strength, and to act in unison with each other. Besides other impediments, it may be remarked, that where there is a consciousness of unjust or dishonorable purposes, communication is always checked by distrust, in proportion to the number whose concurrence is necessary.

Hence it clearly appears, that the same advantage, which a Republic has over a Democracy, in controlling the effects of faction, is enjoyed by a large over a small Republic—is enjoyed by the Union over the States composing it. Does this advantage consist in the substitution of Representatives, whose enlightened views and virtuous sentiments render them superior to local prejudices, and to schemes of injustice? It will not be denied, that the Representation of the Union will be most likely to possess these requisite endowments. Does it consist in the greater security afforded by a greater variety of parties, against the event of any one party being able to outnumber and oppress the rest? In an equal degree does the increased variety of parties, comprised within the Union, increase this security. Does it, in fine, consist in the greater obstacles opposed to the concert and accomplishment of the secret wishes of an unjust and interested majority? Here, again, the extent of the Union gives it the most palpable advantage.

The influence of factious leaders may kindle a flame within their particular States, but will be unable to spread a general conflagration through the other States: a religious sect, may degenerate into a political faction in a part of the Confederacy; but the variety of sects dispersed over the entire face of it, must secure the national Councils against any danger from that source: a rage for paper money, for an abolition of debts, for an equal division of property, or for any other improper or wicked project, will be less apt to pervade the whole body of the Union, than a particular member of it; in the same proportion as such a malady is more likely to taint a particular county or district, than an entire State.

In the extent and proper structure of the Union, therefore, we behold a Republican remedy for the diseases most incident to Republican

Government. And according to the degree of pleasure and pride, we feel in being Republicans, ought to be our zeal in cherishing the spirit, and supporting the character of Federalists.

[November 22, 1787]

No. 12   [Hamilton]

THE UTILITY OF THE UNION IN RESPECT TO REVENUE

The effects of union upon the commercial prosperity of the States have been sufficiently delineated. Its tendency to promote the interests of revenue will be the subject of our present inquiry.

The prosperity of commerce is now perceived and acknowledged, by all enlightened statesmen, to be the most useful as well as the most productive source of national wealth; and has accordingly become a primary object of their political cares.[44] By multiplying the means of gratification, by promoting the introduction and circulation of the precious metals, those darling objects of human avarice and enterprise, it serves to vivify and invigorate the channels[45] of industry, and to make them flow with greater activity and copiousness. The assiduous merchant, the laborious husbandman, the active mechanic, and the industrious manufacturer, all orders of men look forward with eager expectation and growing alacrity to this pleasing reward of their toils. The often-agitated question, between agriculture and commerce, has from indubitable experience received a decision, which has silenced the rivalships, that once subsisted between them, and has proved to the satisfaction[46] of their friends, that their interests are intimately blended and interwoven. It has been found, in various countries, that in proportion as commerce has flourished, land has risen in value. And how could it have happened otherwise? Could that which procures a freer vent for the products of the earth—which furnishes new

---

44. [Compare Hume, "Of Civil Liberty," in *Essays, Moral and Political* (1741): "Trade was never esteemed an affair of state until the last century; and there scarcely is any ancient writer on politics, who has made mention of it. Even the Italians have kept a profound silence with regard to it, though it has now engaged the chief attention, as well of ministers of state, as of speculative reasoners. The great opulence, grandeur, and military achievements of the two maritime powers [i.e., Holland and England] seem first to have instructed mankind in the importance of an extensive commerce."]

45. ["All the channels" in McLean and subsequent editions.]

46. ["The entire satisfaction" in McLean and subsequent editions.]

incitements to the cultivators of land—which is the most powerful instrument in increasing the quantity of money in a state—could that, in fine, which is the faithful handmaid of labor and industry in every shape, fail to augment the value of that article, which is the prolific parent of far the greatest part of the objects upon which they are exerted? It is astonishing, that so simple a truth should ever have had an adversary; and it is one among a multitude of proofs, how apt a spirit of ill-informed jealousy, or of too great abstraction and refinement is to lead men astray from the plainest paths of reason and conviction.

The ability of a country to pay taxes must always be proportioned, in a great degree, to the quantity of money in circulation, and to the celerity with which it circulates. Commerce, contributing to both these objects, must of necessity render the payment of taxes easier, and facilitate the requisite supplies to the treasury. The hereditary dominions of the Emperor of Germany, contain a great extent of fertile, cultivated, and populous territory, a large proportion of which is situated in mild and luxuriant climates. In some parts of this territory are to be found the best gold and silver mines in Europe. And yet, from the want of the fostering influence of commerce, that monarch can boast but slender revenues. He has several times been compelled to owe obligations to the pecuniary succors of other nations, for the preservation of his essential interests; and is unable, upon the strength of his own resources, to sustain a long or continued war.

But it is not in this aspect of the subject alone, that union will be seen to conduce to the purposes of revenue. There are other points of view, in which its influence will appear more immediate and decisive. It is evident from the state of the country, from the habits of the people, from the experience we have had on the point itself, that it is impracticable to raise any very considerable sums by direct taxation. Tax laws have in vain been multiplied—new methods to enforce the collection have in vain been tried—the public expectation has been uniformly disappointed, and the treasuries of the States have remained empty. The popular system of administration, inherent in the nature of popular government, coinciding with the real scarcity of money, incident to a languid and mutilated state of trade, has hitherto defeated every experiment for extensive collections, and has at length taught the different Legislatures the folly of attempting them.

No person, acquainted with what happens in other countries, will be surprised at this circumstance. In so opulent a nation as that of Britain, where direct taxes from superior wealth, must be much more tolerable, and from the vigor of the government, much more practicable, than in America, far the greatest part of the national revenue is derived from taxes of the indirect kind; from imposts and from excises. Duties on imported articles form a large branch of this latter description.

In America it is evident, that we must a long time depend, for the means of revenue, chiefly on such duties. In most parts of it, excises must be confined within a narrow compass. The genius of the people will ill brook the inquisitive and peremptory spirit of excise laws. The pockets of the farmers, on the other hand, will reluctantly yield but scanty supplies in the unwelcome shape of impositions on their houses and lands. And personal property is too precarious and invisible a fund to be laid hold of in any other way, than by the imperceptible agency of taxes on consumption.

If these remarks have any foundation, that state of things, which will best enable us to improve and extend so valuable a resource, must be best adapted to our political welfare. And it cannot admit of a serious doubt, that this state of things must rest on the basis of a general union. As far as this would be conducive to the interests of commerce, so far it must tend to the extension of the revenue to be drawn from that source. As far as it would contribute to rendering regulations for the collection of the duties more simple and efficacious, so far it must serve to answer the purposes of making the same rate of duties more productive, and of putting it in the power of the government to increase the rate, without prejudice to trade.

The relative situation of these States, the number of rivers, with which they are intersected, and of bays that wash their shores, the facility of communication in every direction, the affinity of language, and manners, the familiar habits of intercourse; all these are circumstances, that would conspire to render an illicit trade between them, a matter of little difficulty, and would ensure frequent evasions of the commercial regulations of each other. The separate States, or confederacies would be necessitated by mutual jealousy to avoid the temptations to that kind of trade, by the lowness of their duties. The temper of our governments, for a long time to come, would not permit those rigorous precautions, by which the European nations guard the avenues into their respective countries, as well by land as by water; and which even there are found insufficient obstacles to the adventurous stratagems of avarice.

In France there is an army of patrols (as they are called) constantly employed to secure their[47] fiscal regulations against the inroads of the dealers in contraband trade.[48] Mr. *Neckar* computes the number of these

---

47. ["Their" becomes "her" in McLean and subsequent editions.]

48. ["Trade" omitted in McLean and subsequent editions.]

patrols at upward of twenty thousand.[49] This shows[50] the immense difficulty in preventing that species of traffic, where there is an inland communication, and places in a strong light the disadvantages with which the
collection of duties in this country would be encumbered, if by disunion
the States should be placed in a situation, with respect to each other,
resembling that of France with respect to her neighbors. The arbitrary
and vexatious powers with which the patrols are necessarily armed would
be intolerable in a free country.

If on the contrary, there be but one government pervading all the
States, there will be as to the principal part of our commerce but ONE
SIDE to guard, the ATLANTIC COAST. Vessels arriving directly from foreign countries, laden with valuable cargoes, would rarely choose to hazard[51] themselves to the complicated and critical perils, which would
attend attempts to unlade prior to their coming into port. They would
have to dread both the dangers of the coast, and of detection as well after
as before their arrival at the places of their final destination. An ordinary
degree of vigilance would be competent to the prevention of any material
infractions upon the rights of the revenue. A few armed vessels, judiciously stationed at the entrances of our ports, might at a small expense
be made useful sentinels of the laws. And the government having the
same interests to provide against violations everywhere, the cooperation
of its measures in each State would have a powerful tendency to render
them effectual. Here also we should preserve by union an advantage
which nature holds out to us, and which would be relinquished by separation. The United States lie at a great distance from Europe, and at a
considerable distance from all other places with which they would have
extensive connections of foreign trade. The passage from them to us, in a
few hours, or in a single night, as between the coasts of France and Britain, and of other neighboring nations, would be impracticable. This is a
prodigious security against a direct contraband with foreign countries;
but a circuitous contraband to one State, through the medium of another,
would be both easy and safe. The difference between a direct importation
from abroad and an indirect importation, through the channel of a neighboring State, in small parcels, according to time and opportunity, with
the additional facilities of inland communication, must be palpable to
every man of discernment.

---

49. [Jacques Necker, finance minister under Louis XVI; Hamilton's source is
his *Treatise on the Administration of the Finances of France* (1785).]

50. ["Proves" substituted in McLean and subsequent editions.]

51. ["Expose" substituted in McLean and subsequent editions.]

It is therefore, evident, that one national government would be able, at much less expense, to extend the duties on imports, beyond comparison further, than would be practicable to the States separately, or to any partial confederacies: Hitherto I believe it may safely be asserted, that these duties have not upon an average exceeded in any State three percent. In France they are estimated to be about fifteen percent and in Britain they exceed this proportion.[52] There seems to be nothing to hinder their being increased in this country, to at least treble their present amount. The single article of ardent spirits, under Federal regulation, might be made to furnish a considerable revenue. Upon a ratio to the importation into this State, the whole quantity imported into the United States may[53] be estimated at four million Gallons; which at a shilling per gallon would produce two hundred thousand pounds. That article would well bear this rate of duty: and if it should tend to diminish the consumption of it, such an effect would be equally favorable to the agriculture, to the economy, to the morals, and to the health of the society. There is perhaps nothing so much a subject of national extravagance, as these spirits.[54]

What will be the consequence, if we are not able to avail ourselves of the resource in question in its full extent? A nation cannot long exist without revenue. Destitute of this essential support, it must resign its independence and sink into the degraded condition of a province. This is an extremity to which no government will of choice accede. Revenue therefore must be had at all events. In this country, if the principal part be not drawn from commerce, it must fall with oppressive weight upon land. It has been already intimated, that excises in their true signification are too little in unison with the feelings of the people, to admit of great use being made of that mode of taxation, nor indeed, in the States where almost the sole employment is agriculture, are the objects, proper for excise sufficiently numerous to permit very ample collections in that way. Personal estate, (as has been before remarked) from the difficulty of tracing it cannot be subjected to large contributions, by any other means, than by taxes on consumption. In populous cities, it may be enough the subject of conjecture, to occasion the oppression of individuals, without much aggregate benefit to the State; but beyond these circles it must in a great measure escape the eye and the hand of the taxgatherer. As the necessities of the State, nevertheless, must be satisfied, in some mode or other, the defect of

---

52. If my memory be right they amount to twenty percent. (Publius) [Note omitted in McLean and subsequent editions.]

53. ["May at a low computation be" in McLean and subsequent editions.]

54. ["This very article" in McLean and subsequent editions.]

other resources must throw the principal weight of the public burdens on the possessors of land. And as, on the other hand, the wants of the government can never obtain an adequate supply, unless all the sources of revenue are open to its demands, the finances of the community under such embarrassments, cannot be put into a situation consistent with its respectability, or its security. Thus we shall not even have the consolations of a full treasury to atone for the oppression of that valuable class of the citizens, who are employed in the cultivation of the soil. But public and private distress will keep pace with each other in gloomy concert; and unite in deploring the infatuation of those councils, which led to disunion.

[November 27, 1787]

No. 14   [Madison]

AN OBJECTION DRAWN FROM THE EXTENT OF COUNTRY ANSWERED

We have seen the necessity of the union as our bulwark against foreign danger, as the conservator of peace among ourselves, as the guardian of our commerce and other common interests, as the only substitute for those military establishments which have subverted the liberties of the old world; and as the proper antidote for the diseases of faction, which have proved fatal to other popular governments, and of which alarming symptoms have been betrayed by our own. All that remains, within this branch of our inquiries, is to take notice of an objection, that may be drawn from the great extent of country which the union embraces. A few observations on this subject will be the more proper, as it is perceived that the adversaries of the new constitution are availing themselves of a prevailing prejudice, with regard to the practicable sphere of republican administration, in order to supply by imaginary difficulties, the want of those solid objections, which they endeavor in vain to find.

The error which limits Republican Government to a narrow district, has been unfolded and refuted in preceding papers.[55] I remark here only, that it seems to owe its rise and prevalence chiefly to the confounding of a republic with a democracy: And applying to the former reasonings drawn from the nature of the latter. The true distinction between these forms was also adverted to on a former occasion. It is, that in a democracy, the people meet and exercise the government in person; in a republic they assemble and administer it by their representatives and agents. A

---

55. [See Essays 9 and 10, above.]

democracy consequently must be confined to a small spot. A republic may be extended over a large region.

To this accidental source of the error may be added, the artifice of some celebrated authors, whose writings have had a great share in forming the modern standard of political opinions. Being subjects either of an absolute, or limited monarchy, they have endeavored to heighten the advantages or palliate the evils of those forms; by placing in comparison with them, the vices and defects of the republican, and by citing as specimens of the latter, the turbulent democracies of ancient Greece, and modern Italy. Under the confusion of names, it has been an easy task to transfer to a republic, observations applicable to a democracy only, and among others, the observation that it can never be established but among a small number of people, living within a small compass of territory.

Such a fallacy may have been the less perceived, as most of the popular governments of antiquity were of the democratic species; and even in modern Europe, to which we owe the great principle of representation, no example is seen of a government wholly popular, and founded at the same time wholly on that principle. If Europe has the merit of discovering this great mechanical power in government, by the simple agency of which, the will of the largest political body may be concentered, and its force directed to any object, which the public good requires; America can claim the merit of making the discovery the basis of unmixed and extensive republics. It is only to be lamented, that any of her citizens should wish to deprive her of the additional merit of displaying its full efficacy in the establishment of the comprehensive system now under her consideration.

As the natural limit of a democracy is that distance from the central point, which will just permit the most remote citizens to assemble as often as their public functions demand; and will include no greater number than can join in those functions; so the natural limit of a republic is that distance from the center, which will barely allow the representatives of the people to meet as often as may be necessary for the administration of public affairs. Can it be said, that the limits of the United States exceed this distance? It will not be said by those who recollect that the Atlantic coast is the longest side of the union; that during the term of thirteen years, the representatives of the States have been almost continually assembled; and that the members from the most distant states are not chargeable with greater intermissions of attendance, than those from the States in the neighborhood of Congress.

That we may form a juster estimate with regard to this interesting subject, let us resort to the actual dimensions of the union. The limits as fixed by the treaty of peace are on the east the Atlantic, on the south the latitude of thirty-one degrees, on the west the Mississippi, and on the north an irregular line running in some instances beyond the forty-fifth degree, in others falling as low as the forty-second. The southern shore of lake Erie lies below that latitude. Computing the distance between the thirty-first and forty-fifth degrees, it amounts to nine hundred and seventy-three common miles; computing it from thirty-one to forty-two degrees to seven hundred, sixty-four miles and an half. Taking the mean for the distance, the amount will be eight hundred, sixty-eight miles and three-fourths. The mean distance from the Atlantic to the Mississippi does not probably exceed seven hundred and fifty miles. On a comparison of this extent, with that of several countries in Europe, the practicability of rendering our system commensurate to it, appears to be demonstrable. It is not a great deal larger than Germany, where a Diet, representing the whole empire is continually assembled; or than Poland before the late dismemberment, where another national Diet was the depositary of the supreme power. Passing by France and Spain, we find that in Great Britain, inferior as it may be in size, the representatives of the northern extremity of the island, have as far to travel to the national Council, as will be required of those of the most remote parts of the union.

Favorable as this view of the subject may be, some observations remain which will place it in a light still more satisfactory.

In the first place it is to be remembered, that the general government is not to be charged with the whole power of making and administering laws. Its jurisdiction is limited to certain enumerated objects, which concern all the members of the republic, but which are not to be attained by the separate provisions of any. The subordinate governments which can extend their care to all those other objects, which can be separately provided for, will retain their due authority and activity. Were it proposed by the plan of the convention to abolish the governments of the particular States, its adversaries would have some ground for their objection, though it would not be difficult to show that if they were abolished, the general government would be compelled by the principle of self preservation, to reinstate them in their proper jurisdiction.

A second observation to be made is, that the immediate object of the Federal Constitution is to secure the union of the Thirteen Primitive States, which we know to be practicable; and to add to them such other States, as may arise in their own bosoms, or in their neighborhoods, which we cannot doubt to be equally practicable. The arrangements that may be necessary for those angles and fractions of our territory, which lie on our northwestern frontier, must be left to those whom further discoveries and experience will render more equal to the task.

Let it be remarked in the third place, that the intercourse throughout the union will be daily facilitated by new improvements. Roads will everywhere be shortened, and kept in better order; accommodations for travelers will be multiplied and meliorated; an interior navigation on our eastern side will be opened throughout, or nearly throughout the whole extent of the Thirteen States. The communication between the western and Atlantic districts, and between different parts of each, will be rendered more and more easy by those numerous canals with which the beneficence of nature has intersected our country, and which art finds it so little difficult to connect and complete.

A fourth and still more important consideration is, that as almost every State will on one side or other, be a frontier, and will thus find in a regard to its safety, an inducement to make some sacrifices for the sake of the general protection; so the States which lie at the greatest distance from the heart of the union, and which of course may partake least of the ordinary circulation of its benefits, will be at the same time immediately contiguous to foreign nations, and will consequently stand on particular occasions, in greatest need of its strength and resources. It may be inconvenient for Georgia or the States forming our western or northeastern borders, to send their representatives to the seat of government, but they would find it more so to struggle alone against an invading enemy, or even to support alone the whole expense of those precautions, which may be dictated by the neighborhood of continual danger. If they should derive less benefit therefore from the union in some respects, than the less distant States, they will derive greater benefit from it in other respects, and thus the proper equilibrium will be maintained throughout.

I submit to you my fellow citizens, these considerations, in full confidence that the good sense which has so often marked your decisions, will allow them their due weight and effect; and that you will never suffer difficulties, however formidable in appearance or however fashionable the error on which they may be founded, to drive you into the gloomy and perilous scene into which the advocates for disunion would conduct you. Hearken not to the unnatural voice which tells you that the people of America, knit together as they are by so many cords of affection, can no longer live together as members of the same family; can no longer continue the mutual guardians of their mutual happiness; can no longer be fellow citizens of one great respectable and flourishing empire. Hearken not to the voice which petulantly tells you that the form of government recommended for your adoption is a novelty in the political world; that it has never yet had a place in the theories of the wildest projectors; that it rashly attempts what it is impossible to accomplish. No my countrymen, shut your ears against this unhallowed language. Shut your hearts against the poison which it conveys; the kindred blood which flows in the veins of American citizens, the mingled blood which they have shed in defense of their sacred rights, consecrate their union, and excite horror at the idea of their becoming aliens, rivals, enemies. And if novelties are to be shunned, believe me the most alarming of all novelties, the most wild of all projects, the most rash of all attempts, is that of rending us in pieces, in order to preserve our liberties and promote our happiness. But why is the experiment of an extended republic to be rejected merely because it may comprise what is new? Is it not the glory of the people of America, that whilst they have paid a decent regard to the opinions of former times and other nations, they have not suffered a blind veneration for antiquity, for custom, or for names, to overrule the suggestions of their own good sense, the knowledge of their own situation, and the lessons of their own experience? To this manly spirit, posterity will be indebted for the possession, and the world for the example of the numerous innovations displayed on the American theater, in favor of private rights and public happiness. Had no important step been taken by the leaders of the revolution for which a precedent could not be discovered, no government established of which an exact model did not present itself, the people of the United States might, at this moment, have been numbered among the melancholy victims of misguided councils, must at best have been laboring under the weight of some of those forms which have crushed the liberties of the rest of mankind. Happily for America, happily we trust for the whole human race, they pursued a new and more noble course. They accomplished a revolution which has no parallel in the annals of human society: They reared the fabrics of governments which have no model on the face of the globe. They formed the design of a great confederacy, which it is incumbent on their successors to improve and perpetuate. If their works betray imperfections, we wonder at the fewness of them. If they erred most in the structure of the union, this was the work most difficult to be executed; this is the work which had been new modeled by the act of your Convention, and it is that act on which you are now to deliberate and to decide.

[November 30, 1787]

No. 15   [Hamilton]

CONCERNING THE DEFECTS OF THE PRESENT CONFEDERATION IN RELATION TO THE PRINCIPLE OF LEGISLATION FOR THE STATES IN THEIR COLLECTIVE CAPACITIES

In the course of the preceding papers, I have endeavored, my Fellow Citizens, to place before you in a clear and convincing light, the importance of Union to your political safety and happiness. I have unfolded to you a complication of dangers to which you would be exposed should you permit that sacred knot which binds the people of America together to be severed or dissolved by ambition or by avarice, by jealousy or by misrepresentation. In the sequel of the inquiry, through which I propose to accompany you, the truths intended to be inculcated will receive further confirmation from facts and arguments hitherto unnoticed. If the road, over which you will still have to pass, should in some places appear to you tedious or irksome, you will recollect, that you are in quest of information on a subject the most momentous which can engage the attention of a free people: that the field through which you have to travel is in itself spacious, and that the difficulties of the journey have been unnecessarily increased by the mazes[56] with which sophistry has beset the way. It will be my aim to remove the obstacles to your progress in as compendious a manner, as it can be done, without sacrificing utility to dispatch.

In pursuance of the plan, which I have laid down, for the discussion of the subject, the point next in order to be examined is the "insufficiency of the present confederation to the preservation of the Union." It may perhaps be asked, what need is there of reasoning or proof to illustrate a position, which is not either controverted or doubted; to which the understandings and feelings of all classes of men assent; and which in substance is admitted by the opponents as well as by the friends of the New Constitution? It must in truth be acknowledged that however these may differ in other respects, they in general appear to harmonize in this sentiment at least, that there are material imperfections in our national system, and that something is necessary to be done to rescue us from impending anarchy. The facts that support this opinion are no longer objects of speculation. They have forced themselves upon the sensibility of the people at large, and have at length extorted from those, whose mistaken policy has had the principal share in precipitating the extremity, at which we are arrived, a reluctant confession of the reality of those defects in the scheme of our Federal government, which have been long pointed out and regretted by the intelligent friends of the Union.

We may indeed with propriety be said to have reached almost the last stage of national humiliation. There is scarcely any thing that can wound the pride, or degrade the character of an independent nation, which we do not experience. Are there engagements to the performance of which we are held by every tie respectable among men? These are the subjects of constant and unblushing violation. Do we owe debts to foreigners and to our own citizens contracted in a time of imminent peril, for the preservation of our political existence? These remain without any proper or satisfactory

---

56. ["Mazes" is McLean's correction for the newspapers' "magic."]

provision for their discharge. Have we valuable territories and important posts in the possession of a foreign power,[57] which by express stipulations ought long since to have been surrendered? These are still retained, to the prejudice of our interests not less than of our rights. Are we in a condition to resent, or to repel the aggression? We have neither troops nor treasury nor government.[58] Are we even in a condition to remonstrate with dignity? The just imputations on our own faith, in respect to the same treaty, ought first to be removed.[59] Are we entitled by nature and compact to a free participation in the navigation of the Mississippi? Spain excludes us from it. Is public credit an indispensable resource in time of public danger? We seem to have abandoned its cause as desperate and irretrievable. Is commerce of importance to national wealth? Ours is at the lowest point of declension. Is respectability in the eyes of foreign powers a safeguard against foreign encroachments? The imbecility of our Government even forbids them to treat with us: Our ambassadors abroad are the mere pageants of mimic sovereignty. Is a violent and unnatural decrease in the value of land a symptom of national distress? The price of improved land in most parts of the country is much lower than can be accounted for by the quantity of waste land at market, and can only be fully explained by that want of private and public confidence, which are so alarmingly prevalent among all ranks and which have a direct tendency to depreciate property of every kind. Is private credit the friend and patron of industry? That most useful kind which relates to borrowing and lending is reduced within the narrowest limits, and this still more from an opinion of insecurity than from the scarcity of money. To shorten an enumeration of particulars which can afford neither pleasure nor instruction it may in general be demanded, what indication is there of national disorder, poverty, and insignificance that could befall a community so peculiarly blessed with natural advantages as we are, which does not form a part of the dark catalog of our public misfortunes?

This is the melancholy situation, to which we have been brought by those very maxims and counsels, which would now deter us from adopting the proposed constitution; and which not content with having conducted us to the brink of a precipice, seem resolved to plunge us into the abyss, that awaits us below. Here, my Countrymen, impelled by every motive that ought to influence an enlightened people, let us make a firm

---

57. [Great Britain.]

58. *I mean for the Union.* (Publius)

59. [The American had failed to honor articles IV, V, and VI of the peace treaty with Great Britain of 1783.]

stand for our safety, our tranquillity, our dignity, our reputation. Let us at last break the fatal charm which has too long seduced us from the paths of felicity and prosperity.

It is true, as has been before observed, that facts too stubborn to be resisted have produced a species of general assent to the abstract proposition that there exist material defects in our national system; but the usefulness of the concession, on the part of the old adversaries of federal measures, is destroyed by a strenuous opposition to a remedy, upon the only principles, that can give it a chance of success. While they admit that the Government of the United States is destitute of energy; they contend against conferring upon it those powers which are requisite to supply that energy: They seem still to aim at things repugnant and irreconcilable—at an augmentation of Federal authority without a diminution of State authority—at sovereignty in the Union and complete independence in the members. They still in fine seem to cherish with blind devotion the political monster of an *imperium in imperio*.[60] This renders a full display of the principal defects of the confederation necessary, in order to show, that the evils we experience do not proceed from minute or partial imperfections, but from fundamental errors in the structure of the building which cannot be amended otherwise than by an alteration in the first principles and main pillars of the fabric.

The great and radical vice in the construction of the existing Confederation is in the principle of LEGISLATION for STATES or GOVERNMENTS, in their CORPORATE or COLLECTIVE CAPACITIES and as contradistinguished from the INDIVIDUALS of whom they consist. Though this principle does not run through all the powers delegated to the Union; yet it pervades and governs those, on which the efficacy of the rest depends. Except as to the rule of apportionment, the United States have an indefinite discretion to make requisitions for men and money; but they have no authority to raise either by regulations extending to the individual citizens of America. The consequence of this is, that though in theory their resolutions concerning those objects are laws, constitutionally binding on the members of the Union, yet in practice they are mere recommendations, which the States observe or disregard at their option.

It is a singular instance of the capriciousness of the human mind, that after all the admonitions we have had from experience on this head, there should still be found men, who object to the New Constitution for deviating from a principle which has been found the bane of the old; and which is in itself evidently incompatible with the idea of GOVERNMENT; a principle in short which if it is to be executed at all must substitute the

---

60. [One independent state within another independent state.]

violent and sanguinary agency of the sword to the mild influence of the Magistracy.

There is nothing absurd or impracticable in the idea of a league or alliance between independent nations, for certain defined purposes precisely stated in a treaty; regulating all the details of time, place, circumstance, and quantity; leaving nothing to future discretion; and depending for its execution on the good faith of the parties. Compacts of this kind exist among all civilized nations subject to the usual vicissitudes of peace and war, of observance and nonobservance, as the interests or passions of the contracting powers dictate. In the early part of the present century, there was an epidemical rage in Europe for this species of compacts; from which the politicians of the times fondly hoped for benefits which were never realized. With a view to establishing the equilibrium of power and the peace of that part of the world, all the resources of negotiation were exhausted, and triple and quadruple alliances were formed; but they were scarcely formed before they were broken, giving an instructive but afflicting lesson to mankind how little dependence is to be placed on treaties which have no other sanction than the obligations of good faith; and which oppose general considerations of peace and justice to the impulse of any immediate interest and passion.

If the particular States in this country are disposed to stand in a similar relation to each other, and to drop the project of a general DISCRETIONARY SUPERINTENDANCE, the scheme would indeed be pernicious, and would entail upon us all the mischiefs that have been enumerated under the first head; but it would have the merit of being at least consistent and practicable. Abandoning all views toward a confederate Government, this would bring us to a simple alliance offensive and defensive; and would place us in a situation to be alternately friends and enemies of each other as our mutual jealousies and rivalships nourished by the intrigues of foreign nations should prescribe to us.

But if we are unwilling to be placed in this perilous situation; if we will still adhere to the design of a national government, or which is the same thing of a superintending power under the direction of a common Council, we must resolve to incorporate into our plan those ingredients which may be considered as forming the characteristic difference between a league and a government; we must extend the authority of the union to the persons of the citizens,—the only proper objects of government.

Government implies the power of making laws. It is essential to the idea of a law, that it be attended with a sanction; or, in other words, a penalty or punishment for disobedience. If there be no penalty annexed to disobedience, the resolutions or commands which pretend to be laws will in fact amount to nothing more than advice or recommendation. This penalty, whatever it may be, can only be inflicted in two ways; by the agency of the Courts and Ministers of Justice, or by military force; by the COERCION of the magistracy, or by the COERCION of arms. The first kind can evidently apply only to men—the last kind must of necessity be employed against bodies politic, or communities or States. It is evident, that there is no process of a court by which their observance of the laws can in the last resort be enforced. Sentences may be denounced against them for violations of their duty; but these sentences can only be carried into execution by the sword. In an association where the general authority is confined to the collective bodies of the communities that compose it, every breach of the laws must involve a state of war, and military execution must become the only instrument of civil obedience. Such a state of things can certainly not deserve the name of government, nor would any prudent man choose to commit his happiness to it.

There was a time when we were told that breaches, by the States, of the regulations of the federal authority were not to be expected—that a sense of common interest would preside over the conduct of the respective members, and would beget a full compliance with all the constitutional requisitions of the Union. This language at the present day would appear as wild as a great part of what we now hear from the same quarter will be thought, when we shall have received further lessons from that best oracle of wisdom, experience. It at all times betrayed an ignorance of the true springs by which human conduct is actuated, and belied the original inducements to the establishment of civil power. Why has government been instituted at all? Because the passions of men will not conform to the dictates of reason and justice, without constraint. Has it been found that bodies of men act with more rectitude or greater disinterestedness than individuals? The contrary of this has been inferred by all accurate observers of the conduct of mankind; and the inference is founded upon obvious reasons. Regard to reputation has a less active influence, when the infamy of a bad action is to be divided among a number, than when it is to fall singly upon one. A spirit of faction which is apt to mingle its poison in the deliberations of all bodies of men, will often harry[61] the persons of whom they are composed into improprieties and excesses, for which they would blush in a private capacity.[62]

---

61. [McLean substitutes "hurry."]

62. [Compare Hume, "Of the Independency of Parliament," *Essays, Moral and Political* (1741): "Men are generally more honest in their private than in their public capacity, and will go to greater lengths to serve a party, than when their own private interest is alone concerned. Honour is a great check upon mankind: But where a considerable body of men act together, this check is, in a great measure,

In addition to all this, there is in the nature of sovereign power an impatience of control, that disposes those who are invested with the exercise of it, to look with an evil eye upon all external attempts to restrain or direct its operations. From this spirit it happens that in every political association which is formed upon the principle of uniting in a common interest a number of lesser sovereignties, there will be found a kind of eccentric tendency in the subordinate or inferior orbs, by the operation of which there will be a perpetual effort in each to fly off from the common center. This tendency is not difficult to be accounted for. It has its origin in the love of power. Power controlled or abridged[63] is almost always the rival and enemy of that power by which it is controlled or abridged. This simple proposition will teach us how little reason there is to expect, that the persons, entrusted with the administration of the affairs of the particular members of a confederacy, will at all times be ready, with perfect good humor, and an unbiased regard to the public weal, to execute the resolutions or decrees of the general authority. The reverse of this results from the constitution of human nature.[64]

If therefore the measures of the confederacy cannot be executed, without the intervention of the particular administrations, there will be little prospect of their being executed at all. The rulers of the respective members, whether they have a constitutional right to do it or not, will undertake to judge of the propriety of the measures themselves. They will consider the conformity of the thing proposed or required to their immediate interests or aims, the momentary conveniences or inconveniences that would attend its adoption. All this will be done, and in a spirit of interested and suspicious scrutiny, without that knowledge of national circumstances and reasons of state, which is essential to a right judgment, and with that strong predilection in favor of local objects, which can hardly fail to mislead the decision. The same process must be repeated in every member of which the body is constituted; and the execution of the plans, framed by the councils of the whole, will always fluctuate on the discretion of the ill-informed and prejudiced opinion of every part. Those who have been conversant in the proceedings of popular assemblies; who have seen how difficult it often is, when there is no exterior pressure of circumstances, to bring them to harmonious resolutions on important points, will readily conceive how

---

removed; since a man is sure to be approved of by his own party, for what promotes the common interest; and he soon learns to despise the clamours of adversaries."]

63. ["Abridged" is McLean's correction; the newspapers have "abused."]

64. "Of man" in McLean and later editions.]

impossible it must be to induce a number of such assemblies, deliberating at a distance from each other, at different times, and under different impressions, long to cooperate in the same views and pursuits.

In our case, the concurrence of thirteen distinct sovereign wills is requisite under the confederation to the complete execution of every important measure, that proceeds from the Union. It has happened as was to have been foreseen. The measures of the Union have not been executed; and the delinquencies of the States have step by step matured themselves to an extreme, which has at length arrested all the wheels of the national government, and brought them to an awful stand. Congress at this time scarcely possess the means of keeping up the forms of administration; until the States can have time to agree upon a more substantial substitute for the present shadow of a federal government. Things did not come to this desperate extremity at once. The causes which have been specified produced at first only unequal and disproportionate degrees of compliance with the requisitions of the Union. The greater deficiencies of some States furnished the pretext of example and the temptation of interest to the complying, or to the least delinquent States. Why should we do more in proportion than those who are embarked with us in the same political voyage? Why should we consent to bear more than our proper share of the common burden? These were suggestions which human selfishness could not withstand, and which even speculative men, who looked forward to remote consequences, could not, without hesitation, combat. Each State yielding to the persuasive voice of immediate interest and convenience has successively withdrawn its support, until the frail and tottering edifice seems ready to fall upon our heads and to crush us beneath its ruins.

[December 1, 1787]

No. 16   [Hamilton]

THE SAME SUBJECT CONTINUED IN
RELATION TO THE SAME PRINCIPLE

The tendency of the principle of legislation for States, or communities, in their political capacities, as it has been exemplified by the experiment we have made of it, is equally attested by the events which have befallen all other governments of the confederate kind, of which we have any account, in exact proportion to its prevalence in those systems. The confirmations of this fact will be worthy of a distinct and particular examination.[65]

---

65. [In Essays 18, 19, and 20, not included in this selection.]

I shall content myself with barely observing here, that of all the confederacies of antiquity, which history has handed down to us, the Lycian and
Achaean leagues, as far as there remain vestiges of them, appear to have
been most free from the fetters of that mistaken principle, and were
accordingly those which have best deserved, and have most liberally
received the applauding suffrages of political writers.

This exceptionable principle may as truly as emphatically be styled the
parent of anarchy: It has been seen that delinquencies in the members of
the Union are its natural and necessary offspring; and that whenever they
happen, the only constitutional remedy is force, and the immediate effect
of the use of it, civil war.

It remains to inquire how far so odious an engine of government, in its
application to us, would even be capable of answering its end. If there
should not be a large army, constantly at the disposal of the national government, it would either not be able to employ force at all, or when this
could be done, it would amount to a war between different parts of the
confederacy, concerning the infractions of a league; in which the strongest combination would be most likely to prevail, whether it consisted of
those who supported, or of those who resisted the general authority. It
would rarely happen that the delinquency to be redressed would be confined to a single member, and if there were more than one, who had
neglected their duty, similarity of situation would induce them to unite
for common defense. Independent of this motive of sympathy, if a large
and influential State should happen to be the aggressing member, it
would commonly have weight enough with its neighbors, to win over
some of them as associates to its cause. Specious arguments of danger to
the common[66] liberty could easily be contrived; plausible excuses for the
deficiencies of the party, could, without difficulty be invented, to alarm
the apprehensions, inflame the passions, and conciliate the good will even
of those States which were not chargeable with any violation, or omission
of duty. This would be the more likely to take place, as the delinquencies
of the larger members might be expected sometimes to proceed from an
ambitious premeditation in their rulers, with a view to getting rid of all
external control upon their designs of personal aggrandizement; the better to effect which, it is presumable they would tamper beforehand with
leading individuals in the adjacent States. If associates could not be found
at home, recourse would be had to the aid of foreign powers, who would
seldom be disinclined to encouraging the dissensions of a confederacy,
from the firm Union of which they had so much to fear. When the sword

---

66. ["General" in McLean and later editions.]

is once drawn, the passions of men observe no bounds of moderation. The suggestions of wounded pride, the instigations of irritated resentment, would be apt to carry the States, against which the arms of the Union were exerted to any extremes necessary to revenge the affront, or to avoid the disgrace of submission. The first war of this kind would probably terminate in a dissolution of the Union.

This may be considered as the violent death of the confederacy. Its more natural death is what we now seem to be on the point of experiencing, if the federal system be not speedily renovated in a more substantial form. It is not probable, considering the genius of this country, that the complying States would often be inclined to support the authority of the Union by engaging in a war against the noncomplying States. They would always be more ready to pursue the milder course of putting themselves upon an equal footing with the delinquent members, by an imitation of their example. And the guilt of all would thus become the security of all. Our past experience has exhibited the operation of this spirit in its full light. There would in fact be an insuperable difficulty in ascertaining when force could with propriety be employed. In the article of pecuniary contribution, which would be the most usual source of delinquency, it would often be impossible to decide whether it had proceeded from disinclination, or inability. The pretense of the latter would always be at hand. And the case must be very flagrant in which its fallacy could be detected with sufficient certainty to justify the harsh expedient of compulsion. It is easy to see that this problem alone, as often as it should occur, would open a wide field for the exercise of factious views, of partiality and of oppression, in the majority that happened to prevail in the national council.[67]

It seems to require no pains to prove that the States ought not to prefer a national constitution, which could only be kept in motion by the instrumentality of a large army, continually on foot to execute the ordinary requisitions or decrees of the government. And yet this is the plain alternative involved by those who wish to deny it the power of extending its operations to individuals. Such a scheme, if practicable at all, would instantly degenerate into a military despotism; but it will be found in every light impracticable. The resources of the Union would not be equal to the maintenance of an army considerable enough to confine the larger States within the limits of their duty; nor would the means ever be furnished of forming such an army in the first instance. Whoever considers the populousness and strength of several of these States singly at the present juncture, and looks forward to what they will become, even at the

---

67. ["A wide field to the majority . . . for the exercise. . . ." in McLean and later editions.]

distance of half a century, will at once dismiss as idle and visionary any scheme, which aims at regulating their movements by laws, to operate upon them in their collective capacities, and to be executed by a coercion applicable to them in the same capacities. A project of this kind is little less romantic than that monster-taming spirit, which is attributed to the fabulous heroes and demigods of antiquity.

Even in those confederacies, which have been composed of members smaller than many of our counties, the principle of legislation for sovereign States, supported by military coercion, has never been found effectual. It has rarely been attempted to be employed, but against the weaker members: And in most instances attempts to coerce the refractory and disobedient, have been the signals of bloody wars; in which one-half of the confederacy has displayed its banners against the other half.

The result of these observations to an intelligent mind must be clearly this, that if it be possible at any rate to construct a Federal Government capable of regulating the common concerns and preserving the general tranquillity, it must be founded, as to the objects committed to its care, upon the reverse of the principle contended for by the opponents of the proposed constitution. It must carry its agency to the persons of the citizens. It must stand in need of no intermediate legislations; but must itself be empowered to employ the arm of the ordinary magistrate to execute its own resolutions. The majesty of the national authority must be manifested through the medium of the Courts of Justice. The government of the Union, like that of each State, must be able to address itself immediately to the hopes and fears of individuals; and to attract to its support, those passions, which have the strongest influence upon the human heart. It must in short, possess all the means and have a right to resort to all the methods of executing the powers, with which it is entrusted, that are possessed and exercised by the governments of the particular States.

To this reasoning it may perhaps be objected, that if any State should be disaffected to the authority of the Union, it could at any time obstruct the execution of its laws, and bring the matter to the same issue of force, with the necessity of which the opposite scheme is reproached.

The plausibility of this objection will vanish the moment we advert to the essential difference between a mere NONCOMPLIANCE and a DIRECT and ACTIVE RESISTANCE. If the interposition of the State Legislatures be necessary to give effect to a measure of the Union, they have only NOT TO ACT or TO ACT EVASIVELY, and the measure is defeated. This neglect of duty may be disguised under affected but unsubstantial provisions, so as not to appear, and of course not to excite any alarm in the people for the safety of the constitution. The State leaders may even make a merit of their surreptitious invasions of it, on the ground of some temporary convenience, exemption, or advantage.

But if the execution of the laws of the national government, should not require the intervention of the State Legislatures; if they were to pass into immediate operation upon the citizens themselves, the particular governments could not interrupt their progress without an open and violent exertion of an unconstitutional power. No omissions, nor evasions would answer the end. They would be obliged to act, and in such a manner, as would leave no doubt that they had encroached on the national rights. An experiment of this nature would always be hazardous—in the face of a constitution in any degree competent to its own defense, and of a people enlightened enough to distinguish between a legal exercise and an illegal usurpation of authority. The success of it would require not merely a factious majority in the Legislature, but the concurrence of the courts of justice, and of the body of the people. If the Judges were not embarked in a conspiracy with the Legislature they would pronounce the resolutions of such a majority to be contrary to the supreme law of the land, unconstitutional and void. If the people were not tainted with the spirit of their State representatives, they, as the natural guardians of the constitution, would throw their weight into the national scale, and give it a decided preponderancy in the contest. Attempts of this kind would not often be made with levity[68] or rashness; because they could seldom be made without danger to the authors; unless in cases of a tyrannical exercise of the Federal authority.

If opposition to the national government should arise from the disorderly conduct of refractory, or seditious individuals, it could be overcome by the same means which are daily employed against the same evil, under the State governments. The Magistracy, being equally the Ministers of the law of the land, from whatever source it might emanate, would doubtless be as ready to guard the national as the local regulations from the inroads of private licentiousness. As to those partial commotions and insurrections which sometimes disquiet society, from the intrigues of an inconsiderable faction, or from sudden or occasional ill humors that do not infect the great body of the community, the general government could command more extensive resources for the suppression of disturbances of that kind, than would be in the power of any single member. And as to those mortal feuds, which in certain conjunctures spread a conflagration through a whole nation, or through a very large proportion of it, proceeding either from weighty causes of discontent given by the government, or from the contagion of some violent popular paroxysm, they do not fall

---

68. ["Levity" is McLean's correction. The newspapers have "liberty."]

within any ordinary rules of calculation. When they happen, they commonly amount to revolutions and dismemberments of empire. No form of government can always either avoid or control them. It is in vain to hope to guard against events too mighty for human foresight or precaution, and it would be idle to object to a government because it could not perform impossibilities.

[December 4, 1787]

No. 23   [Hamilton]

THE NECESSITY OF A GOVERNMENT AT LEAST
EQUALLY ENERGETIC WITH THE ONE PROPOSED

The necessity of a Constitution, at least equally energetic with the one proposed, to the preservation of the Union, is the point, at the examination of which we are now arrived.

This inquiry will naturally divide itself into three branches—the objects to be provided for by a Federal Government—the quantity of power necessary to the accomplishment of those objects—the persons upon whom that power ought to operate. Its distribution and organization will more properly claim our attention under the succeeding head.

The principal purposes to be answered by Union are these—The common defense of the members—the preservation of the public peace as well against internal convulsions as external attacks—the regulation of commerce with other nations and between the States—the superintendence of our intercourse, political and commercial, with foreign countries.

The authorities essential to the care of the common defense are these—to raise armies—to build and equip fleets—to prescribe rules for the government of both—to direct their operations—to provide for their support. These powers ought to exist without limitation: *Because it is impossible to foresee or define the extent and variety of national exigencies, or the correspondent extent and variety of the means which may be necessary to satisfy them.* The circumstances that endanger the safety of nations are infinite; and for this reason no constitutional shackles can wisely be imposed on the power to which the care of it is committed. This power ought to be coextensive with all the possible combinations of such circumstances; and ought to be under the direction of the same councils, which are appointed to preside over the common defense.

This is one of those truths, which to a correct and unprejudiced mind, carries its own evidence along with it; and may be obscured, but cannot be made plainer by argument or reasoning. It rests upon axioms as simple as they are universal. The *means* ought to be proportioned to the *end;* the persons, from whose agency the attainment of any *end* is expected, ought to possess the *means* by which it is to be attained.

Whether there ought to be a Federal Government entrusted with the care of the common defense, is a question in the first instance open to discussion; but the moment it is decided in the affirmative, it will follow, that that government ought to be clothed with all the powers requisite to the complete execution of its trust. And unless it can be shown, that the circumstances which may affect the public safety are reducible within certain determinate limits; unless the contrary of this position can be fairly and rationally disputed, it must be admitted, as a necessary consequence, that there can be no limitation of that authority, which is to provide for the defense and protection of the community, in any matter essential to its efficacy; that is, in any matter essential to the *formation, direction,* or *support* of the NATIONAL FORCES.

Defective as the present Confederation has been proved to be, this principle appears to have been fully recognized by the framers of it; though they have not made proper or adequate provision for its exercise. Congress have an unlimited discretion to make requisitions of men and money—to govern the army and navy—to direct their operations. As their requisitions were made constitutionally binding upon the States, who are in fact under the most solemn obligations to furnish the supplies required of them, the intention evidently was, that the United States should command whatever resources were by them judged requisite to "the common defense and general welfare." It was presumed that a sense of their true interests, and a regard to the dictates of good faith, would be found sufficient pledges for the punctual performance of the duty of the members to the Federal Head.

The experiment has, however demonstrated, that this expectation was ill founded and illusory; and the observations made under the last head, will, I imagine, have sufficed to convince the impartial and discerning, that there is an absolute necessity for an entire change in the first principles of the system: That if we are in earnest about giving the Union energy and duration, we must abandon the vain project of legislating upon the States in their collective capacities: We must extend the laws of the Federal Government to the individual citizens of America: We must discard the fallacious scheme of quotas and requisitions, as equally impracticable and unjust. The result from all this is, that the Union ought to be invested with full power to levy troops to build and equip fleets, and to raise the revenues, which will be required for the formation and support of an army and navy, in the customary and ordinary modes practiced in other governments.

If the circumstances of our country are such, as to demand a compound instead of a simple, a confederate instead of a sole government, the essential point which will remain to be adjusted, will be to discriminate the OBJECTS, as far as it can be done, which shall appertain to the different provinces or departments of power; allowing to each the most ample authority for fulfilling the objects committed to its charge. Shall the Union be constituted the guardian of the common safety? Are fleets and armies and revenues necessary to this purpose? The government of the Union must be empowered to pass all laws, and to make all regulations which have relation to them. The same must be the case, in respect to commerce, and to every other matter to which its jurisdiction is permitted to extend. Is the administration of justice between the citizens of the same State, the proper department of the local governments? These must possess all the authorities which are connected with this object, and with every other that may be allotted to their particular cognizance and direction. Not to confer in each case a degree of power, commensurate to the end, would be to violate the most obvious rules of prudence and propriety, and improvidently to trust the great interests of the nation to hands, which are disabled from managing them with vigor and success.

Who so likely to make suitable provisions for the public defense, as that body to which the guardianship of the public safety is confided—which, as the center of information, will best understand the extent and urgency of the dangers that threaten—as the representative of the WHOLE will feel itself most deeply interested in the preservation of every part—which, from the responsibility implied in the duty assigned to it, will be most sensibly impressed with the necessity of proper exertions—and which, by the extension of its authority throughout the States, can alone establish uniformity and concert in the plans and measures, by which the common safety is to be secured? Is there not a manifest inconsistency in devolving upon the Federal Government the care of the general defense, and leaving in the State governments the *effective* powers, by which it is to be provided for? Is not a want of cooperation the infallible consequence of such a system? And will not weakness, disorder, an undue distribution of the burdens and calamities of war, an unnecessary and intolerable increase of expense, be its natural and inevitable concomitants? Have we not had unequivocal experience of its effects in the course of the revolution, which we have just accomplished?[69]

Every view we may take of the subject, as candid inquirers after truth, will serve to convince us, that it is both unwise and dangerous to deny the Federal Government an unconfined authority, as to all those objects

---

69. ["Achieved" in McLean and later editions.]

which are entrusted to its management. It will indeed deserve the most vigilant and careful attention of the people, to see that it be modeled in such a manner, as to admit of its being safely vested with the requisite powers. If any plan which has been, or may be offered to our consideration, should not, upon a dispassionate inspection, be found to answer this description, it ought to be rejected. A government, the Constitution of which renders it unfit to be trusted with all the powers, which a free people *ought to delegate to any government,* would be an unsafe and improper depositary of the NATIONAL INTERESTS. Wherever THESE can with propriety be confided, the coincident powers may safely accompany them. This is the true result of all just reasoning upon the subject. And the adversaries of the plan, promulgated by the Convention, ought to have[70] confined themselves to showing that the internal structure of the proposed government, was such as to render it unworthy of the confidence of the people. They ought not to have wandered into inflammatory declamations, and unmeaning cavils about the extent of the powers. The POWERS are not too extensive for the OBJECTS of Federal administration, or in other words, for the management of our NATIONAL INTERESTS; nor can any satisfactory argument be framed to show that they are chargeable with such an excess. If it be true, as has been insinuated by some of the writers on the other side, that the difficulty arises from the nature of the thing, and that the extent of the country will not permit us to form a government, in which such ample powers can safely be reposed, it would prove that we ought to contract our views, and resort to the expedient of separate Confederacies, which will move within more practicable spheres. For the absurdity must continually stare us in the face of confiding to a government, the direction of the most essential national interests, without daring to trust it with the authorities which are indispensable to their proper and efficient management. Let us not attempt to reconcile contradictions, but firmly embrace a rational alternative.

I trust, however, that the impracticability of one general system cannot be shown. I am greatly mistaken, if anything of weight, has yet been advanced of this tendency; and I flatter myself, that the observations which have been made in the course of these papers, have sufficed[71] to place the reverse of that position in as clear a light as any matter still in the womb of time and experience can be susceptible of. This at all events must be evident, that the very difficulty itself drawn from the extent of the country, is the strongest argument in favor of an energetic government;

---

70. ["Would have given a better impression of their candor if they had" in McLean and later editions.]

71. ["Served" in McLean and later editions.]

for any other can certainly never preserve the Union of so large an empire. If we embrace the tenets of those, who oppose the adoption of the proposed Constitution, as the standard of our political creed, we cannot fail to verify the gloomy doctrines, which predict the impracticability of a national system, pervading the entire limits of the present Confederacy.

[December 18, 1787]

No. 24   [Hamilton]

THE SUBJECT CONTINUED WITH AN ANSWER TO
AN OBJECTION CONCERNING STANDING ARMIES

To the powers proposed to be conferred upon the Federal Government in respect to the creation and direction of the national forces, I have met with but one specific objection; which if I understand it rightly is this— that proper provision has not been made against the existence of standing armies in time of peace; an objection which I shall now endeavor to show rests on weak and unsubstantial foundations.

It has indeed been brought forward in the most vague and general form, supported only by bold assertions—without the appearance of argument—without even the sanction of theoretical opinions, in contradiction to the practice of other free nations, and to the general sense of America, as expressed in most of the existing constitutions. The propriety of this remark will appear the moment it is recollected that the objection under consideration turns upon a supposed necessity of restraining the LEGISLATIVE authority of the nation, in the article of military establishments; a principle unheard of except in one or two of our state constitutions, and rejected in all the rest.

A stranger to our politics, who was to read our newspapers, at the present juncture, without having previously inspected the plan reported by the Convention, would be naturally led to one of two conclusions: Either that it contained a positive injunction that standing armies should be kept up in time of peace, or that it vested in the EXECUTIVE the whole power of levying troops, without subjecting his discretion in any shape to the control of the legislature.

If he came afterward to peruse the plan itself, he would be surprised to discover that neither the one nor the other was the case—that the whole power of raising armies was lodged in the *legislature,* not in the *executive;* that this legislature was to be a popular body, consisting of the representatives of the people, periodically elected; and that, instead of the provision he had supposed in favor of standing armies, there was to be found, in respect to this object, an important qualification even of the legislative discretion, in that clause which forbids the appropriation of money for the support of an army for any longer period than two years: a precaution, which, upon a nearer view of it, will appear to be a great and real security against the keeping up of troops[72] without evident necessity.

Disappointed in his first surmise, the person I have supposed would be apt to pursue his conjectures a little further. He would naturally say to himself, it is impossible that all this vehement and pathetic declamation can be without some colorable pretext. It must needs be, that this people so jealous of their liberties, have in all the preceding models of the constitutions, which they have established, inserted the most precise and rigid precautions on this point, the omission of which in the new plan has given birth to all this apprehension and clamor.

If under this impression he proceeded to pass in review the several State Constitutions, how great would be his disappointment to find that *two* only of them[73] contained an interdiction of standing armies in time of peace; that the other eleven had either observed a profound silence on the subject, or had in express terms admitted the right of the legislature to authorize their existence.

Still however he would be persuaded that there must be some plausible foundation for the cry raised on this head. He would never be able to imagine, while any source of information remained unexplored, that it was nothing more than an experiment upon the public credulity, dictated either by a deliberate intention to deceive or by the overflowing of a zeal too intemperate to be ingenuous. It would probably occur to him that he would be likely to find the precautions he was in search of in the primitive compact between the States. Here, at length, he would expect to meet

---

72. ["Against military establishments" in McLean and later editions.]

73. This statement of the matter is taken from the printed collections of state constitutions—Pennsylvania and North Carolina are the two which contain the interdiction in these words—"as standing armies in time of peace are dangerous to liberty, *they ought not* to be kept up." This is in truth rather a *caution* than a *prohibition*. New Hampshire, Massachusetts, Delaware, and Maryland, have in each of their bills of rights a clause to this effect—"standing armies are dangerous to liberty, and ought not to be raised or kept up *without the consent of the legislature*"; which is a formal admission of the authority of the legislature. NEW YORK has no bill of her rights and her Constitution says not a word about the matter. No bills of rights appear annexed to the constitutions of the other States, except the foregoing, and their constitutions are equally silent. I am told, however, that one or two states have bills of rights which do not appear in this collection, but that those also recognize the right of the legislative authority in this respect. (Publius)

with a solution of the enigma. No doubt he would observe to himself the existing confederation must contain the most explicit provisions against military establishments in time of peace; and a departure from this model in a favorite point has occasioned the discontent which appears to influence these political champions.

If he should now apply himself to a careful and critical survey of the articles of confederation, his astonishment would not only be increased but would acquire a mixture of indignation at the unexpected discovery that these articles instead of containing the prohibition he looked for, and although they had with a jealous circumspection restricted the authority of the State Legislatures in this particular, had not imposed a single restraint on that of the United States. If he happened to be a man of quick sensibility or ardent temper, he could now no longer refrain from regarding these clamors as[74] the dishonest artifices of a sinister and unprincipled opposition to a plan which ought at least to receive a fair and candid examination from all sincere lovers of their country. How else, he would say, could the authors of them have been tempted to vent such loud censures upon that plan, about a point, in which it seems to have conformed itself to the general sense of America as declared in its different forms of government, and in which it has even superadded a new and powerful guard unknown to any of them? If on the contrary he happened to be a man of calm and dispassionate feelings—he would indulge a sigh for the frailty of human nature; and would lament that in a matter so interesting to the happiness of millions the true merits of the question should be perplexed and entangled[75] by expedients so unfriendly to an impartial and right determination. Even such a man could hardly forbear remarking that a conduct of this kind has too much the appearance of an intention to mislead the people by alarming their passions rather than to convince them by arguments addressed to their understandings.

But however little this objection may be countenanced even by precedents among ourselves, it may be satisfactory to take a nearer view of its intrinsic merits. From a close examination it will appear that restraints upon the discretion of the Legislature in respect to military establishments in time of peace[76] would be improper to be imposed, and if imposed, from the necessities of society would be unlikely to be observed.

Though a wide ocean separates the United States from Europe; yet there are various considerations that warn us against an excess of confidence or security. On one side of us and stretching far into our rear are

---

74. ["Pronouncing these clamors to be" in McLean and later editions.]

75. ["Obscured" in McLean and later editions.]

76. ["In time of peace" omitted in McLean and later editions.]

growing settlements subject to the dominion of Britain.[77] On the other side and extending to meet the British settlements are colonies and establishments subject to the dominion of Spain. This situation and the vicinity of the West India islands belonging to these two powers create between them, in respect to their American possessions, and in relation to us, a common interest. The savage tribes on our western frontier ought to be regarded as our natural enemies their natural allies; because they have most to fear from us and most to hope from them. The improvements in the art of navigation have, as to the facility of communication, rendered distant nations in a great measure neighbors. Britain and Spain are among the principal maritime powers of Europe. A future concert of views between these nations ought not to be regarded as improbable. The increasing remoteness of consanguinity is every day diminishing the force of the family compact between France and Spain. And politicians have ever with great reason considered the ties of blood as feeble and precarious links of political connection. These circumstances combined admonish us not to be too sanguine in considering ourselves as entirely out of the reach of danger.

Previous to the revolution, and ever since the peace, there has been a constant necessity for keeping small garrisons on our western frontier. No person can doubt that these will continue to be indispensable, if it should only be against the ravages and depredations of the Indians. These garrisons must either be furnished by occasional detachments from the militia, or by permanent corps in the pay of the government. The first is impracticable; and if practicable, would be pernicious. The militia would not long, if at all, submit to be dragged from their occupations and families to perform that most disagreeable duty in times of profound peace. And if they could be prevailed upon, or compelled to do it, the increased expense of a frequent rotation of service and the loss of labor, and disconcertion of the industrious pursuits of individuals, would form conclusive objections to the scheme. It would be as burdensome and injurious to the public, as ruinous to private citizens. The latter resource of permanent corps in the pay of government amounts to a standing army in time of peace; a small one indeed, but not the less real for being small. Here is a simple view of the subject that shows us at once the impropriety of a constitutional interdiction of such establishments, and the necessity of leaving the matter to the discretion and prudence of the legislature.

In proportion to our increase in strength, it is probable, nay it may be said certain, that Britain and Spain would augment their military establishments in our neighborhood. If we should not be willing to be exposed

---

77. [I.e., Canada.]

in a naked and defenseless condition to their insults or encroachments, we should find it expedient to increase our frontier garrisons in some ratio to the force by which our western settlements might be annoyed. There are and will be particular posts the possession of which will include the command of large districts of territory and facilitate future invasions of the remainder. It may be added that some of those posts will be keys to the trade with the Indian nations. Can any man think it would be wise to leave such posts in a situation to be at any instant seized by one or the other of two neighboring and formidable powers? To act this part would be to desert all the usual maxims of prudence and policy.

If we mean to be a commercial people or even to be secure on our Atlantic side, we must endeavor as soon as possible to have a navy. To this purpose there must be dockyards and arsenals, and, for the defense of these, fortifications and probably garrisons. When a nation has become so powerful by sea, that it can protect its dockyards by its fleets, this supersedes the necessity of garrisons for that purpose; but where naval establishments are in their infancy, moderate garrisons will in all likelihood be found an indispensable security against descents for the destruction of the arsenals and dockyards, and sometimes of the fleet itself.

[December 19, 1787]

No. 28   [Hamilton]

THE SAME SUBJECT CONCLUDED

That there may happen cases, in which the national government may be necessitated to resort to force, cannot be denied. Our own experience has corroborated the lessons taught by the examples of other nations; that emergencies of this sort will sometimes arise[78] in all societies, however constituted; that seditions and insurrections are unhappily maladies as inseparable from the body politic, as tumors and eruptions from the natural body; that the idea of governing at all times by the simple force of law (which we have been told is the only admissible principle of republican government) has no place but in the reveries of those political doctors, whose sagacity disdains the admonitions of experimental instruction.

Should such emergencies at any time happen under the national government, there could be no remedy but force. The means to be employed must be proportioned to the extent of the mischief. If it should be a slight commotion in a small part of a State, the militia of the residue would be

---

78. ["Exist" substituted in McLean and subsequent editions.]

adequate to its suppression: and the natural presumption is, that they would be ready to do their duty. An insurrection, whatever may be its immediate cause, eventually endangers all government: Regard to the public peace, if not to the rights of the Union, would engage the citizens, to whom the contagion had not communicated itself, to oppose the insurgents: And if the general government should be found in practice conducive to the prosperity and felicity of the people, it were irrational to believe that they would be disinclined to its support.

If on the contrary the insurrection should pervade a whole State, or a principal part of it, the employment of a different kind of force might become unavoidable. It appears that Massachusetts found it necessary to raise troops for repressing[79] the disorders within that State;[80] that Pennsylvania, from the mere apprehension of commotions among a part of her citizens, has thought proper to have recourse to the same measure.[81] Suppose the State of New York had been inclined to reestablish her lost jurisdiction over the inhabitants of Vermont; could she have hoped for success in such an enterprise from the efforts of the militia alone?[82] Would she not have been compelled to raise and to maintain a more regular force for the execution of her design? If it must then be admitted that the necessity of recurring to a force different from the militia in cases of this extraordinary nature, is applicable to the State governments themselves, why should the possibility that the national government might be under a like necessity in similar extremities, be made an objection to its existence? Is it not surprising that men, who declare an attachment to the union in the abstract, should urge, as an objection to the proposed constitution, what applies with tenfold weight to the plan for which they contend; and what as far as it has any foundation in truth is an inevitable consequence of civil society upon an enlarged scale? Who would not prefer that possibility to the unceasing agitations and frequent revolutions which are the continual scourages[83] of petty republics?

Let us pursue this examination in another light. Suppose, in lieu of one general system, two or three or even four confederacies were to be formed, would not the same difficulty oppose itself to the operations of

---

79. ["Suppressing" in McLean and subsequent editions.]

80. [Shay's Rebellion.]

81. [The prospect of the secession of the Wyoming Valley.]

82. [Vermont claimed independence in 1777, but was prevented from joining the Union until 1791.]

83. ["Scourage" is an obsolete word, derived from "scour," meaning to skirmish or harass.]

either of these confederacies? Would not each of them be exposed to the same casualties; and, when these happened, be obliged to have recourse to the same expedients for upholding its authority, which are objected to a government for all the States? Would the militia in this supposition be more ready or more able to support the federal authority than in the case of a general union? All candid and intelligent men must upon due consideration acknowledge that the principle of the objection is equally applicable to either of the two cases; and that whether we have one government for all the States, or different governments for different parcels of them, or even if there should be an entire separation of the States,[84] there might sometimes be a necessity to make use of a force constituted differently from the militia to preserve the peace of the community, and to maintain the just authority of the laws against those violent invasions of them which amount to insurrections and rebellions.

Independent of all other reasonings upon the subject, it is a full answer to those who require a more peremptory provision against military establishments in time of peace, that[85] the whole power of the proposed government is to be in the hands of the representatives of the people. This is the essential, and after all the only efficacious security for the rights and privileges of the people which is attainable in civil society.[86]

If the representatives of the people betray their constituents, there is then no resource left but in the exertion of that original right of self-defense, which is paramount to all positive forms of government; and which, against the usurpations of the national rulers, may be exerted with infinitely better prospect of success, than against those of the rulers of an individual State. In a single State, if the persons entrusted with supreme power became usurpers, the different parcels, subdivisions or districts, of which it consists, having no distinct government in each, can take no regular measures for defense. The citizens must rush tumultuously to arms, without concert, without system, without resource; except in their courage and despair. The usurpers, clothed with the forms of legal authority, can too often crush the opposition in embryo. The smaller the extent of territory, the more difficult will it be for the people to form a regular or systematic plan of opposition; and the more easy will it be to defeat their early efforts. Intelligence can be more speedily obtained of their preparations and movements; and the military force in the possession of the

---

84. ["Or as many unconnected governments as there are states" substituted in McLean and later editions.]

85. ["To say that" in McLean and subsequent editions.]

86. Its full efficacy will be examined hereafter. (Publius)

usurpers, can be more rapidly directed against the part where the opposition has begun. In this situation, there must be a peculiar coincidence of circumstances to ensure success to the popular resistance.

The obstacles to usurpation and the facilities of resistance increase with the increased extent of the state; provided the citizens understand their rights and are disposed to defend them. The natural strength of the people in a large community, in proportion to the artificial strength of the government, is greater than in a small; and of course more competent to a struggle with the attempts of the government to establish a tyranny. But in a confederacy the people, without exaggeration, may be said to be entirely the masters of their own fate. Power being almost always the rival of power; the General Government will at all times stand ready to check the usurpations of the state governments; and these will have the same disposition toward the General Government. The people, by throwing themselves into either scale, will infallibly make it preponderate. If their rights are invaded by either, they can make use of the other, as the instrument of redress. How wise will it be in them by cherishing the Union to preserve to themselves an advantage which can never be too highly prized!

It may safely be received as an axiom in our political system, that the state governments will in all possible contingencies afford complete security against invasions of the public liberty by the national authority. Projects of usurpation cannot be masked under pretenses so likely to escape the penetration of select bodies of men as of the people at large. The Legislatures will have better means of information. They can discover the danger at a distance; and possessing all the organs of civil power and the confidence of the people, they can at once adopt a regular plan of opposition, in which they can combine all the resources of the community. They can readily communicate with each other in the different states; and unite their common forces for the protection of their common liberty.

The great extent of the country is a further security. We have already experienced its utility against the attacks of a foreign power. And it would have precisely the same effect against the enterprises of ambitious rulers in the national councils. If the federal army should be able to quell the resistance of one state, the distant states would be able to make head with fresh forces. The advantages obtained in one place must be abandoned to subdue the opposition in others; and the moment the part which had been reduced to submission was left to itself its efforts would be renewed and its resistance revive.

We should recollect that the extent of the military force must at all events be regulated by the resources of the country. For a long time to come, it will not be possible to maintain a large army: and as the means of doing this increase, the population and natural strength of the community will proportionably increase. When will the time arrive, that the federal Government can raise and maintain an army capable of erecting a despotism over the great body of the people of an immense empire; who are in a situation, through the medium of their state governments, to take measures for their own defense with all the celerity, regularity, and system of independent nations? The apprehension may be considered as a disease, for which there can be found no cure in the resources of argument and reasoning.

[December 26, 1787]

No. 31 [Hamilton]

[CONCERNING TAXATION]: THE SAME SUBJECT CONTINUED

In disquisitions of every kind there are certain primary truths or first principles upon which all subsequent reasonings must depend. These contain an internal evidence, which antecedent to all reflection or combination commands the assent of the mind. Where it produces not this effect, it must proceed either from some defect or[87] disorder in the organs of perception, or from the influence of some strong interest, or passion, or prejudice. Of this nature are the maxims in geometry, that "The whole is greater than its part; that things equal to the same are equal to one another; that two straight lines cannot enclose a space; and that all right angles are equal to each other." Of the same nature are these other maxims in ethics and politics, that there cannot be an effect without a cause; that the means ought to be proportioned to the end; that every power ought to be commensurate with its object; that there ought to be no limitation of a power destined to effect a purpose, which is itself incapable of limitation. And there are other truths in the two latter sciences, which if they cannot pretend to rank in the class of axioms, are yet such direct inferences from them, and so obvious in themselves, and so agreeable to the natural and unsophisticated dictates of common sense, that they challenge the assent of a sound and unbiased mind, with a degree of force and conviction almost equally irresistible.[88]

The objects of geometrical inquiry are so entirely abstracted from those pursuits which stir up and put in motion the unruly passions of the

---

87. ["Defect or" omitted in McLean and later editions.]

88. [On the axioms of political science see Hume, "That Politics May Be Reduced to a Science," in *Essays, Moral and Political* (1741).]

human heart, that mankind without difficulty adopt not only the more simple theorems of the science, but even those abstruse paradoxes, which however they may appear susceptible of demonstration, are at variance with the natural conceptions which the mind, without the aid of philosophy, would be led to entertain upon the subject. The INFINITE DIVISIBILITY of matter, or in other words, the INFINITE divisibility of a FINITE thing, extending even to the minutest atom, is a point agreed among geometricians, though not less incomprehensible to common sense, than any of those mysteries in religion, against which the batteries of infidelity have been so industriously leveled.

But in the sciences of morals and politics men are found far less tractable. To a certain degree it is right and useful, that this should be the case. Caution and investigation are a necessary armor against error and imposition. But this untractableness may be carried too far, and may degenerate into obstinacy, perverseness, or disingenuity. Though it cannot be pretended that the principles of moral and political knowledge have in general the same degree of certainty with those of the mathematics; yet they have much better claims in this respect, than to judge from the conduct of men in particular situations, we should be disposed to allow them. The obscurity is much oftener in the passions and prejudices of the reasoner than in the subject. Men upon too many occasions do not give their own understandings fair play; but yielding to some untoward bias they entangle themselves in words and confound themselves in subtleties.

How else could it happen (if we admit the objectors to be sincere in their opposition) that positions so clear as those which manifest the necessity of a general power of taxation in the government of the union, should have to encounter any adversaries among men of discernment? Though these positions have been elsewhere fully stated,[89] they will perhaps not be improperly recapitulated in this place, as introductory to an examination of what may have been offered by way of objection to them. They are in substance as follow:

A government ought to contain in itself every power requisite to the full accomplishment of the objects committed to its care, and to the complete execution of the trusts for which it is responsible; free from every other control, but a regard to the public good and to the sense of the people.

As the duties of superintending the national defense and of securing the public peace against foreign or domestic violence, involve a provision for casualties and dangers, to which no possible limits can be assigned, the power of making that provision ought to know no other bounds than the exigencies of the nation and the resources of the community.

---

89. [In Essay 30, not included here.]

As revenue is the essential engine by which the means of answering the national exigencies must be procured, the power of procuring that article in its full extent, must necessarily be comprehended in that of providing for those exigencies.

As theory and practice conspire to prove that the power of procuring revenue is unavailing, when exercised over the States in their collective capacities, the Federal government must of necessity be invested with an unqualified power of taxation in the ordinary modes.

Did not experience evince the contrary, it would be natural to conclude that the propriety of a general power of taxation in the national government might safely be permitted to rest on the evidence of these propositions, unassisted by any additional arguments or illustrations. But we find in fact, that the antagonists of the proposed constitution, so far from acquiescing in their justness or truth, seem to make their principal and most zealous effort against this part of the plan. It may therefore be satisfactory to analyze the arguments with which they combat it.

Those of them, which have been most labored with that view, seem in substance to amount to this: "It is not true, because the exigencies of the Union may not be susceptible of limitation, that its power of laying taxes ought to be unconfined. Revenue is as requisite to the purposes of the local administrations as to those of the Union; and the former are at least of equal importance with the latter to the happiness of the people. It is therefore as necessary, that the State Governments should be able to command the means of supplying their wants, as, that the National Government should possess the like faculty, in respect to the wants of the Union. But an indefinite power of taxation in the *latter* might, and probably would in time deprive the former of the means of providing for their own necessities; and would subject them entirely to the mercy of the national Legislature. As the laws of the Union are to become the supreme law of the land; as it is to have power to pass all laws that may be NECESSARY for carrying into execution, the authorities with which it is proposed to vest it; the national government might at any time abolish the taxes imposed for State objects, upon the pretense of an interference with its own. It might allege a necessity of doing this, in order to give efficacy to the national revenues: And thus all the resources of taxation might by degrees, become the subjects of federal monopoly, to the entire exclusion and destruction of the State Governments."

This mode of reasoning appears sometimes to turn upon the supposition of usurpation in the national government; at other times it seems to be designed only as a deduction from the constitutional operation of its intended powers. It is only in the latter light, that it can be admitted to have any pretensions to fairness. The moment we launch into conjectures about the usurpations of the federal Government, we get into an unfathomable abyss, and fairly put ourselves out of the reach of all reasoning. Imagination may range at pleasure until it gets bewildered amid the labyrinths of an enchanted castle, and knows not on which side to turn to extricate itself from the perplexities into which it has so rashly adventured.[90] Whatever may be the limits or modifications of the powers of the Union, it is easy to imagine an endless train of possible dangers; and by indulging an excess of jealousy and timidity, we may bring ourselves to a state of absolute skepticism and irresolution. I repeat here what I have observed in substance in another place[91] that all observations founded upon the danger of usurpation, ought to be referred to the composition and structure of the government, not to the nature or extent of its powers. The State governments, by their original constitutions, are invested with complete sovereignty. In what does our security consist against usurpations from that quarter? Doubtless in the manner of their formation, and in a due dependence of those who are to administer them upon the people. If the proposed construction of the Federal Government, be found upon an impartial examination of it, to be such as to afford, to a proper extent, the same species of security, all apprehensions on the score of usurpation ought to be discarded.

It should not be forgotten, that a disposition in the State governments to encroach upon the rights of the Union, is quite as probable, as a disposition in the Union to encroach upon the rights of the State Governments. What side would be likely to prevail in such a conflict, must depend on the means which the contending parties could employ toward ensuring success. As in republics, strength is always on the side of the people; and as there are weighty reasons to induce a belief, that the State governments will commonly possess most influence over them, the natural conclusion is, that such contests will be most apt to end to the disadvantage of the Union; and that there is greater probability of encroachments by the members upon the Federal Head, than by the Federal Head upon the members. But it is evident, that all conjectures of this kind, must be extremely vague and fallible, and that it is by far the safest course to lay them altogether aside; and to confine our attention wholly to the nature and extent of the powers as they are delineated in the constitution. Everything beyond this, must be left to the prudence and firmness of the people; who, as they will hold the scales in their own hands, it is to be hoped, will always take care to preserve the constitutional equilibrium between the

---

90. ["Escape from the apparitions which itself has raised" in McLean and subsequent editions.]

91. [See the conclusion of Essay 23.]

General and the State Governments. Upon this ground, which is evidently the true one, it will not be difficult to obviate the objections which have been made to an indefinite power of taxation in the United States.

[January 1, 1788]

No. 33   [Hamilton]

THE SAME SUBJECT CONTINUED

The residue of the argument against the provisions in the constitution, in respect to taxation, is engrafted upon the following clauses;[92] the last clause of the eighth section of the first article of the plan under consideration, authorizes the national legislature "to make all laws which shall be *necessary* and *proper,* for carrying into execution *the powers* by that Constitution vested in the government of the United States, or in any department or officer thereof"; and the second clause of the sixth article declares, that "the Constitution and the Laws of the United States made *in pursuance thereof,* and the treaties made by their authority shall be the *supreme law* of the land; anything in the constitution or laws of any State to the contrary notwithstanding."

These two clauses have been the sources of much virulent invective and petulant declamation against the proposed constitution, they have been held up to the people, in all the exaggerated colors of misrepresentation, as the pernicious engines by which their local governments were to be destroyed and their liberties exterminated—as the hideous monster whose devouring jaws would spare neither sex nor age, nor high nor low, nor sacred nor profane; and yet strange as it may appear, after all this clamor, to those who may not have happened to contemplate them in the same light, it may be affirmed with perfect confidence, that the constitutional operation of the intended government would be precisely the same, if these clauses were entirely obliterated, as if they were repeated in every article. They are only declaratory of a truth, which would have resulted by necessary and unavoidable implication from the very act of constituting a Federal Government, and vesting it with certain specified powers. This is so clear a proposition, that moderation itself can scarcely listen to the railings which have been so copiously vented against this part of the plan, without emotions that disturb its equanimity.

---

92. [In the newspapers, Essay 33 was printed as the concluding part of Essay 32, and this first clause was absent.]

What is a power, but the ability or faculty of doing a thing? What is the ability to do a thing but the power of employing the *means* necessary to its execution? What is a LEGISLATIVE power but a power of making LAWS? What are the *means* to execute a LEGISLATIVE power but LAWS? What is the power of laying and collecting taxes but a *legislative power,* or a power of *making laws,* to lay and collect taxes? What are the proper means of executing such a power but *necessary* and *proper* laws?

This simple train of inquiry furnishes us at once with a test by which to judge[93] of the true nature of the clause complained of. It conducts us to this palpable truth, that a power to lay and collect taxes must be a power to pass all laws *necessary* and *proper* for the execution of that power; and what does the unfortunate and calumniated provision in question do more than declare the same truth; to wit, that the national legislature to whom the power of laying and collecting taxes had been previously given, might in the execution of that power pass all laws *necessary* and *proper* to carry it into effect? I have applied these observations thus particularly to the power of taxation, because it is the immediate subject under consideration, and because it is the most important of the authorities proposed to be conferred upon the Union. But the same process will lead to the same result in relation to all other powers declared in the constitution. And it is *expressly* to execute these powers, that the sweeping clause, as it has been affectedly called, authorizes the national legislature to pass all *necessary* and *proper* laws. If there is anything exceptionable, it must be sought for in the specific powers, upon which this general declaration is predicated. The declaration itself, though it may be chargeable with tautology or redundancy, is at least perfectly harmless.

But SUSPICION may ask why then was it introduced? The answer is, that it could only have been done for greater caution, and to guard against all caviling refinements in those who might hereafter feel a disposition to curtail and evade the legitimate authorities of the Union. The Convention probably foresaw what it has been a principal aim of these papers to inculcate that the danger which most threatens our political welfare, is, that the State Governments will finally sap the foundations of the Union; and might therefore think it necessary, in so cardinal a point, to leave nothing to construction. Whatever may have been the inducement to it, the wisdom of the precaution is evident from the cry which has been raised against it; as that very cry betrays a disposition to question the great and essential truth which it is manifestly the object of that provision to declare.

But it may be again asked, who is to judge of the *necessity* and *propriety* of the laws to be passed for executing the powers of the Union? I answer

---

93. ["By which to judge" omitted in McLean and later editions.]

first that this question arises as well and as fully upon the simple grant of those powers, as upon the declaratory clause: And I answer in the second place, that the national government, like every other, must judge in the first instance of the proper exercise of its powers; and its constituents in the last. If the Federal Government should overpass the just bounds of its authority, and make a tyrannical use of its powers; the people whose creature it is must appeal to the standard they have formed, and take such measures to redress the injury done to the constitution, as the exigency may suggest and prudence justify. The propriety of a law in a constitutional light, must always be determined by the nature of the powers upon which it is founded. Suppose by some forced constructions of its authority (which indeed cannot easily be imagined) the Federal Legislature should attempt to vary the law of descent in any State; would it not be evident that in making such an attempt it had exceeded its jurisdiction and infringed upon that of the State? Suppose again that upon the pretense of an interference with its revenues, it should undertake to abrogate a land tax imposed by the authority of a State, would it not be equally evident that this was an invasion of that concurrent jurisdiction in respect to this species of tax which its constitution plainly supposes to exist in the State governments? If there ever should be a doubt on this head the credit of it will be entirely due to those reasoners, who, in the imprudent zeal of their animosity to the plan of the Convention, have labored to envelop it in a cloud calculated to obscure the plainest and simplest truths.

But it is said, that the laws of the Union are to be the *supreme law* of the land. But[94] what inference can be drawn from this or what would they amount to, if they were not to be supreme? It is evident they would amount to nothing. A LAW by the very meaning of the term includes supremacy. It is a rule which those to whom it is prescribed are bound to observe. This results from every political association. If individuals enter into a state of society the laws of that society must be the supreme regulator of their conduct. If a number of political societies enter into a larger political society, the laws which the latter may enact, pursuant to the powers entrusted to it by its constitution, must necessarily be supreme over those societies, and the individuals of whom they are composed. It would otherwise be a mere treaty, dependent on the good faith of the parties, and not a government; which is only another word for POLITICAL POWER AND SUPREMACY. But it will not follow from this doctrine that acts of the larger society which are *not pursuant* to its constitutional powers but which are invasions of the residuary authorities of the smaller societies will become the supreme law of the land. These will be merely acts of usurpation and

---

94. ["But" omitted in McLean and later editions.]

will deserve to be treated as such. Hence we perceive that the clause which declares the supremacy of the laws of the Union, like the one we have just before considered, only declares a truth, which flows immediately and necessarily from the institution of a Federal Government. It will not, I presume, have escaped observation that it *expressly* confines this supremacy to laws made *pursuant to the Constitution;* which I mention merely as an instance of caution in the Convention; since that limitation would have been to be understood though it had not been expressed.

Though a law therefore for laying a tax for the use of the United States would be supreme in its nature, and could not legally be opposed or controlled; yet a law for abrogating or preventing the collection of a tax laid by the authority of a State (unless upon imports and exports) would not be the supreme law of the land, but an usurpation of power not granted by the constitution. As far as an improper accumulation of taxes on the same object might tend to render the collection difficult or precarious, this would be a mutual inconvenience not arising from a superiority or defect of power on either side, but from an injudicious exercise of power by one or the other, in a manner equally disadvantageous to both. It is to be hoped and presumed however that mutual interest would dictate a concert in this respect which would avoid any material inconvenience. The inference from the whole is—that the individual States would, under the proposed constitution, retain an independent and uncontrollable authority to raise revenue to any extent of which they may stand in need by every kind of taxation except duties on imports and exports. It will be shown in the next paper[95] that this CONCURRENT JURISDICTION in the article of taxation was the only admissible substitute for an entire subordination, in respect to this branch of power, of the State authority to that of the Union.

[January 2, 1788]

No. 35   [Hamilton][96]

THE SAME SUBJECT CONTINUED

Before we proceed to examine any other objections to an indefinite power of taxation in the Union, I shall make one general remark; which is, that if the jurisdiction of the national government in the article of revenue

---

95. [I.e., Essay 34, not included in this section.]

96. [This essay attacks views identical to those later expressed by Melancton Smith in his speeches of June 21 and 23, 1788.]

should be restricted to particular objects, it will[97] naturally occasion an undue proportion of the public burdens to fall upon those objects. Two evils would spring from this source, the oppression of particular branches of industry, and an unequal distribution of the taxes, as well among the several States as among the citizens of the same State.

Suppose, as has been contended for, the federal power of taxation were to be confined to duties on imports, it is evident that the government, for want of being able to command other resources, would frequently be tempted to extend these duties to an injurious excess. There are persons who imagine that this[98] can never be carried to too great a length;[99] since the higher they are, the more it is alleged they will tend to discourage an extravagant consumption, to produce a favorable balance of trade, and to promote domestic manufactures. But all extremes are pernicious in various ways. Exorbitant duties on imported articles would beget[100] a general spirit of smuggling; which is always prejudicial to the fair trader, and eventually to the revenue itself: They tend to render other classes of the community tributary in an improper degree to the manufacturing classes to whom they give a premature monopoly of the markets: They sometimes force industry out of its more natural channels into others in which it flows with less advantage. And in the last place they oppress the merchant, who is often obliged to pay them himself without any retribution[101] from the consumer. When the demand is equal to the quantity of goods at market, the consumer generally pays the duty; but when the markets happen to be overstocked, a great proportion falls upon the merchant, and sometimes not only exhausts his profits, but breaks in upon his capital. I am apt to think that a division of the duty between the seller and the buyer more often happens than is commonly imagined. It is not always possible to raise the price of a commodity, in exact proportion to every additional imposition laid upon it. The merchant especially, in a country of small commercial capital, is often under a necessity of keeping prices down, in order to a more expeditious sale.

The maxim that the consumer is the payer, is so much oftener true than the reverse of the proposition, that it is far more equitable the duties on imports should go into a common stock, than that they should redound to the exclusive benefit of the importing States. But it is not so

---

97. ["Would" substituted in McLean and subsequent editions.]

98. ["They" in the newspapers.]

99. ["Can never be the case" in McLean and subsequent editions.]

100. ["Serve to beget" in McLean and subsequent editions.]

101. [I.e., compensation.]

generally true as to render it equitable that those duties should form the only national fund. When they are paid by the merchant, they operate as an additional tax upon the importing State; whose citizens pay their proportion of them in the character of consumers. In this view they are productive of inequality among the States; which inequality would be increased with the increased extent of the duties. The confinement of the national revenues to this species of imposts, would be attended with inequality, from a different cause between the manufacturing and the non-manufacturing States. The States which can go furthest toward the supply of their own wants, by their own manufactures, will not, according to their numbers or wealth, consume so great a proportion of imported articles, as those States which are not in the same favorable situation; they would not therefore in this mode alone contribute to the public treasury in a ratio to their abilities. To make them do this, it is necessary that recourse be had to excises; the proper objects of which are particular kinds of manufactures. New York is more deeply interested in these considerations than such of her citizens as contend for limiting the power of the Union to external taxation can be aware of—New York is an importing State, and is not likely speedily to be to any great extent a manufacturing State.[102] She would of course suffer in a double light from restraining the jurisdiction of the Union to commercial imposts.

So far as these observations tend to inculcate a danger of the import duties being extended to an injurious extreme it may be observed, conformably to a remark made in another part of these papers,[103] that the interest of the revenue itself would be a sufficient guard against such an extreme. I readily admit that this would be the case as long as other resources were open; but if the avenues to them were closed HOPE stimulated by necessity would[104] beget experiments fortified by rigorous precautions and additional penalties; which for a time would have the intended effect, until there had been leisure to contrive expedients to elude these new precautions. The first success would be apt to inspire false opinions; which it might require a long course of subsequent experience to correct. Necessity, especially in politics, often occasions false hopes, false reasonings, and a system of measures, correspondently erroneous. But even if this supposed excess should not be a consequence of the limitation of the

---

102. ["And from a greater disproportion between her population and territory, is less likely, than some other states, speedily to become in any considerable degree a manufacturing state" in McLean and subsequent editions.]

103. [In Essay 21, not included in this selection.]

104. ["Might" in McLean and subsequent editions, both here and in the next phrase.]

federal power of taxation the inequalities spoken of would still ensue, though not in the same degree, from the other causes that have been noticed. Let us now return to the examination of objections—

One, which if we may judge from the frequency of its repetition seems most to be relied on, is that the house of representatives is not sufficiently numerous for the reception of all the different classes of citizens; in order to combine the interests and feelings of every part of the community, and to produce a due[105] sympathy between the representative body and its constituents. This argument presents itself under a very specious and seducing form; and is well calculated to lay hold of the prejudices of those to whom it is addressed. But when we come to dissect it with attention it will appear to be made up of nothing but fair-sounding words. The object it seems to aim at is in the first place impracticable, and in the sense in which it is contended for is unnecessary. I reserve for another place the discussion of the question which relates to the sufficiency of the representative body in respect to numbers;[106] and shall content myself with examining here the particular use which has been made of a contrary supposition in reference to the immediate subject of our inquiries.

The idea of an actual representation of all classes of the people by persons of each class is altogether visionary. Unless it were expressly provided in the Constitution that each different occupation should send one or more members the thing would never take place in practice. Mechanics and manufacturers will always be inclined with few exceptions to give their votes to merchants in preference to persons of their own professions or trades. Those discerning citizens are well aware that the mechanic and manufacturing arts furnish the materials of mercantile enterprise and industry. Many of them indeed are immediately connected with the operations of commerce. They know that the merchant is their natural patron and friend; and they are aware that however great the confidence they may justly feel in their own good sense, their interests can be more effectually promoted by the merchant than by themselves. They are sensible that their habits in life have not been such as to give them those acquired endowments, without which in a deliberative assembly the greatest natural abilities are for the most part useless; and that the influence and weight and superior acquirements of the merchants render them more equal to a contest with any spirit which might happen to infuse itself into the public councils unfriendly to the manufacturing and trading interests. These considerations and many others that might be mentioned prove, and experience confirms it, that artisans and manufacturers will

---

105. ["True" substituted in McLean.]
106. [In Essays 54 (not included in this selection) and 55.]

commonly be disposed to bestow their votes upon merchants and those whom they recommend. We must therefore consider merchants as the natural representatives of all these classes of the community.

With regard to the learned professions, little need be observed; they truly form no distinct interest in society; and according to their situation and talents will be indiscriminately the objects of the confidence and choice of each other and of other parts of the community.

Nothing remains but the landed interest; and this in a political view and particularly in relation to taxes I take to be perfectly united from the wealthiest landlord to the poorest tenant. No tax can be laid on land which will not affect the proprietor of millions of acres as well as the proprietor of a single acre. Every landholder will therefore have a common interest to keep the taxes on land as low as possible; and common interest may always be reckoned upon as the surest bond of sympathy. But if we even could suppose a distinction of interest between the opulent landholder and the middling farmer, what reason is there to conclude that the first would stand a better chance of being deputed to the national legislature than the last? If we take fact as our guide and look into our own senate and assembly we shall find that moderate proprietors of land prevail in both; nor is this less the case in the senate which consists of a smaller number than in the Assembly, which is composed of a greater number. Where the qualifications of the electors are the same, whether they have to choose a small or a large number their votes will fall upon those in whom they have most confidence; whether these happen to be men of large fortunes or of moderate property or of no property at all.

It is said to be necessary that all classes of citizens should have some of their own number in the representative body, in order that their feelings and interests may be the better understood and attended to. But we have seen that this will never happen under any arrangement that leaves the votes of the people free. Where this is the case, the representative body, with too few exceptions to have any influence on the spirit of the government, will be composed of landholders, merchants, and men of the learned professions. But where is the danger that the interests and feelings of the different classes of citizens will not be understood or attended to by these three descriptions of men? Will not the landholder know and feel whatever will promote or injure the interests of landed property? and will he not from his own interest in that species of property be sufficiently prone to resist every attempt to prejudice or encumber it? Will not the merchant understand and be disposed to cultivate as far as may be proper the interests of the mechanic and manufacturing arts to which his commerce is so nearly allied? Will not the man of the learned profession, who will feel a neutrality to the rivalships between the different branches of industry, be likely to prove an impartial arbiter between them, ready to promote either, so far as it shall appear to him conducive to the general interests of the society?

If we take into the account the momentary humors or dispositions which may happen to prevail in particular parts of the society, and to which a wise administration will never be inattentive, is the man whose situation leads to extensive inquiry and information less likely to be a competent judge of their nature, extent, and foundation than one whose observation does not travel beyond the circle of his neighbors and acquaintances? Is it not natural that a man who is a candidate for the favor of the people and who is dependent on the suffrages of his fellow citizens for the continuance of his public honors should take care to inform himself of their dispositions and inclinations and should be willing to allow them their proper degree of influence upon his conduct? This dependence, and the necessity of being bound himself and his posterity by the laws to which he gives his assent are the true, and they are the strong chords of sympathy between the representatives and the constituent.

There is no part of the administration of government that requires extensive information and a thorough knowledge of the principles of political economy so much as the business of taxation. The man who understands those principles best will be least likely to resort to oppressive expedients, or to sacrifice any particular class of citizens to the procurement of revenue. It might be demonstrated that the most productive system of finance will always be the least burdensome. There can be no doubt that in order to a judicious exercise of the power of taxation it is necessary that the person in whose hands it is should be acquainted with the general genius, habits, and modes of thinking of the people at large and with the resources of the country. And this is all that can be reasonably meant by a knowledge of the interests and feelings of the people. In any other sense the proposition has either no meaning, or an absurd one. And in that sense let every considerate citizen judge for himself where the requisite qualification is most likely to be found.

[January 5, 1788]

No. 37   [Madison]

CONCERNING THE DIFFICULTIES WHICH THE CONVENTION MUST HAVE EXPERIENCED IN THE FORMATION OF A PROPER PLAN

In reviewing the defects of the existing Confederation, and showing that they cannot be supplied by a Government of less energy than that before the public, several of the most important principles of the latter fell of course under consideration. But as the ultimate object of these papers is to determine clearly and fully the merits of this Constitution, and the expediency of adopting it, our plan cannot be completed without taking a more critical and thorough survey of the work of the Convention; without examining it on all its sides; comparing it in all its parts, and calculating its probable effects. That this remaining task may be executed under impressions conducive to a just and fair result, some reflections must in this place be indulged, which candor previously suggests.

It is a misfortune, inseparable from human affairs, that public measures are rarely investigated with that spirit of moderation which is essential to a just estimate of their real tendency to advance or obstruct the public good; and that this spirit is more apt to be diminished than promoted, by those occasions which require an unusual exercise of it. To those who have been led by experience to attend to this consideration, it could not appear surprising, that the act of the Convention which recommends so many important changes and innovations, which may be viewed in so many lights and relations, and which touches the springs of so many passions and interests, should find or excite dispositions unfriendly both on one side, and on the other, to a fair discussion and accurate judgment of its merits. In some, it has been too evident from their own publications, that they have scanned the proposed Constitution, not only with a predisposition to censure; but with a predetermination to condemn: as the language held by others betrays an opposite predetermination or bias, which must render their opinions also of little moment in the question. In placing however, these different characters on a level, with respect to the weight of their opinions, I wish not to insinuate that there may not be a material difference in the purity of their intentions. It is but just to remark in favor of the latter description, that as our situation is universally admitted to be peculiarly critical, and to require indispensably, that something should be done for our relief, the predetermined patron of what has been actually done, may have taken his bias from the weight of these considerations, as well as from considerations of a sinister nature. The predetermined adversary on the other hand, can have been governed by no venial motive whatever. The intentions of the first may be upright, as they may on the contrary be culpable. The views of the last cannot be upright, and must be culpable. But the truth is, that these papers are not addressed to persons falling under either of these characters. They solicit the attention of those only, who add to a sincere zeal for the happiness of their country, a temper favorable to a just estimate of the means of promoting it.

Persons of this character will proceed to an examination of the plan submitted by the Convention, not only without a disposition to find or to magnify faults; but will see the propriety of reflecting that a faultless plan was not to be expected. Nor will they barely make allowances for the errors which may be chargeable on the fallibility to which the Convention, as a body of men, were liable; but will keep in mind that they themselves also are but men, and ought not to assume an infallibility in rejudging the fallible opinions of others.

With equal readiness will it be perceived, that besides these inducements to candor, many allowances ought to be made for the difficulties inherent in the very nature of the undertaking referred to the Convention.

The novelty of the undertaking immediately strikes us. It has been shown in the course of these papers, that the existing confederation is founded on principles which are fallacious;[107] that we must consequently change this first foundation, and with it, the superstructure resting upon it. It has been shown,[108] that the other confederacies which could be consulted as precedents, have been vitiated by the same erroneous principles, and can therefore furnish no other light than that of beacons, which give warning of the course to be shunned, without pointing out that which ought to be pursued. The most that the Convention could do in such a situation, was to avoid the errors suggested by the past experience of other countries, as well as of our own; and to provide a convenient mode of rectifying their own errors, as future experience may unfold them.

Among the difficulties encountered by the Convention, a very important one must have lain, in combining the requisite stability and energy in Government with the inviolable attention due to liberty, and to the Republican form. Without substantially accomplishing this part of their undertaking, they would have very imperfectly fulfilled the object of their appointment, or the expectation of the public: Yet, that it could not be easily accomplished, will be denied by no one, who is unwilling to betray his ignorance of the subject. Energy in Government is essential to that security against external and internal danger, and to that prompt and salutary execution of the laws, which enter into the very definition of good Government. Stability in government, is essential to national character, and to the advantages annexed to it, as well as to that repose and confidence in the minds of the people, which are among the chief blessings of civil society. An irregular and mutable legislation, is not more an evil in itself, than it is odious to the people; and it may be pronounced with assurance, that the people of this country, enlightened as they are, with regard to the nature, and interested, as the great body of them are, in the

---

107. [See Essays 15 and 16, above.]
108. [In Essays 18, 19, and 20, not included in this selection.]

effects of good Government, will never be satisfied, until some remedy be applied to the vicissitudes and uncertainties, which characterize the State administrations. On comparing, however, these valuable ingredients with the vital principles of liberty, we must perceive at once, the difficulty of mingling them together in their due proportions. The genius of Republican liberty, seems to demand on one side, not only that all power should be derived from the people; but, that those entrusted with it should be kept in dependence on the people, by a short duration of their appointments; and, that, even during this short period, the trust should be placed not in a few, but in a number of hands. Stability, on the contrary, requires, that the hands, in which power is lodged, should continue for a length of time, the same. A frequent change of men will result from a frequent return of elections,[109] and a frequent change of measures, from a frequent change of men: while energy in Government requires not only a certain duration of power, but the execution of it by a single hand. How far the Convention may have succeeded in this part of their work, will better appear on a more accurate view of it. From the cursory view, here taken, it must clearly appear to have been an arduous part.

Not less arduous must have been the task of marking the proper line of partition, between the authority of the general, and that of the State Governments. Every man will be sensible of this difficulty, in proportion, as he has been accustomed to contemplate and discriminate objects, extensive and complicated in their nature. The faculties of the mind itself have never yet been distinguished and defined, with satisfactory precision, by all the efforts of the most acute and metaphysical Philosophers. Sense, perception, judgment, desire, volition, memory, imagination, are found to be separated by such delicate shades, and minute gradations, that their boundaries have eluded the most subtle investigations, and remain a pregnant source of ingenious disquisition and controversy. The boundaries between the great kingdoms of nature, and still more, between the various provinces, and lesser portions, into which they are subdivided, afford another illustration of the same important truth. The most sagacious and laborious naturalists have never yet succeeded, in tracing with certainty, the line which separates the district of vegetable life from the neighboring region of unorganized matter, or which marks the termination of the former and the commencement of the animal empire. A still greater obscurity lies in the distinctive characters, by which the objects in each of these great departments of nature, have been arranged and assorted.

When we pass from the works of nature, in which all the delineations are perfectly accurate, and appear to be otherwise only from the imperfection

---

109. [McLean mistakenly substitutes "electors" for "elections."]

of the eye which surveys them, to the institutions of man, in which the obscurity arises as well from the object itself, as from the organ by which it is contemplated; we must perceive the necessity of moderating still further our expectations and hopes from the efforts of human sagacity. Experience has instructed us that no skill in the science of Government has yet been able to discriminate and define, with sufficient certainty, its three great provinces, the Legislative, Executive, and Judiciary; or even the privileges and powers of the different Legislative branches. Questions daily occur in the course of practice, which prove the obscurity which reigns in these subjects, and which puzzle the greatest adepts in political science.

The experience of ages, with the continued and combined labors of the most enlightened Legislators and jurists, have been equally unsuccessful in delineating the several objects and limits of different codes of laws and different tribunals of justice. The precise extent of the common law, the statute law, the maritime law, the ecclesiastical law, the law of corporations, and other local laws and customs, remain still to be clearly and finally established in Great Britain, where accuracy in such subjects has been more industriously pursued than in any other part of the world. The jurisdiction of her several courts, general and local, of law, of equity, of admiralty, etc. is not less a source of frequent and intricate discussions, sufficiently denoting the indeterminate limits by which they are respectively circumscribed. All new laws, though penned with the greatest technical skill, and passed on the fullest and most mature deliberation, are considered as more or less obscure and equivocal, until their meaning be liquidated and ascertained by a series of particular discussions and adjudications. Besides the obscurity arising from the complexity of objects, and the imperfection of the human faculties, the medium through which the conceptions of men are conveyed to each other, adds a fresh embarrassment. The use of words is to express ideas. Perspicuity therefore requires not only that the ideas should be distinctly formed, but that they should be expressed by words distinctly and exclusively appropriated to them. But no language is so copious as to supply words and phrases for every complex idea, or so correct as not to include many equivocally denoting different ideas. Hence, it must happen, that however accurately objects may be discriminated in themselves, and however accurately the discrimination may be considered, the definition of them may be rendered inaccurate by the inaccuracy of the terms in which it is delivered. And this unavoidable inaccuracy must be greater or less, according to the complexity or novelty of the objects defined. When the Almighty himself condescends to address mankind in their own language, his meaning luminous as it must be, is rendered dim and doubtful, by the cloudy medium through which it is communicated. Here then are three sources of vague and incorrect definitions; indistinctness of the object, imperfection of the organ of conception, inadequateness of the vehicle of ideas. Any one of these must produce a certain degree of obscurity. The Convention, in delineating the boundary between the Federal and State jurisdictions, must have experienced the full effect of them all.

To the difficulties already mentioned, may be added the interfering pretensions of the larger and smaller States. We cannot err in supposing that the former would contend for a participation in the Government, fully proportioned to their superior wealth and importance; and that the latter would not be less tenacious of the equality at present enjoyed by them. We may well suppose that neither side would entirely yield to the other, and consequently that the struggle could be terminated only by compromise. It is extremely probable also, that after the ratio of representation had been adjusted, this very compromise must have produced a fresh struggle between the same parties, to give such a turn to the organization of the Government, and to the distribution of its powers, as would increase the importance of the branches, in forming which they had respectively obtained the greatest share of influence. There are features in the Constitution which warrant each of these suppositions; and as far as either of them is well founded, it shows that the Convention must have been compelled to sacrifice theoretical propriety to the force of extraneous considerations.

Nor could it have been the large and small States only which would marshal themselves in opposition to each other on various points. Other combinations, resulting from a difference of local position and policy, must have created additional difficulties. As every State may be divided into different districts, and its citizens into different classes, which give birth to contending interests and local jealousies; so the different parts of the United States are distinguished from each other, by a variety of circumstances, which produce a like effect on a larger scale. And although this variety of interests, for reasons sufficiently explained in a former paper,[110] may have a salutary influence on the administration of the Government when formed; yet every one must be sensible of the contrary influence which must have been experienced in the task of forming it.

Would it be wonderful if under the pressure of all these difficulties, the Convention should have been forced into some deviations from that artificial structure and regular symmetry, which an abstract view of the subject might lead an ingenious theorist to bestow on a Constitution planned in his closet or in his imagination? The real wonder is, that so many difficulties should have been surmounted; and surmounted with a unanimity

---

110. [Essay 10.]

almost as unprecedented as it must have been unexpected. It is impossible for any man of candor to reflect on this circumstance, without partaking of the astonishment. It is impossible for the man of pious reflection not to perceive in it, a finger of that Almighty hand which has been so frequently and so signally extended to our relief in the critical stages of the revolution. We had occasion in a former paper, to take notice of the repeated trials which have been unsuccessfully made in the United Netherlands,[111] for reforming the baneful and notorious vices of their Constitution. The history of almost all the great councils and consultations, held among mankind for reconciling their discordant opinions, assuaging their mutual jealousies, and adjusting their respective interests, is a history of factions, contentions, and disappointments; and may be classed among the most dark and degrading pictures which display the infirmities and depravities of the human character. If, in a few scattered instances, a brighter aspect is presented, they serve only as exceptions to admonish us of the general truth; and by their luster to darken the gloom of the adverse prospect to which they are contrasted. In revolving the causes from which these exceptions result, and applying them to the particular instance before us, we are necessarily led to two important conclusions. The first is, that the Convention must have enjoyed in a very singular degree, an exemption from the pestilential influence of party animosities; the diseases most incident to deliberative bodies, and most apt to contaminate their proceedings. The second conclusion is, that all the deputations composing the Convention, were either satisfactorily accommodated by the final act; or were induced to accede to it, by a deep conviction of the necessity of sacrificing private opinions and partial interests to the public good, and by a despair of seeing this necessity diminished by delays or by new experiments.

[January 11, 1788]

No. 39   [Madison]

THE CONFORMITY OF THE PLAN TO REPUBLICAN
PRINCIPLES: AN OBJECTION IN RESPECT TO THE
POWERS OF THE CONVENTION EXAMINED

The last paper[112] having concluded the observations which were meant to introduce a candid survey of the plan of government reported by the

---

111. [Essay 20, not included in this selection.]
112. [Essay 38, not included in this selection.]

Convention, we now proceed to the execution of that part of our undertaking. The first question that offers itself is, whether the general form
and aspect of the government be strictly republican? It is evident that
no other form would be reconcilable with the genius of the people of
America; with the fundamental principles of the revolution; or with that
honorable determination, which animates every votary of freedom, to
rest all our political experiments on the capacity of mankind for self-
government. If the plan of the Convention therefore be found to depart
from the republican character, its advocates must abandon it as no longer
defensible.

What then are the distinctive characters of the republican form? Were
an answer to this question to be sought, not by recurring to principles,
but in the application of the term by political writers, to the constitutions
of different States, no satisfactory one would ever be found. Holland, in
which no particle of the supreme authority is derived from the people, has
passed almost universally under the denomination of a republic. The
same title has been bestowed on Venice, where absolute power over the
great body of the people, is exercised in the most absolute manner, by a
small body of hereditary nobles. Poland, which is a mixture of aristocracy
and of monarchy in their worst forms, has been dignified with the same
appellation. The government of England, which has one republican
branch only, combined with a hereditary aristocracy and monarchy, has
with equal impropriety been frequently placed on the list of republics.
These examples, which are nearly as dissimilar to each other as to a genuine republic, show the extreme inaccuracy with which the term has been
used in political disquisitions.

If we resort for a criterion, to the different principles on which different forms of government are established, we may define a republic to be,
or at least may bestow that name on, a government which derives all its
powers directly or indirectly from the great body of the people; and is
administered by persons holding their offices during pleasure, for a limited period, or during good behavior. It is *essential* to such a government,
that it be derived from the great body of the society, not from an inconsiderable proportion, or a favored class of it; otherwise a handful of tyrannical nobles, exercising their oppressions by a delegation of their powers,
might aspire to the rank of republicans, and claim for their government
the honorable title of republic. It is *sufficient* for such a government, that
the persons administering it be appointed, either directly or indirectly, by
the people; and that they hold their appointments by either of the tenures
just specified; otherwise every government in the United States, as well as
every other popular government that has been or can be well organized or
well executed, would be degraded from the republican character. Accord-

ing to the constitution of every State in the Union, some or other of the officers of government are appointed indirectly only by the people. According to most of them the chief magistrate himself is so appointed. And according to one, this mode of appointment is extended to one of the coordinate branches of the legislature. According to all the Constitutions also, the tenure of the highest offices is extended to a definite period, and in many instances, both within the legislative and executive departments, to a period of years. According to the provisions of most of the constitutions, again, as well as according to the most respectable and received opinions on the subject, the members of the judiciary department are to retain their offices by the firm tenure of good behavior.

On comparing the Constitution planned by the Convention, with the standard here fixed, we perceive at once that it is in the most rigid sense conformable to it. The House of Representatives, like that of one branch at least of all the State Legislatures, is elected immediately by the great body of the people. The Senate, like the present Congress, and the Senate of Maryland, derives its appointment indirectly from the people. The President is indirectly derived from the choice of the people, according to the example in most of the States. Even the judges, with all other officers of the Union, will, as in the several States, be the choice, though a remote choice, of the people themselves. The duration of the appointments is equally conformable to the republican standard, and to the model of the State Constitutions. The House of Representatives is periodically elective as in all the States: and for the period of two years as in the State of South Carolina. The Senate is elective for the period of six years; which is but one year more than the period of the Senate of Maryland; and but two more than of the Senates of New York and Virginia. The President is to continue in office for the period of four years; as in New York and Delaware, the chief magistrate is elected for three years, and in South Carolina for two years. In the other States the election is annual. In several of the States however, no constitutional[113] provision is made for the impeachment of the chief magistrate. And in Delaware and Virginia, he is not impeachable until out of office. The President of the United States is impeachable at any time during his continuance in office. The tenure by which the Judges are to hold their places, is, as it unquestionably ought to be, that of good behavior. The tenure of the ministerial offices generally will be a subject of legal regulation, conformably to the reason of the case, and the example of the State Constitutions.

Could any further proof be required of the republican complexion of this system, the most decisive one might be found in its absolute

---

113. [Changed to "explict" in McLean and later editions.]

prohibition of titles of nobility, both under the Federal and the State Governments; and in its express guarantee of the republican form to each of the latter.

But it was not sufficient, say the adversaries of the proposed Constitution, for the Convention to adhere to the republican form. They ought, with equal care, to have preserved the *federal* form, which regards the union as a *confederacy* of sovereign States; instead of which, they have framed a *national* government, which regards the union as a *consolidation* of the States. And it is asked by what authority this bold and radical innovation was undertaken. The handle which has been made of this objection requires, that it should be examined with some precision.

Without inquiring into the accuracy of the distinction on which the objection is founded, it will be necessary to a just estimate of its force, first to ascertain the real character of the government in question; secondly, to inquire how far the Convention were authorized to propose such a government; and thirdly, how far the duty they owed to their country, could supply any defect of regular authority.

First. In order to ascertain the real character of the government it may be considered in relation to the foundation on which it is to be established; to the sources from which its ordinary powers are to be drawn; to the operation of those powers; to the extent of them; and to the authority by which future changes in the government are to be introduced.

On examining the first relation, it appears on one hand that the Constitution is to be founded on the assent and ratification of the people of America, given by deputies elected for the special purpose; but on the other, that this assent and ratification is to be given by the people, not as individuals composing one entire nation; but as composing the distinct and independent States to which they respectively belong. It is to be the assent and ratification of the several States, derived from the supreme authority in each State, the authority of the people themselves. The act therefore establishing the Constitution, will not be a *national* but a *federal* act.

That it will be a federal and not a national act, as these terms are understood by the objectors, the act of the people as forming so many independent States, not as forming one aggregate nation, is obvious from this single consideration, that it is to result neither from the decision of a *majority* of the people of the Union, nor from that of the *majority* of the States. It must result from the *unanimous* assent of the several States that are parties to it, differing no otherwise from their ordinary assent than in its being expressed, not by the legislative authority, but by that of the people themselves. Were the people regarded in this transaction as forming one nation, the will of the majority of the whole people of the United

States, would bind the minority; in the same manner as the majority in each State must bind the minority; and the will of the majority must be determined either by a comparison of the individual votes; or by considering the will of a majority of the States, as evidence of the will of a majority of the people of the United States. Neither of these rules has been adopted. Each State in ratifying the Constitution, is considered as a sovereign body independent of all others, and only to be bound by its own voluntary act. In this relation then the new Constitution will, if established, be a *federal* and not a *national* Constitution.

The next relation is to the sources from which the ordinary powers of government are to be derived. The house of representatives will derive its powers from the people of America, and the people will be represented in the same proportion, and on the same principle, as they are in the Legislature of a particular State. So far the government is *national* not *federal*. The Senate on the other hand will derive its powers from the States, as political and coequal societies; and these will be represented on the principle of equality in the Senate, as they now are in the existing Congress. So far the government is *federal*, not *national*. The executive power will be derived from a very compound source. The immediate election of the President is to be made by the States in their political characters. The votes allotted to them, are in a compound ratio, which considers them partly as distinct and coequal societies; partly as unequal members of the same society. The eventual election, again is to be made by that branch of the Legislature which consists of the national representatives; but in this particular act, they are to be thrown into the form of individual delegations from so many distinct and coequal bodies politic. From this aspect of the Government, it appears to be of a mixed character presenting at least as many *federal* as *national* features.

The difference between a federal and national government, as it relates to the *operation of the Government,* is[114] supposed to consist in this, that in the former, the powers operate on the political bodies composing the confederacy, in their political capacities: In the latter, on the individual citizens, composing the nation, in their individual capacities. On trying the Constitution by this criterion, it falls under the *national,* not the *federal* character; though perhaps not so completely, as has been understood. In several cases and particularly in the trial of controversies to which States may be parties, they must be viewed and proceeded against in their collective and political capacities only. So far the national countenance of the Government on this side seems to be disfigured by a few federal features.

---

114. [McLean inserts "by the adversaries of the plan of the convention" here, perhaps aware that the argument would otherwise be at odds with that of Essay 9.]

But this blemish is perhaps unavoidable in any plan; and[115] the operation of the Government on the people in their individual capacities, in its ordinary and most essential proceedings, may [116] on the whole designate it in this relation a *national* government.

But if the Government be national with regard to the *operation* of its powers, it changes its aspect again when we contemplate it in relation to the *extent* of its powers. The idea of a national Government involves in it, not only an authority over the individual citizens, but an indefinite supremacy over all persons and things, so far as they are objects of lawful Government. Among a people consolidated into one nation, this supremacy is completely vested in the national Legislature. Among communities united for particular purposes, it is vested partly in the general, and partly in the municipal Legislatures. In the former case, all local authorities are subordinate to the supreme; and may be controlled, directed, or abolished by it at pleasure. In the latter the local or municipal authorities form distinct and independent portions of the supremacy, no more subject within their respective spheres to the general authority, than the general authority is subject to them, within its own sphere. In this relation then the proposed Government cannot be deemed a *national* one; since its jurisdiction extends to certain enumerated objects only, and leaves to the several States a residuary and inviolable sovereignty over all other objects. It is true that in controversies relating to the boundary between the two jurisdictions, the tribunal which is ultimately to decide, is to be established under the general Government.[117] But this does not change the principle of the case. The decision is to be impartially made, according to the rules of the Constitution; and all the usual and most effectual precautions are taken to secure this impartiality. Some such tribunal is clearly essential to prevent an appeal to the sword, and a dissolution of the compact; and that it ought to be established under the general, rather than under the local Governments; or to speak more properly, that it could be safely established under the first alone, is a position not likely to be combated.

If we try the constitution by its last relation, to the authority by which amendments are to be made, we find it neither wholly *national*, nor wholly *federal*. Were it wholly national, the supreme and ultimate authority would reside in the *majority* of the people of the Union; and this authority

---

115. [McLean omits the passage from "So far" to here, substituting "but" for "and."]

116. [McLean changes "may" to "will" and inserts "in the sense of its opponents."]

117. [This is the first reference to judicial review. The idea is absent two weeks earlier (above, p. 213).]

would be competent at all times, like that of a majority of every national society, to alter or abolish its established Government. Were it wholly federal on the other hand, the concurrence of each State in the Union would be essential to every alteration that would be binding on all. The mode provided by the plan of the Convention, is not founded on either of these principles. In requiring more than a majority, and particularly, in computing the proportion by *States*, not by *citizens*, it departs from the *national*, and advances toward the *federal* character: In rendering the concurrence of less than the whole number of States sufficient, it loses again the *federal*, and partakes of the *national* character.

The proposed Constitution therefore[118] is in strictness neither a national nor a federal constitution; but a composition of both. In its foundation, it is federal, not national; in the sources from which the ordinary powers of the Government are drawn, it is partly federal, and partly national: in the operation of these powers, it is national, not federal: In the extent of them again, it is federal, not national: And finally, in the authoritative mode of introducing amendments, it is neither wholly federal, nor wholly national.

[January 16, 1788]

No. 47   [Madison]

THE MEANING OF THE MAXIM, WHICH REQUIRES A SEPARATION OF THE DEPARTMENTS OF POWER, EXAMINED AND ASCERTAINED

Having reviewed the general form of the proposed government, and the general mass of power allotted to it: I proceed to examine the particular structure of this government, and the distribution of this mass of power among its constituent parts.

One of the principal objections inculcated by the more respectable adversaries to the constitution, is its supposed violation of the political maxim, that the legislative, executive and judiciary departments ought to be separate and distinct. In the structure of the federal government, no regard, it is said, seems to have been paid to this essential precaution in favor of liberty. The several departments of power are distributed and blended in such a manner, as at once to destroy all symmetry and beauty of form; and to expose some of the essential parts of the edifice to the danger of being crushed by the disproportionate weight of other parts.

---

118. [McLean inserts "even when tested by the rules laid down by its antagonists."]

No political truth is certainly of greater intrinsic value or is stamped with the authority of more enlightened patrons of liberty, than that on which the objection is founded. The accumulation of all powers legislative, executive, and judiciary in the same hands, whether of one, a few, or many, and whether hereditary, self-appointed, or elective, may justly be pronounced the very definition of tyranny. Were the federal constitution therefore really chargeable with this accumulation of power or with a mixture of powers, having a dangerous tendency to such an accumulation, no further arguments would be necessary to inspire a universal reprobation of the system. I persuade myself however, that it will be made apparent to everyone, that the charge cannot be supported, and that the maxim on which it relies, has been totally misconceived and misapplied. In order to form correct ideas on this important subject, it will be proper to investigate the sense, in which the preservation of liberty requires, that the three great departments of power should be separate and distinct.

The oracle who is always consulted and cited on this subject, is the celebrated Montesquieu. If he be not the author of this invaluable precept in the science of politics, he has the merit at least of displaying, and recommending it most effectually to the attention of mankind. Let us endeavor in the first place to ascertain his meaning on this point.

The British constitution was to Montesquieu, what Homer has been to the didactic writers on epic poetry. As the latter have considered the work of the immortal Bard, as the perfect model from which the principles and rules of the epic art were to be drawn, and by which all similar works were to be judged; so this great political critic appears to have viewed the constitution of England, as the standard, or to use his own expression, as the mirror of political liberty; and to have delivered in the form of elementary truths, the several characteristic principles of that particular system. That we may be sure then not to mistake his meaning in this case, let us recur to the source from which the maxim was drawn.

On the slightest view of the British constitution we must perceive, that the legislative, executive, and judiciary departments are by no means totally separate and distinct from each other. The executive magistrate forms an integral part of the legislative authority. He alone has the prerogative of making treaties with foreign sovereigns, which when made have, under certain limitations, the force of legislative acts. All the members of the judiciary department are appointed by him; can be removed by him on the address of the two Houses of Parliament, and form, when he pleases to consult them, one of his constitutional councils. One branch of the legislative department forms also, a great constitutional council to the executive chief; as on another hand, it is the sole depositary of judicial power in cases of impeachment, and is invested with the supreme appellate jurisdiction, in all other cases. The judges again are so far connected with the legislative department, as often to attend and participate in its deliberations, though not admitted to a legislative vote.

From these facts by which Montesquieu was guided it may clearly be inferred, that in saying "there can be no liberty where the legislative and executive powers are united in the same person, or body of magistrates," or "if the power of judging be not separated from the legislative and executive powers," he did not mean that these departments ought to have no *partial agency* in, or no *control* over the acts of each other. His meaning, as his own words import, and still more conclusively as illustrated by the example in his eye, can amount to no more than this, that where the *whole* power of one department is exercised by the same hands which possess the *whole* power of another department, the fundamental principles of a free constitution, are subverted. This would[119] have been the case in the constitution examined by him, if the King who is the sole executive magistrate, had possessed also the complete legislative power, or the supreme administration of justice; or if the entire legislative body had possessed the supreme judiciary, or the supreme executive authority. This however is not among the vices of that constitution. The magistrate in whom the whole executive power resides cannot of himself make a law, though he can put a negative on every law, nor administer justice in person, though he has the appointment of those who do administer it. The judges can exercise no executive prerogative, though they are shoots from the executive stock, nor any legislative function, though they may be advised with by the legislative councils. The entire legislature, can perform no judiciary act, though by the joint act of two of its branches, the judges may be removed from their offices; and though one of its branches is possessed of the judicial power in the last resort. The entire legislature again can exercise no executive prerogative, though one of its branches[120] constitutes the supreme executive magistracy; and another,[121] on the impeachment of a third,[122] can try and condemn all the subordinate officers in the executive department.

The reasons on which Montesquieu grounds his maxim are a further demonstration of his meaning. "When the legislative and executive powers are united in the same person or body" says he, "there can be no liberty, because apprehensions may arise lest *the same* monarch or senate

---

119. [McLean (obviously mistakenly, as Gideon recognizes) inserts "not" here.]
120. [The King.]
121. [The House of Lords.]
122. [The House of Commons.]

should *enact* tyrannical laws, to *execute* them in a tyrannical manner."
Again "Were the power of judging joined with the legislative, the life and
liberty of the subject would be exposed to arbitrary control, for *the judge*
would then be *the legislator*. Were it joined to the executive power, *the
judge* might behave with all the violence of *an oppressor*." Some of these
reasons are more fully explained in other passages; but briefly stated as
they are here, they sufficiently establish the meaning which we have put
on this celebrated maxim of this celebrated author.

If we look into the constitutions of the several states we find that notwithstanding the emphatical, and in some instances, the unqualified
terms in which this axiom has been laid down, there is not a single
instance in which the several departments of power have been kept absolutely separate and distinct. New Hampshire, whose constitution was the
last formed, seems to have been fully aware of the impossibility and inex-
pediency of avoiding any mixture whatever of these departments; and has
qualified the doctrine by declaring "that the legislative, executive and
judiciary powers ought to be kept as separate from, and independent of
each other *as the nature of a free government will admit; or as is consistent
with that chain of connection, that binds the whole fabric of the constitution in
one indissoluble bond of unity and amity*." Her constitution accordingly
mixes these departments in several respects. The senate which is a branch
of the legislative department is also a judicial tribunal for the trial of
impeachments. The president who is the head of the executive department, is the presiding member also of the senate; and besides an equal
vote in all cases, has a casting vote in case of a tie. The executive head is
himself eventually elective every year by the legislative department; and
his council is every year chosen by and from the members of the same
department. Several of the officers of state are also appointed by the legislature. And the members of the judiciary department are appointed by the
executive department.

The constitution of Massachusetts has observed a sufficient though
less pointed caution in expressing this fundamental article of liberty. It
declares "that the legislative department shall never exercise the executive
and judicial powers, or either of them: The executive shall never exercise
the legislative and judicial powers, or either of them: The judicial shall
never exercise the legislative and executive powers, or either of them."
This declaration corresponds precisely with the doctrine of Montesquieu
as it has been explained, and is not in a single point violated by the plan of
the Convention. It goes no further than to prohibit any one of the entire
departments from exercising the powers of another department. In the
very constitution to which it is prefixed, a partial mixture of powers has
been admitted. The Executive Magistrate has a qualified negative on the

Legislative body, and the Senate, which is a part of the Legislature, is a court of impeachment for members both of the executive and judiciary departments. The members of the judiciary department again are appointable by the executive department, and removable by the same authority, on the address of the two legislative branches. Lastly, a number of the officers of government are annually appointed by the legislative department. As the appointment to offices, particularly executive offices, is in its nature an executive function, the compilers of the Constitution have in this last point at least, violated the rule established by themselves.

I pass over the constitutions of Rhode Island and Connecticut, because they were formed prior to the revolution; and even before the principle under examination had become an object of political attention.

The constitution of New York contains no declaration on this subject; but appears very clearly to have been framed with an eye to the danger of improperly blending the different departments. It gives nevertheless to the executive magistrate a partial control over the legislative department; and what is more, gives a like control to the judiciary department, and even blends the executive and judiciary departments in the exercise of this control. In its council of appointment, members of the legislative are associated with the executive authority in the appointment of officers both executive and judiciary. And its court for the trial of impeachments and correction of errors, is to consist of one branch of the legislature and the principal members of the judiciary department.

The constitution of New Jersey has blended the different powers of government more than any of the preceding. The governor, who is the executive magistrate, is appointed by the legislature; is chancellor and ordinary or surrogate of the state; is a member of the supreme court of appeals, and president with a casting vote, of one of the legislative branches. The same legislative branch acts again as executive council to the governor, and with him constitutes the court of appeals. The members of the judiciary department are appointed by the legislative department, and removable by one branch of it, on the impeachment of the other.

According to the constitution of Pennsylvania, the president, who is head of the executive department, is annually elected by a vote in which the legislative department predominates. In conjunction with an executive council, he appoints the members of the judiciary department, and forms a court of impeachment for trial of all officers, judiciary as well as executive. The judges of the supreme court, and justices of the peace, seem also to be removable by the legislature; and the executive power of pardoning in certain cases to be referred to the same department. The members of the executive council are made EX OFFICIO justices of peace throughout the state.

In Delaware, the chief executive magistrate is annually elected by the legislative department. The speakers of the two legislative branches are vice presidents in the executive department. The executive chief, with six others, appointed three by each of the legislative branches, constitute the supreme court of appeals: He is joined with the legislative department in the appointment of the other judges. Throughout the states it appears that the members of the legislature may at the same time be justices of the peace. In this state, the members of one branch of it are EX OFFICIO justices of peace; as are also the members of the executive council. The principal officers of the executive department are appointed by the legislative; and one branch of the latter forms a court of impeachments. All officers may be removed on address of the legislature.

Maryland has adopted the maxim in the most unqualified terms; declaring that the legislative, executive, and judicial powers of government, ought to be forever separate and distinct from each other. Her constitution, notwithstanding makes the executive magistrate appointable by the legislative department; and the members of the judiciary, by the executive department.

The language of Virginia is still more pointed on this subject. Her constitution declares, "that the legislative, executive, and judiciary departments, shall be separate and distinct; so that neither exercises the powers properly belonging to the other; nor shall any person exercise the powers of more than one of them at the same time; except that the justices of the county courts shall be eligible to either house of assembly." Yet we find not only this express exception, with respect to the members of the inferior courts; but that the chief magistrate with his executive council are appointable by the legislature; that two members of the latter are triennially displaced at the pleasure of the legislature; and that all the principal offices, both executive and judiciary, are filled by the same department. The executive prerogative of pardon, also is in one case vested in the legislative department.

The constitution of North Carolina, which declares, "that the legislative, executive, and supreme judicial powers of government, ought to be forever separate and distinct from each other," refers at the same time to the legislative department, the appointment not only of the executive chief, but all the principal officers within both that and the judiciary department.

In South Carolina, the constitution makes the executive magistracy eligible by the legislative department. It gives to the latter also the appointment of the members of the judiciary department, including even justices of the peace and sheriffs; and the appointment of officers in the executive department, down to captains in the army and navy of the state.

In the constitution of Georgia, where it is declared, "that the legislative, executive, and judiciary departments shall be separate and distinct, so that neither exercise the powers properly belonging to the other," we find that the executive department is to be filled by appointments of the legislature; and the executive prerogative of pardon, to be finally exercised by the same authority. Even justices of the peace are to be appointed by the legislature.

In citing these cases in which the legislative, executive, and judiciary departments, have not been kept totally separate and distinct, I wish not to be regarded as an advocate for the particular organizations of the several state governments. I am fully aware that among the many excellent principles which they exemplify, they carry strong marks of the haste, and still stronger of the inexperience, under which they were framed. It is but too obvious that in some instances, the fundamental principle under consideration has been violated by too great a mixture, and even an actual consolidation of the different powers; and that in no instance has a competent provision been made for maintaining in practice the separation delineated on paper. What I have wished to evince is, that the charge brought against the proposed constitution, of violating a sacred maxim of free government, is warranted neither by the real meaning annexed to that maxim by its author; nor by the sense in which it has hitherto been understood in America. This interesting subject will be resumed in the ensuing paper.

[January 30, 1788]

No. 48   [Madison]

THE SAME SUBJECT CONTINUED WITH A VIEW TO THE MEANS
OF GIVING EFFICACY IN PRACTICE TO THAT MAXIM

It was shown in the last paper, that the political apothegm there examined, does not require that the legislative, executive, and judiciary departments should be wholly unconnected with each other. I shall undertake in the next place, to show that unless these departments be so far connected and blended, as to give to each a constitutional control over the others, the degree of separation which the maxim requires as essential to a free government, can never in practice, be duly maintained.

It is agreed on all sides, that the powers properly belonging to one of the departments, ought not to be directly and completely administered by either of the other departments. It is equally evident, that neither of them ought to possess directly or indirectly, an overruling influence over the others in the administration of their respective powers. It will not be denied, that power is of an encroaching nature, and that it ought to be effectually restrained from passing the limits assigned to it. After discriminating therefore in theory, the several classes of power, as they may in their nature be legislative, executive, or judiciary, the next and most difficult task, is to provide some practical security for each against the invasion of the others. What this security ought to be, is the great problem to be solved.

Will it be sufficient to mark with precision the boundaries of these departments in the Constitution of the government, and to trust to these parchment barriers against the encroaching spirit of power? This is the security which appears to have been principally relied on by the compilers of most of the American Constitutions. But experience assures us, that the efficacy of the provision has been greatly overrated; and that some more adequate defense is indispensably necessary for the more feeble, against the more powerful members of the government. The legislative department is everywhere extending the sphere of its activity, and drawing all power into its impetuous vortex.

The founders of our republics have so much merit for the wisdom which they have displayed, that no task can be less pleasing than that of pointing out the errors into which they have fallen. A respect for truth however obliges us to remark, that they seem never for a moment to have turned their eyes from the danger to liberty from the overgrown and all-grasping prerogative of an hereditary magistrate, supported and fortified by an hereditary branch of the legislative authority. They seem never to have recollected the danger from legislative usurpations; which by assembling all power in the same hands, must lead to the same tyranny as is threatened by executive usurpations.

In a government, where numerous and extensive prerogatives are placed in the hands of a hereditary monarch, the executive department is very justly regarded as the source of danger, and watched with all the jealousy which a zeal for liberty ought to inspire. In a democracy, where a multitude of people exercise in person the legislative functions, and are continually exposed by their incapacity for regular deliberation and concerted measures, to the ambitious intrigues of their executive magistrates, tyranny may well be apprehended on some favorable emergency, to start up in the same quarter. But in a representative republic, where the executive magistracy is carefully limited both in the extent and the duration of its power; and where the legislative power is exercised by an assembly, which is inspired by a supposed influence over the people with an intrepid confidence in its own strength; which is sufficiently numerous to feel all the passions which actuate a multitude; yet not so numerous as to be incapable of pursuing the objects of its passions, by means which reason prescribes; it is against the enterprising ambition of this department, that the people ought to indulge all their jealousy and exhaust all their precautions.

The legislative department derives a superiority in our governments from other circumstances. Its constitutional powers being at once more extensive and less susceptible of precise limits, it can with the greater facility, mask under complicated and indirect measures, the encroachments which it makes on the coordinate departments. It is not infrequently a question of real nicety in legislative bodies, whether the operation of a particular measure, will, or will not extend beyond the legislative sphere. On the other side, the executive power being restrained within a narrower compass, and being more simple in its nature; and the judiciary being described by landmarks, still less uncertain, projects of usurpation by either of these departments, would immediately betray and defeat themselves. Nor is this all: As the legislative department alone has access to the pockets of the people, and has in some Constitutions full discretion, and in all, a prevailing influence over the pecuniary rewards of those who fill the other departments, a dependence is thus created in the latter, which gives still greater facility to encroachments of the former.

I have appealed to our own experience for the truth of what I advance on this subject. Were it necessary to verify this experience by particular proofs, they might be multiplied without end. I might find a witness in every citizen who has shared in, or been attentive to, the course of public administrations.[123] I might collect vouchers in abundance from the records and archives of every State in the Union. But as a more concise and at the same time, equally satisfactory evidence, I will refer to the example of two States, attested by two unexceptionable authorities.

The first example is that of Virginia, a State which, as we have seen, has expressly declared in its Constitution, that the three great departments ought not to be intermixed. The authority in support of it is Mr. Jefferson, who, besides his other advantages for remarking the operation of the government, was himself the chief magistrate of it. In order to convey fully the ideas with which his experience had impressed him on this subject, it will be necessary to quote a passage of some length from his very interesting "Notes on the State of Virginia" (p. 195), "All the powers of government, legislative, executive, and judiciary, result to the legislative body. The concentrating these in the same hands is precisely the definition of despotic government. It will be no alleviation that these powers will be exercised by a plurality of hands, and not by a single one. One hundred seventy-three despots would surely be as oppressive as one. Let those who doubt it turn their eyes on the republic of Venice. As little will it avail us that they are chosen by ourselves. An *elective despotism*, was not the government we fought for; but one which should not only be founded

---

123. [This sentence omitted in McLean.]

on free principles, but in which the powers of government should be so divided and balanced among several bodies of magistracy, as that no one could transcend their legal limits, without being effectually checked and restrained by the others. For this reason that Convention which passed the ordinance of government, laid its foundation on this basis, that the legislative, executive, and judiciary departments should be separate and distinct, so that no person should exercise the powers of more than one of them at the same time. *But no barrier was provided between these several powers.* The judiciary and executive members were left dependent on the legislative for their subsistence in office, and some of them for their continuance in it. If therefore the Legislature assumes executive and judiciary powers, no opposition is likely to be made; nor if made can it be effectual; because in that case, they may put their proceeding into the form of an act of Assembly, which will render them obligatory on the other branches. They have accordingly *in many* instances *decided rights* which should have been left to *judiciary controversy*; and *the direction of the executive during the whole time of their session, is becoming habitual and familiar.*"

The other State which I shall take for an example, is Pennsylvania; and the other authority the council of censors which assembled in the years 1783 and 1784.[124] A part of the duty of this body, as marked out by the Constitution was, "to inquire whether the Constitution had been preserved inviolate in every part; and whether the legislative and executive branches of government had performed their duty as guardians of the people, or assumed to themselves, or exercised other or greater powers than they are entitled to by the Constitution." In the execution of this trust, the council were necessarily led to a comparison, of both the legislative and executive proceedings, with the constitutional powers of these departments; and from the facts enumerated, and to the truth of most of which, both sides in the council subscribed, it appears that the Constitution had been flagrantly violated by the Legislature in a variety of important instances.

A great number of laws had been passed violating without any apparent necessity, the rule requiring that all bills of public nature, shall be previously printed for the consideration of the people; although this is one of the precautions chiefly relied on by the Constitution, against improper acts of the Legislature.

The constitutional trial by jury had been violated; and powers assumed, which had not been delegated by the Constitution.

Executive powers had been usurped.

---

124. [The Pennsylvania Constitution of 1776 provided for a council of censors to meet every seven years.]

The salaries of the Judges, which the Constitution expressly requires to be fixed, had been occasionally varied; and cases belonging to the judiciary department, frequently drawn within legislative cognizance and determination.

Those who wish to see the several particulars falling under each of these heads, may consult the Journals of the council which are in print. Some of them, it will be found may be imputable to peculiar circumstances connected with the war: But the greater part of them may be considered as the spontaneous shoots of an ill-constituted government.

It appears also, that the executive department had not been innocent of frequent breaches of the Constitution. There are three observations however, which ought to be made on this head. *First.* A great proportion of the instances, were either immediately produced by the necessities of the war, or recommended by Congress or the Commander in Chief. *Secondly.* In most of the other instances, they conformed either to the declared or the known sentiments of the legislative department. *Thirdly.* The executive department of Pennsylvania is distinguished from that of the other States, by the number of members composing it.[125] In this respect it has as much affinity to a legislative assembly, as to an executive council. And being at once exempt from the restraint of an individual responsibility for the acts of the body, and deriving confidence from mutual example and joint influence; unauthorized measures would of course be more freely hazarded, than where the executive department is administered by a single hand or by a few hands.

The conclusion which I am warranted in drawing from these observations is, that a mere demarcation on parchment of the constitutional limits of the several departments, is not a sufficient guard against those encroachments which lead to a tyrannical concentration of all the powers of government in the same hands.

[February 1, 1788]

No. 49   [Madison]

THE SAME SUBJECT CONTINUED WITH THE SAME VIEW

The author of the "Notes on the state of Virginia," quoted in the last paper, has subjoined to that valuable work, the draft of a constitution

---

125. [The executive under the Pennsylvania Constitution of 1776 was a council with representatives from the city of Philadelphia and from each county of the state.]

which had been prepared in order to be laid before a convention expected to be called in 1783 by the legislature, for the establishment of a constitution for that commonwealth. The plan, like everything from the same pen, marks a turn of thinking original, comprehensive, and accurate; and is the more worthy of attention, as it equally displays a fervent attachment to republican government, and an enlightened view of the dangerous propensities against which it ought to be guarded. One of the precautions which he proposes, and on which he appears ultimately to rely as a palladium to the weaker departments of power, against the invasions of the stronger, is perhaps altogether his own, and as it immediately relates to the subject of our present inquiry, ought not to be overlooked.

His proposition is, "that whenever any two of the three branches of government shall concur in opinion, each by the voices of two-thirds of their whole number, that a convention is necessary for altering the constitution or *correcting breaches of it*, a convention shall be called for the purpose."

As the people are the only legitimate fountain of power, and it is from them that the constitutional charter, under which the several branches of government hold their power, is derived; it seems strictly consonant to the republican theory, to recur to the same original authority, not only whenever it may be necessary to enlarge, diminish, or new-model[126] the powers of government; but also whenever any one of the departments may commit encroachments on the chartered authorities of the others. The several departments being perfectly coordinate by the terms of their common commission, neither of them, it is evident, can pretend to an exclusive or superior right of settling the boundaries between their respective powers; and how are the encroachments of the stronger to be prevented, or the wrongs of the weaker to be redressed; without an appeal to the people themselves; who, as the grantors of the commission, can alone declare its true meaning and enforce its observance?

There is certainly great force in this reasoning, and it must be allowed to prove, that a constitutional road to the decision of the people, ought to be marked out, and kept open, for certain great and extraordinary occasions. But there appear to be insuperable objections against the proposed recurrence to the people, as a provision in all cases for keeping the several departments of power within their constitutional limits.

In the first place, the provision does not reach the case of a combination of two of the departments against a third. If the legislative authority, which possesses so many means of operating on the motives of the other departments, should be able to gain to its interest either of the others, or

---

126. [To "new-model" is to reorganize and transform; the implied reference is to Cromwell's New Model Army.]

even one-third of its members, the remaining department could derive no advantage from this remedial provision. I do not dwell however on this objection, because it may be thought to lie rather against the modification of the principle, than against the principle itself.

In the next place, it may be considered as an objection inherent in the principle, that as every appeal to the people would carry an implication of some defect in the government, frequent appeals would in great measure deprive the government of that veneration, which time bestows on everything, and without which perhaps the wisest and freest governments would not possess the requisite stability. If it be true that all governments rest on opinion,[127] it is no less true that the strength of opinion in each individual, and its practical influence on conduct, depend much on the number which he supposes to have entertained the same opinion. The reason of man, like man himself is timid and cautious, when left alone; and acquires firmness and confidence, in proportion to the number with which it is associated. When the examples, which fortify opinion, are *ancient* as well as *numerous*, they are known to have a double effect. In a nation of philosophers, this consideration ought to be disregarded. A reverence for the laws, would be sufficiently inculcated by the voice of an enlightened reason. But a nation of philosophers is as little to be expected as the philosophical race of kings wished for by Plato. And in every other nation, the most rational government will not find it a superfluous advantage, to have the prejudices of the community on its side.

The danger of disturbing the public tranquillity by interesting too strongly the public passions, is a still more serious objection against a frequent reference of constitutional questions, to the decision of the whole society. Notwithstanding the success which has attended the revisions of our established forms of government, and which does so much honor to the virtue and intelligence of the people of America, it must be confessed, that the experiments are of too ticklish a nature to be unnecessarily multiplied. We are to recollect that all the existing constitutions were formed in the midst of a danger which repressed the passions most unfriendly to order and concord; of an enthusiastic confidence of the people in their patriotic leaders, which stifled the ordinary diversity of opinions on great national questions; of a universal ardor for new and opposite forms, produced by a universal resentment and indignation against the ancient government; and while no spirit of party, connected with the changes to be made, or the abuses to be reformed, could mingle its leaven in the operation. The future situations in which we must

---

127. [A claim made by David Hume in "Of the First Principles of Government" (1741).]

expect to be usually placed, do not present any equivalent security against the danger which is apprehended.

But the greatest objection of all is, that the decisions which would probably result from such appeals, would not answer the purpose of maintaining the constitutional equilibrium of the government. We have seen[128] that the tendency of republican governments is to an aggrandizement of the legislative, at the expense of the other departments. The appeals to the people therefore would usually be made by the executive and judiciary departments. But whether made by one side or the other, would each side enjoy equal advantages on the trial? Let us view their different situations. The members of the executive and judiciary departments, are few in number, and can be personally known to a small part only of the people. The latter by the mode of their appointment, as well as, by the nature and permanency of it, are too far removed from the people to share much in their prepossessions. The former are generally the objects of jealousy: And their administration is always liable to be discolored and rendered unpopular. The members of the legislative department, on the other hand, are numerous. They are distributed and dwell among the people at large. Their connections of blood, of friendship, and of acquaintance, embrace a great proportion of the most influential part of the society. The nature of their public trust implies a personal influence among the people, and that they are more immediately the confidential guardians of the rights and liberties of the people. With these advantages, it can hardly be supposed that the adverse party would have an equal chance for a favorable issue.

But the legislative party would not only be able to plead their cause most successfully with the people. They would probably be constituted themselves the judges. The same influence which had gained them an election into the legislature, would gain them a seat in the convention. If this should not be the case with all, it would probably be the case with many, and pretty certainly with those leading characters, on whom everything depends in such bodies. The convention in short would be composed chiefly of men, who had been, who actually were, or who expected to be, members of the department whose conduct was arraigned. They would consequently be parties to the very question to be decided by them.

It might however sometimes happen, that appeals would be made under circumstances less adverse to the executive and judiciary departments. The usurpations of the legislature might be so flagrant and so sudden, as to admit of no specious coloring. A strong party among themselves might take side with the other branches. The executive power might be in

---

128. [In Essay 48.]

the hands of a peculiar favorite of the people. In such a posture of things, the public decision might be less swayed by prepossessions in favor of the legislative party. But still it could never be expected to turn on the true merits of the question. It would inevitably be connected with the spirit of preexisting parties, or of parties springing out of the question itself. It would be connected with persons of distinguished character and extensive influence in the community. It would be pronounced by the very men who had been agents in, or opponents of the measures, to which the decision would relate. The *passions* therefore not the *reason,* of the public, would sit in judgment. But it is the reason of the public alone that ought to control and regulate the government. The passions ought to be controlled and regulated by the government.

We found in the last paper that mere declarations in the written constitution, are not sufficient to restrain the several departments within their legal limits. It appears in this, that occasional appeals to the people would be neither a proper nor an effectual provision, for that purpose. How far the provisions of a different nature contained in the plan above quoted, might be adequate, I do not examine. Some of them are unquestionably founded on sound political principles, and all of them are framed with singular ingenuity and precision.

[February 2, 1788]

No. 51   [Madison]

THE SAME SUBJECT CONTINUED WITH
THE SAME VIEW AND CONCLUDED

To what expedient then shall we finally resort for maintaining in practice the necessary partition of power among the several departments, as laid down in the constitution? The only answer that can be given is, that as all these exterior provisions are found to be inadequate, the defect must be supplied, by so contriving the interior structure of the government, as that its several constituent parts may, by their mutual relations, be the means of keeping each other in their proper places. Without presuming to undertake a full development of this important idea, I will hazard a few general observations, which may perhaps place it in a clearer light, and enable us to form a more correct judgment of the principles and structure of the government planned by the convention.

In order to lay a due foundation for that separate and distinct exercise of the different powers of government, which to a certain extent, is admitted on all hands to be essential to the preservation of liberty, it is evident that each department should have a will of its own; and consequently should be so constituted, that the members of each should have as little agency as possible in the appointment of the members of the others. Were this principle rigorously adhered to, it would require that all the appointments for the supreme executive, legislative, and judiciary magistracies, should be drawn from the same fountain of authority, the people, through channels, having no communication whatever with one another. Perhaps such a plan of constructing the several departments would be less difficult in practice than it may in contemplation appear. Some difficulties however, and some additional expense, would attend the execution of it. Some deviations therefore from the principle must be admitted. In the constitution of the judiciary department in particular, it might be inexpedient to insist rigorously on the principle; first, because peculiar qualifications being essential in the members, the primary consideration ought to be to select that mode of choice, which best secures these qualifications; secondly, because the permanent tenure by which the appointments are held in that department, must soon destroy all sense of dependence on the authority conferring them.

It is equally evident that the members of each department should be as little dependent as possible on those of the others, for the emoluments annexed to their offices. Were the executive magistrate, or the judges, not independent of the legislature in this particular, their independence in every other would be merely nominal.

But the great security against a gradual concentration of the several powers in the same department, consists in giving to those who administer each department, the necessary constitutional means, and personal motives, to resist encroachments of the others. The provision for defense must in this, as in all other cases, be made commensurate to the danger of attack. Ambition must be made to counteract ambition.[129] The interest of the man must be connected with the constitutional rights of the place. It may be a reflection on human nature, that such devices should be necessary to control the abuses of government. But what is government itself but the greatest of all reflections on human nature? If men were angels, no government would be necessary. If angels were to govern men, neither

---

129. [Compare Hume, "Of the Independency of Parliament" (*Essays, Moral and Political,* 1741): "When there offers, therefore, to our censure and examination, any plan of government, real or imaginary, where the power is distributed among several courts, and several orders of men, we should always consider the separate interest of each court, and each order; and, if we find that, by the skilful division of power, this interest must necessarily, in its operation, concur with public, we may pronounce that government to be wise and happy."]

external nor internal controls on government would be necessary. In framing a government which is to be administered by men over men, the great difficulty lies in this: You must first enable the government to control the governed; and in the next place, oblige it to control itself.[130] A dependence on the people is no doubt the primary control on the government; but experience has taught mankind the necessity of auxiliary precautions.

This policy of supplying by opposite and rival interests, the defect of better motives, might be traced through the whole system of human affairs, private as well as public. We see it particularly displayed in all the subordinate distributions of power; where the constant aim is to divide and arrange the several offices in such a manner as that each may be a check on the other; that the private interest of every individual, may be a sentinel over the public rights.[131] These inventions of prudence cannot be less requisite in the distribution of the supreme powers of the state.

But it is not possible to give to each department an equal power of self-defense. In republican government the legislative authority, necessarily, predominates. The remedy for this inconveniency is, to divide the legislature into different branches; and to render them by different modes of election, and different principles of action, as little connected with each other, as the nature of their common functions, and their common dependence on the society, will admit. It may even be necessary to guard against dangerous encroachments by still further precautions. As the weight of the legislative authority requires that it should be thus divided, the weakness of the executive may require, on the other hand, that it should be fortified. An absolute negative, on the legislature, appears at first view to be the natural defense with which the executive magistrate should be armed. But perhaps it would be neither altogether safe, nor alone sufficient. On ordinary occasions, it might not be exerted with the requisite firmness; and on extraordinary occasions, it might be perfidiously abused. May not

---

130. [For the paradox that government must be made to control itself, see Hume, "Of the Independency of Parliament," *Essays, Moral and Political* (1741): "How, therefore, shall we solve this paradox? And by what means is this member of our constitution [the House of Commons] confined within the proper limits; since, from our very constitution, it must necessarily have as much power as it demands, and can only be confined by itself?"]

131. [Compare Hume, "That Politics May Be Reduced to a Science," *Essays, Moral and Political* (1741): "Effects will always correspond to causes; and wise regulations in any commonwealth are the most valuable legacy that can be left to future ages. In the smallest court or office, the stated forms and methods, by which business must be conducted, are found to be a considerable check upon the natural depravity of mankind."]

this defect of an absolute negative be supplied, by some qualified connection between this weaker department, and the weaker branch of the stronger department, by which the latter may be led to support the constitutional rights of the former, without being too much detached from the rights of its own department?

If the principles on which these observations are founded be just, as I persuade myself they are, and they be applied as a criterion, to the several state constitutions, and to the federal constitution, it will be found, that if the latter does not perfectly correspond with them, the former are infinitely less able to bear such a test.

There are moreover two considerations particularly applicable to the federal system of America, which place that system in a very interesting point of view.

First. In a single republic, all the power surrendered by the people, is submitted to the administration of a single government; and usurpations are guarded against by a division of the government into distinct and separate departments. In the compound republic of America, the power surrendered by the people, is first divided between two distinct governments, and then the portion allotted to each, subdivided among distinct and separate departments. Hence a double security arises to the rights of the people. The different governments will control each other; at the same time that each will be controlled by itself.

Second. It is of great importance in a republic, not only to guard the society against the oppression of its rulers; but to guard one part of the society against the injustice of the other part. Different interests necessarily exist in different classes of citizens. If a majority be united by a common interest, the rights of the minority will be insecure. There are but two methods of providing against this evil: The one by creating a will in the community independent of the majority, that is, of the society itself; the other by comprehending in the society so many separate descriptions of citizens, as will render an unjust combination of a majority of the whole, very improbable, if not impracticable. The first method prevails in all governments possessing an hereditary or self-appointed authority. This at best is but a precarious security; because a power independent of the society may as well espouse the unjust views of the major, as the rightful interests, of the minor party, and may possibly be turned against both parties. The second method will be exemplified in the federal republic of the United States. While all authority in it will be derived from and dependent on the society, the society itself will be broken into so many parts, interests, and classes of citizens, that the rights of individuals or of the minority, will be in little danger from interested combinations of the majority. In a free government, the security for civil rights must be the same as for religious rights. It consists in the one case in the multiplicity of interests, and in the other, in the multiplicity of sects.[132] The degree of security in both cases will depend on the number of interests and sects; and this may be presumed to depend on the extent of country and number of people comprehended under the same government. This view of the subject must particularly recommend a proper federal system to all the sincere and considerate friends of republican government: Since it shows that in exact proportion as the territory of the union may be formed into more circumscribed confederacies or states, oppressive combinations of a majority will be facilitated, the best security under the republican form, for the rights of every class of citizens, will be diminished; and consequently, the stability and independence of some member of the government, the only other security, must be proportionally increased. Justice is the end of government. It is the end of civil society. It ever has been, and ever will be pursued, until it be obtained, or until liberty be lost in the pursuit. In a society under the forms of which the stronger faction can readily unite and oppress the weaker, anarchy may as truly be said to reign, as in a state of nature where the weaker individual is not secured against the violence of the stronger: And as in the latter state even the stronger individuals are prompted by the uncertainty of their condition, to submit to a government which may protect the weak as well as themselves: So in the former state, will the more powerful factions or parties be gradually induced by a like motive, to wish for a government which will protect all parties, the weaker as well as the more powerful. It can be little doubted, that if the state of Rhode Island was separated from the confederacy, and left to itself, the insecurity of rights under the popular form of government within such narrow limits, would be displayed by such reiterated oppressions of factious majorities, that some power altogether independent of the people would soon be called for by the voice of the very factions whose misrule had proved the necessity of it. In the extended republic of the United States, and among the great variety of interests, parties, and sects which it embraces, a coalition of a majority of the whole society could seldom take place on any other principles than those of justice and the general good; and[133] there being thus less danger to a minor from the will of the major party, there must be less pretext also, to provide for the security of the former, by introducing into the government a will not dependent on the latter; or in other words, a will independent of the society itself. It is no

---

132. [See Madison's "Memorial and Remonstrance against Religious Assessments" (June 1785).]

133. ["Whilst" substituted for "and" in McLean and later editions.]

less certain than it is important, notwithstanding the contrary opinions which have been entertained, that the larger the society, provided it lie within a practicable sphere, the more duly capable it will be of self government. And happily for the *republican cause*, the practicable sphere may be carried to a very great extent, by a judicious modification and mixture of the *federal principle.*

[February 6, 1788]

No. 52   [Madison]

CONCERNING THE HOUSE OF REPRESENTATIVES, WITH A
VIEW TO THE QUALIFICATIONS OF THE ELECTORS AND
ELECTED, AND THE TIME OF SERVICE OF THE MEMBERS

From the more general inquiries pursued in the four last papers, I pass on to a more particular examination of the several parts of the government. I shall begin with the House of Representatives.

The first view to be taken of this part of the government, relates to the qualifications of the electors and the elected. Those of the former are to be the same with those of the electors of the most numerous branch of the State Legislatures. The definition of the right of suffrage is very justly regarded as a fundamental article of republican government. It was incumbent on the Convention therefore to define and establish this right, in the Constitution. To have left it open for the occasional regulation of the Congress, would have been improper for the reason just mentioned. To have submitted it to the legislative discretion of the States, would have been improper for the same reason; and for the additional reason, that it would have rendered too dependent on the State Governments, that branch of the Federal Government, which ought to be dependent on the people alone. To have reduced the different qualifications in the different States, to one uniform rule, would probably have been as dissatisfactory to some of the States, as it would have been difficult to the Convention. The provision made by the Convention appears therefore, to be the best that lay within their option. It must be satisfactory to every State; because it is conformable to the standard already established, or which may be established by the State itself. It will be safe to the United States; because, being fixed by the State Constitutions, it is not alterable by the State Governments, and it cannot be feared that the people of the States will alter this part of their Constitutions, in such a manner as to abridge the rights secured to them by the Federal Constitution.

The qualifications of the elected being less carefully and properly defined by the State Constitutions, and being at the same time more susceptible of uniformity, have been very properly considered and regulated by the Convention. A representative of the United States must be of the age of twenty-five years; must have been seven years a citizen of the United States, must at the time of his election, be an inhabitant of the State he is to represent, and during the time of his service must be in no office under the United States. Under these reasonable limitations, the door of this part of the Federal Government, is open to merit of every description, whether native or adoptive, whether young or old, and without regard to poverty or wealth, or to any particular profession of religious faith.

The term for which the Representatives are to be elected, falls under a second view which may be taken of this branch. In order to decide on the propriety of this article, two questions must be considered; first, whether biennial elections will, in this case, be safe; secondly, whether they be necessary or useful.

First. As it is essential to liberty that the government in general, should have a common interest with the people; so it is particularly essential that the branch of it under consideration, should have an immediate dependence on, and an intimate sympathy with the people. Frequent elections are unquestionably the only policy by which this dependence and sympathy can be effectually secured. But what particular degree of frequency may be absolutely necessary for the purpose, does not appear to be susceptible of any precise calculation; and must depend on a variety of circumstances with which it may be connected. Let us consult experience, the guide that ought always to be followed, whenever it can be found.

The scheme of representation, as a substitute for a meeting of the citizens in person, being at most but very imperfectly known to ancient polity; it is in more modern times only, that we are to expect instructive examples. And even here, in order to avoid a research too vague and diffusive, it will be proper to confine ourselves to the few examples which are best known, and which bear the greatest analogy to our particular case. The first to which this character ought to be applied, is the House of Commons in Great Britain. The history of this branch of the English Constitution, anterior to the date of Magna Carta, is too obscure to yield instruction. The very existence of it has been made a question among political antiquaries. The earliest records of subsequent date prove, that Parliaments were to *sit* only, every year; not that they were to be *elected* every year. And even these annual sessions were left so much at the discretion of the monarch, that under various pretexts, very long and dangerous intermissions, were often contrived by royal ambition. To remedy this grievance, it was provided by a statute in the reign of Charles II, that the intermissions should not be protracted beyond a period of three years. On the accession of William III when a revolution took place in the government, the subject was still more seriously resumed, and it was declared to be among the fundamental rights of the people, that Parliaments ought to be held *frequently*. By another statute which passed a few years later in the same reign, the term 'frequently' which had alluded to the triennial period settled in the time of Charles II is reduced to a precise meaning, it being expressly enacted that a new parliament shall be called within three years after the determination of the former. The last change from three to seven years is well-known to have been introduced pretty early in the present century, under an alarm for the Hanoverian succession. From these facts it appears, that the greatest frequency of elections which has been deemed necessary in that kingdom, for binding the representatives to their constituents, does not exceed a triennial return of them. And if we may argue from the degree of liberty retained even under septennial elections, and all the other vicious ingredients in the parliamentary constitution, we cannot doubt that a reduction of the period from seven to three years, with the other necessary reforms, would so far extend the influence of the people over their representatives, as to satisfy us, that biennial elections under the federal system, cannot possibly be dangerous to the requisite dependence of the house of representatives on their constituents.

Elections in Ireland until of late were regulated entirely by the discretion of the crown, and were seldom repeated except on the accession of a new Prince, or some other contingent event. The parliament which commenced with George II was continued throughout his whole reign, a period of about thirty-five years. The only dependence of the representatives on the people consisted, in the right of the latter to supply occasional vacancies, by the election of new members, and in the chance of some event which might produce a general new election. The ability also of the Irish parliament, to maintain the rights of their constituents, so far as the disposition might exist, was extremely shackled by the control of the crown over the subjects of their deliberation. Of late these shackles, if I mistake not, have been broken; and octennial parliaments have besides been established. What effect may be produced by this partial reform, must be left to further experience. The example of Ireland, from this view of it, can throw but little light on the subject. As far as we can draw any conclusion from it, it must be, that if the people of that country have been able, under all these disadvantages, to retain any liberty whatever, the advantage of biennial elections would secure to them every degree of liberty which might depend on a due connection between their representatives and themselves.

Let us bring our inquiries nearer home. The example of these States when British colonies claims particular attention; at the same time that it is so well-known, as to require little to be said on it. The principle of representation, in one branch of the Legislature at least, was established in all of them. But the periods of election were different. They varied from one to seven years. Have we any reason to infer from the spirit and conduct of the representatives of the people, prior to the revolution, that biennial elections would have been dangerous to the public liberties? The spirit which everywhere displayed itself at the commencement of the struggle; and which vanquished the obstacles to independence, is the best of proofs that a sufficient portion of liberty had been everywhere enjoyed to inspire both a sense of its worth, and a zeal for its proper enlargement. This remark holds good as well with regard to the then colonies, whose elections were least frequent, as to those whose elections were most frequent. Virginia was the colony which stood first in resisting the parliamentary usurpations of Great Britain: it was the first also in espousing by public act, the resolution of independence. In Virginia nevertheless, if I have not been misinformed, elections under the former government were septennial. This particular example is brought into view, not as a proof of any peculiar merit, for the priority in those instances, was probably accidental; and still less of any advantage in *septennial* elections, for when compared with a greater frequency they are inadmissible: but merely as a proof, and I conceive it to be a very substantial proof, that the liberties of the people can be in no danger from *biennial* elections.

The conclusion resulting from these examples will be not a little strengthened by recollecting three circumstances. The first is that the Federal Legislature will possess a part only of that supreme legislative authority which is vested completely in the British parliament, and which with a few exceptions was exercised by the colonial Assemblies and the Irish Legislature. It is a received and well-founded maxim, that, where no other circumstances affect the case, the greater the power is, the shorter ought to be its duration; and, conversely, the smaller the power, the more safely may its duration be protracted. In the second place, it has, on another occasion,[134] been shown that the Federal Legislature will not only be restrained by its dependence on the people as other legislative bodies are; but that it will be moreover watched and controlled by the several collateral Legislatures, which other legislative bodies are not. And in the third place, no comparison can be made between the means that will be possessed by the more permanent branches of the Federal Government for seducing, if they should be disposed to seduce, the House of

---

134. [In Essay 46, not in this selection.]

Representatives from their duty to the people; and the means of influence over the popular branch, possessed by the other branches of the governments above cited. With less power therefore to abuse, the Federal Representatives, can be less tempted on one side, and will be doubly watched on the other.

[February 8, 1788]

No. 55   [Madison]

THE SAME SUBJECT CONTINUED IN RELATION
TO THE TOTAL NUMBER OF THE BODY

The number of which the House of Representatives is to consist, forms another, and a very interesting point of view under which this branch of the federal legislature may be contemplated. Scarce any article indeed in the whole constitution seems to be rendered more worthy of attention, by the weight of character and the apparent force of argument, with which it has been assailed. The charges exhibited against it are, first, that so small a number of representatives will be an unsafe depositary of the public interests; secondly, that they will not possess a proper knowledge of the local circumstances of their numerous constituents; thirdly, that they will be taken from that class of citizens which will sympathize least with the feelings of the mass of the people, and be most likely to aim at a permanent elevation of the few on the depression of the many; fourthly, that defective as the number will be in the first instance, it will be more and more disproportionate, by the increase of the people, and the obstacles which will prevent a correspondent increase of the representatives.[135]

In general it may be remarked on this subject, that no political problem is less susceptible of a precise solution, than that which relates to the number most convenient for a representative legislature: Nor is there any point on which the policy of the several states is more at variance; whether we compare their legislative assemblies directly with each other, or consider the proportions which they respectively bear to the number of their constituents. Passing over the difference between the smallest and largest states, as Delaware, whose most numerous branch consists of twenty-one representatives, and Massachusetts, where it amounts to between three and four hundred; a very considerable difference is observable among states nearly equal in population. The number of representatives in

---

135. [See, for example, the speeches of Melancton Smith and Patrick Henry.]

Pennsylvania is not more than one-fifth of that in the state last mentioned. New York, whose population is to that of South Carolina as six to five, has little more than one-third of the number of representatives. As great a disparity prevails between the states of Georgia and Delaware, or Rhode Island. In Pennsylvania the representatives do not bear a greater proportion to their constituents than of one for every four or five thousand. In Rhode Island, they bear a proportion of at least one for every thousand. And according to the constitution of Georgia, the proportion may be carried to one for every ten electors; and must unavoidably far exceed the proportion in any of the other States.

Another general remark to be made is, that the ratio between the representatives and the people, ought not to be the same where the latter are very numerous, as where they are very few. Were the representatives in Virginia to be regulated by the standard in Rhode Island, they would at this time amount to between four and five hundred; and twenty or thirty years hence, to a thousand. On the other hand, the ratio of Pennsylvania, if applied to the state of Delaware, would reduce the Representative assembly of the latter to seven or eight members. Nothing can be more fallacious than to found our political calculations on arithmetical principles. Sixty or seventy men, may be more properly trusted with a given degree of power than six or seven. But it does not follow, that six or seven hundred would be proportionally a better depositary. And if we carry on the supposition to six or seven thousand, the whole reasoning ought to be reversed. The truth is, that in all cases a certain number at least seems to be necessary to secure the benefits of free consultation and discussion, and to guard against too easy a combination for improper purposes: As on the other hand, the number ought at most to be kept within a certain limit, in order to avoid the confusion and intemperance of a multitude. In all very numerous assemblies, of whatever characters composed, passion never fails to wrest the scepter from reason. Had every Athenian citizen been a Socrates; every Athenian assembly would still have been a mob.[136]

It is necessary also to recollect here the observations which were applied to the case of biennial elections.[137] For the same reason that the limited powers of the Congress and the control of the state legislatures, justify less frequent elections than the public safety might otherwise

---

136. [Compare Hume, "Idea of a Perfect Commonwealth," *Political Discourses* (1752): "A large assembly of one thousand, for instance, to represent the people, if allowed to debate, would fall into disorder. . . . Cardinal de RETZ says, that all numerous assemblies, however composed, are mere mob, and swayed in their debates by the least motive."]

137. [In Essay 52.]

require; the members of the Congress need be less numerous than if they possessed the whole power of legislation, and were under no other than the ordinary restraints of other legislative bodies.

With these general ideas in our minds, let us weigh the objections which have been stated against the number of members proposed for the House of Representatives. It is said in the first place, that so small a number cannot be safely trusted with so much power.

The number of which this branch of the legislature is to consist at the outset of the government, will be sixty-five. Within three years a census is to be taken, when the number may be augmented to one for every thirty-thousand inhabitants; and within every successive period of ten years, the census is to be renewed, and augmentations may continue to be made under the above limitation. It will not be thought an extravagant conjecture, that the first census, will, at the rate of one for every thirty thousand raise the number of representatives to at least one hundred. Estimating the Negroes in the proportion of three-fifths, it can scarcely be doubted that the population of the United States will by that time, if it does not already, amount to three million. At the expiration of twenty-five years, according to the computed rate of increase, the number of representatives will amount to two hundred; and of fifty years to four hundred. This is a number which I presume will put an end to all fears arising from the smallness of the body. I take for granted here what I shall in answering the fourth objection hereafter show, that the number of representatives will be augmented from time to time in the manner provided by the constitution. On a contrary supposition, I should admit the objection to have very great weight indeed.

The true question to be decided then is whether the smallness of the number, as a temporary regulation, be dangerous to the public liberty: Whether sixty-five members for a few years, and a hundred or two hundred for a few more, be a safe depositary for a limited and well-guarded power of legislating for the United States? I must own that I could not give a negative answer to this question, without first obliterating every impression which I have received with regard to the present genius of the people of America, the spirit, which actuates the state legislatures, and the principles which are incorporated with the political character of every class of citizens. I am unable to conceive that the people of America in their present temper, or under any circumstances which can speedily happen, will choose, and every second year repeat the choice of sixty-five or a hundred men, who would be disposed to form and pursue a scheme of tyranny or treachery. I am unable to conceive that the state legislatures which must feel so many motives to watch, and which possess so many means of counteracting the federal legislature, would fail either to detect or to defeat a conspiracy of the latter against the liberties of their common constituents. I am equally unable to conceive that there are at this time, or can be in any short time, in the United States any sixty-five or a hundred men capable of recommending themselves to the choice of the people at large, who would either desire or dare within the short space of two years, to betray the solemn trust committed to them. What change of circumstances time and a fuller population of our country may produce, requires a prophetic spirit to declare, which makes no part of my pretensions. But judging from the circumstances now before us, and from the probable state of them within a moderate period of time, I must pronounce that the liberties of America cannot be unsafe in the number of hands proposed by the federal constitution.

From what quarter can the danger proceed? Are we afraid of foreign gold? If foreign gold could so easily corrupt our rulers, and enable them to ensnare and betray their constituents, how has it happened that we are at this time a free and independent nation? The Congress which conducted us through the revolution were a less numerous body than their successors will be; they were not chosen by nor responsible to their fellow citizens at large; though appointed from year to year, and recallable at pleasure, they were generally continued for three years; and prior to the ratification of the federal articles, for a still longer term; they held their consultations always under the veil of secrecy; they had the sole transaction of our affairs with foreign nations; through the whole course of the war, they had the fate of their country more in their hands, than it is to be hoped will ever be the case with our future representatives; and from the greatness of the prize at stake and the eagerness of the party which lost it, it may well be supposed, that the use of other means than force would not have been scrupled; yet we know by happy experience that the public trust was not betrayed; nor has the purity of our public councils in this particular ever suffered even from the whispers of calumny.

Is the danger apprehended from the other branches of the federal government? But where are the means to be found by the President or the Senate, or both? Their emoluments of office it is to be presumed will not, and without a previous corruption of the house of representatives cannot, more than suffice for very different purposes: Their private fortunes, as they must all be American citizens, cannot possibly be sources of danger. The only means then which they can possess, will be in the dispensation of appointments. Is it here that suspicion rests her charge? Sometimes we are told that this fund of corruption is to be exhausted by the President in subduing the virtue of the Senate. Now the fidelity of the other house is to be the victim. The improbability of such a mercenary and perfidious combination of the several members of government standing on as different foundations as republican principles will well admit, and at the same time accountable to the society over which they are placed, ought alone to quiet this apprehension. But fortunately the constitution has provided a still further safeguard. The members of the Congress are rendered ineligible to any civil offices that may be created or of which the emoluments may be increased, during the term of their election. No offices therefore can be dealt out to the existing members, but such as may become vacant by ordinary casualties; and to suppose that these would be sufficient to purchase the guardians of the people, selected by the people themselves, is to renounce every rule by which events ought to be calculated, and to substitute an indiscriminate and unbounded jealousy, with which all reasoning must be vain. The sincere friends of liberty who give themselves up to the extravagancies of this passion are not aware of the injury they do their own cause. As there is a degree of depravity in mankind which requires a certain degree of circumspection and distrust: So there are other qualities in human nature, which justify a certain portion of esteem and confidence. Republican government presupposes the existence of these qualities in a higher degree than any other form. Were the pictures which have been drawn by the political jealousy of some among us, faithful likenesses of the human character, the inference would be that there is not sufficient virtue among men for self-government; and that nothing less than the chains of despotism can restrain them from destroying and devouring one another.[138]

[February 13, 1788]

No. 57   [Madison]

THE SAME SUBJECT CONTINUED IN RELATION TO THE SUPPOSED TENDENCY OF THE PLAN OF THE CONVENTION TO ELEVATE THE FEW ABOVE THE MANY

The *third* charge against the House of Representatives is that it will be taken from that class of citizen which will have least sympathy with the

---

138. [In contrast to the view expressed here, see Hume's claim in "Of the Independency of Parliament" (1741) that "It is, therefore, a just *political* maxim, *that every man must be supposed a knave:* Though at the same time, it appears somewhat strange, that a maxim should be true in *politics,* which is false in *fact.*" In claiming to ground republican government in virtue, the *Federalist* stands in direct opposition to Hume.]

mass of the people, and be most likely to aim at an ambitious sacrifice of the many to the aggrandizement of the few.

Of all the objections which have been framed against the federal Constitution, this is perhaps the most extraordinary. While the objection is leveled against a pretended oligarchy, the principle of it strikes at the very root of republican government.

The aim of every political Constitution is, or ought to be, first to obtain for rulers men who possess most wisdom to discern, and most virtue to pursue, the common good of the society; and in the next place, to take the most effectual precautions for keeping them virtuous while they continue to hold their public trust. The elective mode of obtaining rulers is the characteristic policy of republican government. The means relied on in this form of government for preventing their degeneracy are numerous and various. The most effectual one is such a limitation of the term of appointments as will maintain a proper responsibility to the people.

Let me now ask what circumstance there is in the constitution of the House of Representatives that violates the principles of republican government, or favors the elevation of the few on the ruins of the many? Let me ask whether every circumstance is not, on the contrary, strictly conformable to these principles, and scrupulously impartial to the rights and pretensions of every class and description of citizens?

Who are to be the electors of the Federal Representatives? Not the rich more than the poor; nor the learned more than the ignorant; nor the haughty heirs of distinguished names, more than the humble sons of obscure and unpropitious fortune. The electors are to be the great body of the people of the United States. They are to be the same who exercise the right in every State of electing the correspondent branch of the Legislature of the State.

Who are to be the objects of popular choice? Every citizen whose merit may recommend him to the esteem and confidence of his country. No qualification of wealth, of birth, of religious faith, or of civil profession, is permitted to fetter the judgment or disappoint the inclination of the people.

If we consider the situation of the men on whom the free suffrages of their fellow citizens may confer the representative trust, we shall find it involving every security which can be devised or desired for their fidelity to their constituents.

In the first place, as they will have been distinguished by the preference of their fellow citizens, we are to presume, that in general, they will be somewhat distinguished also, by those qualities which entitle them to it, and which promise a sincere and scrupulous regard to the nature of their engagements.

In the second place, they will enter into the public service under circumstances which cannot fail to produce a temporary affection at least to their constituents. There is in every breast a sensibility to marks of honor, of favor, of esteem, and of confidence, which, apart from all considerations of interest, is some pledge for grateful and benevolent returns. Ingratitude is a common topic of declamation against human nature; and it must be confessed, that instances of it are but too frequent and flagrant both in public and in private life. But the universal and extreme indignation which it inspires, is itself a proof of the energy and prevalence of the contrary sentiment.

In the third place, these ties which bind the representative to his constituents are strengthened by motives of a more selfish nature. His pride and vanity attach him to a form of government which favors his pretensions, and gives him a share in its honors and distinctions. Whatever hopes or projects might be entertained by a few aspiring characters, it must generally happen that a great proportion of the men deriving their advancement from their influence with the people, would have more to hope from a preservation of the favor, than from innovations in the government subversive of the authority of the people.

All these securities however would be found very insufficient without the restraint of frequent elections. Hence, in the fourth place, the House of Representatives is so constituted as to support in the members a habitual recollection of their dependence on the people. Before the sentiments impressed on their minds by the mode of their elevation can be effaced by the exercise of power, they will be compelled to anticipate the moment when their power is to cease, when their exercise of it is to be reviewed, and when they must descend to the level from which they were raised; there for ever to remain, unless a faithful discharge of their trust shall have established their title to a renewal of it.

I will add as a fifth circumstance in the situation of the House of Representatives, restraining them from oppressive measures, that they can make no law which will not have its full operation on themselves and their friends, as well as on the great mass of the society. This has always been deemed one of the strongest bonds by which human policy can connect the rulers and the people together. It creates between them that communion of interests and sympathy of sentiments of which few governments have furnished examples; but without which every government degenerates into tyranny. If it be asked what is to restrain the House of Representatives from making legal discriminations in favor of themselves and a particular class of the society? I answer, the genius of the whole system, the nature of just and constitutional laws, and above all the vigilant and manly spirit which actuates the people of America, a spirit which nourishes freedom, and in return is nourished by it.

If this spirit shall ever be so far debased as to tolerate a law not obligatory on the Legislature as well as on the people, the people will be prepared to tolerate anything but liberty.

Such will be the relation between the House of Representatives and their constituents. Duty, gratitude, interest, ambition itself, are the cords by which they will be bound to fidelity and sympathy with the great mass of the people. It is possible that these may all be insufficient to control the caprice and wickedness of man. But are they not all that government will admit, and that human prudence can devise? Are they not the genuine and characteristic means by which the Republican Government provides for the liberty and happiness of the people? Are they not the identical means on which every State Government in the Union, relies for the attainment of these important ends? What then are we to understand by the objection which this paper has combated? What are we to say to the men who profess the most flaming zeal for Republican Government, yet boldly impeach the fundamental principle of it; who pretend to be champions for the right and the capacity of the people to choose their own rulers, yet maintain that they will prefer those only who will immediately and infallibly betray the trust committed to them?

Were the objection to be read by one who had not seen the mode prescribed by the Constitution for the choice of representatives, he could suppose nothing less than that some unreasonable qualification of property was annexed to the right of suffrage, or that the right of eligibility was limited to persons of particular families or fortunes; or at least that the mode prescribed by the State Constitutions was in some respect or other very grossly departed from. We have seen how far such a supposition would err as to the first two points. Nor would it in fact be less erroneous as to the last. The only difference discoverable between the two cases, is, that each representative of the United States will be elected by five or six thousand citizens; while in the individual States the election of a representative is left to about as many hundred. Will it be pretended that this difference is sufficient to justify an attachment to the State Governments and an abhorrence of the Federal Government? If this be the point on which the objection turns, it deserves to be examined.

Is it supported by *reason*? This cannot be said, without maintaining that five or six thousand citizens are less capable of choosing a fit representative, or more liable to be corrupted by an unfit one, than five or six hundred. Reason, on the contrary, assures us, that as in so great a number, a fit representative would be most likely to be found, so the choice would be less likely to be diverted from him, by the intrigues of the ambitious, or the bribes of the rich.

Is the *consequence* from this doctrine admissible? If we say that five or six hundred citizens are as many as can jointly exercise their right of suffrage, must we not deprive the people of the immediate choice of their public servants in every instance where the administration of the government does not require as many of them as will amount to one for that number of citizens?

Is the doctrine warranted by *facts*? It was shown in the last paper that the real representation in the British House of Common very little exceeds the proportion of one for every thirty thousand inhabitants. Besides a variety of powerful causes, not existing here, and which favor in that country, the pretensions of rank and wealth, no person is eligible as a representative of a county, unless he possess real estate of the clear value of six hundred pounds sterling per year; nor of a city or borough, unless he possess a like estate of half that value. To this qualification on the part of the county representatives, is added another on the part of the county electors, which restrains the right of suffrage to persons having a freehold estate of the annual value of more than twenty pounds sterling according to the present rate of money. Notwithstanding these unfavorable circumstances, and notwithstanding some very unequal laws in the British code, it cannot be said that the representatives of the nation have elevated the few on the ruins of the many.

But we need not resort to foreign experience on this subject. Our own is explicit and decisive. The districts in New Hampshire in which the Senators are chosen immediately by the people are nearly as large as will be necessary for her representatives in the Congress. Those of Massachusetts are larger, than will be necessary for that purpose. And those of New York still more so. In the last State the members of the Assembly, for the cities and counties of New York and Albany, are elected by very nearly as many voters, as will be entitled to a representative in the Congress, calculating on the number of sixty-five representatives only. It makes no difference that in these senatorial districts and counties, a number of representatives are voted for by each elector at the same time. If the same electors, at the same time, are capable of choosing four or five representatives, they cannot be incapable of choosing one. Pennsylvania is an additional example. Some of her counties which elect her State representatives, are almost as large as her districts will be by which her Federal Representatives will be elected. The city of Philadelphia is supposed to contain between fifty and sixty thousand souls. It will therefore form nearly two districts for the choice of Federal Representatives. It forms however but one county, in which every elector votes for each of its representatives in the State Legislature. And what may appear to be still more directly to our purpose, the whole city actually elects a *single member* for the executive council. This is the case in all the other counties in the State.

Are not these facts the most satisfactory proof of the fallacy which has been employed against the branch of the Federal Government under consideration? Has it appeared on trial that the Senators of New Hampshire, Massachusetts, and New York; or the executive council of Pennsylvania; or the members of the Assembly in the two last States, have betrayed any peculiar disposition to sacrifice the many to the few; or are in any respect less worthy of their places than the representatives and magistrates appointed in other States, by very small divisions of the people?

But there are cases of a stronger complexion than any which I have yet quoted. One branch of the Legislature of Connecticut is so constituted that each member of it is elected by the whole State. So is the Governor of that State, of Massachusetts, and of this State, and the President of New Hampshire. I leave every man to decide whether the result of any one of these experiments can be said to countenance a suspicion that a diffusive mode of choosing representatives of the people tends to elevate traitors, and to undermine the public liberty.

[February 19, 1788]

No. 62 [Madison]

CONCERNING THE CONSTITUTION OF THE SENATE WITH
REGARD TO THE QUALIFICATIONS OF THE MEMBERS,
THE MANNER OF APPOINTING THEM, THE EQUALITY OF
REPRESENTATION, THE NUMBER OF THE SENATORS,
AND THE DURATION OF THEIR APPOINTMENTS

Having examined the constitution of the house of representatives, and answered such of the objections against it as seemed to merit notice, I enter next on the examination of the senate. The heads into which this member of the government may be considered, are I. the qualifications of senators. II. the appointment of them by the state legislatures. III. the equality of representation in the senate. IV. the number of senators, and the term for which they are to be elected. V. the powers vested in the senate.[139]

---

139. [The discussion of IV continues in Essay 63, whereas V is discussed in Essays 64, 65, and 66, which are not included in this selection.]

I. The qualifications proposed for senators, as distinguished from those of representatives, consist in a more advanced age, and a longer period of citizenship. A senator must be thirty years of age at least; as a representative, must be twenty-five. And the former must have been a citizen nine years; as seven years are required for the latter. The propriety of these distinctions is explained by the nature of the senatorial trust; which requiring greater extent of information and stability of character, requires at the same time that the senator should have reached a period of life most likely to supply these advantages; and which participating immediately in transactions with foreign nations, ought to be exercised by none who are not thoroughly weaned from the prepossessions and habits incident to foreign birth and education. The term of nine years appears to be a prudent mediocrity between a total exclusion of adopted citizens, whose merit and talents may claim a share in the public confidence; and an indiscriminate and hasty admission of them, which might create a channel for foreign influence on the national councils.

II. It is equally unnecessary to dilate on the appointment of senators by the state legislatures. Among the various modes which might have been devised for constituting this branch of the government, that which has been proposed by the convention is probably the most congenial with the public opinion. It is recommended by the double advantage of favoring a select appointment, and of giving to the state governments such an agency in the formation of the federal government, as must secure the authority of the former; and may form a convenient link between the two systems.

III. The equality of representation in the senate is another point, which, being evidently the result of compromise between the opposite pretensions of the large and the small states, does not call for much discussion. If indeed it be right among a people thoroughly incorporated into one nation, every district ought to have a *proportional* share in the government; and that among independent and sovereign states bound together by[140] simple league, the parties however unequal in size, ought to have an *equal* share in the common councils, it does not appear to be without some reason, that in a compound republic partaking both of the national and federal character, the government ought to be founded on a mixture of the principles of proportional and equal representation. But it is superfluous to try by the standards of theory, a part of the constitution which is allowed on all hands to be the result not of theory, but "of a spirit of amity, and that mutual deference and concession which the peculiarity of our political situation rendered indispensable." A common government with powers equal to its objects, is called for by the voice, and still more

---

140. ["By a" was substituted in the McLean and Hopkins editions.]

loudly by the political situation of America. A government founded on principles more consonant to the wishes of the larger states, is not likely to be obtained from the smaller states. The only option then for the former lies between the proposed government and a government still more objectionable. Under this alternative the advice of prudence must be, to embrace the lesser evil; and instead of indulging a fruitless anticipation of the possible mischiefs which may ensue, to contemplate rather the advantageous consequences which may qualify the sacrifice.

In this spirit it may be remarked, that the equal vote allowed to each state, is at once a constitutional recognition of the portion of sovereignty remaining in the individual states, and an instrument for preserving that residuary sovereignty. So far the equality ought to be no less acceptable to the large than to the small states; since they are not less solicitous to guard by every possible expedient against an improper consolidation of the states into one simple republic.

Another advantage accruing from this ingredient in the constitution of the senate, is the additional impediment it must prove against improper acts of legislation. No law or resolution can now be passed without the concurrence first of a majority of the people, and then of a majority of the states. It must be acknowledged that this complicated check on legislation may in some instances be injurious as well as beneficial; and that the peculiar defense which it involves in favor of the smaller states would be more rational, if any interests common to them, and distinct from those of the other states, would otherwise be exposed to peculiar danger. But as the larger states will always be able by their power over the supplies to defeat unreasonable exertions of this prerogative of the lesser states; and as the facility and excess of law-making seem to be the diseases to which our governments are most liable, it is not impossible that this part of the constitution may be more convenient in practice than it appears to many in contemplation.

IV. The number of senators and the duration of their appointment come next to be considered. In order to form an accurate judgment on both these points, it will be proper to inquire into the purposes which are to be answered by a senate; and in order to ascertain these it will be necessary to review the inconveniences which a republic must suffer from the want of such an institution.

First. It is a misfortune incident to republican government, though in a less degree than to other governments, that those who administer it, may forget their obligations to their constituents, and prove unfaithful to their important trust. In this point of view, a senate, as a second branch of the legislative assembly, distinct from, and dividing the power with, a first, must be in all cases a salutary check on the government. It doubles the security to the people, by requiring the concurrence of two distinct bodies in schemes of usurpation or perfidy, where the ambition or corruption of one, would otherwise be sufficient. This is a precaution founded on such clear principles, and now so well understood in the United States, that it would be more than superfluous to enlarge on it. I will barely remark that as the improbability of sinister combinations will be in proportion to the dissimilarity in the genius of the two bodies; it must be politic to distinguish them from each other by every circumstance which will consist with a due harmony in all proper measures, and with the genuine principles of republican government.

Secondly. The necessity of a senate is not less indicated by the propensity of all single and numerous assemblies, to yield to the impulse of sudden and violent passions, and to be seduced by factious leaders, into intemperate and pernicious resolutions. Examples on this subject might be cited without number; and from proceedings within the United States, as well as from the history of other nations. But a position that will not be contradicted need not be proved. All that need be remarked is that a body which is to correct this infirmity ought itself be free from it, and consequently ought to be less numerous. It ought moreover to possess great firmness, and consequently ought to hold its authority by a tenure of considerable duration.

Thirdly. Another defect to be supplied by a senate lies in a want of due acquaintance with the objects and principles of legislation. It is not possible that an assembly of men called for the most part from pursuits of a private nature, continued in appointment for a short time, and led by no permanent motive to devote the intervals of public occupation to a study of the laws, the affairs, and the comprehensive interests of their country, should, if left wholly to themselves, escape a variety of important errors in the exercise of their legislative trust. It may be affirmed, on the best grounds, that no small share of the present embarrassments of America is to be charged on the blunders of our governments; and that these have proceeded from the heads rather than the hearts of most of the authors of them. What indeed are all the repealing, explaining, and amending laws, which fill and disgrace our voluminous codes, but so many monuments of deficient wisdom; so many impeachments exhibited by each succeeding, against each preceding session; so many admonitions to the people of the value of those aids which may be expected from a well-constituted senate?

A good government implies two things; first, fidelity to the object of government, which is the happiness of the people; secondly, a knowledge of the means by which that object can be best attained. Some governments are deficient in both these qualities: Most governments are deficient in the first. I scruple not to assert that in the American governments, too little attention has been paid to the last. The federal constitution avoids this error; and what merits particular notice, it provides for the last in a mode which increases the security for the first.

Fourthly. The mutability in the public councils, arising from a rapid succession of new members, however qualified they may be, points out in the strongest manner, the necessity of some stable institution in the government. Every new election in the states, is found to change one half of the representatives. From this change of men must proceed a change of opinions; and from a change of opinions, a change of measures. But a continual change even of good measures is inconsistent with every rule of prudence, and every prospect of success. The remark is verified in private life, and becomes more just as well as more important, in national transactions.

To trace the mischievous effects of a mutable government would fill a volume. I will hint a few only, each of which will be perceived to be a source of innumerable others.

In the first place it forfeits the respect and confidence of other nations, and all the advantages connected with national character. An individual who is observed to be inconstant to his plans, or perhaps to carry on his affairs without any plan at all, is marked at once by all prudent people as a speedy victim to his own unsteadiness and folly. His more friendly neighbors may pity him; but all will decline to connect their fortunes with his; and not a few will seize the opportunity of making their fortunes out of his. One nation is to another what one individual is to another; with this melancholy distinction perhaps, that the former with fewer of the benevolent emotions than the latter, are under fewer restraints also from taking undue advantage of the indiscretions of each other. Every nation consequently whose affairs betray a want of wisdom and stability, may calculate on every loss which can be sustained from the more systematic policy of its wiser neighbors. But the best instruction on this subject is unhappily conveyed to America by the example of her own situation. She finds that she is held in no respect by her friends; that she is the derision of her enemies; and that she is a prey to every nation which has an interest in speculating on her fluctuating councils and embarrassed affairs.

The internal effects of a mutable policy are still more calamitous. It poisons the blessings of liberty itself. It will be of little avail to the people that the laws are made by men of their own choice, if the laws be so voluminous that they cannot be read, or so incoherent that they cannot be understood; if they be repealed or revised before they are promulgated, or undergo such incessant changes that no man who knows what the law is today can guess what it will be tomorrow. Law is defined to be a rule of action; but how can that be a rule, which is little known and less fixed?

Another effect of public instability is the unreasonable advantage it gives to the sagacious, the enterprising, and the moneyed few, over the industrious and uninformed mass of the people. Every new regulation concerning commerce or revenue, or in any manner affecting the value of the different species of property, presents a new harvest to those who watch the change, and can trace its consequences; a harvest reared not by themselves but by the toils and cares of the great body of their fellow citizens. This is a state of things in which it may be said with some truth that laws are made for the *few* not for the *many*.

In another point of view great injury results from an unstable government. The want of confidence in the public councils damps every useful undertaking; the success and profit of which may depend on a continuance of existing arrangements. What prudent merchant will hazard his fortunes in any new branch of commerce, when he knows not but that his plans may be rendered unlawful before they can be executed? What farmer or manufacturer will lay himself out for the encouragement given to any particular cultivation or establishment, when he can have no assurance that his preparatory labors and advances will not render him a victim to an inconstant government? In a word no great improvement or laudable enterprise, can go forward, which requires the auspices of a steady system of national policy.

But the most deplorable effect of all is that diminution of attachment and reverence which steals into the hearts of the people, toward a political system which betrays so many marks of infirmity, and disappoints so many of their flattering hopes. No government any more than an individual will long be respected, without being truly respectable, nor be truly respectable without possessing a certain portion of order and stability.

[February 27, 1788]

No. 63   [Madison]

A FURTHER VIEW OF THE CONSTITUTION OF THE SENATE IN REGARD TO THE DURATION OF APPOINTMENT OF ITS MEMBERS

A *fifth* desideratum illustrating the utility of a Senate, is the want of a due sense of national character. Without a select and stable member of the government, the esteem of foreign powers will not only be forfeited by an unenlightened and variable policy, proceeding from the causes already mentioned; but the national councils will not possess that sensibility to the opinion of the world, which is perhaps not less necessary in order to merit, than it is to obtain, its respect and confidence.

An attention to the judgment of other nations is important to every government for two reasons: The one is, that independently of the merits of any particular plan or measure, it is desirable on various accounts, that it should appear to other nations as the offspring of a wise and honorable policy: The second is, that in doubtful cases, particularly where the national councils may be warped by some strong passion, or momentary interest, the presumed or known opinion of the impartial world, may be the best guide that can be followed. What has not America lost by her want of character with foreign nations? And how many errors and follies would she not have avoided, if the justice and propriety of her measures had in every instance been previously tried by the light in which they would probably appear to the unbiased part of mankind?

Yet however requisite a sense of national character may be, it is evident that it can never be sufficiently possessed by a numerous and changeable body. It can only be found in a number so small, that a sensible degree of the praise and blame of public measures may be the portion of each individual; or in an assembly so durably invested with public trust, that the pride and consequence of its members may be sensibly incorporated with the reputation and prosperity of the community. The half-yearly representatives of Rhode Island, would probably have been little affected in their deliberations on the iniquitous measures of that state, by arguments drawn from the light in which such measures would be viewed by foreign nations, or even by the sister states; while it can scarcely be doubted, that if the concurrence of a select and stable body had been necessary, a regard to national character alone, would have prevented the calamities under which that misguided people is now laboring.

I add as a *sixth* defect, the want in some important cases of a due responsibility in the government to the people, arising from that frequency of elections, which in other cases produces this responsibility. This[141] remark will perhaps appear not only new but paradoxical. It must nevertheless be acknowledged, when explained, to be as undeniable as it is important.

Responsibility[142] in order to be reasonable must be limited to objects within the power of the responsible party; and in order to be effectual, must relate to operations of that power, of which a ready and proper judgment can be formed by the constituents. The objects of government may

---

141. ["The" substituted for "This" in McLean and later editions.]

142. [The *Oxford English Dictionary* gives this, misdated to 1787, as the first usage of the word "responsibility," but this is doubly incorrect: the word occurs above in Essays 23 and 48, as well as in the previous paragraph, and was already well-established in a political context. See Gunnar von Proschwitz, "Responsabilité: L'idée et le mot dans le débat politique du XVIIIe siècle," in *Actes du Xe Congrès internationale de linguistique et philologie romane* (1965), 385–97, and above, pp. 21, 68–9, 72–3, for other earlier usages.]

be divided into two general classes; the one depending on measures which have singly an immediate and sensible operation; the other depending on a succession of well-chosen and well-connected measures, which have a gradual and perhaps unobserved operation. The importance of the latter description to the collective and permanent welfare of every country needs no explanation. And yet it is evident, that an assembly elected for so short a term as to be unable to provide more than one or two links in a chain of measures, on which the general welfare may essentially depend, ought not to be answerable for the final result, any more than a steward or tenant, engaged for one year, could be justly made to answer for plans[143] or improvements, which could not be accomplished in less than half a dozen years. Nor is it possible for the people to estimate the *share* of influence which their annual assemblies may respectively have on events resulting from the mixed transactions of several years. It is sufficiently difficult[144]to preserve a personal responsibility in the members of a *numerous* body, for such acts of the body as have an immediate, detached, and palpable operation on its constituents.

The proper remedy for this defect must be an additional body in the legislative department, which, having sufficient permanency to provide for such objects as require a continued attention, and a train of measures, may be justly and effectually answerable for the attainment of those objects.

Thus far I have considered the circumstances which point out the necessity of a well-constructed senate, only as they relate to the representatives of the people. To a people as little blinded by prejudice, or corrupted by flattery, as those whom I address, I shall not scruple to add, that such an institution may be sometimes necessary, as a defense to the people against their own temporary errors and delusions. As the cool and deliberate sense of the community ought in all governments, and actually will in all free governments ultimately prevail over the views of its rulers; so there are particular moments in public affairs, when the people stimulated by some irregular passion, or some illicit advantage, or misled by the artful misrepresentations of interested men, may call for measures which they themselves will afterward be the most ready to lament and condemn. In these critical moments, how salutary will be the interference of some temperate and respectable body of citizens, in order to check the misguided career,[145] and to suspend the blow meditated by the people against

---

143. [All editions before Gideon have "places."]

144. ["At any rate" inserted in McLean.]

145. [In the sense of a gallop or charge; the word did not yet have its modern sense of a course of employment.]

themselves, until reason, justice, and truth, can regain their authority over the public mind? What bitter anguish would not the people of Athens have often escaped, if their government had contained so provident a safeguard against the tyranny of their own passions? Popular liberty might then have escaped the indelible reproach of decreeing to the same citizens, the hemlock on one day, and statues on the next.[146]

It may be suggested that a people spread over an extensive region, cannot like the crowded inhabitants of a small district, be subject to the infection of violent passions; or to the danger of combining in pursuit[147] of unjust measures. I am far from denying that this is a distinction of peculiar importance. I have on the contrary endeavored in a former paper, to show that it is one of the principal recommendations of a confederated republic.[148] At the same time this advantage ought not to be considered as superseding the use of auxiliary precautions. It may even be remarked that the same extended situation which will exempt the people of America from some of the dangers incident to lesser republics, will expose them to the inconvenience of remaining for a longer time, under the influence of those misrepresentations which the combined industry of interested men may succeed in distributing among them.

It adds no small weight to all these considerations, to recollect, that history informs us of no long-lived republic which had not a senate. Sparta, Rome, and Carthage are in fact the only states to whom that character can be applied. In each of the two first there was a senate for life. The constitution of the senate in the last, is less known. Circumstantial evidence makes it probable that it was not different in this particular from the two others. It is at least certain that it had some quality or other which rendered it an anchor against popular fluctuations; and that a smaller council drawn out of the senate was appointed not only for life; but filled up vacancies itself. These examples, though as unfit for the imitation, as they are repugnant to the genius of America, are notwithstanding, when compared with the fugitive and turbulent existence of other ancient republics, very instructive proofs of the necessity of some institution that will blend stability with liberty. I am not unaware of the circumstances which distinguish the American from other popular governments, as well ancient as modern; and which render extreme circumspection necessary in reasoning from the one case to the other. But after allowing due weight

---

146. [Hemlock being a poison employed for public executions; statues being erected to preserve the memory of distinguished citizens.]

147. ["In the pursuit" substituted in McLean and later editions.]

148. [In Essay 10, above.]

to this consideration, it may still be maintained that there are many points of similitude which render these examples not unworthy of our attention. Many of the defects as we have seen, which can only be supplied by a senatorial institution, are common to a numerous assembly frequently elected by the people, and to the people themselves. There are others peculiar to the former, which require the control of such an institution. The people can never willfully betray their own interests: But they may possibly be betrayed by the representatives of the people; and the danger will be evidently greater where the whole legislative trust is lodged in the hands of one body of men, than where the concurrence of separate and dissimilar bodies is required in every public act.

The difference most relied on between the American and other republics, consists in the principle of representation, which is the pivot on which the former move, and which is supposed to have been unknown to the latter, or at least to the ancient part of them. The use which has been made of this difference, in reasonings contained in former papers, will have shown that I am disposed neither to deny its existence nor to undervalue its importance.[149] I feel the less restraint therefore in observing that the position concerning the ignorance of the ancient governments on the subject of representation is by no means precisely true in the latitude commonly given to it. Without entering into a disquisition which here would be misplaced, I will refer to a few known facts in support of what I advance.

In the most pure democracies of Greece, many of the executive functions were performed not by the people themselves, but by officers elected by the people, and *representing* the people in their *executive* capacity.

Prior to the reform of Solon, Athens was governed by nine Archons, annually *elected by the people at large*. The degree of power delegated to them seems to be left in great obscurity. Subsequent to that period, we find an assembly first of four and afterward of six hundred members, annually *elected by the people;* and *partially* representing them in their *legislative* capacity; since they were not only associated with the people in the function of making laws; but had the exclusive right of originating legislative propositions to the people. The senate of Carthage also, whatever might be its power or the duration of its appointment, appears to have been *elective* by the suffrages of the people. Similar instances might be traced in most if not all the popular governments of antiquity.

Lastly in Sparta, we meet with the Ephori, and in Rome with the Tribunes; two bodies, small indeed in number, but annually *elected by the whole body of the people*, and considered as the *representatives* of the people,

---

149. [See Essay 14, above.]

almost in their *plenipotentiary* capacity. The Cosmi of Crete were also annually *elected by the people;* and have been considered by some authors as an institution analogous to those of Sparta and Rome; with this difference only that in the election of that representative body, the right of suffrage was communicated to a part only of the people.

From these facts, to which many others might be added, it is clear that the principle of representation was neither unknown to the ancients, nor wholly overlooked in their political constitutions. The true distinction between these and the American Governments lies *in the total exclusion of the people in their collective capacity* from any share in the *latter,* and not in the *total exclusion of representatives of the people,* from the administration of the *former.* The distinction however thus qualified must be admitted to leave a most advantageous superiority in favor of the United States. But to ensure to this advantage its full effect, we must be careful not to separate it from the other advantage, of an extensive territory. For it cannot be believed that any form of representative government, could have succeeded within the narrow limits occupied by the democracies of Greece.

In answer to all these arguments, suggested by reason, illustrated by examples,[150] and enforced by our own experience, the jealous adversary of the constitution will probably content himself with repeating, that a senate appointed not immediately by the people, and for the term of six years, must gradually acquire a dangerous preeminence in the government, and finally transform it into a tyrannical aristocracy.

To this general answer the general reply ought to be sufficient; that liberty may be endangered by the abuses of liberty, as well as by the abuses of power; that there are numerous instances of the former as well as of the latter; and that the former rather than the latter is apparently most to be apprehended by the United States. But a more particular reply may be given.

Before such a revolution can be effected, the senate, it is to be observed, must in the first place corrupt itself; must next corrupt the state legislatures, must then corrupt the house of representatives, and must finally corrupt the people at large. It is evident that the senate must be first corrupted, before it can attempt an establishment of tyranny. Without corrupting the state legislatures, it cannot prosecute the attempt, because the periodical change of members would otherwise regenerate the whole body. Without exerting the means of corruption with equal success on the house of representatives, the opposition of that coequal branch of the government would inevitably defeat the attempt; and without corrupting the people themselves, a succession of new representatives

---

150. ["By other examples" in the newspapers; corrected in McLean.]

would speedily restore all things to their pristine order. Is there any man who can seriously persuade himself, that the proposed senate can, by any possible means within the compass of human address, arrive at the object of a lawless ambition, through all these obstructions?

If reason condemns the suspicion, the same sentence is pronounced by experience. The constitution of Maryland furnishes the most apposite example. The senate of that state is elected, as the federal senate will be, indirectly by the people; and for a term less by one year only, than the federal senate. It is distinguished also by the remarkable prerogative of filling up its own vacancies within the term of its appointment: and at the same time, is not under the control of any such rotation, as is provided for the federal senate. There are some other lesser distinctions, which would expose the former to colorable objections[151] that do not lie against the latter. If the federal senate therefore really contained the danger which has been so loudly proclaimed, some symptoms at least of a like danger ought by this time to have been betrayed by the senate of Maryland; but no such symptoms have appeared. On the contrary the jealousies at first entertained by men of the same description with those who view with terror the correspondent part of the federal constitution, have been gradually extinguished by the progress of the experiment; and the Maryland constitution is daily deriving from the salutary operations[152] of this part of it, a reputation in which it will probably not be rivaled by that of any state in the union.

But if anything could silence the jealousies on this subject, it ought to be the British example. The senate there, instead: of being elected for a term of six years, and of being unconfined to particular families or fortunes, is an hereditary assembly of opulent nobles. The house of representatives, instead of being elected for two years and by the whole body of the people, is elected for seven years; and in very great proportion, by a very small proportion of the people. Here unquestionably ought to be seen in full display, the aristocratic usurpations and tyranny, which are at some future period to be exemplified in the United States. Unfortunately however for the antifederal argument[153] the British history informs us, that this hereditary assembly has not even been able to defend itself against the continual encroachments of the house of representatives; and that it no sooner lost the support of the monarch, than it was actually crushed by the weight of the popular branch.

---

151. [McLean has "subjections," an evident misprint.]

152. ["Operation" substituted in McLean and later editions.]

153. [The newspapers have "argument in," which is corrected in McLean and later editions.]

As far as antiquity can instruct us on this subject, its examples support the reasoning which we have employed. In Sparta the Ephori, the annual representatives of the people, were found an overmatch for the senate for life, continually gained on its authority, and finally drew all power into their own hands. The tribunes of Rome, who were the representatives of the people, prevailed, it is well-known, in almost every contest with the senate for life, and in the end gained the most complete triumph over it. This fact is the more remarkable, as unanimity was required in every act of the tribunes, even after their number was augmented to ten. It proves the irresistible force possessed by that branch of a free government, which has the people on its side. To these examples might be added that of Carthage, whose senate, according to the testimony of Polybius, instead of drawing all power into its vortex, had at the commencement of the second Punic war, lost almost the whole of its original portion.

Besides the conclusive evidence resulting from this assemblage of facts, that the federal senate will never be able to transform itself, by gradual usurpations, into an independent and aristocratic body; we are warranted in believing that if such a revolution should ever happen from causes which the foresight of man cannot guard against, the house of representatives with the people on their side will at all times be able to bring back the constitution to its primitive form and principles. Against the force of the immediate representatives of the people, nothing will be able to maintain even the constitutional authority of the senate, but such a display of enlightened policy, and attachment to the public good, as will divide with that branch of the legislature, the affections and support of the entire body of the people themselves.

[March 1, 1788]

No. 70   [Hamilton]

[CONCERNING THE CONSTITUTION OF THE PRESIDENT]:
THE SAME SUBJECT CONTINUED IN RELATION TO THE
UNITY OF THE EXECUTIVE, WITH AN EXAMINATION OF
THE PROJECT OF AN EXECUTIVE COUNCIL

There is an idea, which is not without its advocates, that a vigorous executive is inconsistent with the genius of republican government. The enlightened well-wishers to this species of government must at least hope that the supposition is destitute of foundation; since they can never admit its truth, without at the same time admitting the condemnation of their own principles. Energy in the executive is a leading character in the definition of good government. It is essential to the protection of the community against foreign attacks: It is not less essential to the steady administration of the laws, to the protection of property against those irregular and high-handed combinations, which sometimes interrupt the ordinary course of justice, to the security of liberty against the enterprises and assaults of ambition, of faction, and of anarchy. Every man the least conversant in Roman story knows how often that republic was obliged to take refuge in the absolute power of a single man, under the formidable title of dictator, as well against the intrigues of ambitious individuals, who aspired to the tyranny, and the seditions of whole classes of the community, whose conduct threatened the existence of all government, as against the invasions of external enemies, who menaced the conquest and destruction of Rome.

There can be no need however to multiply arguments or examples on this head. A feeble executive implies a feeble execution of the government. A feeble execution is but another phrase for a bad execution: And a government ill executed, whatever it may be in theory, must be in practice a bad government.

Taking it for granted, therefore, that all men of sense will agree in the necessity of an energetic executive; it will only remain to inquire, what are the ingredients which constitute this energy—how far can they be combined with those other ingredients which constitute safety in the republican sense? And how far does this combination characterize the plan, which has been reported by the convention?

The ingredients, which constitute energy in the executive, are first unity, secondly duration, thirdly an adequate provision for its support, fourthly competent powers.[154]

The circumstances[155] which constitute safety in the republican sense are, 1st a due dependence on the people, secondly a due responsibility.

Those politicians and statesmen, who have been the most celebrated for the soundness of their principles, and for the justness of their views, have declared in favor of a single executive and a numerous legislature. They have with great propriety considered energy as the most necessary qualification of the former, and have regarded this as most applicable to power in a single hand; while they have with equal propriety considered the latter as best adapted to deliberation and wisdom, and best calculated to conciliate the confidence of the people and to secure their privileges and interests.

---

154. ["First," "secondly," "thirdly," and "fourthly" omitted in McLean and later editions; similarly, "1st" and "secondly" in the next paragraph.]

155. ["Ingredients" substituted in McLean and later editions.]

That unity is conducive to energy will not be disputed. Decision, activity, secrecy, dispatch[156] will generally characterize the proceedings[157] of one man, in a much more eminent degree, than the proceedings of any greater number; and in proportion as the number is increased, these qualities will be diminished.

This unity may be destroyed in two ways; either by vesting the power in two or more magistrates of equal dignity and authority; or by vesting it ostensibly in one man, subject in whole or in part to the control and cooperation of others, in the capacity of counselors to him. Of the first the two consuls of Rome may serve as an example; of the last we shall find examples in the constitutions of several of the states. New York and New Jersey, if I recollect right, are the only states, which have entrusted the executive authority wholly to single men.[158] Both these methods of destroying the unity of the executive have their partisans; but the votaries of an executive council are the most numerous. They are both liable, if not to equal, to similar objections; and may in most lights be examined in conjunction.

The experience of other nations will afford little instruction on this head. As far however as it teaches anything, it teaches us not to be enamored of plurality in the executive. We have seen that the Achaeans on an experiment of two Praetors, were induced to abolish one.[159] The Roman history records many instances of mischiefs to the republic from the dissensions between the consuls, and between the military tribunes, who were at times substituted to the consuls. But it gives us no specimens of any peculiar advantages derived to the state, from the circumstance of the plurality[160] of those magistrates. That the dissensions between them were not more frequent, or more fatal, is matter of astonishment; until we advert to the singular position in which the republic was almost continually placed and to the prudent policy pointed out by the circumstances of the state, and pursued by the consuls, of making a division of the government between them. The Patricians engaged in a perpetual struggle with the Plebeians for the preservation of their ancient authorities and dignities; the consuls, who were generally chosen out of the former body, were

---

156. ["And dispatch" in McLean and later editions.]

157. ["Proceeding" in the newspapers; corrected in McLean and later editions.]

158. *New York has no council except for the single purpose of appointing to offices; New Jersey has a council, whom the governor may consult. But I think from the terms of the constitution their resolutions do not bind him.* (Publius)

159. [In Essay 18, not in this selection.]

160. ["From the plurality" in McLean and later editions.]

commonly united by the personal interest they had in the defense of the privileges of their order. In addition to this motive of union, after the arms of the republic had considerably expanded the bounds of its empire, it became an established custom with the consuls to divide the administration between themselves by lot; one of them remaining at Rome to govern the city and its environs; the other taking the command in the more distant provinces. This expedient must no doubt have had great influence in preventing those collisions and rivalships, which might otherwise have embroiled the peace of the republic.[161]

But quitting the dim light of historical research, and attaching ourselves purely to the dictates of reason and good sense, we shall discover much greater cause to reject than to approve the idea of plurality in the executive, under any modification whatever.

Wherever two or more persons are engaged in any common enterprise or pursuit, there is always danger of difference of opinion. If it be a public trust or office in which they are clothed with equal dignity and authority, there is peculiar danger of personal emulation and even animosity. From either and especially from all these causes, the most bitter dissensions are apt to spring. Whenever these happen, they lessen the respectability, weaken the authority, and distract the plans and operations of those whom they divide. If they should unfortunately assail the supreme executive magistracy of a country, consisting of a plurality of persons, they might impede or frustrate the most important measures of the government, in the most critical emergencies of the state. And what is still worse, they might split the community into the most[162] violent and irreconcilable factions, adhering differently to the different individuals who composed the magistracy.

Men often oppose a thing merely because they have had no agency in planning it, or because it may have been planned by those whom they dislike. But if they have been consulted and have happened to disapprove, opposition then becomes in their estimation an indispensable duty of self-love. They seem to think themselves bound in honor, and by all the motives of personal infallibility to defeat the success of what has been resolved upon, contrary to their sentiments. Men of upright, benevolent tempers have too many opportunities of remarking with horror, to what desperate lengths this disposition is sometimes carried, and how often the great interests of society are sacrificed to the vanity, to the conceit, and to the obstinacy of individuals, who have credit enough to make their

---

161. ["Embroiled the republic" in McLean and later editions.]

162. ["The most" omitted in McLean and later editions.]

passions and their caprices interesting to mankind. Perhaps the question now before the public may in its consequences afford melancholy proofs of the effects of this despicable frailty, or rather detestable vice in the human character.

Upon the principles of a free government, inconveniences from the source just mentioned must necessarily be submitted to in the formation of the legislature; but it is unnecessary and therefore unwise to introduce them into the constitution of the executive. It is here too that they may be most pernicious. In the legislature, promptitude of decision is oftener an evil than a benefit. The differences of opinion, and the jarrings of parties in that department of the government, though they may sometimes obstruct salutary plans, yet often promote deliberation and circumspection; and serve to check excesses in the majority. When a resolution too is once taken, the opposition must be at an end. That resolution is a law, and resistance to it punishable. But no favorable circumstances palliate or atone for the disadvantages of dissension in the executive department. Here they are pure and unmixed. There is no point at which they cease to operate. They serve to embarrass and weaken the execution of the plan or measure, to which they relate, from the first step to the final conclusion of it. They constantly counteract those qualities in the executive, which are the most necessary ingredients in its composition, vigor, and expedition, and this without any counterbalancing good. In the conduct of war, in which the energy of the executive is the bulwark of the national security, everything would be to be apprehended from its plurality.

It must be confessed that these observations apply with principal weight to the first[163] case supposed, that is to a plurality of magistrates of equal dignity and authority; a scheme the advocates for which are not likely to form a numerous sect: But they apply, though not with equal, yet with considerable weight, to the project of a council, whose concurrence is made constitutionally necessary to the operations of the ostensible executive. An artful cabal in that council would be able to distract and to enervate the whole system of administration. If no such cabal should exist, the mere diversity of views and opinions would alone be sufficient to tincture the exercise of the executive authority with a spirit of habitual feebleness and dilatoriness.

But one of the weightiest objections to a plurality in the executive, and which lies as much against the last as the first plan, is that it tends to conceal faults, and destroy responsibility. Responsibility is of two kinds, to censure and to punishment. The first is the most important of the two;

---

163. ["Full" in the newspapers; corrected in McLean.]

especially in elective office. Man, in public trust, will much oftener act in such a manner as to render him unworthy of being any longer trusted, than in such a manner as to make him obnoxious to legal punishment.[164] But the multiplication of the executive adds to the difficulty of detection in either case. It often becomes impossible, amidst mutual accusations, to determine on whom the blame or the punishment of a pernicious measure, or series of pernicious measures ought really to fall. It is shifted from one to another with so much dexterity, and under such plausible appearances, that the public opinion is left in suspense about the real author. The circumstances which may have led to any national miscarriage or misfortune are sometimes so complicated, that where there are a number of actors who may have had different degrees and kinds of agency, though we may clearly see upon the whole that there has been mismanagement, yet it may be impracticable to pronounce to whose account the evil which may have been incurred is truly chargeable.

"I was overruled by my council. The council were so divided in their opinions, that it was impossible to obtain any better resolution on the point." These and similar pretexts are constantly at hand, whether true or false. And who is there that will either take the trouble or incur the odium of a strict scrutiny into the secret springs of the transaction? Should there be found a citizen zealous enough to undertake the unpromising task, if there happen to be a collusion between the parties concerned, how easy is it to clothe the circumstances with so much ambiguity, as to render it uncertain what was the precise conduct of any of those parties?

In the single instance in which the governor of this state is coupled with a council, that is in the appointment to offices, we have seen the mischiefs of it in the view now under consideration.[165] Scandalous appointments to important offices have been made. Some cases indeed have been so flagrant, that ALL PARTIES have agreed in the impropriety of the thing. When inquiry has been made, the blame has been laid by the governor on the members of the council; who on their part have charged it upon his nomination: While the people remain altogether at a loss to determine by whose influence their interests have been committed to hands so unqualified, and so manifestly improper. In tenderness to individuals, I forbear to descend to particulars.

It is evident from these considerations, that the plurality of the executive tends to deprive the people of the two greatest securities they can have for the faithful exercise of any delegated power; first, the restraints

---

164. ["Men . . . them . . . them" in McLean and later editions.]
165. [In Essay 69, not in this selection.]

of public opinion, which lose their efficacy as well on account of the division of the censure attendant on bad measures among a number, as on account of the uncertainty on whom it ought to fall; and secondly, the opportunity of discovering with facility and clearness the misconduct of the persons they trust, in order either to their removal from office, or to their actual punishment, in cases which admit of it.

In England the king is a perpetual magistrate; and it is maxim, which has obtained for the sake of the public peace, that he is unaccountable for his administration, and his person sacred. Nothing therefore can be wiser in that kingdom than to annex to the king a constitutional council, who may be responsible to the nation for the advice they give. Without this there would be no responsibility whatever in the executive department; an idea inadmissible in a free government. But even there the king is not bound by the resolutions of his council, though they are answerable for the advice they give. He is the absolute master of his own conduct, in the exercise of his office; and may observe or disregard the council given to him at his sole discretion.

But in a republic, where every magistrate ought to be personally responsible for his behavior in office, the reason which in the British constitution dictates the propriety of a council not only ceases to apply, but turns against the institution. In the monarchy of Great Britain, it furnishes a substitute for the prohibited responsibility of the chief magistrate; which serves in some degree as a hostage to the national justice for his good behavior. In the American republic it would serve to destroy, or would greatly diminish the intended and necessary responsibility of the chief magistrate himself.

The idea of a council to the executive, which has so generally obtained in the state constitutions, has been derived from that maxim of republican jealousy, which considers power as safer in the hands of a number of men than of a single man. If the maxim should be admitted to be applicable to the case, I should contend that the advantage on that side would not counterbalance the numerous disadvantages on the opposite side. But I do not think the rule at all applicable to the executive power. I clearly concur in opinion in this particular with a writer[166] whom the celebrated Junius[167] pronounces to be "deep, solid and ingenious," that, "the executive power is more easily confined when it is one":[168] That it is far more safe there

---

166. [Jean Louis de Lolme.]

167. [Junius, *Stat Nominis Umbra* (1772).]

168. De Lostme. (Publius) [So in the newspapers; De Lome in McLean and De Lolme in later editions; i.e., Jean Louis de Lolme, *The Constitution of England* (first published in French in 1771, and in English in 1775).]

should be a single object for the jealousy and watchfulness of the people; and in a word that all multiplication of the executive is rather dangerous than friendly to liberty.

A little consideration will satisfy us, that the species of security sought for in the multiplication of the executive is unattainable. Numbers must be so great as to render combination difficult; or they are rather a source of danger than of security. The united credit and influence of several individuals must be more formidable to liberty than the credit and influence of either of them separately. When power therefore is placed in the hands of so small a number of men, as to admit of their interests and views being easily combined in a common enterprise, by an artful leader, it becomes more liable to abuse and more dangerous when abused, than if it be lodged in the hands of one man; who from the very circumstance of his being alone will be more narrowly watched and more readily suspected, and who cannot unite so great a mass of influence as when he is associated with others. The Decemvirs of Rome, whose name denotes their number,[169] were more to be dreaded in their usurpation than any ONE of them would have been. No person would think of proposing an executive much more numerous than that body, from six to a dozen have been suggested for the number of the council. The extreme of these numbers is not too great for an easy combination; and from such a combination America would have more to fear, than from the ambition of any single individual. A council to a magistrate, who is himself responsible for what he does, are generally nothing better than a clog upon his good intentions; are often the instruments and accomplices of his bad, and are almost always a cloak to his faults.

I forbear to dwell upon the subject of expense; though it be evident that if the council should be numerous enough to answer the principal end, aimed at by the institution, the salaries of the members, who must be drawn from their homes to reside at the seat of government, would form an item in the catalog of public expenditures, too serious to be incurred for an object of equivocal utility.

I will only add, that prior to the appearance of the constitution, I rarely met with an intelligent man from any of the states, who did not admit as the result of experience, that the UNITY of the Executive of this state was one of the best of the distinguishing features of our constitution.

[March 15, 1788]

---

169. *Ten.* (Publius)

No. 78   [Hamilton]

A VIEW OF THE CONSTITUTION OF THE JUDICIAL DEPARTMENT
IN RELATION TO THE TENURE OF GOOD BEHAVIOR

We proceed now to an examination of the judiciary department of the proposed government.

In unfolding the defects of the existing confederation, the utility and necessity of a federal judicature have been clearly pointed out.[170] It is the less necessary to recapitulate the considerations there urged; as the propriety of the institution in the abstract is not disputed: The only questions which have been raised being relative to the manner of constituting it, and to its extent. To these points therefore our observations shall be confined.

The manner of constituting it seems to embrace these several objects— First. The mode of appointing the judges. Second. The tenure by which they are to hold their places. Third. The partition of the judiciary authority between different courts, and their relations to each other.

First. As to the mode of appointing the judges: This is the same with that of appointing the officers of the union in general, and has been so fully discussed in the two last numbers,[171] that nothing can be said here which would not be useless repetition.

Second.[172] As to the tenure by which the judges are to hold their places: This chiefly concerns their duration in office; the provisions for their support; and the precautions for their responsibility.

According to the plan of the convention, all the judges who may be appointed by the United States are to hold their offices *during good behavior,* which is conformable to the most approved of the state constitutions; and among the rest, to that of this state. Its propriety having been drawn into question by the adversaries of that plan, is no light symptom of the rage for objection which disorders their imaginations and judgments. The standard of good behavior for the continuance in office of the judicial magistracy is certainly one of the most valuable of the modern improvements in the practice of government. In a monarchy it is an excellent barrier to the despotism of the prince: In a republic it is a no less excellent barrier to the encroachments and oppressions of the representative body. And it is the best expedient which can be devised in any government to secure a steady, upright, and impartial administration of the laws.

---

170. [In Essay 22, not included in this selection.]

171. [Essays 76 and 77, not included in this selection.]

172. [*Third* is dealt with in Essay 80, not included in this selection.]

Whoever attentively considers the different departments of power must perceive, that in a government in which they are separated from each other, the judiciary, from the nature of its functions, will always be the least dangerous to the political rights of the constitution; because it will be least in a capacity to annoy or injure them. The executive not only dispenses the honors, but holds the sword of the community. The legislature not only commands the purse, but prescribes the rules by which the duties and rights of every citizen are to be regulated. The judiciary on the contrary has no influence over either the sword or the purse, no direction either of the strength or of the wealth of the society, and can take no active resolution whatever. It may truly be said to have neither Force nor Will, but merely judgment; and must ultimately depend upon the aid of the executive arm even for the efficacy of its judgments.

This simple view of the matter suggests several important consequences. It proves incontestably that the judiciary is beyond comparison the weakest of the three departments of power;[173] that it can never attack with success either of the other two; and that all possible care is requisite to enable it to defend itself against their attacks. It equally proves, that though individual oppression may now and then proceed from the courts of justice, the general liberty of the people can never be endangered from that quarter: I mean, so long as the judiciary remains truly distinct from both the legislative[174] and executive. For I agree that "there is no liberty, if the power of judging be not separated from the legislative and executive powers."[175] And it proves, in the last place, that as liberty can have nothing to fear from the judiciary alone, but would have everything to fear from its union with either of the other departments; that as all the effects of such an union must ensue from a dependence of the former on the latter, notwithstanding a nominal and apparent separation; that as from the natural feebleness of the judiciary, it is in continual jeopardy of being overpowered, awed, or influenced by its coordinate branches; and that as nothing can contribute so much to its firmness and independence, as permanency in office, this quality may therefore be justly regarded as an indispensable ingredient in its constitution; and in a great measure as the citadel of the public justice and the public security.

The complete independence of the courts of justice is peculiarly essential in a limited constitution. By a limited constitution I understand one

---

173. The celebrated Montesquieu speaking of them says, "of the three powers above mentioned, the JUDICIARY is next to nothing." Spirit of Laws, volume 1, page 186. (Publius) [i.e., book 11, chapter 6.]

174. ["Legislature" in Gideon.]

175. Idem, page 181. (Publius)

which contains certain specified exceptions to the legislative authority; such for instance as that it shall pass no bills of attainder, no *ex post facto* laws, and the like. Limitations of this kind can be preserved in practice no other way than through the medium of the courts of justice; whose duty it must be to declare all acts contrary to the manifest tenor of the constitution void. Without this, all the reservations of particular rights or privileges would amount to nothing.

Some perplexity respecting the right of the courts to pronounce legislative acts void, because contrary to the constitution, has arisen from an imagination that the doctrine would imply a superiority of the judiciary to the legislative power. It is urged that the authority which can declare the acts of another void, must necessarily be superior to the one whose acts may be declared void. As this doctrine is of great importance in all the American constitutions, a brief discussion of the grounds on which it rests cannot be unacceptable.

There is no position which depends on clearer principles than that every act of a delegated authority, contrary to the tenor of the commission under which it is exercised, is void. No legislative act therefore contrary to the constitution can be valid. To deny this would be to affirm that the deputy is greater than his principal; that the servant is above his master; that the representatives of the people are superior to the people themselves; that men acting by virtue of powers may do not only what their powers do not authorize, but what they forbid.

If it be said that the legislative body are themselves the constitutional judges of their own powers, and that the construction they put upon them is conclusive upon the other departments, it may be answered, that this cannot be the natural presumption, where it is not to be collected from any particular provisions in the constitution. It is not otherwise to be supposed that the constitution could intend to enable the representatives of the people to substitute their *will* to that of their constituents. It is far more rational to suppose that the courts were designed to be an intermediate body between the people and the legislature, in order, among other things, to keep the latter within the limits assigned to their authority. The interpretation of the laws is the proper and peculiar province of the courts. A constitution is in fact, and must be, regarded by the judges as a fundamental law. It therefore belongs to them to ascertain its meaning as well as the meaning of any particular act proceeding from the legislative body. If there should happen to be an irreconcilable variance between the two, that which has the superior obligation and validity ought of course to be preferred; or in other words, the constitution ought to be preferred to the statute, the intention of the people to the intention of their agents.

Nor does this conclusion by any means suppose a superiority of the judicial to the legislative power. It only supposes that the power of the people is superior to both; and that where the will of the legislature declared in its statutes, stands in opposition to that of the people declared in the constitution, the judges ought to be governed by the latter, rather than the former. They ought to regulate their decisions by the fundamental laws, rather than by those which are not fundamental.

This exercise of judicial discretion in determining between two contradictory laws, is exemplified in a familiar instance. It not uncommonly happens, that there are two statutes existing at one time, clashing in whole or in part with each other, and neither of them containing any repealing clause or expression. In such a case, it is the province of the courts to liquidate and fix their meaning and operation: So far as they can by any fair construction be reconciled to each other; reason and law conspire to dictate that this should be done. Where this is impracticable, it becomes a matter of necessity to give effect to one, in exclusion of the other. The rule which has obtained in the courts for determining their relative validity is that the last in order of time shall be preferred to the first. But this is a mere rule of construction, not derived from any positive law, but from the nature and reason of the thing. It is a rule not enjoined upon the courts by legislative provision, but adopted by themselves, as consonant to truth and propriety, for the direction of their conduct as interpreters of the law. They thought it reasonable, that between the interfering acts of an *equal* authority, that which was the last indication of its will, should have the preference.

But in regard to the interfering acts of a superior and subordinate authority, of an original and derivative power, the nature and reason of the thing indicate the converse of that rule as proper to be followed. They teach us that the prior act of a superior ought to be preferred to the subsequent act of an inferior and subordinate authority; and that, accordingly, whenever a particular statute contravenes the constitution, it will be the duty of the judicial tribunals to adhere to the latter, and disregard the former.

It can be of no weight to say, that the courts on the pretense of a repugnancy, may substitute their own pleasure to the constitutional intentions of the legislature. This might as well happen in the case of two contradictory statutes; or it might as well happen in every adjudication upon any single statute. The courts must declare the sense of the law; and if they should be disposed to exercise WILL instead of JUDGMENT, the consequence would equally be the substitution of their pleasure to that of the legislative body. The observation, if it proved anything, would prove that there ought to be no judges distinct from that body.

If then the courts of justice are to be considered as the bulwarks of a limited constitution against legislative encroachments, this consideration will afford a strong argument for the permanent tenure of judicial offices, since nothing will contribute so much as this to that independent spirit in the judges, which must be essential to the faithful performance of so arduous a duty.

This independence of the judges is equally requisite to guard the constitution and the rights of individuals from the effects of those ill humors which the arts of designing men, or the influence of particular conjunctures, sometimes disseminate among the people themselves, and which, though they speedily give place to better information and more deliberate reflection, have a tendency in the meantime to occasion dangerous innovations in the government, and serious oppressions of the minor party in the community. Though I trust the friends of the proposed constitution will never concur with its enemies[176] in questioning that fundamental principle of republican government, which admits the right of the people to alter or abolish the established constitution whenever they find it inconsistent with their happiness; yet it is not to be inferred from this principle, that the representatives of the people, whenever a momentary inclination happens to lay hold of a majority of their constituents incompatible with the provisions in the existing constitution, would on that account be justifiable in a violation of those provisions; or that the courts would be under a greater obligation to connive at infractions in this shape, than when they had proceeded wholly from the cabals of the representative body. Until the people have by some solemn and authoritative act annulled or changed the established form, it is binding upon themselves collectively, as well as individually; and no presumption, or even knowledge of their sentiments, can warrant their representatives in a departure from it, prior to such an act. But it is easy to see that it would require an uncommon portion of fortitude in the judges to do their duty as faithful guardians of the constitution, where legislative invasions of it had been instigated by the major voice of the community.

But it is not with a view to infractions of the constitution only that the independence of the judges may be an essential safeguard against the effects of occasional ill humors in the society. These sometimes extend no

---

176. Vide Protest of the minority of the convention of Pennsylvania, Martin's speech, etc. (Publius) [This is a reference to "The Address and Reasons of Dissent of the Minority of the Convention of the State of Pennsylvania to their Constituents," published December 18, 1787 (above, pp. 3–24); Luther Martin, member of the Constitutional Convention but opponent of the proposed constitution, addressed the Maryland House of Delegates on January 27, 1788.]

farther than to the injury of the private rights of particular classes of citizens, by unjust and partial laws. Here also the firmness of the judicial magistracy is of vast importance in mitigating the severity, and confining the operation of such laws. It not only serves to moderate the immediate mischiefs of those which may have been passed, but it operates as a check upon the legislative body in passing them; who, perceiving that obstacles to the success of an iniquitous intention are to be expected from the scruples of the courts, are in a manner compelled by the very motives of the injustice they meditate, to qualify their attempts. This is a circumstance calculated to have more influence upon the character of our governments, than but few may be aware of. The benefits of the integrity and moderation of the judiciary have already been felt in more states than one; and though they may have displeased those whose sinister expectations they may have disappointed, they must have commanded the esteem and applause of all the virtuous and disinterested. Considerate men of every description ought to prize whatever will tend to beget or fortify that temper in the courts; as no man can be sure that he may not be tomorrow the victim of a spirit of injustice, by which he may be a gainer today. And every man must now feel that the inevitable tendency of such a spirit is to sap the foundations of public and private confidence, and to introduce in its stead, universal distrust and distress.

That inflexible and uniform adherence to the rights of the constitution and of individuals, which we perceive to be indispensable in the courts of justice, can certainly not be expected from judges who hold their offices by a temporary commission. Periodical appointments, however regulated, or by whomsoever made, would in some way or other be fatal to their necessary independence. If the power of making them was committed either to the executive or legislature, there would be danger of an improper complaisance to the branch which possessed it; if to both, there would be an unwillingness to hazard the displeasure of either; if to the people, or to persons chosen by them for the special purpose, there would be too great a disposition to consult popularity, to justify a reliance that nothing would be consulted but the constitution and the laws.

There is yet a further and a weighty reason for the permanency of the judicial offices; which is deducible from the nature of the qualifications they require. It has been frequently remarked with great propriety, that a voluminous code of laws is one of the inconveniences necessarily connected with the advantages of a free government. To avoid an arbitrary discretion in the courts, it is indispensable that they should be bound down by strict rules and precedents, which serve to define and point out their duty in every particular case that comes before them; and it will readily be conceived from the variety of controversies which grow out of the folly and wickedness of mankind, that the records of those precedents must unavoidably swell to a very considerable bulk, and must demand long and laborious study to acquire a competent knowledge of them. Hence it is that there can be but few men in the society, who will have sufficient skill in the laws to qualify them for the stations of judges. And making the proper deductions for the ordinary depravity of human nature, the number must be still smaller of those who unite the requisite integrity with the requisite knowledge. These considerations apprise us, that the government can have no great option between fit characters; and that a temporary duration in office, which would naturally discourage such characters from quitting a lucrative line of practice to accept a seat on the bench, would have a tendency to throw the administration of justice into hands less able, and less well-qualified to conduct it with utility and dignity. In the present circumstances of this country, and in those in which it is likely to be for a long time to come, the disadvantages on this score would be greater than they may at first sight appear; but it must be confessed that they are far inferior to those which present themselves under the other aspects of the subject.

Upon the whole there can be no room to doubt that the convention acted wisely in copying from the models of those constitutions which have established *good behavior* as the tenure of their judicial offices in point of duration; and that so far from being blamable on this account, their plan would have been inexcusably defective if it had wanted this important feature of good government. The experience of Great Britain affords an illustrious comment on the excellence of the institution.

[May 28, 1788]

No. 83   [Hamilton]

A FURTHER VIEW OF THE JUDICIAL DEPARTMENT
IN RELATION TO THE TRIAL BY JURY

The objection to the plan of the convention, which has met with most success in this state, and perhaps in several of the other states, is *that* relative to *the want of a constitutional provision* for the trial by jury in civil cases. The disingenuous form in which this objection is usually stated, has been repeatedly adverted to and exposed; but continues to be pursued in all the conversations and writings of the opponents of the plan. The mere silence of the constitution in regard to *civil causes,* is represented as an abolition of the trial by jury; and the declamations to which it has afforded a pretext, are artfully calculated to induce a persuasion that this pretended abolition is complete and universal; extending not only to every species of civil, but even to *criminal causes*. To argue with respect to the latter, would, however, be as vain and fruitless, as to attempt the serious proof of the *existence* of *matter*, or to demonstrate any of those propositions which by their own internal evidence force conviction, when expressed in language adapted to convey their meaning.

With regard to civil causes, subtleties almost too contemptible for refutation, have been adopted to countenance the surmise that a thing, which is only *not provided for*, is entirely *abolished*. Every man of discernment must at once perceive the wide difference between *silence* and *abolition*. But as the inventors of this fallacy have attempted to support it by certain *legal maxims* of interpretation, which they have perverted from their true meaning, it may not be wholly useless to explore the ground they have taken.

The maxims on which they rely are of this nature, "a specification of particulars is an exclusion of generals"; or, "the expression of one thing is the exclusion of another." Hence, say they, as the constitution has established the trial by jury in criminal cases, and is silent in respect to civil, this silence is an implied prohibition of trial by jury in regard to the latter.

The rules of legal interpretation are rules of *common sense*, adopted by the courts in the construction of the laws. The true test therefore, of a just application of them, is its conformity to the source from which they are derived. This being the case, let me ask if it is consistent with reason or common sense to suppose, that a provision obliging the legislative power to commit the trial of criminal causes to juries, is a privation of its right to authorize or permit that mode of trial in other cases? Is it natural to suppose, that a command to do one thing, is a prohibition to the doing of another, which there was a previous power to do, and which is not incompatible with the thing commanded to be done? If such a supposition would be unnatural and unreasonable, it cannot be rational to maintain that an injunction of the trial by jury in certain cases is an interdiction of it in others.

A power to constitute courts, is a power to prescribe the mode of trial; and consequently, if nothing was said in the constitution on the subject of juries, the legislature would be at liberty either to adopt that institution, or to let it alone. This discretion in regard to criminal causes is abridged by the express injunction of trial by jury in all such cases; but it is of course left at large in relation to civil causes, there being a total silence on this head. The specification of an obligation to try all criminal causes in a particular mode, excludes indeed the obligation or necessity of employing the same mode in civil causes, but does not abridge *the power* of the legislature to exercise that mode if it should be thought proper. The pretense therefore, that the national legislature would not be at full liberty to submit all the civil causes of federal cognizance to the determination of juries, is a pretense destitute of all just foundation.

From these observations, this conclusion results, that the trial by jury in civil cases would not be abolished, and that the use attempted to be made of the maxims which have been quoted, is contrary to reason and common sense, and therefore not admissible. Even if these maxims had a precise technical sense, corresponding with the ideas of those who employ them upon the present occasion, which, however, is not the case, they would still be inapplicable to a constitution of government. In relation to such a subject, the natural and obvious sense of its provisions, apart from any technical rules, is the true criterion of construction.

Having now seen that the maxims relied upon will not bear the use made of them, let us endeavor to ascertain their proper use and true meaning. This will be best done by examples. The plan of the convention declares that the power of congress or in other words of the *national legislature*, shall extend to certain enumerated cases. This specification of particulars evidently excludes all pretension to a general legislative authority; because an affirmative grant of special powers would be absurd as well as useless, if a general authority was intended.

In like manner, the judicial authority of the federal judicatures, is declared by the constitution to comprehend certain cases particularly specified. The expression of those cases marks the precise limits beyond which the federal courts cannot extend their jurisdiction; because the objects of their cognizance being enumerated, the specification would be nugatory if it did not exclude all ideas of more extensive authority.

These examples might be sufficient to elucidate the maxims which have been mentioned, and designate the manner in which they should be used. But that there may be no possibility of misapprehension upon this subject I shall add one case more, to demonstrate the proper use of these maxims, and the abuse which has been made of them.

Let us suppose that by the laws of this state, a married woman was incapable of conveying her estate, and that the legislature, considering this as an evil, should enact that she might dispose of her property by deed executed in the presence of a magistrate. In such a case there can be no doubt but the specification would amount to an exclusion of any other mode of conveyance; because the woman having no previous power to alienate her property, the specification determines the particular mode which she is, for that purpose, to avail herself of. But let us further suppose that in a subsequent part of the same act it should be declared that no woman should dispose of any estate of a determinate value without the consent of three of her nearest relations, signified by their signing the deed; could it be inferred from this regulation that a married woman might not procure the approbation of her relations to a deed for conveying property of inferior value? The position is too absurd to merit a refutation, and yet this is precisely the position which those must establish who contend that the trial by juries, in civil cases, is abolished, because it is expressly provided for in cases of a criminal nature.[177]

From these observations it must appear unquestionably true that trial by jury is in no case abolished by the proposed constitution, and it is equally true that in those controversies between individuals in which the great body of the people are likely to be interested, that institution will remain precisely in the same situation in which it is placed by the state constitutions, and will be in no degree altered or influenced by the adoption of the plan under consideration. The foundation of this assertion is that the national judiciary will have no cognizance of them, and of course they will remain determinable as heretofore by the state courts only, and in the manner which the state constitutions and laws prescribe. All land causes, except where claims under the grants of different states come into question, and all other controversies between the citizens of the same state, unless where they depend upon positive violations of the articles of union by acts of the state legislatures, will belong exclusively to the jurisdiction of the state tribunals. Add to this that admiralty causes, and almost all those which are of equity jurisdiction are determinable under our own government without the intervention of a jury, and the inference from the whole will be that this institution, as it exists with us at present, cannot possibly be affected to any great extent by the proposed alteration in our system of government.

The friends and adversaries of the plan of the convention, if they agree in nothing else, concur at least in the value they set upon the trial by jury: Or if there is any difference between them, it consists in this; the former regard it as a valuable safeguard to liberty, the latter represent it as the very palladium of free government. For my own part, the more the operation of the institution has fallen under my observation, the more reason I have discovered for holding it in high estimation; and it would be altogether superfluous to examine to what extent it deserves to be esteemed useful or essential in a representative republic, or how much more merit it may be entitled to as a defense against the oppressions of an hereditary monarch, than as a barrier to the tyranny of popular magistrates in a popular

---

177. [In Hopkins this and the preceding paragraph become one sentence: "These examples are sufficient to elucidate the maxims which have been mentioned, and designate the manner in which they should be used."]

government. Discussions of this kind would be more curious than beneficial, as all are satisfied of the utility of the institution, and of its friendly
aspect to liberty. But I must acknowledge that I cannot readily discern the
inseparable connection between the existence of liberty and the trial by
jury in civil cases. Arbitrary impeachments, arbitrary methods of prose-
cuting pretended offenses, and arbitrary punishments upon arbitrary convictions have ever appeared to me to be the great engines of judicial
despotism; and these have all relation to criminal proceedings. The trial by
jury in criminal cases, aided by the *habeas corpus* act,[178] seems therefore to
be alone concerned in the question. And both of these are provided for in
the most ample manner in the plan of the convention.

It has been observed, that trial by jury is a safeguard against an
oppressive exercise of the power of taxation. This observation deserves to
be canvassed.

It is evident that it can have no influence upon the legislature, in
regard to the *amount* of the taxes to be laid, to the *objects* upon which they
are to be imposed, or to the *rule* by which they are to be apportioned. If it
can have any influence therefore, it must be upon the mode of collection,
and the conduct of the officers entrusted with the execution of the revenue laws.

As to the mode of collection in this state, under our own constitution,
the trial by jury is in most cases out of use. The taxes are usually levied by
the more summary proceeding of distress and sale, as in cases of rent. And
it is acknowledged on all hands, that this is essential to the efficacy of the
revenue laws. The dilatory course of a trial at law to recover the taxes
imposed on individuals, would neither suit the exigencies of the public,
nor promote the convenience of the citizens. It would often occasion an
accumulation of costs, more burdensome than the original sum of the tax
to be levied.

And as to the conduct of the officers of the revenue, the provision in
favor of trial by jury in criminal cases, will afford the security aimed at.
Willful abuses of a public authority, to the oppression of the subject, and
every species of official extortion, are offenses against the government; for
which, the persons who commit them, may be indicted and punished
according to the circumstances of the case.

The excellence of the trial by jury in civil cases, appears to depend on
circumstances foreign to the preservation of liberty. The strongest argument in its favor is, that it is a security against corruption. As there is

---

178. [The Habeas Corpus Act of 1679 clarified the Common Law procedure
under which the authorities could be required to produce someone in custody
before a court. It thus prevented subjects from being arbitrarily imprisoned.]

always more time and better opportunity to tamper with a standing body
of magistrates than with a jury summoned for the occasion, there is room
to suppose, that a corrupt influence would more easily find its way to the
former than to the latter. The force of this consideration, is however,
diminished by others. The sheriff who is the summoner of ordinary
juries, and the clerks of courts who have the nomination of special juries,
are themselves standing officers, and acting individually, may be supposed
more accessible to the touch of corruption than the judges, who are a collective body. It is not difficult to see that it would be in the power of those
officers to select jurors who would serve the purpose of the party as well
as a corrupted bench. In the next place, it may fairly be supposed that
there would be less difficulty in gaining some of the jurors promiscuously
taken from the public mass, than in gaining men who had been chosen by
the government for their probity and good character. But making every
deduction for these considerations the trial by jury must still be a valuable
check upon corruption. It greatly multiplies the impediments to its success. As matters now stand, it would be necessary to corrupt both court
and jury; for where the jury have gone evidently wrong, the court will
generally grant a new trial, and it would be in most cases of little use to
practice upon the jury, unless the court could be likewise gained. Here
then is a double security; and it will readily be perceived that this complicated agency tends to preserve the purity of both institutions. By increasing the obstacles to success it discourages attempts to seduce the integrity
of either. The temptations to prostitution, which the judges might have to
surmount, must certainly be much fewer while the cooperation of a jury is
necessary, than they might be if they had themselves the exclusive determination of all causes.

Notwithstanding therefore the doubts I have expressed as to the essen-
tiality of trial by jury, in civil cases, to liberty, I admit that it is in most
cases, under proper regulations, an excellent method of determining questions of property; and that on this account alone it would be entitled to a
constitutional provision in its favor, if it were possible to fix the limits
within which it ought to be comprehended. There is however, in all cases,
great difficulty in this; and men not blinded by enthusiasm, must be sensible that in a federal government which is a composition of societies whose
ideas and institutions in relation to the matter materially vary from each
other, that difficulty must be not a little augmented. For my own part, at
every new view I take of the subject, I become more convinced of the reality of the obstacles, which we are authoritatively informed, prevented the
insertion of a provision on this head in the plan of the convention.

The great difference between the limits of the jury trial in different
states is not generally understood. And as it must have considerable influ-

ence on the sentence we ought to pass upon the omission complained of, in regard to this point, an explanation of it is necessary. In this state our judicial establishments resemble more nearly, than in any other, those of Great Britain. We have courts of common law, courts of probates (analogous in certain matters to the spiritual courts in England), a court of admiralty, and a court of chancery. In the courts of common law only the trial by jury prevails, and this with some exceptions. In all the others a single judge presides and proceeds in general either according to the course of the canon[179] or civil law, without the aid of a jury.[180] In New Jersey there is a court of chancery which proceeds like ours, but neither courts of admiralty, nor of probates, in the sense in which these last are established with us. In that state the courts of common law have the cognizance of those causes, which with us are determinable in the courts of admiralty and of probates, and of course the jury trial is more extensive in New Jersey than in New York. In Pennsylvania this is perhaps still more the case, for there is no court of chancery in that state, and its common-law courts have equity jurisdiction. It has a court of admiralty, but none of probates, at least on the plan of ours. Delaware has in these respects imitated Pennsylvania. Maryland approaches more nearly to New York, as does also Virginia, except that the latter has a plurality of chancellors. North Carolina bears most affinity to Pennsylvania; South Carolina to Virginia. I believe however that in some of those states which have distinct courts of admiralty, the causes depending in them are tryable by juries. In Georgia there are none but common-law courts, and an appeal of course lies from the verdict of one jury to another, which is called a special jury, and for which a particular mode of appointment is marked out. In Connecticut they have no distinct courts, either of chancery or of admiralty, and their courts of probates have no jurisdiction of causes. Their common-law courts have admiralty, and to a certain extent, equity jurisdiction. In cases of importance their general assembly is the only court of chancery. In Connecticut therefore the trial by jury extends in *practice* further than in any other state yet mentioned. Rhode Island is I believe in this particular pretty much in the situation of Connecticut. Massachusetts and New Hampshire, in regard to the blending of law,[181] equity, and admiralty, jurisdictions are in a similar predicament. In the four eastern

---

179. [The canon law is the law applied in Church Courts.]

180. It has been erroneously insinuated, with regard to the court of chancery, that this court generally tries disputed facts by a jury. The truth is, that references to a jury in that court rarely happen, and are in no case necessary, but where the validity of a devise of land comes into question. (Publius)

181. [I.e., common law.]

states the trial by jury not only stands upon a broader foundation than in the other states, but it is attended with a peculiarity unknown in its full extent to any of them. There is an appeal *of course*[182] from one jury to another until there have been two verdicts out of three on one side.

From this sketch it appears, that there is a material diversity as well in the modification as in the extent of the institution of trial by jury in civil cases in the several states; and from this fact, these obvious reflections flow. First, that no general rule could have been fixed upon by the convention which would have corresponded with the circumstances of all the states; and secondly, that more, or at least as much might have been hazarded, by taking the system of any one state for a standard, as by omitting a provision altogether, and leaving the matter as it has been left, to legislative regulation.

The propositions which have been made for supplying the omission, have rather served to illustrate than to obviate the difficulty of the thing. The minority of Pennsylvania[183] have proposed this mode of expression for the purpose—"trial by jury shall be as heretofore"—and this I maintain would be absolutely senseless and nugatory. The United States, in their united or collective capacity, are the OBJECT to which all general provisions in the constitution must necessarily be construed to refer. Now it is evident, that though trial by jury with various limitations is known in each state individually, yet in the United States *as such*, it is at this time altogether unknown, because the present federal government has no judiciary power whatever; and consequently there is no proper antecedent or previous establishment to which the term *heretofore* could relate. It would therefore be destitute of a precise meaning, and inoperative from its uncertainty.

As on the one hand, the form of the provision would not fulfill the intent of its proposers, so on the other, if I apprehend that intent rightly, it would be in itself inexpedient. I presume it to be, that causes in the federal courts should be tried by jury, if in the state where the courts sat, that mode of trial would obtain in a similar case in the state courts—that is to say admiralty causes should be tried in Connecticut by a jury, and in New York without one. The capricious operation of so dissimilar a method of trial in the same cases, under the same government, is of itself sufficient to indispose every well-regulated judgment toward it. Whether the cause should be tried with or without a jury would depend in a great number of cases, on the accidental situation of the court and parties.

---

182. [I.e., routinely.]

183. [The Pennsylvania Ratifying Convention had adopted the Constitution on December 15 by a vote of 46 to 23; the minority had sought fourteen amendments, including the ones discussed here (above, p. 9).]

But this is not in my estimation the greatest objection. I feel a deep and deliberate conviction, that there are many cases in which the trial by jury is an ineligible one. I think it so particularly in cases which concern the public peace with foreign nations; that is in most cases where the question turns wholly on the laws of nations. Of this nature among others are all prize causes. Juries cannot be supposed competent to investigations, that require a thorough knowledge of the laws and usages of nations, and they will sometimes be under the influence of impressions which will not suffer them to pay sufficient regard to those considerations of public policy which ought to guide their inquiries. There would of course be always danger that the rights of other nations might be infringed by their decisions, so as to afford occasions of reprisal and war. Though the proper province of juries be to determine matters of fact, yet in most cases legal consequences are complicated with fact in such a manner as render a separation impracticable.

It will add great weight to this remark in relation to prize causes to mention that the method of determining them has been thought worthy of particular regulation in various treaties between different powers of Europe, and that pursuant to such treaties they are determinable in Great Britain in the last before the king himself in his privy council, where the fact as well as the law undergoes a reexamination. This alone demonstrates the impolicy of inserting a fundamental provision in the constitution which would make the state systems a standard for the national government in the article under consideration, and the danger of encumbering the government with any constitutional provisions, the propriety of which is not indisputable.

My convictions are equally strong that great advantages result from the separation of the equity from the law jurisdiction; and that the causes which belong to the former would be improperly committed to juries. The great and primary use of a court of equity is to give relief *in extraordinary cases,* which are *exceptions*[184] to general rules. To unite the jurisdiction of such cases with the ordinary jurisdiction must have a tendency to unsettle the general rules and to subject every case that arises to a *special* determination. While the separation of the one from the other has the contrary effect of rendering one a sentinel over the other, and of keeping each within the expedient limits. Besides this the circumstances that constitute cases proper for courts of equity, are in many instances so nice and intricate, that they are incompatible with the genius of trials by jury. They

---

184. It is true that the principles by which that relief is governed are now reduced to a regular system, but it is not the less true that they are in the main, applicable to SPECIAL circumstances which form exceptions to general rules. (Publius)

require often such long, deliberate, and critical investigation as would be impracticable to men called from their occupations and obliged to decide before they were permitted to return to them. The simplicity and expedition which form the distinguishing characters of this mode of trial require that the matter to be decided should be reduced to some single and obvious point; while the litigations usual in chancery frequently comprehend a long train of minute and independent particulars.

It is true that the separation of the equity from the legal jurisdiction is peculiar to the English system of jurisprudence; which is the model that has been followed in several of the states. But it is equally true, that the trial by jury has been unknown in every case in which they have been united. And the separation is essential to the preservation of that institution in its pristine purity. The nature of a court of equity will readily permit the extension of its jurisdiction to matters of law, but it is not a little to be suspected, that the attempt to extend the jurisdiction of the courts of law to matters of equity will not only be unproductive of the advantages which may be derived from courts of chancery, on the plan upon which they are established in this state, but will tend gradually to change the nature of the courts of law, and to undermine the trial by jury, by introducing questions too complicated for a decision in that mode.

These appear to be conclusive reasons against incorporating the systems of all the states in the formation of the national judiciary; according to what may be conjectured to have been the intent of the Pennsylvania minority. Let us now examine how far the proposition of Massachusetts is calculated to remedy the supposed defect.[185]

It is in this form—"In civil actions between citizens of different states, every issue of fact, arising in *actions at common law*, may be tried by a jury, if the parties, or either of them, request it."

This at best is a proposition confined to one description of causes; and the inference is fair either that the Massachusetts convention considered that as the only class of federal causes, in which the trial by jury would be proper; or that if desirous of a more extensive provision, they found it impracticable to devise one which would properly answer the end. If the first, the omission of a regulation respecting so partial an object, can never be considered as a material imperfection in the system. If the last, it affords a strong corroboration of the extreme difficulty of the thing.

But this is not all: If we advert to the observations already made respecting the courts that subsist in the several states of the union, and the different powers exercised by them, it will appear, that there are no

---

185. [Massachusetts had ratified the Constitution, but had recommended nine amendments, including the one discussed here.]

expressions more vague and indeterminate than those which have been employed to characterize *that* species of causes which it is intended shall be entitled to a trial by jury. In this state the boundaries between actions at common law and actions of equitable jurisdiction are ascertained in conformity to the rules which prevail in England upon that subject. In many of the other states, the boundaries are less precise. In some of them, every cause is to be tried in a court of common law, and upon that foundation every action may be considered as an action at common law, to be determined by a jury, if the parties or either of them choose it. Hence the same irregularity and confusion would be introduced by a compliance with this proposition, that I have already noticed as resulting from the regulation proposed by the Pennsylvania minority. In one state a cause would receive its determination from a jury, if the parties or either of them requested it; but in another state a cause exactly similar to the other must be decided without the intervention of a jury, because the state judicatories varied as to common-law jurisdiction.

It is obvious therefore that the Massachusetts proposition, upon this subject, cannot operate as a general regulation until some uniform plan, with respect to the limits of common law and equitable jurisdictions shall be adopted by the different states. To devise a plan of that kind is a task arduous in itself, and which it would require much time and reflection to mature. It would be extremely difficult, if not impossible, to suggest any general regulation that would be acceptable to all the states in the union, or that would perfectly quadrate with the several state institutions.

It may be asked, why could not a reference have been made to the constitution of this state, taking that, which is allowed by me to be a good one, as a standard for the United States? I answer that it is not very probable the other states should entertain the same opinion of our institutions which we do ourselves. It is natural to suppose that they are hitherto more attached to their own, and that each would struggle for the preference. If the plan of taking one state as a model for the whole had been thought of in the convention, it is to be presumed that the adoption of it in that body, would have been rendered difficult by the predilection of each representation in favor of its own government; and it must be uncertain which of the states would have been taken as the model. It has been shown that many of them would be improper ones. And I leave it to conjecture whether, under all circumstances, it is most likely that New York or some other state would have been preferred. But admit that a judicious selection could have been effected in the convention, still there would have been great danger of jealousy and disgust in the other states, at the partiality which had been shown to the institutions of one. The enemies of the plan would have been furnished with a fine pretext for raising a host of local prejudices against it, which perhaps might have hazarded in no inconsiderable degree, its final establishment.

To avoid the embarrassments of a definition of the cases which the trial by jury ought to embrace, it is sometimes suggested by men of enthusiastic tempers, that a provision might have been inserted for establishing it in all cases whatsoever. For this I believe no precedent is to be found in any member of the union; and the considerations which have been stated in discussing the proposition of the minority of Pennsylvania, must satisfy every sober mind that the establishment of the trial by jury in *all* cases, would have been an unpardonable error in the plan.

In short, the more it is considered, the more arduous will appear the task of fashioning a provision in such a form, as not to express too little to answer the purpose, or too much to be advisable; or which might not have opened other sources of opposition to the great and essential object of introducing a firm national government.

I cannot but persuade myself on the other hand, that the different lights in which the subject has been placed in the course of these observations, will go far toward removing in candid minds, the apprehensions they may have entertained on the point. They have tended to show that the security of liberty is materially concerned only in the trial by jury in criminal cases, which is provided for in the most ample manner in the plan of the convention; that even in far the greatest proportion of civil cases, and those in which the great body of the community is interested, that mode of trial will remain in its full force, as established in the state constitutions, untouched and unaffected by the plan of the convention: That it is in no case abolished[186] by that plan; and that there are great if not insurmountable difficulties in the way of making any precise and proper provision for it in a constitution for the United States.

The best judges of the matter will be the least anxious for a constitutional establishment of the trial by jury in civil cases, and will be the most ready to admit that the changes which are continually happening in the affairs of society, may render a different mode of determining questions of property, preferable in many cases, in which that mode of trial now prevails. For my own part, I acknowledge myself to be convinced that even in this state, it might be advantageously extended to some cases to which it does not at present apply, and might as advantageously be abridged in others. It is conceded by all reasonable men, that it ought not to obtain in all cases. The examples of innovations which contract its ancient limits, as well in these

---

186. Vide No. LXXXI [not included in this selection], in which the supposition of its being abolished by the appellate jurisdiction in matters of fact being vested in the supreme court is examined and refuted. (Publius)

states as in Great Britain, afford a strong presumption that its former extent has been found inconvenient; and give room to suppose that future experience may discover the propriety and utility of other exceptions. I suspect it to be impossible in the nature of the thing, to fix the salutary point at which the operation of the institution ought to stop; and this is with me a strong argument for leaving the matter to the discretion of the legislature.

This is now clearly understood to be the case in Great Britain, and it is equally so in the state of Connecticut; and yet it may be safely affirmed, that more numerous encroachments have been made upon the trial by jury in this state since the revolution, though provided for by a positive article of our constitution, than has happened in the same time either in Connecticut or Great Britain. It may be added that these encroachments have generally originated with the men who endeavor to persuade the people they are the warmest defenders of popular liberty, but who have rarely suffered constitutional obstacles to arrest them in a favorite career.[187] The truth is that the general GENIUS of a government is all that can be substantially relied upon for permanent effects. Particular provisions, though not altogether useless, have far less virtue and efficacy than are commonly ascribed to them; and the want of them will never be with men of sound discernment a decisive objection to any plan which exhibits the leading characters of a good government.

It certainly sounds not a little harsh and extraordinary to affirm that there is no security for liberty in a constitution which expressly establishes the trial by jury in criminal cases, because it does not do it in civil also; while it is a notorious fact that Connecticut, which has been always regarded as the most popular state in the union, can boast of no constitutional provision for either.

[May 28, 1788]

No. 84   [Hamilton]

CONCERNING SEVERAL MISCELLANEOUS OBJECTIONS

In the course of the foregoing review of the constitution I have taken notice of, and endeavored to answer, most of the objections which have appeared against it. There however remain a few which either did not fall naturally under any particular head, or were forgotten in their proper places. These shall now be discussed; but as the subject has been drawn

---

187. [In the sense of a gallop or charge; the word did not yet have its modern sense of a course of employment.]

into great length, I shall so far consult brevity as to comprise all my observations on these miscellaneous points in a single paper.

The most considerable of these remaining objections is, that the plan of the convention contains no bill of rights. Among other answers given to this, it has been upon different occasions remarked, that the constitutions of several of the states are in a similar predicament. I add, that New York is of this number. And yet the opposers of the new system in this state, who profess an unlimited admiration for its constitution, are among the most intemperate partisans of a bill of rights. To justify their zeal in this matter, they allege two things; one is, that though the constitution of New York has no bill of rights prefixed to it, yet it contains in the body of it various provisions in favor of particular privileges and rights, which in substance amount to the same thing; the other is, that the constitution adopts in their full extent the common and statute law of Great Britain, by which many other rights not expressed in it are equally secured.

To the first I answer, that the constitution proposed by the convention contains, as well as the constitution of this state, a number of such provisions.

Independent of those, which relate to the structure of the government, we find the following: Article I. section 3. clause 7. "Judgment in cases of impeachment shall not extend further than to removal from office, and disqualification to hold and enjoy any office of honor, trust or profit under the United States; but the party convicted shall nevertheless be liable and subject to indictment, trial, judgment and punishment, according to law." Section 9. of the same article, clause 2. "The privilege of the writ of *habeas corpus* shall not be suspended, unless when in cases of rebellion or invasion the public safety may require it." Clause 3. "No bill of attainder[188] or *ex post facto* law[189] shall be passed." Clause 7.[190] "No title of nobility shall be granted by the United States: And no person holding any office of profit or trust under them, shall, without the consent of the congress, accept of any present, emolument, office or title, of any kind whatever, from any king, prince or foreign state." Article III. section 2. clause 3. "The trial of all crimes, except in cases of impeachment, shall be by jury; and such trial shall be held in the state where the said crimes shall have been committed; but when not committed within any state, the trial shall be at such place or places as the congress may by law have directed." Section 3, of the same article, "Treason against the United States shall consist only in levying war against them, or in adhering to their enemies,

---

188. [I.e., a bill introduced to declare a person, who has not been tried, guilty.]

189. [I.e., legislation that declares illegal actions performed before the law was passed.]

190. [Clause 8 in the modern Constitution.]

giving them aid and comfort. No person shall be convicted of treason unless on the testimony of two witnesses to the same overt act, or on confession in open court." And clause 3,[191]of the same section. "The congress shall have power to declare the punishment of treason, but no attainder of treason shall work corruption of blood,[192] or forfeiture, except during the life of the person attainted."

It may well be a question whether these are not upon the whole, of equal importance with any which are to be found in the constitution of this state. The establishment of the writ of *habeas corpus,* the prohibition of *ex post facto* laws, and of TITLES OF NOBILITY, *to which we have no corresponding provisions in our constitution,* are perhaps greater securities to liberty and republicanism than any it contains. The creation of crimes after the commission of the fact, or in other words, the subjecting of men to punishment for things which, when they were done, were breaches of no law, and the practice of arbitrary imprisonments have been in all ages the favorite and most formidable instruments of tyranny. The observations of the judicious Blackstone[193] in reference to the latter, are well worthy of recital. "To bereave a man of life (says he) or by violence to confiscate his estate, without accusation or trial, would be so gross and notorious an act of despotism, as must at once convey the alarm of tyranny throughout the whole nation; but confinement of the person by secretly hurrying him to jail, where his sufferings are unknown or forgotten, is a less public, a less striking, and therefore *a more dangerous engine* of arbitrary government." And as a remedy for this fatal evil, he is everywhere peculiarly emphatic in his encomiums on the *habeas corpus* act, which in one place he calls "the BULWARK of the British constitution."[194]

Nothing need be said to illustrate the importance of the prohibition of titles of nobility. This may truly be denominated the cornerstone of republican government; for so long as they are excluded, there can never be serious danger that the government will be any other than that of the people.

To the second, that is, to the pretended establishment of the common and statute law by the constitution, I answer, that they are expressly made subject "to such alterations and provisions as the legislature shall from time to time make concerning the same." They are therefore at any moment liable to repeal by the ordinary legislative power, and of course

---

191. [Clause 2 in the modern Constitution.]

192. [Under English law, those attainted were deemed to have suffered corruption of blood, which meant no one could inherit from them.]

193. Vide Blackstone's Commentaries, volume 1, page 136. (Publius) [The first edition of Blackstone's *Commentaries on the Laws of England* appeared in 1765–9.]

194. Idem, volume 4, page 438. (Publius)

have no constitutional sanction. The only use of the declaration was to recognize the ancient law, and to remove doubts which might have been occasioned by the revolution. This consequently can be considered as no part of a declaration of rights, which under our constitutions must be intended as limitations of the power of the government itself.

It has been several times truly remarked, that bills of rights are in their origin, stipulations between kings and their subjects, abridgments of prerogative in favor of privilege, reservations of rights not surrendered to the prince. Such was MAGNA CARTA, obtained by the Barons, sword in hand, from king John.[195] Such were the subsequent confirmations of that charter by subsequent princes. Such was the *petition of right* assented to by Charles the First, in the beginning of his reign.[196] Such also was the declaration of right presented by the lords and commons to the prince of Orange in 1688, and afterward thrown into the form of an act of parliament, called the bill of rights. It is evident, therefore, that according to their primitive signification, they have no application to constitutions professedly founded upon the power of the people, and executed by their immediate representatives and servants. Here, in strictness, the people surrender nothing, and as they retain everything, they have no need of particular reservations. "WE THE PEOPLE of the United States, to secure the blessings of liberty to ourselves and our posterity, do *ordain* and *establish* this constitution for the United States of America." Here is a better recognition of popular rights than volumes of those aphorisms which make the principal figure in several of our state bills of rights, and which would sound much better in a treatise of ethics than in a constitution of government.

But a minute detail of particular rights is certainly far less applicable to a constitution like that under consideration, which is merely intended to regulate the general political interests of the nation, than to a constitution which has the regulation of every species of personal and private concerns. If therefore the loud clamors against the plan of the convention on this score, are well-founded, no epithets of reprobation will be too strong for the constitution of this state. But the truth is, that both of them contain all, which in relation to their objects, is reasonably to be desired.

I go further, and affirm that bills of rights, in the sense and to the extent in which they are contended for, are not only unnecessary in the proposed constitution, but would even be dangerous. They would contain various exceptions to powers which are not granted; and on this very account, would afford a colorable pretext to claim more than were granted. For why declare that things shall not be done which there is no

---

195. [In 1215.]
196. [In 1628.]

power to do? Why for instance, should it be said, that the liberty of the press shall not be restrained, when no power is given by which restrictions may be imposed? I will not contend that such a provision would confer a regulating power; but it is evident that it would furnish, to men disposed to usurp, a plausible pretense for claiming that power. They might urge with a semblance of reason, that the constitution ought not to be charged with the absurdity of providing against the abuse of an authority, which was not given, and that the provision against restraining the liberty of the press afforded a clear implication, that a power to prescribe proper regulations concerning it, was intended to be vested in the national government. This may serve as a specimen of the numerous handles which would be given to the doctrine of constructive powers, by the indulgence of an injudicious zeal for bills of rights.

On the subject of the liberty of the press, as much has been said, I cannot forbear adding a remark or two: In the first place, I observe that there is not a syllable concerning it in the constitution of this state, and in the next, I contend that whatever has been said about it in that of any other state, amounts to nothing. What signifies a declaration that "the liberty of the press shall be inviolably preserved?" What is the liberty of the press? Who can give it any definition which would not leave the utmost latitude for evasion? I hold it to be impracticable; and from this, I infer, that its security, whatever fine declarations may be inserted in any constitution respecting it, must altogether depend on public opinion, and on the general spirit of the people and of the government.[197] And here, after all, as intimated upon

---

197. To show that there is a power in the constitution by which the liberty of the press may be affected, recourse had been had to the power of taxation. It is said that duties may be laid upon publications so high as to amount to a prohibition. I know not by what logic it could be maintained that the declaration in the state constitutions, in favor of the freedom of the press, would be a constitutional impediment to the imposition of duties upon publications by the state legislatures. It cannot certainly be pretended that any degree of duties, however low, would be an abridgment of the liberty of the press. We know that newspapers are taxed in Great Britain, and yet it is notorious that the press nowhere enjoys greater liberty than in that country. And if duties of any kind may be laid without a violation of that liberty, it is evident that the extent must depend on legislative discretion, regulated by public opinion; so that after all, general declarations respecting the liberty of the press will give it no greater security than it will have without them. The same invasions of it may be effected under the state constitutions which contain those declarations through the means of taxation, as under the proposed constitution which has nothing of the kind. It would be quite as significant to declare that government ought to be free, that taxes ought not to be excessive, etc., as that the liberty of the press ought not to be restrained. (Publius)

another occasion, must we seek for the only solid basis of all our rights. There remains but one other view of this matter to conclude the point. The truth is, after all the declamation we have heard, that the constitution is itself in every rational sense, and to every useful purpose, A BILL OF RIGHTS. The several bills of rights, in Great Britain, form its constitution, and conversely the constitution of each state is its bill of rights. And the proposed constitution, if adopted, will be the bill of rights of the union. Is it one object of a bill of rights to declare and specify the political privileges of the citizens in the structure and administration of the government? This is done in the most ample and precise manner in the plan of the convention, comprehending various precautions for the public security, which are not to be found in any of the state constitutions. Is another object of a bill of rights to define certain immunities and modes of proceeding, which are relative to personal and private concerns? This we have seen has also been attended to, in a variety of cases, in the same plan. Adverting therefore to the substantial meaning of a bill of rights, it is absurd to allege that it is not to be found in the work of the convention. It may be said that it does not go far enough, though it will not be easy to make this appear; but it can with no propriety be contended that there is no such thing. It certainly must be immaterial what mode is observed as to the order of declaring the rights of the citizens, if they are to be found in any part of the instrument which establishes the government. And hence it must be apparent that much of what has been said on this subject rests merely on verbal and nominal distinctions, which are entirely foreign from the substance of the thing.

Another objection, which has been made, and which from the frequency of its repetition it is to be presumed is relied on, is of this nature:—It is improper (say the objectors) to confer such large powers, as are proposed, upon the national government; because the seat of that government must of necessity be too remote from many of the states to admit of a proper knowledge on the part of the constituent, of the conduct of the representative body. This argument, if it proves anything, proves that there ought to be no general government whatever. For the powers which it seems to be agreed on all hands, ought to be vested in the union, cannot be safely entrusted to a body which is not under every requisite control. But there are satisfactory reasons to show that the objection is in reality not well-founded. There is in most of the arguments which relate to distance a palpable illusion of the imagination. What are the sources of information by which the people in Montgomery county[198] must regulate their

---

198. [The county of New York State furthest from the city of New York. The Hopkins edition substitutes "is any distant county," and omits the last sentence of the paragraph.]

judgment of the conduct of their representatives in the state legislature? Of personal observation they can have no benefit. This is confined to the citizens on the spot. They must therefore depend on the information of intelligent men, in whom they confide—and how must these men obtain their information? Evidently from the complexion of public measures, from the public prints, from correspondences with their representatives, and with other persons who reside at the place of their deliberation. This does not apply to Montgomery county only, but to all the counties, at any considerable distance from the seat of government.

It is equally evident that the same sources of information would be open to the people, in relation to the conduct of their representatives in the general government; and the impediments to a prompt communication which distance may be supposed to create, will be overbalanced by the effects of the vigilance of the state governments. The executive and legislative bodies of each state will be so many sentinels over the persons employed in every department of the national administration; and as it will be in their power to adopt and pursue a regular and effectual system of intelligence, they can never be at a loss to know the behavior of those who represent their constituents in the national councils, and can readily communicate the same knowledge to the people. Their disposition to apprise the community of whatever may prejudice its interests from another quarter, may be relied upon, if it were only from the rivalship of power. And we may conclude with the fullest assurance, that the people, through that channel, will be better informed of the conduct of their national representatives, than they can be by any means they now possess of that of their state representatives.

It ought also to be remembered, that the citizens who inhabit the country at and near the seat of government, will in all questions that affect the general liberty and prosperity, have the same interest with those who are at a distance; and that they will stand ready to sound the alarm when necessary, and to point out the actors in any pernicious project. The public papers will be expeditious messengers of intelligence to the most remote inhabitants of the union.

Among the many extraordinary objections which have appeared against the proposed constitution, the most extraordinary and the least colorable one, is derived from the want of some provision respecting the debts due *to* the United States. This has been represented as a tacit relinquishment of those debts, and as a wicked contrivance to screen public defaulters. The newspapers have teemed with the most inflammatory railings on this head; and yet there is nothing clearer than that the suggestion is entirely void of foundation, and is the offspring of extreme ignorance or extreme dishonesty. In addition to the remarks I have made upon the subject in another place,[199] I shall only observe, that as it is a plain dictate of common sense, so it is also an established doctrine of political law, that *"States neither lose any of their rights, nor are discharged from any of their obligations by a change in the form of their civil government."*[200]

The last objection of any consequence which I at present recollect, turns upon the article of expense. If it were even true that the adoption of the proposed government would occasion a considerable increase of expense, it would be an objection that ought to have no weight against the plan. The great bulk of the citizens of America, are with reason convinced that union is the basis of their political happiness. Men of sense of all parties now, with few exceptions, agree that it cannot be preserved under the present system, nor without radical alterations; that new and extensive powers ought to be granted to the national head, and that these require a different organization of the federal government, a single body being an unsafe depositary of such ample authorities. In conceding all this, the question of expense must be given up, for it is impossible, with any degree of safety, to narrow the foundation upon which the system is to stand. The two branches of the legislature are in the first instance, to consist of only sixty-five persons, which is the same number of which congress, under the existing confederation, may be composed. It is true that this number is intended to be increased; but this is to keep pace with the increase of the population and resources of the country. It is evident, that a less number would, even in the first instance, have been unsafe; and that a continuance of the present number would, in a more advanced stage of poopulation, be a very inadequate representation of the people.

Whence is the dreaded augmentation of expense to spring? One source pointed out, is the multiplication of offices under the new government. Let us examine this a little.

It is evident that the principal departments of the administration under the present government, are the same which will be required under the new. There are now a secretary at war, a secretary for foreign affairs, a secretary for domestic affairs, board of treasury consisting of three persons, a treasurer, assistants, clerks, etc. These offices are indispensable under any system and will suffice under the new as well as under the old. As to ambassadors and other ministers and agents in foreign countries,

---

199. [Essay 43, not included in this selection.]

200. Vide Rutherford's Institutes, volume 2, book II, chapter x, sections xiv and xv.—Vide also Grotius, book II, chapter ix, sections viii and ix. (Publius) [Thomas Rutherforth, *Institutes of Natural Law: Being the Substance of a Course of Lectures on Grotius' de Jure Belli et Pacis* (2 vols.: Cambridge, 1754–6); Grotius' *Of the Laws of War and Peace* was first published in 1625.]

the proposed constitution can make no other difference, than to render their characters, where they reside, more respectable, and their services more useful. As to persons to be employed in the collection of the revenues, it is unquestionably true that these will form a very considerable addition to the number of federal officers; but it will not follow, that this will occasion an increase of public expense. It will be in most cases nothing more than an exchange of state officers for national officers. In the collection of all duties, for instance, the persons employed will be wholly of the latter description. The states individually will stand in no need of any for this purpose. What difference can it make in point of expense, to pay officers of the customs appointed by the state, or those appointed by the United States? There is no good reason to suppose, that either the number or the salaries of the latter, will be greater than those of the former.[201]

Where then are we to seek for those additional articles of expense which are to swell the account to the enormous size that has been represented to us? The chief item which occurs to me, respects the support of the judges of the United States. I do not add the president, because there is now a president of congress, whose expenses may not be far, if anything, short of those which will be incurred on account of the president of the United States. The support of the judges will clearly be an extra expense, but to what extent will depend on the particular plan which may be adopted in practice in regard to this matter. But it can upon no reasonable plan amount to a sum which will be an object of material consequence.

Let us now see what there is to counterbalance any extra expenses that may attend the establishment of the proposed government. The first thing that presents itself is, that a great part of the business, which now keeps congress sitting through the year, will be transacted by the president. Even the management of foreign negotiations will naturally devolve upon him according to general principles concerted with the senate, and subject to their final concurrence. Hence it is evident, that a portion of the year will suffice for the session of both the senate and the house of representatives: We may suppose about a fourth for the latter, and a third or perhaps a half for the former. The extra business of treaties and appointments may give this extra occupation to the senate. From this circumstance we may infer, that until the house of representatives shall be increased greatly beyond its present number, there will be a considerable saving of expense from the difference between the constant session of the present, and the temporary session of the future congress.

But there is another circumstance, of great importance in the view of economy. The business of the United States has hitherto occupied the

---

201. [This sentence omitted in Hopkins.]

state legislatures as well as congress. The latter has made requisitions which the former have had to provide for. Hence it has happened that the sessions of the state legislatures have been protracted greatly beyond what was necessary for the execution of the mere local business of the states. More than half their time has been frequently employed in matters which related to the United States. Now the members who compose the legislatures of the several states amount to two thousand and upward; which number has hitherto performed what under the new system will be done in the first instance by sixty-five persons, and probably at no future period by above fourth or a fifth of that number. The congress under the proposed government will do all the business of the United States themselves, without the intervention of the state legislatures, who thenceforth will have only to attend to the affairs of their particular states, and will not have to sit in any proportion as long as they have heretofore done. This difference, in the time of the sessions of the state legislatures, will be all clear gain, and will alone form an article of saving, which may be regarded as an equivalent for any additional objects of expense that may be occasioned by the adoption of the new system.

The result from these observations is, that the sources of additional expense from the establishment of the proposed constitution are much fewer than may have been imagined, that they are counterbalanced by considerable objects of saving, and that while it is questionable on which side the scale will preponderate, it is certain that a government less expensive would be incompetent to the purposes of the union.

[May 28, 1788]

No. 85   [Hamilton]

CONCLUSION

According to the formal division of the subject of these papers, announced in my first number, there would appear still to remain for discussion, two points, "the analogy of the proposed government to your own state constitution," and "the additional security, which its adoption will afford to republican government, to liberty, and to property." But these heads have been so fully anticipated and exhausted in the progress of the work, that it would now scarcely be possible to do anything more than repeat, in a more dilated form, what has been heretofore said; which the advanced stage of the question, and the time already spent upon it conspire to forbid.

It is remarkable, that the resemblance of the plan of the convention to the act which organizes the government of this state holds, not less with regard to many of the supposed defects, than to the real excellencies of the former. Among the pretended defects, are the reeligibility of the executive, the want of a council, the omission of a formal bill of rights, the omission of a provision respecting the liberty of the press: These and several others, which have been noted in the course of our inquiries, are as much chargeable on the existing constitution of this state, as on the one proposed for the Union. And a man must have slender pretensions to consistency, who can rail at the latter for imperfections which he finds no difficulty in excusing in the former. Nor indeed can there be a better proof of the insincerity and affectation of some of the zealous adversaries of the plan of the convention among us, who profess to be the devoted admirers of the government under which they live, than the fury with which they have attacked that plan, for matters in regard to which our own constitution is equally, or perhaps more vulnerable.

The additional securities to republican government, to liberty, and to property, to be derived from the adoption of the plan under consideration, consist chiefly in the restraints which the preservation of the union will impose on local factions and insurrections, and on the ambition of powerful individuals in single states, who might acquire credit and influence enough, from leaders and favorites, to become the despots of the people; in the diminution of the opportunities to foreign intrigue, which the dissolution of the confederacy would invite and facilitate; in the prevention of extensive military establishments, which could not fail to grow out of wars between the states in a disunited situation; in the express guarantee of a republican form of government to each; in the absolute and universal exclusion of titles of nobility; and in the precautions against the repetition of those practices on the part of the state governments, which have undermined the foundations of property and credit, have planted mutual distrust in the breasts of all classes of citizens, and have occasioned an almost universal prostration of morals.

Thus have I, my fellow citizens, executed the task I had assigned to myself; with what success, your conduct must determine. I trust at least you will admit, that I have not failed in the assurance I gave you respecting the spirit with which my endeavors should be conducted. I have addressed myself purely to your judgments, and have studiously avoided those asperities which are too apt to disgrace political disputants of all parties, and which have been not a little provoked by the language and conduct of the opponents of the constitution. The charge of a conspiracy against the liberties of the people, which has been indiscriminately brought against the advocates of the plan, has something in it too wanton and too malignant not to excite the indignation of every man who feels in his own bosom a refutation of the calumny. The perpetual charges which have been rung upon the wealthy, the wellborn and the great, have been such as to inspire the disgust of all sensible men. And the unwarrantable concealments and misrepresentations which have been in various ways practiced to keep the truth from the public eye, have been of a nature to demand the reprobation of all honest men. It is not impossible that these circumstances may have occasionally betrayed me into intemperances of expression which I did not intend: It is certain that I have frequently felt a struggle between sensibility and moderation, and if the former has in some instances prevailed, it must be my excuse that it has been neither often nor much.

Let us now pause and ask ourselves whether, in the course of these papers, the proposed constitution has not been satisfactorily vindicated from the aspersions thrown upon it, and whether it has not been shown to be worthy of the public approbation, and necessary to the public safety and prosperity. Every man is bound to answer these questions to himself, according to the best of his conscience and understanding, and to act agreeably to the genuine and sober dictates of his judgment. This is a duty, from which nothing can give him a dispensation. It is one that he is called upon, nay, constrained by all the obligations that form the bands of society, to discharge sincerely and honestly. No partial motive, no particular interest, no pride of opinion, no temporary passion or prejudice, will justify to himself, to his country, or to his posterity, an improper election of the part he is to act. Let him beware of an obstinate adherence to party. Let him reflect that the object upon which he is to decide is not a particular interest of the community, but the very existence of the nation. And let him remember that a majority of America has already given its sanction to the plan, which he is to approve or reject.

I shall not dissemble, that I feel an entire confidence in the arguments, which recommend the proposed system to your adoption; and that I am unable to discern any real force in those which by it has been opposed. I am persuaded, that it is the best which our political situation, habits, and opinions will admit, and superior to any the revolution has produced.

Concessions on the part of the friends of the plan, that it has not a claim to absolute perfection, have afforded matter of no small triumph to its enemies. Why, say they, should we adopt an imperfect thing? Why not amend it, and make it perfect before it is irrevocably established? This may be plausible enough, but it is only plausible. In the first place I remark, that the extent of these concessions has been greatly exaggerated. They have been stated as amounting to an admission, that the plan is radically defective; and that, without material alterations, the rights and the interests of the community cannot be safely confided to it. This, as far as I have understood the meaning of those who make the concessions, is an entire perversion of their sense. No advocate of the measure can be found who will not declare as his sentiment, that the system, though it may not be perfect in every part, is upon the whole a good one, is the best that the present views and circumstances of the country will permit, and is such an one as promises every species of security which a reasonable people can desire.

I answer in the next place, that I should esteem it the extreme of imprudence to prolong the precarious state of our national affairs, and to expose the union to the jeopardy of successive experiments, in the chimerical pursuit of a perfect plan. I never expect to see a perfect work from imperfect man. The result of the deliberations of all collective bodies must necessarily be a compound as well of the errors and prejudices, as of the good sense and wisdom of the individuals of whom they are composed. The compacts which are to embrace thirteen distinct states, in a common bond of amity and union, must as necessarily be a compromise of as many dissimilar interests and inclinations. How can perfection spring from such materials?

The reasons assigned in an excellent little pamphlet lately published in this city[202] are unanswerable to show the utter improbability of assembling a new convention, under circumstances in any degree so favorable to a happy issue, as those in which the late convention met, deliberated, and concluded. I will not repeat the arguments there used, as I presume the production itself has had an extensive circulation. It is certainly well worthy the perusal of every friend to his country. There is however one point of light in which the subject of amendments still remains to be considered; and in which it has not yet been exhibited to public view. I cannot resolve to conclude, without first taking a survey of it in this aspect.

It appears to me susceptible of absolute demonstration, that it will be far more easy to obtain subsequent than previous amendments to the constitution. The moment an alteration is made in the present plan, it becomes, to the purpose of adoption, a new one, and must undergo a new decision of each state. To its complete establishment throughout the union, it will therefore require the concurrence of thirteen states. If, on the contrary, the constitution proposed should once be ratified by all the states as it stands, alterations in it may at any time be effected by nine states. Here

---

202. Entitled "An Address to the people of the state of New York." (Publius) [The pamphlet was written by John Jay and published in April 1788.]

then the chances are as thirteen to nine[203] in favor of subsequent amendments, rather than of the original adoption of an entire system.

This is not all. Every constitution for the United States must inevitably consist of a great variety of particulars, in which thirteen independent states are to be accommodated in their interests or opinions of interest. We may of course expect to see, in any body of men charged with its original formation, very different combinations of the parts upon different points. Many of those who form the majority on one question may become the minority on a second, and an association dissimilar to either may constitute the majority on a third. Hence the necessity of molding and arranging all the particulars which are to compose the whole in such a manner as to satisfy all the parties to the compact; and hence also an immense multiplication of difficulties and casualties in obtaining the collective assent to a final act. The degree of that multiplication must evidently be in a ratio to the number of particulars and the number of parties.

But every amendment to the constitution, if once established would be a single proposition, and might be brought forward singly. There would then be no necessity for management or compromise, in relation to any other point, no giving nor taking. The will of the requisite number would at once bring the matter to a decisive issue. And consequently whenever nine or rather ten states, were united in the desire of a particular amendment, that amendment must infallibly take place. There can therefore be no comparison between the facility of effecting an amendment, and that of establishing in the first instance a complete constitution.

In opposition to the probability of subsequent amendments it has been urged, that the persons delegated to the administration of the national government, will always be disinclined to yield up any portion of the authority of which they were once possessed. For my own part I acknowledge a thorough conviction that any amendments which may, upon mature consideration, be thought useful, will be applicable to the organization of the government, not to the mass of its powers; and on this account alone, I think there is no weight in the observation just stated. I also think there is little weight in it on another account. The intrinsic difficulty of governing THIRTEEN STATES at any rate, independent of calculations upon an ordinary degree of public spirit and integrity, will, in my opinion, constantly *impose* on the national rulers the *necessity* of a spirit of accommodation to the reasonable expectations of their constituents. But there is yet a further consideration, which proves beyond the possibility

---

203. It may rather be said TEN, for though two-thirds may set on foot the measure, three-fourths must ratify. (Publius)

of doubt, that the observation is futile. It is this, that the national rulers, whenever nine states concur, will have no option upon the subject. By the fifth article of the plan the congress will be *obliged,* "on the application of the legislatures of two-thirds of the states, (which at present amounts to nine) to call a convention for proposing amendments, which *shall be valid* to all intents and purposes, as part of the constitution, when ratified by the legislatures of three-fourths of the states, or by conventions in three-fourths thereof." The words of this article are peremptory. The congress *"shall* call a convention." Nothing in this particular is left to the discretion of that body. And of consequence all the declamation about their disinclination to a change, vanishes in air. Nor however difficult it may be supposed to unite two-thirds or three-fourths of the state legislatures, in amendments which may affect local interests, can there be any room to apprehend any such difficulty in a union on points which are merely relative to the general liberty or security of the people. We may safely rely on the disposition of the state legislatures to erect barriers against the encroachments of the national authority.

If the foregoing argument is a fallacy, certain it is that I am myself deceived by it; for it is, in my conception, one of those rare instances in which a political truth can be brought to the test of mathematical demonstration. Those who see the matter in the same light with me, however zealous they may be for amendments, must agree in the propriety of a previous adoption as the most direct road to their own object.

The zeal for attempts to amend, prior to the establishment of the constitution, must abate in every man, who, is ready to accede to the truth of the following observations of a writer, equally solid and ingenious: "To balance a large state or society (says he) whether monarchical or republican, on general laws, is a work of so great difficulty, that no human genius, however comprehensive, is able by the mere dint of reason and reflection, to effect it. The judgment of many must unite in the work: EXPERIENCE must guide their labor: TIME must bring it to perfection: And the FEELING of inconveniences must correct the mistakes which they *inevitably* fall into, in their first trials and experiments."[204] These judicious reflections contain a lesson of moderation to all the sincere lovers of the union, and ought to put them upon their guard against hazarding anarchy, civil war, a perpetual alienation of the states from each other, and perhaps the military despotism of a victorious demagogue, in the pursuit of what they are not likely to obtain, but from TIME and EXPERIENCE. It may be in me a defect of political fortitude, but I acknowledge, that I cannot entertain an

---

204. Hume's Essays, volume I, page 128.—The rise of arts and sciences. (Publius) [*Essays, Moral and Political,* volume 2, 1742.]

equal tranquillity with those who affect to treat the dangers of a longer continuance in our present situation as imaginary. A NATION without a NATIONAL GOVERNMENT is, in my view, an awful spectacle. The establishment of a constitution, in time of profound peace, by the voluntary consent of a whole people, is a PRODIGY, to the completion of which I look forward with trembling anxiety. I can reconcile it to no rules of prudence to let go the hold we now have, in so arduous an enterprise, upon seven out of the thirteen states; and after having passed over so considerable a part of the ground to recommence the course. I dread the more the consequences of new attempts, because I KNOW that POWERFUL INDIVIDUALS, in this and in other states, are enemies to a general national government, in every possible shape.

[May 28, 1788]

The Constitutional Documents

[July 9, 1778]

Act of Confederation of the United States of America

TO ALL TO WHOM THESE PRESENTS SHALL COME, WE THE UNDERSIGNED DELEGATES OF THE STATES AFFIXED TO OUR NAMES, SEND GREETINGS.

Whereas the Delegates of the United States of America in Congress assembled did on the 15th day of November in the Year of our Lord One Thousand Seven Hundred and Seventy-seven, and in the Second Year of the Independence of America agree to certain articles of Confederation and perpetual Union between the states of New Hampshire, Massachusetts Bay, Rhode Island and Providence Plantations, Connecticut, New York, New Jersey, Pennsylvania, Delaware, Maryland, Virginia, North Carolina, South Carolina, and Georgia in the Words following, viz.

Articles of Confederation and Perpetual Union between the States of New Hampshire, Massachusetts Bay, Rhode Island and Providence Plantations, Connecticut, New York, New Jersey, Pennsylvania, Delaware, Maryland, Virginia, North Carolina, South Carolina, and Georgia

Article I. The Style of this confederacy shall be "The United States of America."

Article II. Each State retains its Sovereignty, freedom, and independence, and every Power, Jurisdiction, and right, which is not by this confederation expressly delegated to the United States in Congress assembled.

Article III. The said states hereby severally enter into a firm league of friendship with each other, for their common defense, the security of their Liberties, and their mutual and general welfare, binding themselves to assist each other, against all force offered to, or attacks made upon them, or any of them, on account of religion, sovereignty, trade, or any other pretense whatever.

Article IV. The better to secure and perpetuate mutual friendship and intercourse among the people of the different states in this union, the free

317

inhabitants of each of these states, paupers, vagabonds, and fugitives from Justice excepted, shall be entitled to all privileges and immunities of free citizens in the several states, and the people of each state shall have free ingress and regress to and from any other state, and shall enjoy therein all the privileges of trade and commerce, subject to the same duties, impositions, and restrictions as the inhabitants thereof respectively, provided that such restrictions shall not extend so far as to prevent the removal of property imported into any state, to any other state of which the Owner is an inhabitant, provided also that no imposition, duties, or restriction shall be laid by any state, on the property of the united states, or either of them.

If any Person guilty of, or charged with treason, felony, or other high misdemeanor in any state, shall flee from Justice, and be found in any of the united states, he shall upon demand of the Governor or executive power, of the state from which he fled, be delivered up and removed to the state having jurisdiction of his offense.

Full faith and credit shall be given in each of these states to the records, acts, and judicial proceedings of the courts and magistrates of every other state.

Article V. For the more convenient management of the general interest of the united states, delegates shall be annually appointed in such manner as the legislature of each state shall direct, to meet in Congress on the first Monday in November, in every year, with a power reserved to each state, to recall its delegates, or any of them, at any time within the year, and to send others in their stead, for the remainder of the Year.

No state shall be represented in Congress by less than two, nor by more than seven Members; and no person shall be capable of being a delegate for more than three years in any term of six years; nor shall any person, being a delegate, be capable of holding any office under the united states, for which he, or another for his benefit receives any salary, fees, or emolument of any kind.

Each state shall maintain its own delegates in a meeting of the states, and while they act as members of the committee of the states.

In determining questions in the united states, in Congress assembled, each state shall have one vote.

Freedom of speech and debate in Congress shall not be impeached or questioned in any Court, or place out of Congress, and the members of congress shall be protected in their persons from arrests and imprisonments, during the time of their going to and from, and attendance on congress, except for treason, felony, or breach of the peace.

Article VI. No state without the Consent of the united states in congress assembled, shall send any embassy to, or receive any embassy from, or enter into any conference, agreement, alliance, or treaty with any King, prince, or state; nor shall any person holding any office of profit or trust under the united states, or any of them, accept of any present, emolument, office, or title of any kind whatever from any king, prince, or foreign state; nor shall the united states in congress assembled, or any of them, grant any title of nobility.

No two or more states shall enter into any treaty, confederation, or alliance whatever between them, without the consent of the united states in congress assembled, specifying accurately the purposes for which the same is to be entered into, and how long it shall continue.

No state shall lay any imposts or duties, which may interfere with any stipulations in treaties, entered into by the united states in congress assembled with any king, prince, or state, in pursuance of any treaties already proposed by congress to the courts of France and Spain.

No vessels of war shall be kept up in time of peace by any state, except such number only, as shall be deemed necessary by the united states in congress assembled, for the defense of such state, or its trade; nor shall any body of forces be kept up by any state, in time of peace, except such number only, as in the judgment of the united states, in congress assembled, shall be deemed requisite to garrison the forts necessary for the defense of such state; but every state shall always keep up a well-regulated and disciplined militia, sufficiently armed and accoutred, and shall provide and constantly have ready for use, in public stores, a due number of fieldpieces and tents, and a proper quantity of arms, ammunition, and camp equipage.

No state shall engage in any war without the consent of the united states in congress assembled, unless such state be actually invaded by enemies, or shall have received certain advice of a resolution being formed by some nation of Indians to invade such state, and the danger is so imminent as not to admit of a delay, until the united states in congress assembled can be consulted: nor shall any state grant commissions to any ships or vessels of war, nor letters of marque or reprisal, except it be after a declaration of war by the united states in Congress assembled, and then only against the kingdom or state and the subjects thereof, against which war has been so declared, and under such regulations as shall be established by the united states in congress assembled, unless such state be infested by pirates, in which case vessels of war may be fitted out for that occasion, and kept so long as the danger shall continue, or until the united states in congress assembled shall determine otherwise.

Article VII. When land forces are raised by any state for the common defense, all officers of or under the rank of colonel, shall be appointed by the legislature of each state respectively by whom such forces shall be raised, or in such manner as such state shall direct, and all vacancies shall be filled up by the state which first made the appointment.

Article VIII. All charges of war, and all other expenses that shall be incurred for the common defense or general welfare, and allowed by the united states in congress assembled, shall be defrayed out of a common treasury, which shall be supplied by the several states, in proportion to the value of all land within each state, granted to or surveyed for any Person, as such land and the buildings and improvements thereon shall be estimated according to such mode as the united states in congress assembled, shall from time to time direct and appoint.

The taxes for paying that proportion shall be laid and levied by the authority and direction of the legislatures of the several states within the time agreed upon by the united states in congress assembled.

Article IX. The united states in congress assembled, shall have the sole and exclusive right and power of determining on peace and war, except in the cases mentioned in the sixth article—of sending and receiving ambassadors—entering into treaties and alliances, provided that no treaty of commerce shall be made whereby the legislative power of the respective states shall be restrained from imposing such imposts and duties on foreigners, as their own people are subjected to, or from prohibiting the exportation or importation of any species of goods or commodities whatsoever—of establishing rules for deciding in all cases, what captures on land or water shall be legal, and in what manner prizes taken by land or naval forces in the service of the united states shall be divided or appropriated—of granting letters of marque and reprisal in times of peace—appointing courts for the trial of piracies and felonies committed on the high seas and establishing courts for receiving and determining finally appeals in all cases of captures, provided that no member of congress shall be appointed a judge of any of the said courts.

The united states in congress assembled shall also be the last resort on appeal in all disputes and differences now subsisting or that hereafter may arise between two or more states concerning boundary, jurisdiction, or any other cause whatever, which authority shall always be exercised in the manner following. Whenever the legislative or executive authority or lawful agent of any state in controversy with another shall present a petition to congress stating the matter in question and praying for a hearing, notice thereof shall be given by order of congress to the legislative or executive authority of the other state in controversy, and a day assigned for the appearance of the parties by their lawful agents, who shall then be directed to appoint by joint consent, commissioners or judges to constitute a court for hearing and determining the matter in question: but if they cannot agree, congress shall name three persons out of each of the united states, and from the list of such persons each party shall alternately strike out one, the petitioners beginning, until the number shall be reduced to thirteen; and from that number not less than seven, nor more than nine names as congress shall direct, shall in the presence of congress be drawn out by lot, and the persons whose names shall be so drawn or any five of them, shall be commissioners or judges, to hear and finally determine the controversy, so always as a major part of the judges who shall hear the cause shall agree in the determination: and if either party shall neglect to attend at the day appointed, without showing reasons, which congress shall judge sufficient, or being present shall refuse to strike, the congress shall proceed to nominate three persons out of each state, and the secretary of congress shall strike in behalf of such party absent or refusing; and the judgment and sentence of the court to be appointed, in the manner before prescribed, shall be final and conclusive; and if any of the parties shall refuse to submit to the authority of such court, or to appear or defend their claim or cause, the court shall nevertheless proceed to pronounce sentence, or judgment, which shall in like manner be final and decisive, the judgment or sentence and other proceedings being in either case transmitted to congress, and lodged among the acts of congress for the security of the parties concerned: provided that every commissioner, before he sits in judgment, shall take an oath to be administered by one of the judges of the supreme or superior court of the state, where the cause shall be tried, "well and truly to hear and determine the matter in question, according to the best of his judgment without favor, affection or hope of reward": provided also that no state shall be deprived of territory for the benefit of the united states.

All controversies concerning the private right of soil claimed under different grants of two or more states, whose jurisdictions as they may respect such lands, and the states which passed such grants are adjusted, the said grants or either of them being at the same time claimed to have originated antecedent to such settlement of jurisdiction, shall on the petition of either party to the congress of the united states, be finally determined as near as may be in the same manner as is before prescribed for deciding disputes respecting territorial jurisdiction between different states.

The united states in congress assembled shall also have the sole and exclusive right and power of regulating the alloy and value of coin struck by their own authority, or by that of the respective states—fixing the standard of weights and measures throughout the united states—regulating the trade and managing all affairs with the Indians, not members of any of the states, provided that the legislative right of any state within its own limits be not infringed or violated—establishing and regulating post offices from one state to another, throughout all the united states, and exacting such postage on the papers passing through the same as may be requisite to defray the expenses of the said office—appointing all officers of the land forces, in the service of the united states, excepting regimental officers—appointing all the officers of the naval forces, and commissioning all officers whatever in the service of the united states—making rules for the government and regulation of the said land and naval forces, and directing their operations.

The united states in congress assembled shall have authority to appoint a committee, to sit in the recess of congress, to be denominated "A Committee of the States," and to consist of one delegate from each state; and to appoint such other committees and civil officers as may be necessary for managing the general affairs of the united states under their direction—to appoint one of their number to preside, provided that no person be allowed to serve in the office of president more than one year in any term of three years; to ascertain the necessary sums of Money to be raised for the service of the united states, and to appropriate and apply the same for defraying the public expenses—to borrow money, or emit bills on the credit of the united states, transmitting every half year to the respective states an account of the sums of moneys so borrowed or emitted—to build and equip a navy—to agree upon the number of land forces, and to make requisition from each state for its quota, in proportion to the number of white inhabitants in such state; which requisitions shall be binding, and thereupon the legislature of each state shall appoint the regimental officers, raise the men and clothe, arm, and equip them in a soldier-like manner, at the expense of the united states; and the officers and men so clothed, armed, and equipped shall march to the place appointed, and within the time agreed on by the united states in congress assembled: But if the united states in congress assembled shall, on consideration of circumstances judge proper that any state should not raise men, or should raise a smaller number than its quota, and that any other state should raise a greater number of men than the quota thereof, such extra number shall be raised, officered, clothed, armed, and equipped in the same manner as the quota of such state, unless the legislature of such state shall judge that such extra number cannot be safely spared out of the same, in which case they shall raise, officer, clothe, arm, and equip as many of such extra number as they judge can be safely spared. And the officers and men so clothed, armed, and equipped, shall march to the place appointed, and within the time agreed on by the united states in congress assembled.

The united states in congress assembled shall never engage in a war, nor grant letters of marque and reprisal in time of peace, nor enter into any treaties or alliances, nor coin money, nor regulate the value thereof, nor ascertain the sums and expenses necessary for the defense and welfare of the united states, or any of them, nor emit bills, nor borrow money on the credit of the united states, nor appropriate money, nor agree upon the number of vessels of war, to be built or purchased, or the number of land or sea forces to be raised, nor appoint a commander in chief of the army or navy, unless nine states assent to the same; nor shall a question on any other point, except for adjourning from day to day be determined, unless by the votes of a majority of the united states in congress assembled.

The congress of the united states shall have power to adjourn to any time within the year, and to any place within the united states, so that no period of adjournment be for a longer duration than the space of six Months, and shall publish the Journal of their proceedings monthly, except such parts thereof relating to treaties, alliances, or military operations as in their judgment require secrecy; and the yeas and nays of the delegates of each state on any question shall be entered on the Journal, when it is desired by any delegate; and the delegates of a state, or any of them, at his or their request shall be furnished with a transcript of the said Journal, except such parts as are above excepted, to lay before the legislatures of the several states.

Article X. The committee of the states, or any nine of them, shall be authorized to execute, in the recess of congress such of the powers of congress as the united states in congress assembled, by the consent of nine states, shall from time to time think expedient to vest them with; provided that no power be delegated to the said committee, for the exercise of which, by the articles of confederation, the voice of nine states in the congress of the united states assembled is requisite.

Article XI. Canada acceding to this confederation, and joining in the measures of the united states, shall be admitted into, and entitled to all the advantages of this union: but no other colony shall be admitted into the same, unless such admission be agreed to by nine states.

Article XII. All bills of credit emitted, moneys borrowed, and debts contracted by, or under the authority of congress, before the assembling of the united states, in pursuance of the present confederation, shall be deemed and considered as a charge against the united states, for payment and satisfaction whereof the said united states, and the public faith are hereby solemnly pledged.

Article XIII. Every state shall abide by the determinations of the united states in congress assembled, on all questions which by this confederation are submitted to them. And the Articles of this confederation shall be inviolably observed by every state, and the union shall be perpetual; nor shall any alteration at any time hereafter be made in any of them; unless such alteration be agreed to in a congress of the united states, and be afterward confirmed by the legislatures of every state.

AND WHEREAS it has pleased the Great Governor of the World to incline the hearts of the legislatures we respectively represent in congress, to approve of, and to authorize us to ratify the said articles of confederation and perpetual union. KNOW YE that we the undersigned delegates, by virtue of the power and authority to us given for that purpose, do by these presents, in the name and in behalf of our respective constituents, fully and entirely ratify and confirm each and every of the said articles of confederation and perpetual union, and all and singular the matters and things therein contained: And we do further solemnly plight and engage the faith of our respective constituents, that they shall abide by the determinations of the united states in congress assembled, on all questions, which by the said confederation are submitted to them. And that the articles thereof shall be inviolably observed by the states we respectively represent and that the union shall be perpetual.

IN WITNESS whereof we have hereunto set our hands in Congress. DONE at Philadelphia in the state of Pennsylvania the ninth Day of July in the Year of our Lord one Thousand seven Hundred and Seventy-eight, and in the third year of the independence of America. [the signatures of the delegates follow]

THE VIRGINIA PLAN

Resolutions proposed by Mr. Randolph in Convention, May 29, 1787

1. Resolved that the Articles of Confederation ought to be so corrected and enlarged as to accomplish the objects proposed by their institution; namely, "common defense, security of liberty, and general welfare."

2. Resolved therefore that the rights of suffrage in the National Legislature ought to be proportioned to the Quotas of contribution, or to the number of free inhabitants, as the one or the other rule may seem best in different cases.

3. Resolved that the National Legislature ought to consist of two branches.

4. Resolved that the members of the first branch of the national Legislature ought to be elected by the people of the several States every   for the term of   ; to be of the age of   years at least, to receive liberal stipends by which they may be compensated for the devotion of their time to public service; to be ineligible to any office established by a particular

State, or under the authority of the United States, except those peculiarly belonging to the functions of the first branch, during the term of service, and for the space of   after its expiration; to be incapable of reelection for the space of   after the expiration of their term of service, and to be subject to recall.

5. Resolved that the members of the second branch of the National Legislature ought to be elected by those of the first, out of a proper number of persons nominated by the individual Legislatures, to be of the age of   years at least; to hold their offices for a term sufficient to ensure their independency; to receive liberal stipends, by which they may be compensated for the devotion of their time to public service; and to be ineligible to any office established by a particular State, or under the authority of the United States, except those peculiarly belonging to the functions of the second branch, during the term of service, and for the space of   after the expiration thereof.

6. Resolved that each branch ought to possess the right of originating Acts; that the national Legislature ought to be empowered to enjoy the Legislative Rights vested in Congress by the Confederation and moreover to legislate in all cases to which the separate States are incompetent, or in which the harmony of the United States may be interrupted by the exercise of individual Legislation; to negative all laws passed by the several States, contravening in the opinion of the National Legislature the articles of Union, and to call forth the force of the Union against any member of the Union failing to fulfill its duty under the articles thereof.

7. Resolved that a National Executive be instituted; to be chosen by the National Legislature for the term of   years, to receive punctually at stated times a fixed compensation for the services rendered, in which no increase or diminution shall be made so as to affect the Magistracy, existing at the time of increase or diminution, and to be ineligible a second time; and that besides a general authority to execute the National laws, it ought to enjoy the Executive rights vested in Congress by the Confederation.

8. Resolved that the Executive and a Convenient number of the National Judiciary, ought to compose a Council of revision with authority to examine every act of the National Legislature before it shall operate, and every act of a particular Legislature before a Negative thereon shall be final; and that the dissent of the said Council shall amount to a rejection, unless the Act of the National Legislature be again passed, or that of a particular Legislature be again negatived by   of the members of each branch.

9. Resolved that a National Judiciary be established to consist of one or more supreme tribunals, and of inferior tribunals to be chosen by the National Legislature, to hold their offices during good behavior; and to

receive punctually at stated times fixed compensation for their services, in which no increase or diminution shall be made so as to affect the persons actually in office at the time of such increase or diminution. That the jurisdiction of the inferior tribunals shall be to hear and determine in the first instance, and of the supreme tribunal to hear and determine in the dernier resort, all Piracies and felonies on the high seas, captures from an enemy; cases in which foreigners or citizens of other States applying to such jurisdictions may be interested, or which respect the collection of the National revenue; impeachments of any national officers, and questions which may involve the national peace and harmony.

10. Resolved that provision ought to be made for the admission of States lawfully arising within the limits of the United States, whether from a voluntary junction of Government and Territory or otherwise, with the consent of a number of voices in the National legislature less than the whole.

11. Resolved that a Republican Government and the territory of each State, except in the instance of a voluntary junction of Government and territory, ought to be guaranteed by the United States to each State.

12. Resolved that provision ought to be made for the continuance of Congress and their authorities and privileges, until a given day after the reform of the articles of Union shall be adopted, and for the completion of all their engagements.

13. Resolved that provision ought to be made for the amendment of the Articles of Union whensoever it shall seem necessary, and that the assent of the National Legislature ought not to be required thereto.

14. Resolved that the Legislative Executive and Judiciary powers within the several States ought to be bound by oath to support the articles of Union.

15. Resolved that the amendments which shall be offered to the Confederation, by the Convention ought at a proper time, or times, after the approbation of Congress to be submitted to an assembly or assemblies of Representatives, recommended by the several Legislatures to be expressly chosen by the people to consider and decide thereon.

CONSTITUTION OF THE UNITED STATES OF AMERICA

WE THE PEOPLE of the United States, in Order to form a more perfect Union, establish Justice, insure domestic Tranquillity, provide for the common defense, promote the general Welfare, and secure the Blessings of Liberty to ourselves and our Posterity, do ordain and establish this CONSTITUTION for the United States of America.

Article I

Section 1. All legislative Powers herein granted shall be vested in a Congress of the United States, which shall consist of a Senate and House of Representatives.

Section 2. The House of Representatives shall be composed of Members chosen every second Year by the People of the several States, and the Electors in each State shall have the Qualifications requisite for Electors of the most numerous Branch of the State Legislature.

No Person shall be a Representative who shall not have attained to the Age of twenty-five Years, and been seven Years a Citizen of the United States, and who shall not, when elected, be an Inhabitant of that State in which he shall be chosen.

Representatives and direct Taxes shall be apportioned among the several States which may be included within this Union, according to their respective Numbers, which shall be determined by adding to the whole Number of free Persons, including those bound to Service for a Term of Years, and excluding Indians not taxed, three-fifths of all other Persons. The actual Enumeration shall be made within three Years after the first Meeting of the Congress of the United States, and within every subsequent Term of ten Years, in such Manner as they shall by Law direct. The Number of Representatives shall not exceed one for every thirty Thousand, but each State shall have at Least one Representative; and until such enumeration shall be made, the State of New Hampshire shall be entitled to choose three, Massachusetts eight, Rhode Island and Providence Plantations one, Connecticut five, New York six, New Jersey four, Pennsylvania eight, Delaware one, Maryland six, Virginia ten, North Carolina five, South Carolina five, and Georgia three.

When vacancies happen in the Representation from any State, the Executive Authority thereof shall issue Writs of Election to fill such Vacancies.

The House of Representatives shall choose their Speaker and other Officers; and shall have the sole Power of Impeachment.

Section 3. The Senate of the United States shall be composed of two Senators from each State, chosen by the Legislature thereof, for six Years; and each Senator shall have one Vote.

Immediately after they shall be assembled in Consequence of the first Election, they shall be divided as equally as may be into three Classes. The Seats of the Senators of the first Class shall be vacated at the Expiration of the Second Year, of the second Class at the Expiration of the fourth Year, and of the third Class at the Expiration of the sixth Year; so that one-third may be chosen every second Year; and if Vacancies happen by Resignation, or otherwise, during the Recess of the Legislature of any State, the Executive thereof may make temporary Appointments until the next Meeting of the Legislature, which shall then fill such Vacancies.

No Person shall be a Senator who shall not have attained to the Age of thirty Years, and been nine Years a Citizen of the United States, and who shall not, when elected, be an Inhabitant of that State for which he shall be chosen.

The Vice President of the United States shall be President of the Senate, but shall have no Vote, unless they be equally divided.

The Senate shall choose their other Officers, and also a President pro tempore, in the absence of the Vice President, or when he shall exercise the Office of President of the United States.

The Senate shall have the sole Power to try all Impeachments. When sitting for that Purpose, they shall be on Oath or Affirmation. When the President of the United States is tried, the Chief Justice shall preside: And no Person shall be convicted without the Concurrence of two-thirds of the Members present.

Judgment in Cases of Impeachment shall not extend further than to removal from Office, and disqualification to hold and enjoy any Office of honor, Trust, or Profit under the United States: but the Party convicted shall nevertheless be liable and subject to Indictment, Trial, Judgment, and Punishment, according to Law.

Section 4. The Time, Places, and Manner of holding Elections for Senators and Representatives, shall be prescribed in each State by the Legislature thereof; but the Congress may at any time by Law make or alter such Regulations, except as to the Places of choosing Senators.

The Congress shall assemble at least once in every Year, and such Meeting shall be on the first Monday in December, unless they shall by Law appoint a different Day.

Section 5. Each House shall be the Judge of the Elections, Returns, and Qualifications of its own Members, and a Majority of each shall constitute a Quorum to do Business; but a smaller Number may adjourn from day to day, and may be authorized to compel the Attendance of absent Members, in such Manner, and under such Penalties as each House may provide.

Each House may determine the Rules of its Proceedings, punish its Members for disorderly Behavior, and, with the Concurrence of two-thirds, expel a Member.

Each House shall keep a Journal of its Proceedings, and from time to time publish the same, excepting such Parts as may in their Judgment require Secrecy; and the Yeas and Nays of the Members of either House on any question shall, at the Desire of one-fifth of those Present be entered on the Journal.

Neither House, during the Session of Congress, shall, without the Consent of the other, adjourn for more than three days, nor to any other Place than that in which the two Houses shall be sitting.

Section 6. The Senators and Representatives shall receive a Compensation for their Services, to be ascertained by Law, and paid out of the Treasury of the United States. They shall in all Cases, except Treason, Felony, and Breach of the Peace, be privileged from Arrest during their Attendance at the Session of their respective Houses, and in going to and returning from the same; and for any Speech or Debate in either House, they shall not be questioned in any other Place.

No Senator or Representative shall, during the Time for which he was elected, be appointed to any civil Office under the Authority of the United States, which shall have been created, or the Emoluments whereof shall have been increased during such time; and no Person holding any Office under the United States, shall be a Member of either House during his Continuance in Office.

Section 7. All Bills for raising Revenue shall originate in the House of Representatives; but the Senate may propose or concur with Amendments as on other Bills.

Every Bill which shall have passed the House of Representatives and the Senate, shall, before it become a Law, be presented to the President of the United States; if he approve he shall sign it, but if not he shall return it, with his Objections to that House in which it shall have originated, who shall enter the Objections at large on their Journal, and proceed to reconsider it. If after such Reconsideration two-thirds of that House shall agree to pass the Bill, it shall be sent, together with the Objections, to the other House, by which it shall likewise be reconsidered, and if approved by two-thirds of that House, it shall become a Law. But in all such Cases the Votes of both Houses shall be determined by Yeas and Nays, and the Names of the Persons voting for and against the Bill shall be entered on the Journal of each House respectively. If any Bill shall not be returned by the President within ten Days (Sundays excepted) after it shall have been presented to him, the Same shall be a Law, in like Manner as if he had signed it, unless the Congress by their Adjournment prevent its Return, in which Case it shall not be a Law.

Every Order, Resolution, or Vote to which the Concurrence of the Senate and House of Representatives may be necessary (except on a question of Adjournment) shall be presented to the President of the United

States; and before the Same shall take Effect, shall be approved by him, or being disapproved by him, shall be repassed by two-thirds of the Senate and House of Representatives, according to the Rules and Limitations prescribed in the Case of a Bill.

Section 8. The Congress shall have Power To lay and collect Taxes, Duties, Imposts, and Excises, to pay the Debts and provide for the common Defense and general Welfare of the United States; but all Duties, Imposts, and Excises shall be uniform throughout the United States;

To borrow Money on the credit of the United States;

To regulate Commerce with foreign Nations, and among the several States, and with the Indian Tribes;

To establish an uniform Rule of Naturalization, and uniform Laws on the subject of Bankruptcies throughout the United States;

To coin Money, regulate the Value thereof, and of foreign Coin, and fix the Standard of Weights and Measures;

To provide for the Punishment of counterfeiting the Securities and current Coin of the United States;

To establish Post Offices and post Roads;

To promote the Progress of Science and useful Arts, by securing for limited Times to Authors and Inventors the exclusive Right to their respective Writings and Discoveries;

To constitute Tribunals inferior to the supreme Court;

To define and punish Piracies and Felonies committed on the high Seas, and Offenses against the Law of Nations;

To declare War, grant Letters of Marque and Reprisal and make Rules concerning Captures on Land and Water;

To raise and support Armies, but no Appropriation of Money to that Use shall be for a longer Term than two Years;

To provide and maintain a Navy;

To make Rules for the Government and Regulation of the land and naval Forces;

To provide for calling forth the Militia to execute the Laws of the Union, suppress Insurrections, and repel Invasions;

To provide for organizing, arming, and disciplining the Militia, and for governing such Part of them as may be employed in the Service of the United States, reserving to the States respectively, the Appointment of the Officers, and the Authority of training the Militia according to the discipline prescribed by Congress;

To exercise exclusive Legislation in all Cases whatsoever, over such District (not exceeding ten Miles square) as may, by Cession of particular States, and the Acceptance of Congress, become the Seat of the Government of the United States, and to exercise like Authority over all Places purchased by the Consent of the Legislature of the State in which the Same shall be, for the Erection of Forts, Magazines, Arsenals, Dockyards, and other needful Buildings;—And

To make all Laws which shall be necessary and proper for carrying into Execution the foregoing Powers, and all other Powers vested by this Constitution in the Government of the United States, or in any Department or Officer thereof.

Section 9. The Migration or Importation of Such Persons as any of the States now existing shall think proper to admit, shall not be prohibited by the Congress prior to the Year one thousand eight hundred and eight, but a tax or duty may be imposed on such Importation, not exceeding ten dollars for each Person.

The privilege of the Writ of Habeas Corpus shall not be suspended, unless when in Cases of Rebellion or Invasion the public Safety may require it.

No Bill of Attainder or ex post facto Law shall be passed.

No capitation, or other direct, Tax shall be laid, unless in Proportion to the Census or Enumeration herein before directed to be taken.

No Tax or Duty shall be laid on Articles exported from any State.

No preference shall be given by any Regulation of Commerce or Revenue to the Ports of one State over those of another: nor shall Vessels bound to, or from, one State be obliged to enter, clear, or pay Duties in another.

No money shall be drawn from the Treasury, but in Consequence of Appropriations made by Law; and a regular Statement and Account of the Receipts and Expenditures of all public Money shall be published from time to time.

No Title of Nobility shall be granted by the United States: And no Person holding any Office of Profit or Trust under them, shall, without the Consent of the Congress, accept of any present, Emolument, Office, or Title, of any kind whatever, from any King, Prince, or foreign State.

Section 10. No State shall enter into any Treaty, Alliance, or Confederation; grant Letters of Marque and Reprisal; coin Money; emit Bills of

Credit; make any Thing but gold and silver Coin a Tender in Payment of Debts; pass any Bill of Attainder, ex post facto Law, or Law impairing the Obligation of Contracts, or grant any Title of Nobility.

No State shall, without the Consent of the Congress, lay any Imposts or Duties on Imports or Exports, except what may be absolutely necessary for executing its inspection Laws: and the net Produce of all Duties and Imposts, laid by any State on Imports or Exports, shall be for the Use of the Treasury of the United States; and all such Laws shall be subject to the Revision and Control of the Congress.

No State shall, without the Consent of Congress, lay any duty of Tonnage, keep Troops, or Ships of War in time of Peace, enter into any Agreement or Compact with another State, or with a foreign Power, or engage in War, unless actually invaded, or in such imminent Danger as will not admit of delay.

Article II

Section 1. The executive Power shall be vested in a President of the United States of America. He shall hold his Office during the Term of four years, and, together with the Vice President, chosen for the same Term, be elected, as follows:

Each State shall appoint, in such Manner as the Legislature thereof may direct, a Number of Electors, equal to the whole Number of Senators and Representatives to which the State may be entitled in the Congress: but no Senator or Representative, or Person holding an Office of Trust or Profit under the United States, shall be appointed an Elector.

The Electors shall meet in their respective States, and vote by Ballot for two persons, of whom one at least shall not be an Inhabitant of the same State with themselves. And they shall make a List of all the Persons voted for, and of the Number of Votes for each; which List they shall sign and certify, and transmit sealed to the Seat of the Government of the United States, directed to the President of the Senate. The President of the Senate shall, in the Presence of the Senate and House of Representatives, open all the Certificates, and the Votes shall then be counted. The Person having the greatest Number of Votes shall be the President, if such Number be a Majority of the whole Number of Electors appointed; and if there be more than one who have such Majority, and have an equal Number of Votes, then the House of Representatives shall immediately choose by Ballot one of them for President; and if no Person have a Majority, then from the five highest on the List the said House shall in like Manner choose the President. But in choosing the President, the Votes shall be taken by States, the Representation from each State having one Vote; A quorum for this Purpose shall consist of a Member or Members from two-thirds of the States, and a Majority of all the States shall be necessary to a Choice. In every Case, after the Choice of the President, the Person having the greatest Number of Votes of the Electors shall be the Vice President. But if there should remain two or more who have equal Votes, the Senate shall choose from them by Ballot the Vice President.

The Congress may determine the Time of choosing the Electors, and the Day on which they shall give their Votes; which Day shall be the same throughout the United States.

No person except a natural-born Citizen, or a Citizen of the United States, at the time of the Adoption of this Constitution, shall be eligible to the Office of President; neither shall any Person be eligible to that Office who shall not have attained to the Age of thirty-five Years, and been fourteen Years a Resident within the United States.

In case of the Removal of the President from Office, or of his Death, Resignation, or Inability to discharge the Powers and Duties of the said Office, the same shall devolve on the Vice President, and the Congress may by Law provide for the Case of Removal, Death, Resignation, or Inability, both of the President and Vice President, declaring what Officer shall then act as President, and such Officer shall act accordingly, until the Disability be removed, or a President shall be elected.

The President shall, at stated Times, receive for his Services, a Compensation, which shall neither be increased nor diminished during the Period for which he shall have been elected, and he shall not receive within that Period any other Emolument from the United States, or any of them.

Before he enter on the Execution of his Office, he shall take the following Oath or Affirmation:—"I do solemnly swear (or affirm) that I will faithfully execute the Office of President of the United States, and will to the best of my Ability, preserve, protect, and defend the Constitution of the United States."

Section 2. The President shall be Commander-in-Chief of the Army and Navy of the United States, and of the Militia of the several States, when called into the actual Service of the United States; he may require the Opinion, in writing, of the principal Officer in each of the executive Departments, upon any subject relating to the Duties of their respective Offices, and he shall have Power to grant Reprieves and Pardons for Offenses against the United States, except in Cases of Impeachment.

He shall have Power, by and with the Advice and Consent of the Senate, to make Treaties, provided two-thirds of the Senators present concur; and he shall nominate, and by and with the Advice and Consent of the Senate, shall appoint Ambassadors, other public Ministers and Consuls,

Judges of the supreme Court, and all other Officers of the United States, whose Appointments are not herein otherwise provided for, and which shall be established by law; but the Congress may by Law vest the Appointment of such inferior Officers, as they think proper, in the President alone, in the Courts of Law, or in the Heads of Departments.

The President shall have Power to fill up all Vacancies that may happen during the Recess of the Senate, by granting Commissions which shall expire at the End of their next Session.

Section 3. He shall from time to time give to the Congress Information of the State of the Union, and recommend to their Consideration such Measures as he shall judge necessary and expedient; he may, on extraordinary Occasions, convene both Houses, or either of them, and in Case of Disagreement between them, with Respect to the Time of Adjournment, he may adjourn them to such Time as he shall think proper; he shall receive Ambassadors and other public Ministers; he shall take Care that the Laws be faithfully executed, and shall Commission all the Officers of the United States.

Section 4. The President, Vice President, and all civil Officers of the United States, shall be removed from Office on Impeachment for, and Conviction of, Treason, Bribery, or other high Crimes and Misdemeanors.

Article III

Section 1. The judicial Power of the United States, shall be vested in one supreme Court, and in such inferior Courts as the Congress may from time to time ordain and establish. The Judges, both of the supreme and inferior Courts, shall hold their offices during good Behavior, and shall, at stated Times, receive for their Services a Compensation which shall not be diminished during their Continuance in Office.

Section 2. The judicial Power shall extend to all Cases, in Law and Equity, arising under this Constitution, the Laws of the United States, and Treaties made, or which shall be made, under their Authority;—to all Cases affecting Ambassadors, other public Ministers and Consuls;—to all Cases of admiralty and maritime Jurisdiction;—to Controversies to which the United States shall be a Party;—to Controversies between two or more States;—between a State and Citizens of another State;—between Citizens of different States;—between Citizens of the same State claiming Lands under Grants of different States, and between a State, or the Citizens thereof, and foreign States, Citizens, or Subjects.

In all Cases affecting Ambassadors, other public Ministers and Consuls, and those in which a State shall be Party, the supreme Court shall have original Jurisdiction. In all the other Cases before mentioned, the supreme Court shall have appellate Jurisdiction, both as to Law and Fact, with such Exceptions, and under such Regulations as the Congress shall make.

The trial of all Crimes, except in Cases of Impeachment, shall be by Jury; and such Trial shall be held in the State where the said Crimes shall have been committed; but when not committed within any State, the Trial shall be at such Place or Places as the Congress may by Law have directed.

Section 3. Treason against the United States, shall consist only in levying War against them, or in adhering to their Enemies, giving them Aid and Comfort. No Person shall be convicted of Treason unless on the Testimony of two Witnesses to the same overt Act, or on Confession in open Court.

The Congress shall have power to declare the Punishment of Treason, but no Attainder of Treason shall work Corruption of Blood, or Forfeiture except during the Life of the Person attainted.

Article IV

Section 1. Full Faith and Credit shall be given in each State to the public Acts, Records, and judicial Proceedings of every other State. And the Congress may by general Laws prescribe the Manner in which such Acts, Records, and Proceedings shall be proved, and the Effect thereof.

Section 2. The Citizens of each State shall be entitled to all Privileges and Immunities of Citizens in the several States.

A Person charged in any State with Treason, Felony, or other Crime, who shall flee from Justice, and be found in another State, shall on demand of the executive Authority of the State from which he fled, be delivered up, to be removed to the State having Jurisdiction of the Crime.

No Person held to Service or Labor in one State, under the Laws thereof, escaping into another, shall, in Consequence of any Law or Regulation therein, be discharged from such Service or Labor, but shall be delivered up on Claim of the Party to whom such Service or Labor may be due.

Section 3. New States may be admitted by the Congress into this Union; but no new State shall be formed or erected within the Jurisdiction of any other State; nor any State be formed by the Junction of two or more States, or parts of States, without the Consent of the Legislatures of the States concerned as well as of the Congress.

The Congress shall have Power to dispose of and make all needful Rules and Regulations respecting the Territory or other Property belonging to the United States; and nothing in this Constitution shall be so construed as to Prejudice any Claims of the United States, or of any particular State.

Section 4. The United States shall guarantee to every State in this Union a Republican Form of Government, and shall protect each of them against Invasion; and on Application of the Legislature, or of the Executive (when the Legislature cannot be convened) against domestic Violence.

Article V

The Congress, whenever two-thirds of both Houses shall deem it necessary, shall propose Amendments to this Constitution, or, on the Application of the Legislatures of two-thirds of the several States, shall call a Convention for proposing Amendments, which, in either Case, shall be valid to all Intents and Purposes, as part of this Constitution, when ratified by the Legislatures of three-fourths of the several States, or by Conventions in three-fourths thereof, as the one or the other Mode of Ratification may be proposed by the Congress; Provided that no Amendment which may be made prior to the Year One thousand eight hundred and eight shall in any Manner affect the first and fourth Clauses in the Ninth Section of the first Article, and that no State without its Consent, shall be deprived of its equal Suffrage in the Senate.

Article VI

All Debts contracted and Engagements entered into, before the Adoption of this Constitution shall be as valid against the United States under this Constitution, as under the Confederation.

This Constitution, and the Laws of the United States which shall be made in Pursuance thereof, and all Treaties made, or which shall be made, under Authority of the United States, shall be the supreme Law of the Land, and the Judges in every State shall be bound thereby, any Thing in the Constitution or Laws of any State to the Contrary notwithstanding.

The Senators and Representatives before mentioned, and the Members of the several State Legislatures, and all executive and judicial Officers, both of the United States and of the several States, shall be bound by Oath or Affirmation, to support this constitution; but no religious Test shall ever be required as a Qualification to any Office or public Trust under the United States.

Article VII

The Ratification of the Conventions of nine States shall be sufficient for the Establishment of this Constitution between the States so ratifying the

Same. Done in Convention by the Unanimous Consent of the States present the Seventeenth Day of September in the Year of our Lord one thousand seven hundred and Eighty-seven and of the Independence of the United States of America the Twelfth. In witness whereof We have hereunto subscribed our Names, [the names of the delegates follow]

BILL OF RIGHTS (ADOPTED AS AMENDING THE
CONSTITUTION, DECEMBER 15, 1791)

Amendment I

Congress shall make no law respecting an establishment of religion, or prohibiting the free exercise thereof; or abridging the freedom of speech, or of the press; or the right of the people peaceably to assemble, and to petition the Government for a redress of grievances.

Amendment II

A well-regulated Militia, being necessary to the security of a free State, the right of the people to keep and bear Arms, shall not be infringed.

Amendment III

No Soldier shall, in time of peace be quartered in any house, without the consent of the Owner, nor in time of war, but in a manner to be prescribed by law.

Amendment IV

The right of the people to be secure in their persons, houses, papers, and effects, against unreasonable searches and seizures, shall not be violated, and no Warrants shall issue, but upon probable cause, supported by Oath or affirmation, and particularly describing the place to be searched, and the persons or things to be seized.

Amendment V

No person shall be held to answer for a capital, or otherwise infamous crime, unless on a presentment or indictment of a Grand Jury, except in cases arising in the land or naval forces, or in the Militia, when in actual service in time of War or public danger; nor shall any person be subject for the same offenses to be twice put in jeopardy of life or limb; nor shall be compelled in any criminal case to be a witness against himself, nor be deprived of life, liberty, or property, without due process of law; nor shall private property be taken for public use, without just compensation.

Amendment VI

In all criminal prosecutions, the accused shall enjoy the right to a speedy and public trial, by an impartial jury of the State and district wherein the crime shall have been committed, which district shall have been previously ascertained by law, and to be informed of the nature and cause of the accusation; to be confronted with the witnesses against him; to have compulsory process for obtaining witnesses in his favor, and to have the Assistance of Counsel for his defense.

Amendment VII

In suits at common law, where the value in controversy shall exceed twenty dollars, the right of trial by jury shall be preserved, and no fact tried by a jury, shall be otherwise reexamined in any Court of the United States, than according to the rules of the common law.

Amendment VIII

Excessive bail shall not be required, nor excessive fines imposed, nor cruel and unusual punishments inflicted.

Amendment IX

The enumeration in the Constitution, of certain rights, shall not be construed to deny or disparage others retained by the people.

Amendment X

The powers not delegated to the United States by the Constitution, nor prohibited by it to the States, are reserved to the States respectively, or to the people.

Index

340